About the Authors

Alfred Diamant was born in 1917 in Vienna to Slovakian Jewish merchants. He was fascinated by classical music and history. However, the sociopolitical circumstances created by the Nazis forced him to abandon his dream of teaching history for a career in the textile industry. Freddy miraculously managed to survive Kristallnacht, and eventually, he escaped to Kitchener Camp in England, and then to the United States.

During WWII, Freddy again miraculously survived when he was critically injured as a parachutist in the 82nd Airborne. He went on to pursue his academic dreams, studying at Indiana University and at Yale. During his 40-year career in political science, he remained devoted to excellence in research and teaching.

Ann Redmon Diamant was born in 1913 near Columbus, Indiana, to Protestant farmers descended from early pioneer families, the Quicks and the Vanskikes. With her keen intellect, Ann seemed destined for academics. However, the Depression and family tragedy struck, and economic circumstances forced her to enter the workforce.

Ann became an ardent feminist and supporter of human rights. Her strength of character served her well during her life's many challenges. Throughout her lifetime, she remained devoted to her love for learning and teaching through her work with Christian education and the League of Women Voters. Ann had an enduring passion for beauty and color, which was expressed through her interest in the arts.

Ann and Freddy met at Fort Benjamin Harrison in Indianapolis and married during WWII. Despite their vastly different backgrounds, they forged a happy marriage of more than sixty years. Their academic life began at Indiana University in Bloomington in the early 1940s, and took them to such places as Yale in New Haven, the University of Florida in Gainesville, Haverford College in Pennsylvania, UCLA at Berkeley, across Europe, and eventually back to Indiana University and Bloomington during the campus unrest of the 60s and 70s. Along the way, they came numerous adversities, and their lives touched others in memorable ways.

A Word from the Editor

When Alice Diamant first asked me to work on her parents' memoirs, I was intrigued by her description of their life events. A few weeks later, FedEx delivered a large box containing their 777-page manuscript. As I made my way through the crowded typed pages, I was rewarded with some very pleasing discoveries....

I was immediately struck by the charming way Ann and Freddy related their life events. It was evident that both were gifted writers, and that their observations were often profound and thought-provoking.

Then, as their memoirs unfolded, I also discovered that their story was intriguing—it was that good read we all yearn for. Their life events were that mixture of the commonplace and the remarkable that instantly captivates the reader, inviting us to relate to the ordinary and to ponder the extraordinary.

It is impossible to read Ann's story and not be charmed, for instance, by young Ann, growing up in rural Indiana, and her determined efforts to escape wearing one of the huge hair bows that were all the rage in the early nineteen-teens. It is impossible not to relate to her determined efforts to attain a postsecondary education during the Great Depression and to her determined struggle to navigate those seemingly insurmountable obstacles that life hands us all.

It is equally impossible not to be engaged, for instance, by young Freddy, growing up in Vienna, wanting simply to study and teach history—an absurd dream for anyone Jewish during the rise of Nazism. It is impossible not to be intrigued as Freddy manages to survive Kristallnacht, to escape from Nazi Austria, and to survive parachuting into occupied France during WWII, and likewise, as he struggles to overcome the obstacles that an immigrant faces as he works to attain his dream of an academic career.

Worlds Apart, Worlds United: A European Story, The Memoirs of Ann and Alfred Diamant is, I quickly discovered, the story of two quite remarkable people. The reader will be charmed, intrigued, enlightened.

Elyse K. Abraham, Ph.D.
Consulting Editor
Bloomington, Indiana
August 2009

Worlds Apart, Worlds United

A European-American Story,

The Memoirs of Ann and Alfred Diamant

Ann Redmon Diamant
Alfred Diamant

authorHOUSE®

AuthorHouse™
1663 Liberty Drive
Bloomington, IN 47403
www.authorhouse.com
Phone: 1-800-839-8640

First published by AuthorHouse 8/11/2010

ISBN: 978-1-4490-0375-3 (hc)
ISBN: 978-1-4490-0376-0 (sc)

Library of Congress Control Number: 2009907681

Printed in the United States of America
Bloomington, Indiana

This book is printed on acid-free paper.

Edited by Elyse K. Abraham, Ph.D.

Attention Corporations, Universities, Colleges, and professional organizations: Quantity discounts are available on bulk purchases of this book for educational or gift purposes, or for use as premiums to increase magazine subscriptions or renewals. Special books or book excerpts can also be created. For more information, please contact the publisher.

*For all our Family & Friends,
who have enriched our lives
and our marriage.*

*For Ann (04.09.13 to 02.27.03),
whose love and devotion to my
work became the foundation
for sixty years of marriage.*

Contents

Introduction   1

Our Early Years
Chapter 1. Ann's Story (1913-1942)   5
Chapter 2. Freddy's Story: Vienna (1917-1938)   67
Chapter 3. Freddy's Story: America (1938-1942)   123

Our Paths Cross
Chapter 4. A Wartime Courtship & Marriage (1942-1944)   169
     Ann's Account   169
     Freddy's Account   192

Our Life Together: Ann's Story
Chapter 5. Bloomington & New Haven (1945-1950)   223
Chapter 6. Gainesville & New Haven Again (1950-1960)   251
Chapter 7. Haverford (1960-1966)   293
Chapter 8. Europe (1966-1967)   331
Chapter 9. Bloomington (1967-1993)   365

Our Life Together: Freddy's Story
Chapter 10. Bloomington & New Haven (1945-1950)   407
Chapter 11. Gainesville & New Haven Again (1950-1960)   431
Chapter 12. Haverford (1960-1966)   451
Chapter 13. Europe (1966-1967)   465
Chapter 14. Bloomington (1967-1993)   475

Conclusion   519

Epilogue   523

Family Trees
Family Tree for Ann Redmon & Freddy Diamant   527
Descendants of Tunis Quick & Susannah Records   528
Descendants of James Hoagland Quick & Martha Ellen
     Vanskike   529
Vanskike (van Shoyk) Family Tree   530
Everson Family Tree   531

Descendants of George Washington Quick & Anna
    Mae Everson   532
Descendants of Mary Louetta Quick & Carl Hugh Redmon   533
Descendants of Joseph Christopher Redmon & Mary
    Elizabeth King   539
King Family Tree   540
Diamant Family Tree   542
Weiss-Herzog Family Tree   543
Descendants of Julia Herzog & Ignatz Diamant   544
Diamant-Unger Family Tree   545
Diamant-Hartmann Family Tree   546

Preface

My parents, Ann and Freddy Diamant, have always been beacons of love, stability, and clarity for me and, I think, for countless others—many of whom are described in these memoirs. Coming from vastly different worlds and cultural backgrounds, they met by happenstance during a time of war, instability, and confusion. In spite of these differences, something sparked and ignited between them—something so strong and so deep that it overcame those differences and united them in a love and communion spanning 60 years.

These memoirs are their story, first each in her or his separate world and then together in their shared life. Their shared life was rich, deep, and beautiful, founded as it was on a common understanding and feeling for thoughts and ideas, beauty in the world, and their relationships—not just with each other but with many, many friends, colleagues, and loved ones.

Additionally, the memoirs are a historical record of other times and places, a glimpse into a window that is now closed or at least darkened for most of today's generations. As such, their story is an insightful eyewitness account that offers us an understanding of those times and places.

Still, as I have indicated, this is first and foremost a love story. It is a testament to the strength, durability, and beauty of Ann's and Freddy's profound love—one that bridged and overcame worlds separated by geography, history, and culture and united them in thoughts, words, and deeds to the enrichment and betterment of themselves and all those whose lives they touched.

Alice Diamant
Castroville, Texas
September 2007

Introduction

It is a dictum of marriage counselors, at least in western societies, that partners in marriage should get to know each other during courtship. They should also be matched as to ethnicity, family background, social standing, and religion. Marriages not built on such a foundation are likely to end in disaster when the partners discover a range of incompatibilities as they try to construct a family life.

Fortunately, we did not consult a marriage counselor when we decided to get married in the midst of the tumult of World War II.

As our account will make clear, our chance encounter at Fort Harrison in the line of duty initiated a relationship that has endured precisely because it was built on a foundation of common values, interests, and concerns— a foundation that transcended our contrasting family, religious, and cultural backgrounds.

The son of a Central European Jewish merchant family and the daughter of Protestant Indiana farmers discovered common bonds more profound and more lasting than mere social characteristics. Our story will speak for itself.

Freddy & Ann Diamant
Treasure Cay, Abaco Island
The Bahamas, c. 1988

Ann Redman Diamant

Alfred Diamant

Treasure Cay, The Bahamas
January 1988

Ann and Freddy's Family Tree

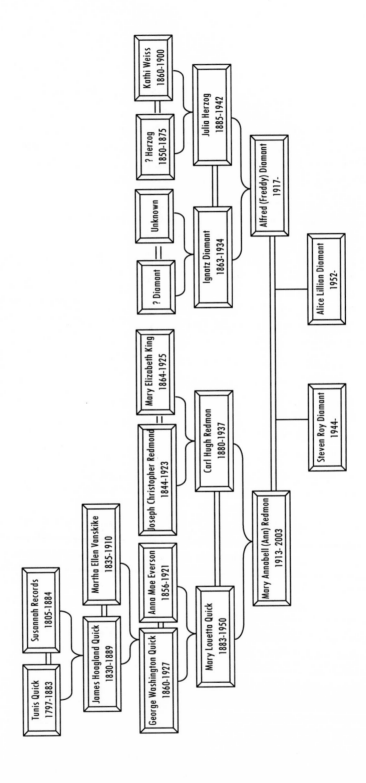

Part I

Our Early Years

Chapter 1

Ann's Story

(1913-1942)

The families of both of my parents came to the New World years before the American Revolution. I know a great deal more about my mother's family than my father's, for her great-grandfather, Tunis Gorrell Quick, was a pioneer in Indiana, in Bartholomew County, where I, some one hundred years later, was born.

Growing up in rural Indiana

Tunis Quick had married Susannah Records, whose father was also a pioneer in Bartholomew County, so I grew up among a whole county full of my mother's relatives. Books have been written about both the Records and the Quicks, so I will not go into great detail about either of these families.

I have the pleasure of owning a book written by my mother's great-aunt Rachel Quick Butz, the youngest daughter of Tunis G. Quick, in which she relates a great deal about both her parents and their backgrounds. Her book

Susannah Records
(1805-1884)

is entitled *A Hoosier Girlhood*, and Indiana University has a copy in its collection.

My father's family resided in Asheville, North Carolina, when the first United States Census was taken in 1790. Two brothers, Stephen and Christopher Redmond, with their families, were counted in that census. My grandfather Joseph Christopher Redmond was a direct descendant of Christopher. These Redmonds were businessmen: mill owners involved in lumber, weaving, and related enterprises. Stephen Redmond and his family were generally professional people: medical doctors, lawyers, surveyors, and so on.

There were some large reunions of Redmond descendants in the 1960s and 1970s in Asheville. I did not attend any of them, but my younger brother Roy and his wife, Paulene, did. I have some doubts about the accuracy of the research material they obtained there, since I recognize in it a number of gaps and errors about my father's family.

It is believed that these two brothers were born in Virginia, lived for a time in Sevier, Tennessee, and then went to Asheville, North Carolina, about the time the American Revolution ended. Since the family came to Virginia, it is safe to conjecture that they came from England, Ireland, or Scotland, because there were Redmonds in all these countries. As far as

Tunis Quick
(1797-1883)

I know, none were Roman Catholic in their religion, whatever that might indicate about their place of origin.

My parents met in church, a very typical meeting place in their time. It was a Baptist church—which does not accord with their backgrounds, for neither of their families was Baptist. What it does point to is the fluidity and ease with which American Protestants move from one sect to another. When my parents were young, going to church was in a sense a social thing. My father had a sweet tenor voice, though untrained, and he loved to sing. He sang as a visitor with a quartet at that church.

At that time, my mother, Louetta Quick, was living with her grandmother Ellen Vanskike Quick and her uncle Evan. Ellen, a widow, had come to keep house for her son Evan and help raise his children. When Mother was a child of nine or ten, she had been very ill with rheumatic fever, which had affected her heart, and thus she was never strong. She lived with and was cared for by a variety of relatives, and when able, she was employed to help a busy farmwife with her children. I think she loved and regarded her uncle Evan as a father and her cousins Earl and Edna as brother and sister. Anyway, it was they who were attending the Flatrock Baptist Church, a small country church in a very small community just north of Hope, Indiana.

*Martha Ellen Vanskike Quick,
Ann's great-grandmother*

My father, Hugh Redmond, had come from Asheville to visit his mother's sister Cally (Caroline), who had moved with her husband from Asheville to St. Paul, Indiana. There was, then, always a need for farm labor, so my father had started working for farmers in the area. He attended this church in Flatrock with his Uncle John King, who had also come to Indiana from Asheville. John was his mother's youngest brother and only a few years older than my father, so they were very like brothers. John had a very good bass voice, and like my father, loved to sing. So it was he who had taken Dad to this church. They provided the male voices in the quartet that led the singing.

My parents were married in Shelby County, Indiana, and their first home was a tenant house on a farm a few miles north of Hope, Indiana. My sister Mae and my brother Joe were born there. William Jacob Norton, our dear family doctor, attended Mother at their births. Dr. Norton practiced medicine in Hope and had married a cousin of Great-grandmother Ellen Quick. He really was a family doctor in the best sense and tradition of the word during my entire childhood. We all loved him.

I was born to Hugh and Louetta Redmon the third of nine children on April 9, 1913. Just here, I think I should explain the change in the spelling of our family name. When my parents were issued their marriage license, the clerk who sold them the document left the *d* off Redmond when he wrote in their names. The license was a very ornate form with roses, cupids, and fancy lettering. It was mounted in a heavily decorated frame made from dried vines woven together, and it hung on our living room wall. Dad had decided that it mattered not whether he spelled his name with or without the *d* so left the license as it was. All this points to the poor education of small office holders in local government in the early twentieth century in Indiana, and probably in many other states as well.

Hugh & Louetta Redmon
On their Wedding Day
September 10, 1907

Exactly when my parents moved to the house where I was born, I do not know. Great-grandmother Ellen Quick had died before the move was made. Probably she was helping Mother after Joe was born, for she died at my parents' house after an accident. She had mistakenly opened the door to the cellar and fell down the stairs. She suffered a concussion and never regained consciousness.

It was after that when my great-grandmother's brother Francis Vanskike hired my father to work for him. (The original family name was van Schoyck before the anglicized form of Vanskike was used.) If I remember correctly, the arrangement was that Uncle Francis provided a house for my parents and all the capital, and in return for his labor, my father received a percentage of the year's profits. All the farm animals, farming machinery, and tools belonged to Uncle Francis.

These were the World War I years—probably the best years ever, financially, for farmers in the United States. Even so, Uncle Francis must have been a benevolent employer, for my parents began to accumulate some capital and some capital goods.

I have happy memories of events during those years in Uncle Francis' house. Uncle Francis and his wife, Belle (who had been a Homsher), had no children. They treated us as kindly as grandparents would have done. I have a very happy memory of a winter outfit I wore and loved. I had a red coat someone had given me, probably as a hand-me-down. Aunt Belle had crocheted a matching red hood for me to wear with it and had given me a little red muff in a material that matched the coat. The most wonderful thing about the muff was its small clasp-fastening purse. How I loved that outfit!

Our house was separated from Uncle Francis' by a large untilled plot we called the barn lot. It was separate from the barnyard, but the barn opened into it and during temperate weather, the cows and horses were kept there overnight. This made bringing the cows in for milking or the horses for harnessing a much easier and quicker chore every morning. Going to and from the Vanskike house, we crossed this lot. I do not remember gates, so I expect that it had a rail fence. Of course, we always had to go to the barn before we went any place because the vehicles were kept there. I have no idea whether the horses, buggy, and carriage belonged to us or to Uncle Francis, but they were our transportation to Hope, church, and Columbus.

The Redmons
Joe, Hugh, Louetta,
Mae, & Ann, c. 1914

We attended the Sharon Baptist Church, some four or five miles from our house. While we waited for Dad to harness the horses to the carriage, I always went into Uncle Francis' house where Aunt Belle put a penny in the little purse in my muff for me to put in the collection plate at church. When I was not wearing the muff, she tied the penny into a corner of my handkerchief and tucked it into my pocket. Maybe there were exceptions, but I seem to remember that our dresses always had pockets. Where else could children carry that very necessary handkerchief?

Aunt Belle had inherited adjoining acres with a house (the Homsher house), and Uncle Francis also farmed this land. Exactly when Uncle Francis hired my father's uncle John King, and when Uncle John and Aunt Rose moved into the Homsher house, I cannot recall. It must have been after I was born, for my cousin Imogene was not born there, and she is four months younger than me.

Imogene was my first and best playmate for years. Since my sister Mae and my brother Joe were both older than me, and had already formed a close companionship by the time I was born, I did not often participate in their games. So having Imogene near-by was wonderful. I spent a lot of time in her home, and I dearly loved her mother, Aunt Rose.

Uncle John and his family also attended Sharon Church, where he and Daddy continued their quartet singing. Nora May, the wife of Charlie May, a neighbor, sang the alto parts, and Katie Kissling played the piano and sang soprano. One of the congregation's fa-vorites was "The Old Rugged Cross," and I think the quartet liked it, too. I enjoyed having a father who was admired and applauded by the congregation.

During the summer months, it was the custom to invite friends to accompany a family home from church for dinner. Often we went to another home for dinner, and often we hosted dinner for others. Sunday dinner was always the most opulent of the week, and when describing other dinners, the comparison was always to Sunday dinner, when we usually had fried chicken, mashed pota-toes, cream gravy, coleslaw, green beans, corn, sliced tomatoes, sliced cucumbers, relishes, and jellies, and often hot rolls or bis-cuits, cakes, and pies (usually there was a choice of light or dark cake and cream or fruit pie).

I was never too happy about these visits or dinners, mainly because of a physical problem I have always had. I need to have food at regular intervals. If I am too long without food and then try to eat, my head begins to ache. After the ache begins, if it is too long before I eat, the headache develops into a migraine, and I am violently ill for hours.

I can remember going to my mother and saying that I was getting a headache, and she would say, "You'll be all right when you eat, and we are going to eat soon." However, in those days in many houses, adults ate at the first sitting, and children ate at the second sitting, often with the hostess.

My parents seemed to feel that my problem was childish un-ruliness and bad manners. Perhaps I was regarded as impertinent because I needed food. In retrospect, I still do not understand why Mother could not have given me a bit of bread, or taken from home a few saltines for me to eat! However, Mother was a very shy person with an extreme feeling of inferiority. She would never intrude or do anything she regarded as unusual in any way. So she could never bring herself to ask for something for me to eat before we were called for dinner.

So, as I have said, visiting friends after church was not my favorite event. I must hasten to add that family dinners were no problem. I felt free to ask for a bite and was given it. My mother's sister Mabel was always most kind and understanding about my problem. I always had her attentive sympathy.

I have always felt guilty about finding fault with my mother for her inattention or lack of sympathy. She was totally unfitted for the part in life that she was given to play, and I have never known anyone as totally good and innocent as she was. All of our relatives spoke of her as a saint. She was loved by everyone. However, when I was a child, I did not always appreciate these qualities, and I often wished for a neater, cleaner house, more imaginative cooking, and most of all, time to myself without having to babysit my siblings! I vowed I would *never* marry and *never, never* have children.

Visiting Mother's family in Indianapolis

We lived less than three miles from the tiny village of Nortonburg, which was a stop for the Big 4 Railroad. The grocer at the general store there would raise a red flange to indicate to the train engineer when he should stop for a passenger or packages. My family used the train stop with some frequency, especially to visit my mother's family.

My mother's mother, Anna Everson Quick, and her two married children, Mabel and Charles, all lived in Indianapolis. Uncle Charles and his wife, Bertha, had a daughter, Dorothy, who was closer to me than any of my cousins for many years. Grandma lived with and kept house for Aunt Mabel, who was married to William Kimberlin. They had no children.

Aunt Mabel worked outside the home, a fairly unusual thing in those days. She had a very good job in a printing press concern, the kind of job usually held by a man (I think she was a typesetter). Aunt Mabel was a true feminist when it was very tough to be one. Her brother, sisters, nieces, and nephews respected her very much.

I visited Grandma, Aunt Mabel, and Uncle Bill frequently. Whenever I visited, Aunt Mabel would buy materials, and Aunt Bertha would make a new dress for me. Aunt Bertha loved to sew, and she was very proficient at it. She and Uncle Charles were married about the time Mother was pregnant with me, and my aunt had hand-sewed a most exquisite baby dress for me, which I still have. I vaguely remember a hand-embroidered and lace-trimmed cap, but that has disappeared.

I was not always appreciative of Aunt Bee's taste, for she loved bows and lace trimmings, and I really preferred plain things. I had overheard adults speaking of me and saying I was a plain little thing, which I believed, and I thought that excessive decoration only served to emphasize my plainness.

Ann and the hair bow

Once when I was visiting, Aunt Bertha made matching dresses for Dorothy and me. She even bought broad ribbons of the same color to make hair bows to wear with the dresses. My hair had not been cut to accommodate fastening bows, so Grandma took me by trolley to downtown Indianapolis to have my hair cut.

Riding downtown in the trolley was an exciting adventure. I loved it. We went to L. S. Ayres, the eminent downtown department store, where we met Aunt Bertha and Dorothy. It was a wonderful place to this country girl who usually went with her father to a barbershop in

Ann & her grandmother
Anna Everson Quick
c. 1917

Hope for haircuts. The waiting room of the hair salon had been arranged as a play area with a small slide and even a large sandbox!

Then came the haircut, with my aunt supervising. She had bought a barrette for clasping the bow on my hair. The woman barber parted and trimmed my hair and fastened on the bow. They called Dorothy and Grandma to come see and admire me. I clearly remember the weight of that bow on my head and seeing my image in the mirror. I liked neither the feel nor the sight of it. I was an unusually tiny child. My head and face were small. The bow, I thought, was almost as big as my head!

We went home after that. In the afternoon Grandma usually had a nap, and she would put me to bed for a nap as well. I never slept, for at home I did not take naps, but usually I would lie still and try to be quiet so that Grandma could rest. That day she was very tired, so she went to sleep quickly. Well, I decided that I was *not* going to wear that hair bow! I knew where Grandma kept her sewing shears in the top drawer of a chest, and I worked out in my mind how to get them. I pulled out the lower drawers and climbed them to get to the scissors. Then I sat on top of the dresser and cut off the hank of hair that held the bow!

How I looked did not worry me one bit. I have always been a bit indifferent about my looks. I fully expected to be severely punished for my actions. I knew what I was doing, but I decided that punishment could be endured more easily than wearing that horrid bow. I recall receiving little more than surprisingly light reprimands.

Grandma, Aunt Mabel, and Mother were never able to be particularly severe with me because they could not look at me without laughing. But I am sure it upset and hurt Aunt Bertha very much. After that, Grandma took me home on the train. We transferred in Columbus, detrained at Nortonburg, left our luggage in the store to be collected later, and walked home, surprising Mother who had *not* been expecting us.

We move and I start school

In 1919, the year I was six, my parents moved. Father had accumulated enough capital to buy the equipment needed for farming on his own. The year before we moved, he bought his first car, a Model T Ford sedan. I am sure he was very pleased and proud of it. I am also sure that many of our friends and relations must have thought it a highly imprudent purchase.

For some reason, I cannot recall many events of this particular period, except that two more children, Paul and George, were born before we moved. I rather think that Uncle Francis was failing in health. I do not remember whether he died before we moved or soon thereafter. But there was one event we children found rather fascinatingly horrible that took place while Dad still worked for him. Uncle Francis had a diseased eye that had to be removed. Why they did not take him to the hospital in Columbus, I do not know, for the Bartholomew County Hospital was built in 1913.

Instead, Dr. Norton did the eye surgery in Uncle's house, and my father assisted. Joe and I talked about it a great deal. I remember that we sat on the rail fence and discussed it at length. Mae could not bear to think of it, and she was thoroughly disgusted with us because we found it so interesting. After that, Uncle wore a patch over his eye.

In 1919, Father arranged with Curtis R. New (who lived out-of-state) to farm his and his wife's acres some four or five miles further east down our road. Mr. New's wife had been Bertha May. The Mays were a prominent family in the area and owned the largest and most luxurious house in the neighborhood (one of the largest in the county in fact). I believe they had about 160 acres. Originally, this land had been in the Trotter-Vanskike family (ancestors of my mother). Bertha May New's family must have bought it fifty or more years before.

About half the land had never been tilled. It was low-lying and swampy, but also rich, black, and loamy. According to a local legend, thirty or more of our acres and the acreage immediately behind it had been awarded to a bodyguard of General George Washington at the conclusion of the American Revolution. There is a grave in the Sharon Church cemetery of an American Revolutionary War soldier, which is decorated every Memorial Day by the DAR. This soldier was probably the first owner of that land.

I remember Dad clearing two fields and laying tile drainage ditches in most of the fields during the first year we lived there. But the really important thing for me was that I started school the year we moved. From that day on, the most important thing in my life was going to school!

Chapter 1. Ann's Story (1913-1942)   15

While we lived in the Vanskike house, Joe and Mae had gone to a one-room school in Clay Township near Petersville. Mae was incredibly shy, and she was left-handed, so in her interest, our parents delayed her going to school until she was seven. At that time, school was compulsory for ages seven to sixteen, so she was not required to go until then.

The schoolteacher there was a stern disciplinarian, very abrupt, and sarcastic. He did not permit left-hand writing. However, our parents must have persuaded him to allow Mae to write with her left hand, because she did, and still does so. Nevertheless, they were not very pleased with his teaching.

When we moved to the new farm, we were a great deal farther away from the Petersville School. So we would have had to walk an even further distance, for Clay Township provided no transportation. However, Flatrock, the next township to the north of us, had a consolidated elementary school and high school in Clifford, and it also provided transportation. In fact, the horse-drawn school hack went past our door.

Hawcreek Township, Hope, also provided these amenities and was across the road to the east. However, the Hawcreek hack did not come as far south as we were because there were no students going to Hope on that road. Our father consulted our township trustee, who agreed to transfer us to the Clifford School. (This meant that our township paid our tuition to Flatrock Township.) We then rode to school to Clifford. That was good luck for me, for I am sure that the long walk would have been too physically taxing for me.

I was so very small and not strong. Running was something I was never able to do well, and I hated it because I was so breathless almost at once. Whenever I had colds, they always became chest colds and caused me to cough for weeks afterwards. I cannot recall my height when I entered school, but my weight was *thirty-two* pounds! I remember it because it was talked about a great deal, and I was always encouraged to eat more and drink more milk. And to my great chagrin, my classmates were always picking me up and carrying me around.

We had a wonderful teacher, Miss Nora Mohr. I loved her dearly, as did all the students. The world should have more Nora Mohrs. I do not think any student of hers ever advanced to another grade without knowing how to read, write, add, and subtract. I sometimes overheard adults lamenting her looks, which always angered me. What did it matter how she looked?

She was so good, so kind, so loving and understanding to us all. If there was a child that needed shoes or a coat, she found some for her or him. If a child had no lunch, she gave hers. I am sure that there was some mischievous behavior in her classes, but there were never any acts of cruelty or great unkindness among the children under her supervision.

My chief friend was a lovely little girl with large brown eyes and naturally curly hair (greatly prized in the days before permanent waves). Evelyn Linson Pugh is still my friend today, even though we have periods of being apart.

I had another friend who lived closer, on a farm within walking distance of our home—Beulah Harris Schaffer, who still lives in Hope, and with whom I talk on the phone when I am in Hope.

Beulah's mother was a large woman with an equally large heart. I remember most vividly a birthday cake decorated with pink candles that Mrs. Harris baked for me. My and Beulah's birthdays were in April (hers later than mine), but the cake was for me. It was the first I had ever had, even though it was my seventh birthday. Mrs. Harris gave me the partially burnt candles to take home; they remained among my treasures for years.

I cannot recall exactly when birthday cakes with candles entered my family's customs. I could guess that it was my prodding and insisting together with Mae's initiative (she baked the cakes) that brought it about. Producing two babies every five years was taking its toll on our mother. She had been losing her teeth for some years, and she finally had all of them pulled after Roy was born.

That was a difficult pregnancy for Mother. In the early spring of that year, the whole family, except Dad, had influenza. He might have had a slight case in 1917-18 when the great scourge hit the country, but the rest of us had escaped, only to have it in the second epidemic of 1922. Mother and Paul were especially ill. I remember that many neighbors were ill and that there were several deaths. I remember, too, that in the summer months between my first and second grades, a little boy who had been in my grade died of lockjaw (tetanus).

I know that these sad happenings had an effect on me. Many people, including young children, died in those days, people who would live today because of the rapid development of life-saving drugs and immunizations. I was beginning to learn of tragedy—that not all of life's happenings are humanly controllable, and that not all stories have happy endings.

I had learned to read almost at once, and by the second grade I could read almost anything set before me. But understanding all of it came only gradually. My first readings were largely happy-ending stories. Later our readers at school contained excerpts from sophisticated writers. Of course, they had little application to the lives of country children. It was the teacher's task to make them relevant. That is education. Why should we read just about the life we know? Awakening our minds to a larger world is the role of our teachers. With me, they were very successful.

Grandma Anna and Grandpa George

As I said earlier, Mother was less strong after her sixth child. When I was eight or nine, she was expecting again. It was about this time that her mother, Anna Everson Quick, died. I was told that Grandma Anna had a most unhappy life and not much interest in living. Her husband, George Washington Quick, had never helped her make a home, had been only an intermittent provider of financial help, and had disappeared from time to time for months, even years, without communicating with her.

Because of her weak heart from rheumatic fever, Mother seldom lived at home. She often was cared for by relatives who would provide a home for her. For a time, she lived with her great-aunt Hannah Quick. Hannah, who never married, cared for her parents, Tunis and Susannah Quick, the original pioneers in Indiana, and inherited Heartsease, the home place.

Mother's great-aunt Rachel and her husband, Samuel Butz, who was a medical doctor, and their daughter, Mabel, lived with Hannah. (Rachel wrote *A Hoosier Girlhood*, an account of much of that family's story.) Mother may have lived with them during her illness so Uncle Butz (as she always called him) could supervise and provide medical help when needed. After that, Mother lived with her uncle Evan and her grandmother Ellen Vanskike Quick.

Mother's brother and sister, Charles and Mabel, lived with their mother (Grandma Anna), but I have no recollection of where they lived at that time, except that it was in Columbus. At one time, their father (Grandpa George) had moved the family to Kansas, then to Nebraska, and then to the Oklahoma Territory. The only thing Mother told us about this was that the house in which they lived bordered on an Indian reservation and that Grandma Anna was terrified of the Indians.

When Grandpa George left them there with no money at all, some kind relative must have sent money for their return to Columbus. Great-grandmother Everson survived on a federal pension, since her husband had been a soldier in the Civil War (1861-1865). Perhaps they went to her; I do not really know.

George Washington Quick,
Ann's grandfather

Grandma Anna took in washing (as the phrase was for a laundress), and money from that work is all they had to live on. At some time during this early period, Grandpa George returned, and there was another child, Inez. How long he lived with his family after Inez's birth, I do not know. He enlisted as a volunteer from Columbus during the Spanish-American War in 1898. He said he never went all the way to Cuba; he was still training in Florida when the war was over.

By this time, Uncle Charles and Aunt Mabel had become full-time wage earners. Mother told me that Grandfather, after one of his disappearing acts, had returned, but Aunt Mabel and Uncle Charles refused to let him live in any house for which they were paying. He left again, and it was years before any of his family saw him again.

Grandpa George sometimes appeared at our house, and Mother, who never found it in her heart to be vindictive, took him in and allowed him to live with us for months at a time. He was there during the summer and always planted and maintained an excellent kitchen garden.

Mother said Grandma Anna, who was living in Indianapolis with Aunt Mabel, would have liked to see him, but she would not be disloyal to her son and daughter. In all the pictures that I have seen of her, she looked sad, and Mother always said that this was the foremost reason for her death—years of grief.

My year in Indianapolis (1922)

In the summer after Grandma Anna died, and when I was nine years old, my mother's family gathered to spend a weekend together with Aunt Inez and Uncle Sheddy (Shedrick Wright) near Madison, Indiana. I suppose I had suffered a cold during that spring and continued to cough—I cannot recall the exact details. One night Aunt Mabel became aware of my coughing, and the next day she talked at length to my mother about it and induced my parents to permit her to take me home with her. She proposed to take me to doctors in Indianapolis for a thorough medical examination.

My guess is that the family presumed I had tuberculosis, because one of the first tests I had was for that. The test was negative. Tuberculosis was a very prevalent and deadly disease at the time, and a number of my father's family had died of it (a brother and at least three sisters). In assuming I had TB, Aunt Mabel could easily have been correct.

In Indianapolis, there was a home and school for tubercular children, and she took me to look at it. The chief thing I remember were the dormitories where the children slept in the open air—three sides of the rooms had French doors that were opened wide every night. Over the years, I have noticed that in Indianapolis and in other cities I have visited or lived in, sleeping porches were commonly added to homes built in that era.

Although I did not have TB, I lived with Aunt Mabel and Uncle Bill through that school year. I was then nine years old and had grown hardly at all since I was six. Again I remember my weight, *forty-two* pounds, because it was the subject of so much attention. When the medical doctors found I did not have tuberculosis and, I assume, could not diagnose my problem, Aunt Mabel took me to a chiropractic college in Indianapolis. She had gone there to be practiced upon by the senior students. The woman who gave us both treatments graduated soon after and opened her own office where we went regularly.

There must have been an interview with the principal of the local elementary school (No. 57) in Indianapolis, for my school days varied from the other students. The difference was in my exercise program and what I was given at snack time. I remember having a rest period that I spent in the nurse's office. I also remember being given graham crackers, rather than the usual saltines, and milk with a higher fat content. Who had set up the program for me, I have no idea, but I thrived!

I often think about this year in an Indianapolis public school, and I marvel at the flexibility that allowed this individualized care. I thrived academically, too. My chief interest was always in learning, and during this time, my interests were broadened, especially in art and music, subjects that were included in the curriculum in most city systems but not in rural schools.

My ability to read and write and my knowledge of mathematics were at least equal to that of my fellow students. As a matter of fact, I was given a written and oral examination when I entered, and my performance was so advanced that the principal suggested that I be placed in fifth rather than fourth grade—but Aunt Mabel refused. She believed that what I needed was to become healthy and grow.

Aunt Mabel never told me that I could have gone into fifth grade. Mother told me years later. Had the choice been mine, I expect I would have chosen the higher grade. It would have been characteristic of me. However, I wonder whether I would have survived had it not been for my aunt's timely intervention and decisive action.

I went home for Christmas that year. Whether someone took me or whether I went on the interurban to Columbus and my father met me there, I cannot remember. What does stand out for me is that on Christmas Eve, we were presented with a new baby brother, Robert William. That is all I recall of that Christmas. I returned to Indianapolis after Christmas to finish the school year. However, Aunt Mabel, Uncle Bill, and I did go back once: Baby

Robert William died, and we returned for the funeral. That event remains vivid. As a family, we all truly mourned.

Rural schools in Indiana finished their school year much earlier than the city schools because farm children usually worked in the fields, and that work began in April. The Indianapolis schools were in session until mid-June. When school finished, I wanted to go home. My health had improved many times over, and though Aunt Mabel and Uncle Bill said I could stay with them and be their daughter, I was drawn back by my family. There were many material advantages to being a single child in a household, and I enjoyed being the center of attention, but my family was *my* family and I had to be with them.

Perhaps the death of our little brother had affected me. I am unable to say. As much as I often resented having the responsibility of caring for my younger brothers, I sincerely loved them. As well, my sister Mae and I had grown close—in a family such as ours we had to rely upon each other. We were very independent and made most of our decisions in our own way. Usually the rules were very general, and we were remarkably free of close parental supervision.

One other noteworthy event took place that year in Indianapolis. I was baptized and joined a church. My parents had met in a Baptist Church, and we had attended Sharon Church until about the time I started school. That was when the scandal happened. The main prop of our church had been the Kissling Family, Katie Kissling being generally in charge of the music. It would not have been a subject for young ears, so I am not clear in all the details, but there was a monstrous scandal involving Uncle John King and the unmarried Katie Kissling.

I do know that as a result, Aunt Rose filed for divorce and returned to Asheville, taking her three youngest children with her. Her three older children remained with their father, but my chief playmate, Imogene, was gone. After that we ceased attending the church, and there was a long coolness between Dad and Uncle John.

All the Eversons, including Grandma Anna, were members of the First Christian Church in Columbus, and my mother had been baptized in it. Aunt Mabel had not. It is a church exclusive of outside organizational ties, so any member living outside its area needs to find another affiliation. Grandma never had. After Grandma died, Aunt Mabel started attending the First Methodist Church in Irvington, the Indianapolis suburb in which she lived.

Aunt Mabel enrolled me in Sunday school there, and I loved that, too. Our teacher, Mrs. Whitney, was a lovely woman who took her role seriously, so our classes were interesting and rewarding. One of the memorable events of the year was receiving my own Bible with beautifully-colored ribbon markers as an award for learning to recite all the books of the Bible. That Bible I still have. Around Easter, Mrs. Whitney gave the children who wanted to be baptized special instruction in her home on Saturday afternoons. So it was that one Sunday morning, my aunt and I were baptized and taken into the church at the same time.

The prosperous and tranquil 1920s

At some point after my return home, our family started attending Sunday school at the Petersville Methodist Church. Since the church shared its minister with a church at Newbern, church services were only every other Sunday. Even so, we seldom stayed for them; we went home after Sunday school.

At first, our father took us and stayed for the classes. But he soon found himself in such violent disagreement over politics with the other men that he vowed not to go to a church full of know-nothings who were sure only Republicans could go to heaven. He did not object to our going. He felt everyone was entitled to make her or his own decisions about religious and political affiliations. It was true that an overwhelming percentage of Methodists were Republicans. I remained a Methodist for a long time, but I never became a Republican.

So it was then that after a year in Indianapolis, I resumed life with my family and in my school. The following year, those of our family still in elementary school were no longer transferred out of the township but instead, attended Clay Township's new consolidated school at Petersville, riding in the system's new buses. With the change in schools came a change in my friends and interests.

By this time (1920–1930), farmers were entering the mechanized age. We, too, had a tractor, though we still had horses, as did most farmers. New implements, like plows, rakes, cultivators, mowers, and reapers, which could be pulled by tractors, were replacing the smaller horse-drawn equipment.

My father was enjoying these changes and doing comparatively well economically. He had a small herd of milk cows, fed a number of pigs, and rotated his fields with wheat, corn, and clover. Often he planted rye in the fields where the wheat had been harvested, and let the cows and horses graze on the new rye plants. I look back on those years as a pleasant, tranquil interlude.

We did not have electricity in our house, or running water. So one task that the children in our family shared was hand-pumping water into tanks for the farm animals. It had to be done twice a day, and in the evening, the tanks required more water than in the morning. We complained too often, and we accused each other of scamping a turn. In short, we did what we could to avoid the pumping. Another shared task was carrying coal and wood into the house for our heating and cooking stoves.

What I disliked most was feeding and watering the chickens. I never liked having chickens around. I suspect I was allergic to them, for I now know that I had asthma as a child, though I cannot remember that it was ever diagnosed.

Ann, Mae, & Dorothy
May 30, 1924

The morning chores of feeding, watering, milking, and harnessing were done by the males (and sometimes in later years by a female) while Mother prepared breakfast. My father was up first, and he made the fires. Then came Mother to prepare the meal.

For him, biscuits, fried eggs, coffee, and cereal were the norm. In the summer, we had corn flakes, but sometimes in winter, we had hot oatmeal. Mother or Mae prepared the oats before going to bed at night, cooking them all night over water in a double boiler.

The jelly and preserves made during the summer seldom lasted into the winter, so on our table was always a small pitcher of corn syrup. We must have made a large contribution to the Pennant Syrup Factory in Edinburgh, which was co-owned by our great uncle Harold Hughes. I remember how my brothers loved syrup with peanut butter on their biscuits.

We bought our staples in quantity: flour and sugar came in 25-, 50-, and 100-pound cloth bags. Saltines came in a very large box, perhaps 14 inches by 14 inches by 16 inches. Nothing like that now exists in supermarkets, but then most of our buying was done in a locally owned and managed grocery. Very occasionally, we would also have a box of that size filled with cookies for our school lunches.

On alternate days, we had beans and potatoes—white beans cooked with white bacon, and boiled peeled potatoes with butter, salt, and pepper. Too often for me, our school lunch was peanut butter between two slices of bread. (I came to dislike peanut butter, and not until my children asked for it did I ever keep any in my pantry.) The peanut butter and the syrup came in one-gallon tin pails. Packaging was simple then.

On Saturdays, our parents took us to Columbus to shop. We usually ate lunch in Kitzinger's Bakery. What a lovely-smelling place it was! Daddy often bought sweet rolls, buns, sliced bologna, and cheddar cheese. We sat at wooden tables in the back of the bakery. I loved the mustard. The Kitzingers made it themselves, and it sat in pots on the tables. Sometimes we also had a cookie, but usually not, for the sweet rolls were enough. Dessert at our house was a special treat. We did not have it every day.

Just a few stores away from Kitzinger's was a candy and ice cream store that everyone called "The Greeks" though their sign read Zaharako. Once in a while we bought ice cream in cones there. At Christmas time, both at school and at church, children were given a gift, typically a bag of candy and an orange. Some bus drivers also gave us the same treats. The candy most longed for and joyfully received was that from The Greeks. They made

The Redmon children
Paul, George, Ann holding Betty, Joe, Mae, & Roy
Hope, Indiana, c. 1926

quality confections. The store existed through two generations in one family, and it was always a popular place.

After Mae had a course in cooking as part of the required domestic science course in school, she introduced some new dishes into our meals, which had generally been very monotonous and uninteresting. Some of Mother's cooking was really superb, but overall she had little interest in either cooking or eating. My father's family hardly knew what yeast bread was; they ate soda biscuits or cornbread at every meal. For breakfast, we usually had hot biscuits. I have never tasted any as good as those Mother made.

Eventually, Mae began doing much of the cooking, and she introduced us to chili con carne. How that particular dish came to be taught to eighth-grade girls in Indiana in the 1920s, I have no clue. It was a popular dish in our house and in many others. Schools began to have chili suppers to raise money for those extra things never provided for in the budget. Sometimes there was simply the supper: chili, salad, and a choice of cake or pie for dessert.

I can remember making my first cake, standing on a chair to do the mixing. Mae was an expert long before I was, but I did fairly well, too. Truly, our cakes were better than Mother's. She sort of threw everything into the bowl and stirred it up, and sometimes the cakes came out lumpy and not well blended. Mae taught me to follow the recipe: sift the dry ingredients, beat the eggs separately, and blend gradually.

Our cakes were good, but Mother beat us hands down at making pie crusts. Her crusts were invariably flaky and crisp, just as they should be. After long years, I finally learned the secret: unlike cakes, pie crusts should be mixed quickly and handled as little as possible—just as our overworked mother made them.

Mae and I learned to make flaky crusts about the same time, even though years later we lived miles apart. Once when we were visiting, we thought about it at the same moment and turned to each other to say simultaneously, "I can make really good pie crust." Some of our children were present, and they hooted and laughed. But we

Mae & Ann
1931

understood the significance of it. It was so wonderful, after so many years of trying, to be finally able to make flaky crusts!

In spite of the difference in our ages, Mae and I were good friends and companions. We assumed household responsibilities and worked together. She was intensely shy, and I was not, so often I led the way. When we went to the movies, I bought the tickets. When an order was to be placed, I placed it. I realized that many older relatives spoke disparagingly of my "bold" behavior (you see, my early years were still of the children-should-be-seen-and-not-heard variety). I was sorry for it, but I did not change my ways.

In many ways, I was not an exemplary child. Another task I thoroughly hated was picking blackberries. A neighbor had a large blackberry patch, and every year we were given days when we could pick. I was one of the pickers, but I never did a satisfactory job. I did try, and I did get some berries, but I was so terribly uncomfortable!

We were dressed in our brothers' overalls and shirts, and rag strips soaked in kerosene were tied around our ankles, wrists, and necks to discourage chiggers and mosquitoes. The pesky rascals were perhaps deterred but never eliminated, and since I always suffered a definite reaction to their bites, the whole expedition filled me with dread.

I can remember enormous welts, even a generalized edematous reaction over my whole body, and a fever from the chigger bites. Allergic reactions were not a part of the medical lore in those days. One was merely told, "It won't kill you. You'll get over it." In a few days one did. Blackberries are still not my favorite food.

Graduation from eighth grade (1926)

The year I graduated from eighth grade, Mae graduated from high school. Both events were celebrated with special ceremonies at night that included music, a speech by a local dignitary, and the awarding of diplomas and honors. It was an occasion for dressing up. My dress was a gift from Aunt Mabel and Aunt Bertha. In the usual way, Mabel bought the material, and Bertha made the dress. I did not like my dress at all.

Ann Redmon
Eighth Grade Graduation
1926

In fact, I struggled not to cry when I saw it. I tried to thank them, but I must have done a poor job, for my father took me aside, scolded me severely, and threatened to whip me if I did not behave in a more grateful manner. I suppose the dress was in the same category as the hair bow of years earlier.

At the graduation ceremony, I received a wonderful accolade that made me so happy that the dress no longer mattered. In those days, the state required rural students to pass a state-prepared written examination before being admitted to high school. The speaker for my graduation ceremony, Judge Julian Sharpnack from Columbus, spoke of the need for education and congratulated the township officials on their building. Then he congratulated the teachers and said how well they had done their jobs, since one of the students they were graduating that night had performed especially well on the state examination.

He went on to say that in fact, the student had placed third in the county, and only a very few points from first and second place, and in the top three percent in the state. Then he said *my* name! It made me so happy, and when the local newspaper printed a story about the examination, together with the names of the top performers, I was given a lot of attention.

My high school years begin

Graduation from the eighth grade constituted another turning point for me. There being no high school in Clay Township, a family had to choose a high school for their child after graduation from eighth grade. The township would pay the tuition to the high school, but the cost of transportation and the means was left to the family. Both Joe and Mae had continued to attend school at Clifford, riding in the school bus, which passed our home. I am sure it was assumed I would go there, too. As you may guess, I wanted to go to Columbus, not Clifford.

While attending school at Petersville, I had formed new friendships, in particular, with Doris Taylor and Thelma Glick. Doris and I attended the same church, as did Ruth Talley, who was one grade ahead of us and a neighbor of the Taylors. At various times in my Sunday school years, Mrs. Talley and Mrs. Taylor had taught the class I was in. I loved them both. They stimulated my thinking, and they talked to me about the books I read and suggested others to read. Though they were not widely traveled, they had the means to go to places like Chicago, Philadelphia, and New York, so their interests went beyond the local scene.

So I wanted to continue with these friends and go to school in Columbus, not in Clifford or Hope. I think I expressed my wishes to

Mother first; I usually did. As I recall, she was neither sympathetic nor unsympathetic. She merely pointed out that I could get a high school diploma at either Hope or Clifford, and that transportation to these schools was readily available at no cost, which I already knew. So I approached my father.

Daddy was not overjoyed with my wishes, but neither was he unsympathetic. Within a few days, he told me that he had talked with his friend Charlie May, who had bought a small car for his son Donald to drive to school. It was Donald's car, so if Donald wished to take another passenger, he could. Ruth Finkel, another neighbor's daughter, had ridden to school with Donald the previous year. Our school at Petersville was so small (usually less than 125 students in eight grades) that there were no strangers. Those in one's age group were normally one's close friends, but one also had more casual friends in other grades. So I knew both Ruth and Donald before we drove, crowded into his little roadster, to school in Columbus for two years.

On the whole, my high school years in Columbus were both happy and intellectually satisfying. I did not think about it then, but I have since reflected upon it, and I know that I had the benefit of some really excellent teachers. On the first day, those of us who had not graduated from the Columbus schools were required to take an examination. I am not sure why, for it was very like the one the state had required for our graduation from eighth grade. We were also given a schedule of classes, and the principal, Mr. Lambert, told us what would be required to get a high school diploma. He emphasized that if you were preparing for college, you would need the required hours of math, foreign language, history, and science.

At that time in Indiana, though many students dropped out of school at age sixteen, the majority graduated from high school. However, only a small percentage went on to college. I loved learning, and I knew that I wanted to go on and on, as far as I could go. I was not greatly endowed in any particular way, and I had not been exposed to great art or to great music. But I read everything that came my way, and I did have some exposure to great literature.

I thought I would like to write, and there, I think, was one of the gaps. I recently looked back over some things I wrote then, and although they were not very good, the possibilities were there. It seems to me that I should have been corrected more, and I should never have been praised. Perhaps I could have been a fairly good writer if my life had gone in such a way as to have required more creative writing. In high school, I substituted journalism for English one semester, and I loved it. I would have been happy to pursue journalistic writing.

Extracurricular activities were difficult to arrange for rural students, but some were possible for me because both Donald and Ruth were very cooperative and accommodating about driving home an hour or so late. We shopped a little (though no one had extra cash for nonessentials in those years), and then usually we went to the local county library and studied until we were all ready to go home.

In my second year in high school, I was asked to join Sorosis. Ruth and Donald told me it was an honor, so it was agreed that I should join. They said they would be happy to wait for me on the evenings I would be going to meetings. Sorosis was a current events club sponsored by Mildred Murray, one of the English teachers. Each fall the Sorosis members chose new members from a group of names selected from the top female scholars of the previous year.

At our meetings, we engaged in discussions of current events. Each member took her turn reporting orally on an item of prevailing interest that was selected from a news magazine or journal. We were asked to be as neutral as possible in our presentation and to give as much information as was readily available to us. We met twice a week for an hour after class, so of course, we were not asked to do in-depth reporting, but we did try to be objective.

Mildred Murray directed, criticized, and participated. She was an excellent sponsor, and I, for one, learned a lot about researching a topic, organizing the material, and participating in meaningful discussions. Sorosis was a definite *plus* in my educational experience.

The struggle for Women's Suffrage had been in the experience of my teachers. In fact, it had been an amendment to the American Constitution only about ten years before my high school days. I think one reason for the excellence of my teachers (about sixty percent female) was that there was then almost no other profession open to women for earning a living. They came from high middle-class homes, and their families had been able to finance their education. Most of them lived with their mothers or perhaps a sister. They had not traveled abroad but they did go to Chicago or New York for further education and to seek cultural recreation not available in Columbus.

I remember, in particular, Miss Murray, whose Mecca was Columbia University in New York City. She studied for a master's degree in their then-famous school of education, and she saw every play and attended every musical event that she could manage, given the constraints of time and money. Not all of my teachers did this. The men, for instance, were married, and had homes to make, and families to support. So in this regard, the females had more freedom. However, on the whole, my teachers were an aware, lively, and able group.

The recession and hard times

I was so happily engrossed in school that I was only dimly aware of the worsening national economy—not only its immediate effects on my family, but the very personal troubles that were building into tragedies in my parents' lives. Both my parents were ill-prepared for the life circumstances they were given to lead. Dad had wanted to break away from his past. He wanted an atmosphere other than the post-Civil War gloom of the entire South.

Dad's father had every reason for gloom. His family had once been prosperous. They had owned land and mills. (The mills were operated by waterpower and so, especially suited for that part of North Carolina.) But the mills had been wrecked by Northern soldiers, and he had no money left to replace them or even to pay property taxes on his acres.

I do not know much about Grandfather's youth, but I deduce that having been born with a clubfoot, he cherished resentment for having a handicap all his days. From reading the history of that period, I realize that he salvaged a living for himself and his large family in the way that was most successful throughout the South. He set up a general store on his reduced acres, and though he was never wealthy again, neither were they poor. However, alcoholism may have been a genetic fault in his family, for he drank heavily and was abusive to his family often. My father wanted to get away from that.

Dad had concluded that hard work and careful planning were the requirements for success. From what I have read, I think that was the prevailing thought of the time. Remember, this was when Horatio Alger was a great success with his books about poor, honest, hardworking young boys earning great riches by their toil, upright behavior, and honesty. At any rate, Dad was very ambitious and very hardworking, but many other things enter the equation for success, and the negatives were already entering.

Among the capital goods that Dad had acquired for farming were milk cows and pigs. In his time, farms in Indiana were highly diversified operations. Only some of the corn, clover, and wheat grown was sold; much of it was used for animal feed. Chickens were usually the domain of the wife. She and the children cared for the chickens, and the revenue from the eggs and fryers was her private income. But Mother could never manage to care for a sufficient number of chickens to increase her income significantly. She struggled mightily to be the helpmate a farmwife was expected to be, but she had neither the strength nor the health.

I vaguely remember one time when disease struck the pigs and most of them died—truly a disaster for someone who had no cash reserves to speak of. Hard work and honesty did not help the pigs at all. They died.

Then there was a time during my high school days when the cows started dying. The vet dosed them with vast quantities of medicines poured through a funnel down their throats. This treatment, it seems, actually killed them. We discovered that sometime later, when after losing many cows, Dad quit calling the vet, and some of them, without treatment, recovered.

This disaster had in part come about because of Dad's ambition to be a first-class farmer. He was one of the first to grow soybeans as a main crop. I am a little hazy about the details, but I assume that the soybeans were cut and stored much as clover was. Clover was cut, turned, and allowed to dry, then carried by wagon to the barns where it was lifted into the loft, or mews, as we called them. Evidently, that was not the way to handle soybeans. The soybeans had moldered, and eating them had caused the cows to become greatly bloated. The veterinarian's treatment of drenching the cows had caused fluid to surround their lungs, and so they had died.

Losing the cows was a tough blow for someone like my father, who was already close to the edge. About then, I expect, was when his faith in himself began to wane. I am only guessing about his health, but it is an educated guess based on my own disabilities. He spoke of his rheumatism, and you could see that he moved with difficulty. His ways changed. He was not eager to work, and much of the labor was done by his children, mostly by my brothers, but we all contributed.

Mae had gone to Indianapolis, where she worked as a receptionist and bookkeeper for two medical doctors. My youngest sibling, Martha, was born while I was in high school, and that completed our family: four boys and four girls. I have often thought that the four youngest probably had a less happy childhood than the four who preceded them. But there were pluses and minuses for all of us. We have been a loyal, loving group, united largely by our remarkable mother. I am sure our father adored her. However, when I once said this to her, she gave me a very surprised and somewhat skeptical look and replied, "Well, I think I disappointed him because I never could do as much work as other farmwives did."

That may have been true, but it was only one of many problems they had to face in their life together. My father had not really understood the economics of farming. It is not just labor-intensive; it is capital-intensive as well, as has been demonstrated in this country time after time for many years.

So then, when I was in high school, our country's economy was falling into a deep recession. I was aware of it, naturally. Wasn't it one of the chief matters for discussion in Sorosis? Nevertheless, I was happy in school.

In my senior year, I was offered the editorship of both the high school newspaper and the annual yearbook for our class. The second was the greater honor, but I knew I would like editing the newspaper better. The advisor was my journalism teacher, who was also a good friend, not much older than me. And I liked the work; I had been doing feature stories for the paper since I had taken the journalism course.

However, I was persuaded to edit the yearbook by Mr. Lambert, the principal, and by the yearbook advisor, Otto Hughes, who had been my seventh grade teacher at Petersville, and again my teacher in one of the history courses in high school. Being editor of the yearbook did indeed add another dimension to my education, for it required organization and management skills, and it took hours of my time. It also gave me a glimpse into an adult world. Contracts had to be awarded to a photographer and a printer, and that was my job.

Working on the yearbook was not new just to me, it was new for Mr. Hughes. Unfortunately, he knew only about as much as I did. I am something of a perfectionist, so I never felt too pleased with our book. Nevertheless, we did produce a yearbook, it arrived in good time, and we did not go beyond our budget. Both Mr. Lambert and Mr. Hughes regarded it as a successful venture.

What I have not talked much about is the state of my health since the year in Indianapolis with Aunt Mabel. After that year, my health was much improved, and I grew slowly. When I graduated from high school, I actually had doubled my weight to eighty-four pounds. But I always had horrible chest colds and coughed for weeks afterwards. Colds and coughing took a great toll on my strength, and my aims often went beyond my ability to accomplish them. I was also forced to miss many days of school.

As with my mother, kind relatives did helpful things for me from time to time. I had stayed with Aunt Ett (Henrietta Strobel), my grandmother's sister, who lived in Columbus, one summer when she had a broken leg. I ran errands for her, did some cooking, and enjoyed the experience. Her husband, Uncle Charlie, worked at the local foundry. Their daughter Edna Keller and her son, James, and an unmarried daughter, Hazel, lived with them. Hazel worked for the telephone company, and Edna at Reliance Manufacturing Company, the local shirt factory. I felt close to them after that, and I could always count on a bed there whenever I needed to stay overnight in Columbus.

Also, I lived for several weeks with my great-aunt Lily (Lillian) and her husband, Hal (Harold) Hughes. I do not recall exactly when or why. Theirs was a different household than any I had known before. Uncle Harold was a superb businessman. He was also a quiet, almost shy, person, and I never felt I knew him very well.

I think that he and my father had a good relationship. Dad farmed his and Aunt Lily's acres. When Uncle Francis Vanskike died, Aunt Lily had inherited some acreage from him, and when Aunt Belle died soon after, Uncle Hal had bought some of the Homsher acres. So they had about eighty acres, which my father farmed along with Mr. New's. Mother and Aunt Lily had been in the same household for some years when Mother had lived with her Uncle Evan. I never knew Aunt Lily's age. She was my grandfather George Washington Quick's sister, but she was likely less than ten years older than Mother.

When I lived with them, Uncle Hal was vice-president and general manager of Union Starch and Refining Company. The president was William Irwin. Columbus, Indiana, though not a city, was always a busy, prosperous county seat with a variety of manufacturing concerns. The Irwin family had established one of the two banks—the Irwin Bank, which was generally used by the manufacturing community. The other, the First National Bank, was used by the farmers.

Mr. Irwin was a financier and an entrepreneur, who invested in many things. He had bought the Hughes brothers' syrup factory in Edinburgh and merged it with a factory he owned in Illinois that produced Argo starch and Karo syrup. So Uncle Hal was an important part of the largest investment group in Columbus. Being part of this household expanded my world quite a lot, even though I certainly was not an intrinsic part of it. So then, like my mother, I came to participate in the lives of my relatives: her mother's family, the Eversons, and her father's family, the Quicks.

We had less contact with my father's family, the Redmonds, because they lived in North Carolina. The exceptions were those members of his mother's family (the Kings) who had moved to Indiana—two of her brothers, John and George, and her sister Cally (Caroline). As well, over the years, three of my father's sisters, Florence, Clara, and Grace, had each come to live with us and assist Mother with the housework.

Daddy went back to Asheville by train several times. The summer of the year before I started high school, he also made a visit by car and took with him Mae, Joe, and me, as well as Uncle John King. We stayed about ten days. My memory is not clear about much of it. We stayed in my grandparents' house, and we visited a different relative every day, it seemed. One day we went to Chimney Rock, a scenic spot for visitors. Everyone was extremely friendly, and the area was beautiful, but I did not feel at home and had no desire to stay.

The Great Depression

As I try to recall my senior year in high school, I sense that I was less happy (or maybe less joyous is a better word) than I had been the three preceding years. The Great Depression was upon us. My home conditions were worsening.

After Martha's birth, Mother was even less strong and her interests more restricted. Father had begun to fall into alcoholism. I have never settled in my own mind how much of alcoholism is a genetic fault and how much is simply an inability to face realities of pain or weakness. Perhaps it is some of each. I have observed other alcoholics, and they do not seem to fall into common behavior patterns. One reads constantly in the news of fights, brawls, and violent behavior by people who have consumed too much alcohol. This was not the case with my father.

He had previously been an extremely hardworking man, very impatient with his children, exacting in his business transactions, and not at all forbearing or forgiving to weak people, adults or children. Drink gentled him. It must have taken the edge from his miseries. He was less impatient with his children, but then, he was also not responsive to their needs. It was as if he was there but had opted out.

I remember once trying to talk to Mother about plans for the future. She only cried bitterly and said she could not understand what had happened to my father. He had hated his own father's drinking habits and had left home because of them. He had vowed he would not behave in such a way. Yet, here he was repeating that behavior. She could not plan or think about the future.

As I have said, small disasters in the big world were close to fatal ones in our small one. Our family existed on such a narrow economic margin that when the animals died and the sale of the crops brought in less money than had been required to sow, tend, reap, and market them, we were in very dire straits.

There was no one anywhere whom I, or any of us, could confide in or seek help from. Conditions in the world at large had shaken the lives of so many others. I reported on these national and international happenings in our Sorosis discussions. What I never reported was that they were happening to me.

Our relatives had their own changes and problems. During my high school years, my mother's youngest sister, Inez, committed suicide, leaving six young children behind. I understood that it was a matter of poor living conditions, an irresponsible husband, and an unwanted pregnancy. Unwanted pregnancies were numerous and very real in those times.

Aunt Mabel took one of the little ones, a girl, into her home. Two boys went to their father's relatives, and three children remained with their father. I heard their lives were fairly miserable. Their father did little more than pay the rent on a poor house. The eldest, a girl just a year younger than me, and two younger brothers, literally cared for themselves.

I was profoundly aware that I was not living in the best of all possible worlds. There should have existed in our society some agency to provide moral support and guidance, especially for children. If there were social workers available, I never heard of them. Certainly there were none in the schools. Some churches may have filled this role, but none that we were a part of in rural life could have done so. As for Aunt Inez and her children, they were probably not regular church members. They had moved about a lot, for Uncle Sheddy changed jobs frequently. Church and family were the usual support for people. Neither government nor society played an organized role.

The Depression years were not too dreadful for many, but they did have an impact on most people. Aunt Mabel's husband, Bill Kimberlin, was a hardwood floor contractor. He did very specialized and beautiful work. During those years, he had very few contracts for floors, and not many in his specialty. Their income barely covered their needs, and they only saved their house after Franklin D. Roosevelt's New Deal provided a program, the FHA (Federal Housing Administration), which allowed them to extend their mortgage.

My father was very wry about this. He was a staunch Democrat, and all the Eversons and Quicks were especially staunch Republicans. I heard him telling my mother that he hoped they would have sense enough to vote their interests after this. My mother's brother, Uncle Charles, was also affected. He was a machinist and worked in a manufacturing plant in Indianapolis. His workdays were cut back drastically. They moved into Aunt Bertha's mother's house and rented their own.

In Columbus, there were fewer changes in our relatives' lives. In counties all around us, banks were closing, but in neither Hope nor Columbus did a single bank close. However, Uncle Hal began to have health problems. He had always smoked a pipe, and he developed cancer on his lip where the pipe had rested. He was at the Kellogg Health Center in Battle Creek, Michigan, receiving treatment for this condition when the stock market crash of 1929 occurred. He lost a great deal in that debacle, although not so much as to upset his family's living patterns. But then, they had always lived modestly.

He was semiretired after this, for the cancer, though delayed, remained and continued to grow. He maintained his position with the Irwin investments, but he had little to do with the Cummins Engine Company, which became that family's greatest moneymaker. He may have helped lay the groundwork for the corporation while it was in the early experimental stage.

My quest for postsecondary education

During my senior year, when many of my classmates were planning for the next year at university, college, technical school, nursing schools attached to hospitals, and so forth, I was casting about for opportunities. Unless one had financial backing, there just were not any.

Mr. Lambert tried to be helpful. He called me in to talk with him and suggested that my father also talk to him. But my father never went. When I told him that Mr. Lambert wanted to see him and why, he replied that there was no point in going. He could not even pay the family bills, and he had to buy seed and gasoline on credit to keep farming. If I wanted to go on to school, I would have to find my own way.

I pursued all the avenues suggested to me and even some I read about or thought about on my own. I was interviewed by a number of small colleges. I even spent weekends at Franklin and Hanover, both of which offered scholarships for relief of about one-third of my tuition. But I had no money at all. And I would need to provide the remainder of my tuition, a place to live, food, books, and clothing. I saw no way to get any of this. Earlham College also offered a scholarship in part tuition relief. It would have been my choice.

It became very clear to me that I probably could not even earn enough to support myself, never mind having anything left over to save for going to school in the future. I had gotten a job while a senior in high school, working at Woolworth's on Saturdays. My pay for the day was $1.25. Even in 1932 that was an extremely poor wage.

Our hours were 8 a.m. to 12 noon, and 1 p.m. to 5 or 6 p.m., an hour for a meal, then back on the floor until 10 p.m. This was paid time, but in addition, we had to be there before opening to have the counters ready for sales, and we remained in the evening to clean up and restock. How busy we had been and how long it took us to straighten our wares determined the time we could leave. I was always so tired at closing time that I felt sure I could not walk to find our car, but of course, I did.

Often it was a long wait until my father appeared to drive the two of us home. Usually he brought me to work in the morning and then stayed in town, playing cards and drinking at the Elks or the Eagles, and too often not coming to the car until near midnight. One time when it was after midnight, I complained and said some quite nasty things to him about being so tired and yet having to wait to go home to bed. He slapped my face very hard and said something to the effect that it was his car and his business. I did not complain again.

With my salary of $1.25, I usually bought a pair of hose for 95¢. Later, I found that one could buy rejects from the Real Silk Hosiery Mill in Indianapolis for 79¢. But while I was still in high school, I had no time or way to get the rejects. I did buy them for a good many years after, until wartime when silk was used for parachutes not hose.

But I have digressed from the business of scholarships, their availability, and their meagerness. Another fact of life was revealed to me that year. Male and female are not equal. It became abundantly clear to me that a male student with my performance record could have received a great deal more help in securing an education than I, a female, could.

It was very commonly said that it was a waste of time and money to give higher education to women, because they only married, had children, and kept house anyway. When I heard statements like that, I really saw red. I could see then, and I can see now, the very real need for educating women.

At that time DePauw University in Greencastle, Indiana, offered a Rector Scholarship to the male student with the highest grade ranking of the graduates in his public high school anywhere in Indiana. A good friend of mine who had been in my journalism class and who was editor of the school newspaper in my senior year went to DePauw with a Rector Scholarship. I was glad for him, I really was, but I was sad for me.

Another friend, Ben Niemoeller, from a farm family, was awarded a scholarship with full tuition paid to Franklin. Ben did not have much cash either. He drove to Franklin daily with some other students in a ramshackle old touring car. This was one of the early open cars that used storm curtains that were fastened to the car with snaps in inclement weather and so, were not greatly protec-

tive. One day Ben and his friends were caught in a snowstorm. He caught a cold from which he never fully recovered. His condition worsened with tuberculosis, and Ben died. As I said, the Depression touched most of our lives.

My senior year came to an end not too happily. Not only had I found no prospects for continuing my education, but I had absolutely no prospects for any kind of well-paying job. Not even dishwashing jobs were being advertised in the newspapers. There was no need to advertise. If anyone wanted work to be done, there were several bodies available among acquaintances. Employment openings were passed by word of mouth to relatives and friends.

Ann Redmon
**High School Graduation,
1931**

Life as a working woman

Aunt Mabel had said that if I could get a scholarship to Butler College in Indianapolis, I could live with her while going to school. I had told Mr. Lambert this, and he had contacted Butler on my behalf, but they had found nothing for me. Again, there were only possibilities for men interested in the ministry.

I went to Indianapolis anyway. Of course, Aunt Mabel's position had changed. For one, they had adopted my younger cousin Ruth, Aunt Inez' daughter, and for another, Uncle Bill had very little work, and the jobs he did get had to be performed at less profit. Watching the want ads, the only possibility I found for one with my background was a housework-babysitting job. I was reluctant, but Aunt Mabel insisted, so I applied. They hired me. I was to live in, and I would get $4 for the week's work (seven days with Sunday afternoons free).

It was a Jewish household and very strange to me. I really think that the woman meant to be good to me. She showed me how to do everything. I did no cooking, for they were kosher, but I served the meals, washed all the dishes and pots, and kept the kitchen immaculate. In addition, I did all the washing, ironing, and cleaning. All of this I did—though not very efficiently, I am sure. She even talked with me about higher education. She was very understanding of my ambition and said perhaps her family could help one day.

My pitfall was the little boy. I did not like him very much. He was very spoiled, petulant, and demanding. He whined continuously and asked questions incessantly. Now, I had cared for my siblings all their lives, and I loved them enormously, but this child annoyed me to distraction.

My employer criticized my behavior. She told me that I must never ignore any questions but try to answer them and act more kindly toward him. I tried, but he really was a spoiled brat, and when he threw his food on the floor and at me, I knew I could not stay and hold my temper, so I told her I would have to leave. Her husband and even her brother who was visiting tried to persuade me to stay. I appreciated their kindness, but I held my ground and left at the end of two weeks.

I went home, and the next week I went back to Woolworth's in Columbus, but full-time. My salary was $8 a week, and the hours were 8 a.m. to 6 p.m., except on Saturday when the store closed at 10 p.m. Just as when I worked only on Saturday, we employees gave Woolworth's an extra hour before opening and after closing—at least six hours a week more.

There were always applicants for the jobs because few skills were required; only endurance was needed. So one did not split hairs about time. As our manager pointed out, we were not hourly workers; we were salaried employees. It was true that if one had to perform a personal errand, the manager had the option of allowing the time without cutting one's pay.

One of my problems when I worked in Columbus was transportation. During the summer and fall of that year, I found rides with workers going from Hope to Columbus. My father was still capable of doing some work then, and I believe he did. For some time now, I have repressed the unhappy events of those years, so I am not sure I can be accurate about the time of all the events for my family, although I can for myself.

It was in 1932, the year after my graduation from high school that Franklin Roosevelt was elected president. Most of the people I knew were Republicans, so it was only in my immediate family that there was great rejoicing. He was inaugurated in March and immediately started programs that put many small people to work. It is almost impossible to describe the lifting of spirits. There was a perceptible lessening of gloomy foreboding that gave rise to hope for the future for the laboring class and the youth.

Let me not give the wrong impression—this was not a universal condition. Columbus was full of businessmen who were thunderstruck with dismay over Roosevelt's New Deal and programs such as the NRA (National Recovery Administration), WPA (Works Projects Administration), and AAA (Agricultural Adjustment Administration). In fact, there was a backlash, and the lowly clerks at Woolworth's were made to feel it.

A time clock was installed, and we had to punch it. No matter what the hourly rate had been, Woolworth's was determined, under the new rules of a higher hourly wage rate, to pay us no more than the $8 per week that had been our salary. Actually, my take-home pay was only $7.50 under the new rules, but I had more time for myself, and I was much less tired. I was not a zombie any more. I could read, and I could study again.

I looked about me once more and tried again to think of what I might do to improve my skills and find a better job, ideally one with a future. There was a branch of the Indiana Business College in Columbus, and I went to talk to the manager (a woman) about night courses, hours, and tuition costs. Eventually, I saved enough for tuition, but I had another problem to solve. I would have to find a place to live in Columbus, for it would be impossible to find rides home after ten at night.

I begin night school

Fortunately, I had come to know a family named Stadler in Columbus. I had known their daughter Mary in school and had been in their house. Mrs. Stadler was an elementary schoolteacher, a widow with five children. I have never known anyone who worked harder than she did. I liked and admired her greatly. I do not remember how it came about, but she offered me a bed in her attic, where two of her daughters slept. For a small amount, she even gave me breakfast and dinner.

Actually, it was Mrs. Stadler who had graded the state examination I took when I graduated from the eighth grade. She remembered it, and when Mary brought me home one day, we met for the first time. She was very direct and did not mind speaking her opinion. She hated pretense. And she had compassion, particularly for the underdog. Mrs. Stadler deserves a place in heaven, and I hope she is there enjoying it now.

I lived with the Stadlers for a good many months while I worked and went to night classes. It was a crowded house with no place for study or reading, but I did not have much time for either. Besides, one could always go to the library to study.

What I really could not fit in was the bookkeeping-accounting course, which had great flat spreadsheets for working out problems. When a problem was set, it took me two or three hours to work it all out on a spreadsheet. There was no place I could occupy for that length of time. That may sound silly. But when you have no place of your own, and some dear generous people are sharing their small bit with you, it is not right to make yourself a nuisance. I talked with the manager of the school, and she deferred bookkeeping to a later date.

It was at some time during that period that Aunt Lily and Uncle Hal returned to Columbus. When the lip cancer had spread to his face, they had sold their house on Franklin Street and moved to Denver, Colorado. For years Aunt Lily had spent summers with their daughter in Evergreen, west of Denver in the foothills of the Rockies. (They both had suffered with hay fever and asthma in Indiana, but not in Evergreen or Denver.) I suspect that Uncle Harold was not that ill and did not find much to do away from business. So they returned to Columbus and bought a smaller, pleasant house on Lafayette Street.

I saw Aunt Lily infrequently. Although she was very enthusiastic about my night school program, I never felt that she had any understanding at all of the physical stamina required. But then, she was very occupied with taking care of her husband, whose condition was pretty horrid. Later I learned another reason for their leaving Denver: they were quite unhappy with their daughter's marriage. Their son had died of an acute mastoid infection when he was about twenty years old, so they had grown to care even more deeply about their daughter, Helen, who was a very beautiful and sweet person.

I do not recall how long I lived with the Stadlers, or quite when I moved to the Moores' house. Robert (Bucky) Moore had been in my high school class and had taken me (wearing a borrowed dress) to the prom. I always thought he asked me to go because I was small. Bucky was only about three inches taller than me. His parents admired my school record and me, and I am sure they wanted me for a daughter-in-law. Bucky and I had very few interests in common, but we had remained friendly, and once in a while, he took me to a ballgame or a movie. His mother and Mrs. Stadler went to the same church and likely talked together about me.

One day Mrs. Moore came into the store and invited me to their house for an evening meal. That evening she asked me whether I would like to rent their extra bedroom, and soon after, I moved there. I had a room alone for the first time since the fourth grade! I paid Mrs. Moore just the same amount I had paid Mrs. Stadler.

I had always gone home on weekends and continued to do so, even though it had become an increasingly depressing experience. My brother Joe had more or less taken over the role of breadwinner for the family. He supervised as well as did all the farm work.

My father had been given a small political plum under the road-building program of the New Deal. He supervised the road crew that repaired the county roads. He could now give Mother a few dollars to meet our basic needs, but I suspect that most of his salary just went for whiskey and gasoline. His behavior was never really discussed among family members. We did not need to; we all saw it as a hopeless situation.

Illness and a new job

One summer, after I had been at Woolworth's for more than two years, I became very ill. It started out as an intestinal flu that did not go away. When I began to faint—not once, but every time I tried to stand up—Mrs. Moore called the doctor. He said that I had acute colitis and that I needed a long rest more than anything else.

Dear Dr. Norton had known me all my life, and Mother for a great part of hers. He always loved my mother in a good, kindly sort of way, and it seems to me that he felt a kind of deep-seated anger toward my father for falling into alcoholism. I haven't the foggiest notion what medication he gave me, but I know I was always sleepy. I could sleep for hours on end. I am sure Mrs. Moore would have kept me, but I was not about to stay there without money to pay for my room and food, so I went back to the farm for about six or eight weeks.

After I recovered, Aunt Lily came up with a job for me. Uncle Hal, after returning from Denver, had resumed treatment at the Kellogg Center in Battle Creek. He often was there for a month or more. While he was away, I visited my aunt, as did Mother. Aunt Lily was a woman with a good mind and many interests. One of her interests, and this she shared with her husband, was the establishment of a chapter of the Boys Club of America in Columbus. As a memorial to their son, they had given generously to the club. Aunt Lily interested herself in the program and went to the club to play games with the boys.

The director of the club was Walter Hall, a physical education teacher at the high school. Each fall there was a fund drive, very like present-day United Fund appeals. That fall Aunt Lily suggested to Mr. Hall that they employ me as a sort of clerk-assistant. Mr. Hall had one child, a little boy, who was desperately ill, and he wanted to help his wife care for their child rather than direct the fund campaign.

Yandell Cline, the treasurer of Noblitt-Sparks Industries (now called Arvin Industries), had been named chairperson for the fund drive, so although Walter Hall hired me, I actually worked for Mr. Cline. Evelyn Cline, his sister, had been my journalism teacher and good friend in high school. She adored her big brother and had talked about him, so I knew something of him. He was a great person to work with, and I really enjoyed the experience. I was rather much on my own, but I liked that. I was told what the chairperson needed to know and what needed doing. Then it was left to me to organize my activities. I was very busy, but even though I was just recovering from my illness, it was not too tiring.

My part of the fund drive lasted about three weeks. One day during the last week, Mr. Cline engaged me in a conversation. He asked me about myself, and whether I needed a job. Soon after, he said he would be happy to have me work in his division at Noblitt-Sparks. For the first time since my school days, I felt that lovely glow of satisfaction from having turned in a good performance and it being acknowledged. Before we wound up the affairs of the fund drive, Mr. Hall thanked me for my work. His son was past the critical point of his illness, and he said it had been so great to be able to help take care of the boy and not worry about the day-to-day work of the drive.

I begin working at Noblitt-Sparks

The next Monday I went to see Mr. Cline in his office at Noblitt-Sparks. He called in his executive aide, Earl Robinson, introduced me, and said I would be working under his supervision. I do not know whether Mr. Robinson had been consulted, or whether he had simply been told he was to have another clerk. But for a very long time I had the feeling that I was given made work. I had no special place in the organizational structure. Indeed, I had no special skills or qualifications.

The company had two distinct manufacturing divisions. The division that Mr. Noblitt had first created made mufflers for automobiles under contract to General Motors, Ford, and Chrysler. As the company prospered, their research and engineering division created other products, including car accessories such as heaters and radios.

I thought at the time, and still do, that I was given a job that served no great purpose. My job was to record shipping invoice numbers beside serial numbers in a ledger. I recall only one instance when I was asked for information about a serial number and invoice. This was after months of writing numbers down. However, over time I was assigned duties all about the department. I even ran the file department for about three months while the file clerk was ill.

Overall, it was a pleasant, smoothly run office and a friendly place. We did a lot of work, but seldom were we under pressure. One of my workmates was my first school friend, Evelyn Linson. We resumed our friendship and had many pleasant, happy hours together, both in and out of the office.

One day I ran across Mrs. Moore, and she offered to rent me a room again. They had changed houses, but she said they had an extra room if I would like to use it. So I returned to living with the Moores. After I had been living there for a while, a horridly ugly thing happened for which I was not prepared, and which I was very uncertain how to handle.

One evening, Mr. Moore and I were alone in the house, and he suggested we sit on the porch together, or maybe I went out on the porch where he was. Anyway, I was sitting on the swing, and he came and sat beside me. I became aware that his arm was around me and that he was fondling my breast. Scared, shocked, and angry, I started to get up, but he held me and attempted to kiss me. It was awful!

I was so upset I must have had a great surge of adrenalin, for I gave a mighty shove and nearly upset the swing and him. I raced to my room where I slammed and locked the door. He came and talked to me through the door, and begged me to come out and pardon him. He said that I was just so sweet that he had been overcome, but that he would not do it again.

This went on for a time, while I sat inside and pondered what to do. I prayed for Bucky or Mrs. Moore to come home. Time went on, and I decided I could not spend another night under that roof. I took the screen out of a side window as silently as possible. I saw the people next door, and I thought I could scream if need be. I took my door key and climbed out the window. There was about a three-foot drop from the sill, but I made it safely and walked to the Stadlers.

I knew Mrs. Stadler would understand and she did. One of the girls walked back to the Moores' with me. Mrs. Moore was surprised to see me coming in the front door when she had supposed me asleep in my room behind the locked door.

Margie and I had made up a tale as to why I would be spending the night with her, and then we packed a suitcase and I left. I regretted having to leave Mrs. Moore without giving her a good reason, but I did not feel that I could tell her that her husband was an old goat who had sexually assaulted me. I simply said my mother wanted me to come home for a while, and my father went with me to collect my belongings.

Back home on the farm

Again I joined a car pool to travel to and from work in Columbus while living at home in Hope. The situation at home had only worsened. My mother was truly wonderful. It seemed to me that what she could not do anything about she ignored, and that she concentrated on doing the very best with what she had for her younger children who remained at home.

My brother Joe deserves many stars—a whole heavenful, in fact—for continuing to maintain the farm and for giving a home to Mother and the children. I loved being with my family. I tried to think of pleasant little things we could do together. I came up with new ideas for food and cooking to change the monotonous menus. I thought of new games to play. I often bought clothing for them, even though I could have used better clothing for myself. It broke my heart that they had so little.

In 1937 my sister Mae married Glenn Klipsch. Although the Klipsch family had lived and farmed in our area for a long time, we only knew them by sight. I was the first to become acquainted with them. My dear friend Doris Taylor was dating Edward Ketner, a young man from Hope. Edward and Glenn Klipsch were friends. So I came to know Doris' young man and his friend, and we all went to the movies a few times. Then one Sunday afternoon,

Glenn stopped by to see me when Mae was there. He lost no time in following up on the introduction.

Mae's various jobs in Indianapolis had dwindled, and she was working in Columbus as a chauffeur/housekeeper for an elderly woman and her daughter. This allowed her to develop a relationship with Glenn. Times were tough, and they wanted to marry, but they could not afford a home of their own. Mae would need to continue working, and wanted to. Eventually, she found a position in the office of a trucking company, and the Klipsches gave them two rooms in their home for a small apartment. So they were able to get married.

My father's death

Only a few months later, my father committed suicide. It was an act that affected me profoundly. I found him dead, and he had used a gun that I had purchased. His death had a devastating effect on me, one that still lingers. My two young brothers had become interested in guns, especially Roy. They had learned of a rifle for sale and begged me to buy it for them. Dad used that gun.

I vowed then that I would never buy another gun. In fact, I am really rabid on the subject of guns. When my children were small, I would not even let them play with toy guns. Guns are instruments of death; they are not playthings for either children or adults. Of course our father was sick. He had been sick for years. And if he had not used that gun or that means, he would have used another. I know all that. I know all that, but I never again want to feel the responsibility of causing a death.

I was overwhelmed with a depth of sadness that is hard to explain. Although I was fairly young and limited in experience, I found it so poignantly sad that his life had ended in such a way. Perhaps we were enough alike in our personalities that I could feel a profound sympathy for one who had started out with so much faith in himself, who was so sure that hard work and common sense would bring success, and yet who had failed so miserably. At this time in my life, I already knew how it felt to see your endeavors become failures. I made no great outward changes in my life, but my reading and my philosophy took a sharp turn to the left.

The hours, days, and weeks following Dad's death could not, however, be spent musing. There were tasks to perform and decisions to make immediately (the undertaker, the coroner, the cemetery, the funeral), and relations to notify, and at the end, finding money to pay for it all. The latter I looked upon as a crass thought, but it was a real problem, and it had to be solved. I remember one of the first things the undertaker said, "Who is going to be financially responsible?" Mother was almost numb. She seemed incapable of making any decisions, even trivial ones. If my memory is correct, Joe and I together made them all.

There must have been a dearth of news in Bartholomew County that weekend, for the county newspaper gave us their boldest and biggest black headlines the next day. Evelyn Cline would have called it lurid journalism. But at least we were spared the photographers. The funeral was in our church in Petersville. It must have been the largest ever held there. Some part of me was amazed by the crowd of people.

Grandmother Redmond came from Asheville accompanied by her daughter Belle. Her brother, our uncle John King, met them at the train and brought them to the church. Mama was completely surprised; she had no idea they were coming. They appeared just as we were entering the church as a family, and Mama fainted away in the doorway. Her children held her up, and we all but carried her into our pew. We provided good drama for the crowd.

I suppose all my brothers and sisters were as numb as I was. The service was not in the least comforting or helpful. We endured it. Grandmother Redmond added to the discomfort. She wept and moaned and muttered to herself. The gist of her grief was that she could not and would not accept the fact that her son had committed suicide. She was saying that someone had killed her boy, and she hoped they would find him. She was making dire threats to the murderer and hoping all manner of evil would befall him. I now understand that to her and all his family, he had been much loved and admired.

Finally it was over, both the funeral and the burial, which I do not remember. I expect we went back to the church where refreshments would have been provided by the Ladies Aid, and the family would have received the condolences of their friends and neighbors in the communal area of the church. I cannot even recall any of Mother's relatives being there, although I am sure they were. Sometime during the sermon, I tuned out. I suppose habit and concern for Mama carried me through the rest of the day.

What I do remember is the great and genuine sympathy with which I was greeted when I returned to work. Teletype machines (both Western Union and American) had been installed in our division, and I had been put in charge of receiving and distributing telegrams, as well as sending them out. In this way, I came in contact with the whole office, including all the division heads and the engineering department.

My co-workers were kind and sympathetic. There were even flowers on my desk. One older man, an engineer, continued bringing me flowers from his garden for a long time, until it became a subject of comment, and Mr. Robinson suggested to me that perhaps it should stop. He offered to speak to the fellow. I consented and the bouquets stopped.

One expression of sympathy is particularly worthy of note. Mr. Cline had asked Mr. Robinson to send me into his office when I returned to work. When I look back on it now fifty years later, I can see how wise and thoughtful Mr. Cline was. I sensed it then, and I realize it now.

In no way had Mr. Cline ever singled me out after handing me over to Mr. Robinson for work assignment when I had first arrived. He was always aloof and impersonal, so I never had to suffer surreptitious giggling and behind-the-hand remarks from my co-workers. Even Mr. Robinson had probably wondered. I see now how difficult it must have been for one in Mr. Cline's position to confer a kind act on a young woman without causing gossip.

So when I went in to see him that morning after my father's death, it was in fact the first time I had sat in his office and talked with him since my arrival. He expressed his sympathy. He must have been very adroit in his conversation, for he found out the financial situation of my family. He asked me if it would help if he purchased my stock certificates. I was amazed but managed to say that indeed it would.

On two different occasions, during stock expansion, the company had given each office employee one share of stock. I assumed that they were worth perhaps $5 each and never thought much about how to sell them. Mr. Noblitt had made a little speech at the time of the distribution, speaking of his gratitude to the workforce, his hope for our loyalty to the company, and his wish that we would hold the stock and acquire more when possible. I believe that Mr. Cline wanted to help me financially and that this was his way of doing it quietly and without giving rise to talk.

Mr. Noblitt's secretary handled the transaction in his office. I turned over the certificates, and Mr. Hartley gave me Yandell Cline's check for just under $100. I cannot remember ever before having that great a sum of money in my hands. It was wonderful to be able to give it to Joe to help with the expenses.

My broadening horizons

In spite of my grief and sadness and my concern for Mother's sadness, Father's death also brought us a relief from the tension and strain of the past several years. When it was all over, I felt far more capable of lifting up my head and giving my future some thought once again.

About that time, some neighbors of ours were making changes in their lives. Kate and Earl Finkel and their family lived near us on a farm that Earl had inherited from his father. (Earl was distantly related to Mother—there was hardly a pioneer family that was not.) Ruth Finkel and I had been passengers in Donald May's car during my first year in high school. She had been the driver of her own car and I the passenger during the following years, and we had always had a good friendship. Ruth's brother Paul and my brother Joe had been dating buddies. Now Paul was getting married, and his father was turning over the farm to him.

The elder Finkels had bought a house in Columbus and moved there with the two youngest children, Kathleen and Joby. Ruth had married a year or two before that. In fact, in 1937 I was the only unmarried one of my group of friends from Petersville School. The Finkels' new home was only about a block from the Noblitt-Sparks office in which I worked. Kate had offered me a room in their house even before Dad died. So then, soon after his death, I moved into their home. Living with them was a real joy. Kathleen and Joby were like a younger sister and brother, and the elder Finkels treated me very much like another daughter.

Soon after going there to live, I finished my bookkeeping course. Once again, I had time and a place to read comfortably.

My life became far more normal. I interacted with all my co-workers—going to movies, attending athletic events, and even learning to play bridge and joining a bridge club.

Another dimension was added to my life when I was able to drive to Indianapolis with a co-worker and her father to attend classes in Indiana University's extension program. I completed courses in history (one American, the other European) and the first-year economics course.

As far as I was concerned, it was pure joy. I still loved school. However, I found that I was selective about the courses I did joyfully and the ones I did as tasks to be gotten through. Bookkeeping was monotonous, and I actively disliked typing and shorthand. Business English I thought stilted and stupid. Having already had a bookkeeping course, which included accounting basics, I found economics to be fun. It opened my mind to the larger world of finance and marketing.

My life was pleasant enough. I was not actively unhappy, but I realized that I was running in place insofar as my work was concerned, and that I had no secure financial base for my future. In our office, clerks and typists came and went. Most of the female employees lived at home with their parents, or were married and working to help their husbands buy a house, a car, and furniture—the usual accoutrements for a new household. All the supervisory jobs were held by males.

When I observed young men being brought in and taught their jobs by the women already working there, I felt very deep anger and resentment at the business world's refusal to consider women for even minor executive appointments. I watched these same young men as they stood around the cola machine, drinking colas, smoking cigarettes, rehashing sporting events, and talking about their cars or golf scores. A woman who did the same thing would find a new stack of work on her desk when she returned, and she might even be asked to stay late to complete it.

I had only one pay raise in all the time I was there. My beginning salary was $12 per week, only a little more than at Woolworth's, and after my apprentice period, I was paid $15. I finally realized, very sadly, that no matter how competent or how versatile I became, my future at Noblitt-Sparks would be limited because of my sex.

That most of the European countries were in turbulence impinged somewhere on the periphery of my consciousness, but I did not have enough background knowledge to relate to most of the reports I read. Nor do I remember gaining much of the background information that I needed from newspapers. I felt very much at sea when reading about the Spanish Civil War, because so little was reported in any newspaper I read.

It might very well be that the reviews in the Book-of-the-Month Club were my greatest resource. I remember being greatly interested in Ernest Hemingway's *For Whom the Bell Tolls*. However, the only persons I talked with about world and international events were my Petersville Sunday school teachers Eva and Charles Tally. Both were very well read, and I loved discussions with them. I think they were sometimes alarmed, if not appalled, by some of the books I read, since some might have been written by communists. But they were certainly able to refute some of the statements I made.

While the Spanish Civil War confused me, I felt no confusion at all about Hitler and Mussolini. Perhaps because my early years were lived in an atmosphere of anti-Germanism, I never had any doubts that Adolf Hitler was an evil man and that he and his ideas should be—had to be—eliminated. Mussolini, somehow, was more like the evil giant in Jack and the Beanstalk. Some Jack should come along and eliminate him. At any rate, I viewed President Roosevelt's rather tentative and half-hearted increases in the navy and the army affirmatively.

Indianapolis and Fort Benjamin Harrison

My cousin Dorothy was married in the same year as Mae. Her husband, Sherman Stevens, had been in the ROTC while in college and had majored in science and mathematics, but graduating in the Depression years, he had trouble finding a satisfactory job. Aunt Bertha had a dear friend of many years whose husband was a civilian administrator at Fort Benjamin Harrison, just outside Indianapolis. Mr. Locke was one of the first to be aware that the military establishment was on the alert and enlarging. I think it was he who gave Sherman a job in the Quartermaster Corps at Fort Harrison.

Soon after starting to work there, Sherman was given a commission in the Finance Corps because of his ROTC training, and he was assigned to the Fifth Army Corps headquartered in Columbus, Ohio. However, his first duties kept him at Fort Harrison and in Indianapolis. When Sherman learned that Mr. Locke was hiring additional clerks in the Quartermaster Corps, Dorothy asked Mr. Locke about a job for me.

If I remember correctly, I did not go for an interview, take an exam, or anything else. Dorothy and Sherman told me that the job was there and insisted that I resign from Noblitt-Sparks and move to Indianapolis. I could live with Aunt Mabel and Uncle Bill and share a room with Ruth.

Even though I knew they were right and I realized I must go to work at Fort Harrison, I did not leave Columbus joyfully. As much as anything else, I hated giving up my room in the Finkels' house. I liked having a room all to myself. I would have to return to sharing, though of course I was grateful that Ruth was willing to share with me. Then, too, Noblitt-Sparks was a pleasant place to work, and all my friends were in the Columbus area. And I spent most weekends at home with Mother and my two younger sisters, so I would miss seeing them, too.

My brother Joe had married and was still farming Mr. New's farm. Mother, Betty, and Martha had moved into a small house about a half-mile away. I was contributing as much as I could to their expenses, but it was such a pittance. My salary at Fort Harrison would give me about thirty percent more—$90 a month. So I moved to Indianapolis in April of 1941.

When I reported to Mr. Locke and filled out the forms for employment, he told me that this was a civil service appointment at the lowest clerk salary and that I would have to take the civil service examination when one was next given. How well I did on the exam would determine whether or not I would be promoted to a higher rating and increased salary.

I worked there some months before I took the exam. I was very apprehensive about taking it, because it was almost solely to determine proficiency in typing and shorthand. It had been several years since my schooling in both, and I had not been great in either, only passable. My work since then had required very little of either. Not even in my present work at Fort Harrison did I use them. As usually happens, when one wants most to feel well, one does not. I had a cold. I took the test anyway, and I felt greatly relieved afterwards because I thought I had not done too badly.

Some time later, I was called in to see Mr. Locke about my performance on the exam. He let me know at once that he would never have hired me if he had first had my grades in hand. When I saw them, I thought they were pretty good (my typing grade was 97% and my shorthand was 89%). But he said that all those who were hired after me had scored 97-99%. So, no raise in salary for me.

At that time, I was working with a young soldier and learning his job, for he would soon be transferred. He was an interesting fellow with an able, incisive mind, and no trace of reverence, humility, or modesty in his whole makeup. His name was Hearst Butler and his mother was Randolph Hearst's sister. He was in the army because he had a drinking problem. It was such a treat to my drooping spirits to hear what he had to say about civil service exams, administrators, the army, and the world, including Hitler and Roosevelt. I have never known another like him.

I am very glad he was there with me just then, because he gave me a shot of confidence when I needed it. He told me that there was another exam for supervisors and administrators, and that I should find out when it would be given and take it. He was right. Such an exam was given a few weeks later. I took it and came out with a very high score. As a result, I advanced to a supervisory position and received a raise in salary to $125 a month—even though I was still doing exactly the same work I had been doing from the beginning. The civil service world is a strange one.

Living in Indianapolis, one of the things I missed most was the library at Columbus. There was a branch of the Indianapolis library on Washington Street in Irvington, but it was a long walk from Aunt Mabel's house and had far fewer materials than the Columbus library. It was also a long walk to the East Tenth Street trolley stop, and Aunt Mabel worried quite a lot for my safety. I never worried, possibly because of my ignorance and naiveté. Luckily I never had any bad experiences.

However, there were compensations to be gained by living in the city. Before moving to Indianapolis, I was enrolled in an Indiana University extension course, which I was now able to easily finish. Also, it was possible to go downtown to the big movie theaters, where they often had live entertainment with big band performances.

Much of the music was jazz, and the remainder was popular music from the operettas, musical plays, and films of Broadway productions. I went to a lot of films, usually with someone from my office. In my second year in Indianapolis, I bought a season ticket for performances of the Indianapolis Symphony Orchestra to which I went alone.

My early experiences with the arts

As I look back upon my life now, I recognize that there was always within me some instinctive response to the arts in all forms. For years the only art form I had access to was language and literature. The first literature to appeal to children is poetry, and in my early years of reading, I loved the long epic poems.

Whenever one of my mother's relatives changed houses, moved away, or disposed of a deceased's possessions, our household was the natural repository for leftover libraries. So we had a house full of literature. There were books and magazines of a wide variety. We had Shakespeare, Ruskin, Emerson, and Hawthorne, and we had *Physical Culture* magazines and others of that caliber whose names I do not recall.

Since our reading was totally unsupervised, and I read everything, I learned some basic facts about the human body and human behavior, but I also read the most beautiful and profound thoughts in the English language. I loved Shakespeare and Emerson, and I found Hawthorne and Ruskin interesting. My recitations of "Hiawatha" were a showpiece for visiting friends and relatives.

In our society, children were often called upon to entertain guests, singing, for example, or playing the piano or another musical instrument. Having no musical training, I did my parents proud by reciting poetry. If I wanted to make it short, I recited Tennyson's "Thanatopsis." My love of the exquisite use of the English language was formed then, and it still exists, quite apart from reading for knowledge.

When I first heard real music—music that sweeps the universe and reaches to the heavens searching for the meaning of life, the relationship of man and God—I cannot really remember. What I do know is that while I enjoyed popular music, I realized that it was only transient entertainment. It is almost impossible to understand the great void that existed outside large cities for beautiful music before the advent of radio and TV made it uniformly available.

While working at Noblitt-Sparks, I bought our first radio. It was *an event*. Radios had been around for a while, but we had not owned one, probably because until Roosevelt's Rural Electrification Administration, we had no electricity. The utility company that served Columbus and Hope did not service areas where there were miles between customers. Wealthy farmers might have their own generating plants, but many like us used oil lamps for lighting, and wood and coal for heating and cooking.

So it was with that first radio that I started listening to *The Telephone Hour* and *The Firestone Hour*. My choices were not popular with my family. I was not so selfish as to impose my programs on everyone else all the time, and as long as my father was there, he often overruled me. However, I did hear music to which I responded and which seemed to fill a void in my soul.

After moving to Indianapolis, I pursued various interests that had been awakened during high school. I went to the public library frequently. I read a lot in the journals we used in our Sorosis discussions. My awareness of politics had been aroused during the second Roosevelt election campaign.

In our office, the management was loudly and solidly Republican. Each time a new social program was put into effect, we all heard endlessly how business could not survive. When the Social Security Act went into effect, there were so many remarks addressed to the lowly clerks that we could have wondered whether we were really guilty of biting those benevolent hands that were feeding and clothing us so generously.

Of course, I was passionately in favor of all those programs. I began to read the works of the social thinkers of the time, probably some of them communists.

For the research paper for my American History course at Indiana University, I chose the American labor movement. I did not read only about Samuel Gompers, but since it was he who determined the philosophy and actions of all labor unions, I read mostly about him. John L. Lewis, the leader of the United Mine Workers, was often in the news then, and I followed his activities with interest, but not much admiration. The paper could be only a few pages long, but after finishing it, I read all the books suggested by my professor. It was so wonderful! How I loved Lincoln Steffens' autobiography.

I joined the Book-of-the-Month Club and still have many volumes I bought then. One that affected me very much was Pierre van Paasen's *Days of Our Years*. I was not totally alone in my reading. Mae loved books, too. She read quite a lot. But we rarely discussed together what we read, and after her marriage, not at all.

Life as a civil servant

Those first months of working at Fort Harrison were almost leisurely. They gave me and the other civil servants an opportunity to become acquainted with how the US Army operated and with the many army regulations that guided every move (practically) that everyone made.

In quartermaster supply where I worked, we were concerned with clothing and personal equipment only—no firearms, no food, no medical supplies (those were administered in entirely different divisions). Fortunately, the good fairy who endowed me at birth gave me a simply phenomenal memory, close to photographic recall. It was a marvelous possession that I never appreciated so much until this job at Fort Harrison.

I came to be the person who checked every requisition submitted to the quartermaster's office. Each requisition had to be in compliance with army regulations for my initials to be placed on it, and so my initials came to be the key that opened the door for each supply sergeant to draw his supplies from the warehouse. In my first months, it was fairly quiet at Fort Harrison, which gave me time to learn both the system and the kind of people, both army and civilians, that I worked with. Our working hours were from 8 a.m. to 5 p.m., five days each week.

Free time was greatly needed, not only for personal shopping but also for laundering, hair-washing, room cleaning, all those small tasks that women must do for themselves. This was my most basic and bitter complaint through all my working days. Men could have their shirts laundered and cleaning done for about one-third the cost that women would pay—if women could find someone to do it for them. And I never heard of a male boarder cleaning his own room or helping with the dishes, but women usually were expected to.

I must be fair and say that laundries came into being to serve working men, who comprised at least eighty percent of the labor force. However, men could find women to do all their washing, ironing, and mending, while working women always had to care for their own clothing. Doing so really was a burden. These were the days before wash and wear fabrics, when blouses and dresses were slow-drying and had to be ironed.

When I lived with the Finkels, dear Mrs. Finkel often did much of my laundry. She was so efficient, hardworking, and kind. I so appreciated her. When I came to live again with Aunt Mabel in Indianapolis, she was not well. In addition to this, Uncle Bill's work was sporadic and had been for some years, so she had many worries. Ruth and I got along very well sharing her room in spite of the differences in our ages and personalities. She was a senior in high school that year, and I was already seven years past that age. We were all sharing.

I was not wildly happy, but I was finding life interesting. Most of the people I encountered daily were different than any that I had closely interacted with before. I usually enjoy change, so I coped well with my job and with lots of new people from very different backgrounds. I was intrigued and even entertained, but I did not form any close relationships.

Pearl Harbor and WWII

One Sunday afternoon during my first year in Indianapolis, Aunt Mabel and I went to hear a local group perform Handel's *Messiah*. During the performance, someone came on the stage and announced that the Japanese had attacked the American base at Pearl Harbor in Hawaii. The musicians continued with the *Messiah*, but the audience was certainly less attentive. Uncle Bill picked us up, and we drove home in a very sober mood. The bombing was a surprise to all of us. We had been paying far more attention to the war in Europe.

Because I had always found China and the Chinese fascinating, I had read quite a lot about them. So I was well aware of the Japanese invasion of China. I had also talked with people in the navy who realized the nature and importance of the military in Japan. But somehow, it never occurred to me that they would actually bomb our ships in Hawaii. I was not alone; it shocked all Americans.

The declaration of war came from President Roosevelt almost at once. It was followed immediately by our alliance with England against the German and Italian forces in Europe and Northern Africa. Fort Harrison quickly became a great beehive, and I was back to working six days a week. I had to drop my classes at Indiana University, and once again, activities like personal shopping and laundry became another problem with which to cope.

All America responded to the challenge. To those who have not gone through that experience, it is hard to describe the general aura and atmosphere. There was a great feeling of awakening and change, and of good humor and cooperation. Nowhere could it have been more apparent than at Fort Harrison. Regular Army officers and enlisted men soon disappeared and were replaced by reservists and reserve officers called to active duty.

Fort Harrison was a small place, and even with many additions, we remained small. We served small groups for specialized training, such as cooks, bakers, medical technicians, and chaplains. They all had supply officers and supply sergeants who came to our office with their requisitions to draw their supplies.

Few enlisted men or officers knew anything at all about army regulations, and certainly not the part pertaining to supplies, so I was busy every moment, most of the time trying to teach these people how to follow ARs (army regulations) and get the supplies they needed. My acquaintances became many and varied as I interacted with many people from many places. I got along remarkably well with all these people and generally enjoyed my work.

I decide to join the WACs

When the Women's Army Corps (WACs) was established, I decided to request being transferred into it. My dream of a college degree still existed, and I could see that the piecemeal way I had been going about it would never bring me one. I would have to spend a year or more on a campus at some point, and I could see no way of saving enough money to do that, ever.

It must be observed that nothing was given to me—not the roof over my head, not my transportation, not medical care, not food, not clothing, nothing. And I had always tried to assist my brother in caring for Mother and the younger ones, though my help was pitifully small.

My sisters Betty and Martha were still in school, but my two youngest brothers had been mobilized with the Indiana National Guard and were in training in a field camp in Louisiana. Mother was receiving a dependent's allowance from them. It was not a great deal, but until then, she had been reliant entirely on Joe and me. It really pleased her to have money of her own, and she was as content as I ever knew her to be.

To join the WACs, I needed the permission of my chief officer, a colonel. I talked first to the commanding officer of the WAC unit, a captain who was willing to assist me. She was quite enthusiastic. However, in my office I encountered a stone wall. I did not even get in to talk to the colonel. Neither Mr. Locke nor my captain would allow me access to him. Neither could see my point of view. They insisted that the work I was doing was important to the war effort and that they would suffer a loss if I joined the WACs.

I thought then, and think now, that both men were very offended that women had been allowed to enter the armed forces. By refusing my transfer, they had some vengeful satisfaction.

I was not dumb or conceited enough to think that I was necessary to the operation of Fort Harrison. I did a good job where I was, and I knew far more about the quartermaster supply unit than anyone else there except Mr. Locke. However, my civil service rating and my salary were by no means the highest in the unit. Several older men had been in the civil service most of their lives and had transferred in at a much higher rating than mine. If I were so important, why had I not been given a rating commensurate with my position?

Appendicitis

In the early summer of 1942, an incident happened that brought my financial vulnerability home to me with an almost frightening and certainly sobering impact. I had been visiting Mother, going on a Saturday evening and intending to return on Sunday evening. Whoever had enough gasoline coupons picked me up and took me back to the bus. By this time, all of the civilian section of the United States was rationed, and we had coupons for food supplies and gasoline. I think that for Americans the gasoline rationing was toughest to bear.

On this particular Sunday, I felt one of my migraine headaches coming on, and when it came time to leave, I was already sick enough to have begun the vomiting that always accompanied it. I have no memory of getting back to Indianapolis. The next day I was still unable to retain food, so Aunt Mabel called her doctor for advice. He told her to give me a laxative, an enormous dose, and to report to him the next day.

When she reported back the next day, I was feeling well, weak but not nauseous. He ordered an ambulance sent for me, and he scared her mightily by telling her not to let me move at all. I was to stay absolutely quiet and let the ambulance aides lift me onto a stretcher. The doctor met me in the emergency room at St. Vincent's Hospital, and I had an appendectomy that evening.

My appendix had ruptured, and I was very ill. In these days of antibiotics, recovery from a ruptured appendix is far more assured than it was in 1942. After I came home from the hospital, I felt very weak and wretched for many weeks.

At Aunt Mabel's insistence, when I first arrived in Indianapolis, I had bought an ordinary pay-at-death life insurance policy and medical insurance. However, the insurance company paid only a very small portion of my expenses. I submitted all the bills, and they sent me a check—it was only enough to pay the doctor.

I tried to borrow money to pay the hospital but had no luck. What institution would lend to someone who owned nothing, even though she had a relatively secure job? I went to my brother, who borrowed it for me. I also spent two weeks with Mother before returning to work.

After I came home from the hospital, but before going to Mother's, I received a phone call from Mr. Locke. He wanted to know how I was and when I planned to return to work. When I told him that I needed two more weeks, he reminded me that I had only one more week of sick leave with pay available, something I already knew. Nevertheless, I did need two more weeks. So we agreed I would take them, one with and one without pay.

I never learned whether he felt I was being petulant because I had not been given consent to transfer into the armed forces. I suppose he did. He could not easily check with my relatives, because Dorothy, Sherman, and Aunt Bertha had moved to Columbus, Ohio. In any case, in less than a month I was back at Fort Harrison, almost thirty pounds lighter in weight and very weak.

My first encounter with Alfred Diamant

When I returned to work, there were a few new faces among the supply sergeants who brought their requisitions to my desk. Actually, the one who brought the requisition from Headquarters Company was only a corporal. I recall that I noted him especially because it was the first time he had presented a requisition, and yet it was *perfectly* done.

I was astounded. I did not remember that ever happening before—the right nomenclature, the right quantities, the size and type of company making the request, and yes, even the correct army regulation citation. Everything was right!

It was so remarkable that I took another look at the corporal, and I almost laughed. He was surely the most ludicrous looking fellow who had ever come to my desk.

He was in fatigues, still blue denims in 1942, and they were too small and too tight for him. His spectacles were army issue. His denim fatigue hat was pulled down, and neither the hat nor the glasses concealed the fact that his face was over-large. He had a heavy German accent, but his turn of phrase was British English.

I think I praised the quality of the form he had presented and initialed it. Really, that is all I remember of my first encounter with Alfred Diamant.

Chapter 2

Freddy's Story: Vienna

(1917-1938)

For some, the reminiscences of childhood are like a rich, detailed tapestry stretching several generations into the past. For others, childhood reminiscences are more like Mussorgsky's *Pictures at an Exhibition*, consisting of more or less short strolls from one picture to the next. My own experience is more like the latter pattern: there are some vivid tableaux, but too, there are long stretches of little or no recollection at all.

I have often puzzled about the reasons for this. Was it perhaps the nature of our family life? Was I simply not a very imaginative child? Or was it that after the wrenching events of the 1930s and my emigration to the United States, there was much that I really wanted to forget? Was it that my efforts to make sense of my life in a new and radically different environment resulted in the blotting out of at least some of that earlier tapestry?

My early childhood

I was born in Vienna into a Jewish family that operated a successful dry goods retail store. My father and mother were born in small villages in Slovakia in 1863 and 1885 respectively. Slovakia was then in the Hungarian part of the Austro-Hungarian Empire. Their villages resembled those in Poland and Russia, pictured seriously and entertainingly in *Life is with People* and *Fiddler on the Roof*. The latter needs no explanation; the former is a sociological study based on interviews with former inhabitants of these villages. However, in the Slovakian villages, Jews lived a more integrated life than the Jewish inhabitants of the *shtetl*.

It seems that my father was dissatisfied with the possibilities of village life, for he made his way to Vienna. There he served an apprenticeship and then worked as a salesclerk in a store very much like the one he founded in 1891, and which I remember as Ignatz Diamant & Sohn (the son being my older half-brother, Oscar).

My father must have been a successful retail merchant. He married the daughter of his former boss and he was able to open his own store, which prospered even into the Depression years of the 1930s.

The store was located in one of Vienna's reddest working-class districts (the sixteenth, *Ottakring)*, which meant that our customers were Gentiles of modest means. My father always seemed to sense correctly what would sell. He had a very acute sense of what his customers wanted, so he knew what merchandise to stock. In turn this produced a steady turnover of stock and a continued profit for the owners.

Two children were born into what turned out to be my father's first marriage: Oscar (1891) and Valerie (1901?). Given the number of years between their births and my own (1917), it should be clear that our relationships were not those of typical siblings. Among my early childhood recollections are their weddings in the late 1920s and their subsequently establishing their own households. The two were more like an additional set of parents. Oscar became the head of the family and of the family firm after my father's death in 1934. I remained Little Freddy for the two of them until the events in the world around us drove us into emigration or death in the Holocaust.

My father's first wife died shortly before the outbreak of World War I. I never knew the exact date, and I do not recall either Oscar or Valli (as my sister was called) ever making any reference to their mother. My father was only in his early fifties, with an adult son and a young daughter. I find it interesting that in searching for a second wife he returned to Slovakia, not to his own village, but to one very much like it and only a short distance away, Vrbové. It was common among Jewish families to employ the services of a *shadchen* (marriage broker), but I do not know whether he used such an intermediary.

In some way, my father came to know the Herzog family, who had four daughters and a son. My father offered marriage to Julia, who was twenty-two years his junior. I have a hazy recollection that Mama mentioned that her marriage age was thirty. That would place their marriage in 1915.

I was born on September 25, 1917, one day short of my father's fifty-fourth birthday. Thus, in my early recollections, when I was a schoolboy, my father was in his early sixties. To what extent he took an interest or involved himself in my education I cannot recall. He was a somewhat distant parent, as is often the case with fathers of his age.

What I might have to say about my mother's life as the wife of a much older husband, and in a household that contained a teen-aged stepdaughter and a stepson only six years her junior, derives less from anything Mama said than what I began to surmise much later in my own life.

What I do recall is the love and attention she lavished on me, and her deep concern for her *Fredikind* (Freddy child). She was the one who directed my upbringing—even while she oversaw the running of the household and spent most of each day of a six-day workweek in the store that absorbed the attention of my father, Oscar, and a force of about a half-dozen salesclerks. As I grew up I, too, spent many hours in the store.

The store took up most of the ground floor of a Victorian apartment house. We occupied a large apartment directly above the store from well before I was born until after we were forced to surrender the store after the *Anschluss*. Though I enjoyed the company of the salesclerks who played with me, and though I made an effort to make a meaningful contribution to the functioning of the store, I came to dislike it all mostly because I did not seem to have the personal qualities that made a successful salesperson. Perhaps much of my later life and career can be seen as an effort to escape the world of business.

In spite of my emerging dislike of the business world (or at least of retail), I tried to be helpful in the store. I helped run the cash register, I replaced merchandise on shelves after it had been displayed to customers on the store counter, and I wrapped purchases for customers. Wrapping packages was not a negligible task in those days. Brown wrapping paper on big rolls and brown twine in big balls were the only wrapping materials available. In-deed, presenting a customer with a neatly wrapped package was considered one of the hallmarks of a store that took its customers seriously.

Wrapping packages neatly and effectively has remained the one legacy from my days in the dry goods business. Given the wide variety of highly sophisticated wrapping materials available these days, I can produce mightily neat packages for birthdays, new babies, and all other occasions. That seems to be the only aspect of my life in the Brunnengasse store that not only has survived all the decades, but has continued to be useful and even pleasur-able.

With all her other household and business duties, Mama found time to be with me, to play with me, and to transmit to me her love for music. She enjoyed the theater and the opera, in particu-lar the more popular music of the operettas. She had grown up in an area shared by three cul-tures: the German culture of the governing monarchy, the Magyar culture that domi-nated the Hungarian half of the Empire, and the Slovak culture of the Roman Catho-lic peasantry. Both she and my father were trilingual, and from time to time, they would converse in Magyar if the conversation were not for my ears.

My mother was sensitive to the music and literature of the various cultures that made up her world in her Slovak village. Perhaps my most distinct recollection is Mama's love for Hungarian and Gypsy folk music and for those composers who used it in their own work. Liszt's

Julia Herzog Diamant
Freddy's mother
At the Czech spa
Karlovy Vary, c. 1931

Hungarian Rhapsodies were among her favorites. However, she also knew the words of the folk songs on which this music was based, music that subsequently found itself into the creative impulses of Bartok and Dohnanyi, and also into such operettas as *Der Zigeunerbaron* (*The Gypsy Baron*).

Childhood friends

Mama's delight in theater and literature was recalled to me by one of the few friends I made in my twelve years of schooling. Franzl Fürst was a classmate in grade school who lived around the corner from us in one of the tenements that made up our working-class neighborhood. His father was a headwaiter and his mother a cook in a café. Franzl was mad about theater. He had a play theater with small puppets, and we performed plays by sharing the reading of the various roles.

I do not mean to convey an impression of high-minded literary activity on the part of grade schoolers. We also enacted all kinds of what we called Wild West stuff. We were inspired no doubt by the works of Karl May,

Freddy Diamant
1926

whose tales of adventures, not only in the American West, but also in the Balkans and the Arabian Peninsula, have fascinated the German-speaking world for generations. I believe we enacted scenes from *Winnetou*, the three-volume centerpiece of May's Wild West tales.

May was a prolific writer who produced dozens of these adventure tales, each more than five hundred pages long! It seems that he wrote them while never straying far from his native Radebeul, near Dresden, and while serving jail sentences for fraud. What truly attests to May's claim to universality in German culture is that his work attained the imprimatur of the Third Reich. I suppose that places him in the same pantheon as Goethe, Schiller, Bach, and Beethoven, surviving Kaiserreich, Weimar, Hitler, Bonn, and I would predict, unification.

After grade school, our paths diverged, but Franzl and I still met occasionally. Franzl completed terminal secondary school and was admitted to Max Reinhardt's acting studio in Vienna. We continued play-reading, but I now helped Franzl to rehearse the roles assigned him by the Reinhardt studio, including German classics such as *Faust*.

My own recollection is limited to bits and pieces of the prologue to *Faust I*. Franzl's recollections were more extensive, as I discovered many years later. However, his incipient acting career was interrupted (permanently, as it turned out) by World War II. He served in the German army as a troop entertainer and married one of his fellow performers. After the war, which ended for him when he let himself be captured by the Americans, Franzl spent the rest of his life teaching English to US Embassy personnel in Bonn; he died in 1978.

We resumed contact in the 1950s through a friend from my University of Florida days who spent a year in Bonn as a Fulbright professor. He had met Franzl as a neighbor in the housing that was provided for visiting Americans and embassy employees. Later when Ann and I spent a year in Bad Godesberg in 1973-74, we celebrated a genuine renewal of our friendship of fifty years earlier.

It was in the course of the endless reminiscences in which we indulged that Franzl recalled how Mama had joined him and me in dramatic readings in our apartment. He virtually shamed me by the scope of his recollections of Mama, whom he admired greatly. After all, she had great enthusiasm for the theater, just as he did.

My relationship to Franzl seems to have been part of a pattern that was often repeated in my life. He was the friend who exercised leadership and I was the one who followed. That pattern persisted through my years in Vienna, and in an attenuated form, it followed me across the Atlantic.

Nevertheless, it was not long before I managed to find a way to grow beyond being simply a follower. Perhaps it was delayed maturation. After all, I was only twenty-two years old when I landed in New York. Or perhaps it was the impetus of a new society and the confrontation with war.

Apart from Franzl, I can recall only two other friends from my school years. Lacking fortuitous reencounters such as the one with Franzl, my memories of them are rather sparse. My other grade school friend was a boy whose name I have forgotten. Like Franzl, he lived less than a block from us. His father was a mailman (a curious bit of information to recall half a century later). Whereas Franzl's household functioned on an odd schedule (both his parents worked evening shifts at a café while Franzl was looked after by a live-in grandmother), my other friend's household had a definite petit bourgeois primness. It included a mother devoted to housework and a father in the civil service. The family was devoutly Roman Catholic. I heard later that my friend studied for the priesthood.

The other friend was a boy named Walter with whom I formed a friendship grounded in intellectual interests, especially music. Walter led me to literature beyond that imposed on us by the five hour per week, eight year long requirement of German language and literature instruction. It was Walter who triggered my teenage Wagner mania, an experience I would not have wanted to miss.

The Wagner craze was reinforced by one of our teachers, who spread the cult assiduously among his students. He attended Bayreuth Festivals regularly, and his apartment (so I was told) was filled with Wagner and Bayreuth memorabilia.

Whether my plunge into Wagner preceded Hitler's coming to power in Germany I cannot tell, but it would seem that at least at that time, my Wagner mania was untouched by the subsequent disagreement among Jews (and non-Jews as well) about one's duty to ostracize the man and his music because of the lavish support his work and his family had received from the Third Reich. At that time, at least, one could be both Jewish and a Wagnerian.

Walter's father was a middle-level municipal civil servant and thus, undoubtedly a devout card-carrying Social Democrat. They lived in one of the apartment houses built by the Socialist city government of Vienna after World War I. The apartments were normally made available to union-member workers and to those employed by the city. Their apartment was smaller, but lighter and more airy, than our mid-Victorian accommodations, which were located in an apartment house built to yield a comfortable return to its owner.

I discovered later that because of rent control laws enacted during World War I and never repealed, owning rental property had become a nearly losing proposition in Vienna. My family owned a truly historic rental property built in the eighteenth century. Yet, it yielded just enough rent to pay taxes and to keep the ancient structure from falling down. An American bomb during World War II finally put it out of its misery. After the rubble was removed, we were finally able to sell the property at some profit to serve as a used-car lot. The eighteenth century was finally forced to yield to the twentieth.

My association with Walter came to an end with graduation from secondary school in 1935. I learned later that Walter died soon after we graduated. Many years later, in a book that I had brought with me to America, I discovered a Viennese streetcar coupon with a message from Walter on the reverse side, a meticulously neat handwriting in Gothic script.

Steffi and Anna

In reflecting on my boyhood, I see another central figure, or rather a series of figures, who presided over my daily routines. Most European middle-class families, certainly down to World War II, considered a live-in maid an essential element in the functioning of a household. In our case, a maid was particularly essential because Mama constituted, for all practical purposes, a full-time addition to the store's workforce.

With the store open from 8 a.m. to 6 p.m. six days a week, and hardly any additional closing days except Christmas and New Year, Mama needed a maid-housekeeper-babysitter around-the-clock. Given that, it is not surprising that a succession of maids played an important role in my daily life. I remember clearly only two: Steffi and Anna.

Steffi is a shadowy figure from my earliest years. I remember only that she was a lively young woman. The high point of my life with Steffi occurred one evening after my parents had gone out, when Steffi decided that the only way to enjoy some time at a pub with her boyfriend was to take me along. Frequenting a *Gasthaus* was not something on the social calendar of a Jewish business family. I do not know whether my parents ever learned about this excursion, but it left a deep impression on me.

Since I was the only child of a Jewish family that lived and worked in a Gentile and working-class district, my life was very much like that of a (nearly) sole inhabitant of a desert island. I kept seeing lights of passing ships and wondering what life there might be like. This was reinforced, I am sad to say, by my mother's constant reminders not to be like the goyim.

This reflects, no doubt, the constant tension in Jewish life in the city that practically invented modern anti-Semitism. Mama's admonitions probably had a perverse effect, as such admonitions usually have on children: I wanted to know what the goyim were doing, and even do whatever it was that seemed to make them so happy-go-lucky!

Middle-class housewives like my mother tried to recruit peasant girls directly from the country and train them, so that eventually most of the household, including shopping and cooking, could be entrusted to them without detailed supervision. That was the case with Anna, who came to our house while I was in grade school, and who stayed with us until Germany's racial laws forbade the employment of a female Aryan houseworker in a Jewish family containing young males.

Anna came from a small wine-growing village two or three hours by train from Vienna. I visited her native village with her one weekend. I vaguely remember sleeping in a big featherbed but little else beyond a few glimpses of rural life in Lower Austria.

Usually these young recruits from the countryside became trained household workers, but some had to be dismissed because they were untrainable. Eventually most of them found the other thing that had lured them to the big city: a husband who would not require them to milk cows, work in the fields, and feed a small army of children and field hands. Having found their mates, they ended their *paid* domestic careers.

Anna was an exception to this common pattern. She married, found an apartment nearby, and continued to come in for the day only, an arrangement that suited Mama well, especially after my father's death in 1934, which reduced our household to two persons. Also unlike most of her contemporaries, Anna remained childless.

Anna was a thoroughly friendly and even-tempered person, and I have no recollection of friction between her and Mama. However, I cannot possibly detail any of her personal characteristics, even though she clearly was a household presence in her own right for well over a decade. That she was not more of a person to me might well reflect the class distance and class bias built into our relationships. She was among us, but not one of us.

Thus does social distance shape what we see in the first place and what we remember later. Except for the occasional adventure, we all were locked into our social class structures and roles.

Family life

Ours was a bourgeois Jewish family—the order of the adjectives is meant to suggest the relative significance of these traits. Since I had almost no direct contact with the family life of middle-class Viennese Gentiles, I am reluctant to judge the extent to which ours was a more or less assimilated lifestyle. However, my contacts with a small number of my non-Jewish classmates, as infrequent as they were, lead me to think that I grew up in a rather undifferentiated matrix of Viennese middle-class life.

Though my mother tried to impress me with the importance of not being like the goyim, my father never raised such a concern as far as I can remember. By comparative American standards, we practiced a conservative brand of Judaism. I gathered that in my father's family there had been rabbis in several generations. According to Mama, my father reflected that heritage, having been absorbed in the Jewish schooling in his native village of Dolná Krupá.

Even so, he did not demand that dietary laws be observed in our household. I am sure Mama was grateful for this latitudinarian attitude, for the burden of maintaining a kosher household falls entirely on the women of the household. The only prohibition that we rigorously maintained was the ban on pork. Yet among my father's favorite snack foods was sliced boiled ham. Why he considered this acceptable, I was never able to learn.

Our family had regularly reserved seats in the sixteenth district synagogue, but our attendance was pretty much limited to the high holidays. For the rest of the year the synagogue had to rely on a corps of regular attenders to assure the presence of the necessary ten worshippers (the minyan) for its services. Even on Rosh Hoshan and Yom Kippur, whose fast we observed most scrupulously, our store remained open entrusted to our sales staff, most of whom had been with us for years.

My one vivid recollection of Yom Kippur is that I ended each annual fast with a raging headache that made it impossible to enjoy the coffee with whipped cream and the accompanying pastry (the ubiquitous *Gugelhupf)* with which we broke our fast. I eagerly consumed it all, but within a short time, there were devastating consequences from which I did not recover until the next morning.

Passover remains vivid in my memory. Our observance extended to one Seder, which took place on either the first or second night, depending on negotiations with Oscar and Valli about when their in-law families had scheduled their Seders. These negotiations were not without their tense moments about whose family should be given preference on the first evening and whose family had to be content with the second.

I well remember the Haggadas with their quaint medieval illustrations of each of the plagues, of Pharaoh's daughter finding Moses in the bulrushes, of the Red Sea parting to permit the Exodus from Egypt, and so on.

In our Seders, I was always the youngest male child present. Thus it fell to me to recite the *mani stanu,* the questions and answers about why this particular night was different from all others. Passover was for us clearly a joyous celebration of liberation, of the life of a free people. The abundant dishes that were served symbolized our freedom and well-being, even in those years of rising anti-Semitism. The pitfall for me was the need to memorize this material. Without fail, I would get stuck after the first few questions, amid frowns from the adults about my inattention to my task.

At the age of thirteen, I was confirmed as an adult male member of the Jewish people through the observance of the bar mitzvah. This required being called up in the synagogue to read the Torah passage appointed for that day. To be able to do this, I had to have lessons from our synagogue cantor so I could read the Hebrew text of the scrolls. This was difficult for a beginner because the text did not contain the enclitic marks that identify the vowels underneath the consonants.

Bar mitzvah did not occasion any great festivities, as it now does in the United States. I received my own prayer shawl and ritual prayer straps in a little velvet kit with a drawstring. I also remember the gift of a lovely sterling silver knife from Aunt Gisa, which I insisted on carrying to school and promptly lost, making Mama very angry.

My one involvement in daily prayer was during the year of mourning for my father, who died of a heart embolism following surgery in 1934, shortly before his seventy-first birthday. Tradition requires twice-daily prayer for a year following a death in the immediate family. I do not remember how it was suggested to me or by whom, but I carried out this religious duty because it seemed to please and comfort Mama, who was left widowed at not yet fifty years old.

It seemed to me that her sister Gisa and I were her entire world in this great city of two million people, and I wanted very much to do what would comfort her. Thus, during my last year of *Gymnasium*, I stopped at the synagogue en route to school and returned later in the day for evening prayer.

The only other holiday observance that remains in my memory is Hanukkah. It was one of the few times I did things with my father. We lit the candles, said the prayers, and sang the songs, all of which my father could recite from memory.

What is amusing to me even now is that we did not have a regular menorah for the candles. Every year I was instructed to scavenge in the store for a flat board (yard goods came wound around flat boards). We then fastened the appropriate number of candles to the board with dripping wax and proceeded with the ritual.

What is so puzzling to me is that I do not remember my father being tight about money in any other way. We never missed the observance of Hanukkah as long as he was alive, but we also never had a regular menorah.

Because of the constitutional links between church and state in Austria, children were required to participate in twelve years of religion instruction with the state paying the salaries of the instructors. This law applied not only for Roman Catholics, but also for Jewish and Protestant (Lutheran) religion instruction. In my darker anticlerical moments, I am wont to consider compulsory religion instruction and/or prayer in school a means of destroying religion forever in the hearts and minds of children. However, I actually have no really unpleasant memories of these years of religion instruction. At the same time, none of it prevented me from drifting steadily into a secularized and assimilated intellectualism. It took me a long time to rediscover a religious and spiritual dimension in my life.

Thus, I grew up in an assimilated Jewish middle-class family in a city whose powers of assimilation were formidable. This has been demonstrated, for instance, by the prominent participation of secularized and assimilated Jews in the intellectual, artistic, political, and economic life of the city. (About ten percent of the Viennese population was Jewish, the largest percentage of any European city.) Viennese culture was alluring in many ways, as has been detailed by others. In my case, this assimilative force was particularly powerful because my family lived and worked in a working-class district where Jews were an almost minuscule minority.

In my twelve years of public school, I was often the only Jewish pupil in my class of about twenty to thirty. At most there were two or three of us. Not until I was eighteen did I establish a friendship, male and Jewish, that was not part of our extended family circles. Yet I have no recollection that being a solitary Jewish fish in a vast Gentile sea raised feelings of isolation or bitterness in me, at least during my preteen and early teen years.

But by then, the Great Depression had descended on us and with it, the rise of right-wing extremism with its anti-Semitic crusades. I was fully aware of being different, but I ascribed that to class rather than to religious-ethnic differences. Perhaps my ideology distorted my perception of the reality around me.

The isolation I have suggested here was reinforced by my family's social life, which centered entirely on the several family circles with which our family intersected. Both my parents had a number of siblings, but only few lived in Vienna. On Mama's side there was Aunt Gisa, married and without children. Mama felt very close to her sister, the only relative she could claim in her own right in this big city. The feeling was clearly mutual and was reinforced by Aunt Gisa's affection for me, in place of the children she was unable to bear.

Mama and I spent many Sunday afternoons in Aunt Gisa's company. This was a time my father had re-served for a standing card game in one of Vienna's numerous coffeehouses. These coffeehouses not only provided newspapers

Josef Diamant
Freddy's uncle

and endless glasses of water, but they were also homes to card games that convened with great regularity and at the same table every day or every week.

My father's brothers Adolf and Josef and their families with two and three children respectively constituted another socializing circle. I remember them all very well, especially Uncle Adolf's two daughters, Terri and Helli (Theresa and Helena), and Uncle Josef's children Eric and Fritzi (Fredrica).

Although visits with them were not quite as frequent as visits with Mama's sister, ties were close for a variety of reasons. Terri

Fredrica, Eric, & Egon Diamant
Freddy's cousins

was an accountant and came regularly to take care of our firm's books. Fritzi, who had obtained a teaching license, was my first English language tutor.

Although my uncles Josef and Adolf both died before 1938, as did my father, most of their children were able to emigrate. The most dramatic story was that of Uncle Josef's widow, Judith, who together with her son Eric, emigrated to the Shanghai international settlement. Eric was able to leave Shanghai before the outbreak of the war and come to the United States where his sister Fritzi had already established herself with her family. However, Aunt Judith spent the war years in Shanghai before joining her children in the United States.

The Jewish refugee community in the Shanghai international settlement constitutes one of the more bizarre episodes of the Jewish escape from the Third Reich. Why did thoroughly westernized European Jews choose to immigrate to China? The simple answer is that it was one of the few places that was willing to receive them. The United States was the most generous recipient of Jewish immigrants after 1933 (1938 in the case of Austria). But American immigration laws had a number of restrictions and absurdities. It was such quirks in the law that permitted Eric to enter the United States before Pearl Harbor, while Aunt Judith had to endure internment by the Japanese until after their surrender.

Aunt Judith was obviously a strong and determined woman. She was able to spend the rest of her life in Newark, New Jersey, surrounded by her children and grandchildren (she died at age ninety-six). I have fond memories of a number of visits with her and her family during the years we lived in

Judith Berdach Diamant
Joseph Diamant's wife
Newark, August 1951

New Haven and later in Haverford, Pennsylvania. She continued to cook, bake, and sew until the very end of her life.

Another socializing circle was the huge Unger clan, whose members I addressed as aunt, uncle, or cousin, even though they were not related to me. Father's first wife had been an Unger, so Oscar and Valli, especially the former, kept in close contact with them.

Uncle Adolf Unger, the patriarch of the clan, had introduced men's ready-to-wear to Vienna and had seen the enterprise flourish. Their wealth placed them in a different social category from us and enabled them to patronize Little Freddy in a variety of ways. Both Mama and Oscar worried much about my behaving properly in such august company.

As a sort of Ripley's believe-it-or-not note, I might add that Uncle Adolf's granddaughter Lilly married John Kautsky, a grandson of Karl Kautsky, one of Europe's great social theorists and political leaders. They met at the University of Chicago after World War II. John Kautsky is now retired from the Washington University Political Science Department.

When Oscar married Liesl (Alice) Hartmann in 1929, still another overlapping circle was added, a most lively, interesting one. Liesl's mother was a career woman long before it was common to be. She was a buyer for E. Braun and Company, one of Vienna's great luxury establishments. Liesl had followed in her mother's footsteps. Her sister Lonnie operated a women's clothing store that was a Hartmann family enterprise. The other two sisters, Mary and Margret, followed a more conventional pattern.

All four sisters married and all except Liesl had several children of my generation with whom I socialized occasionally. It was sometimes arranged that I would escort one of my female cousins to an event. I did so because I was an obedient child, but I probably got pretty low scores as an escort.

A special place in my recollections of the Hartmanns is reserved for the father, the one male in this female array. He worked as a manufacturer's representative and commanded the proverbial salesman's fund of stories and wisecracks. He also reveled in being surrounded by all this female talent.

When Valli married Fritz Backenroth in 1925 or 1926, she added still another dimension to my life. Within a year she gave birth to a son, Erwin, and I could proudly announce that I had become an uncle while still less than ten years old.

I occasionally visited Oscar and Liesl at their apartment and luxuriated in their tiled bathtub instead of having to go to a municipal bath, but I remember much more the time I spent with Valli, Erwin, and Fritz. Valli seemed to feel closer ties between us, which I certainly reciprocated. In particular, I remember two summers I spent with her and Erwin in a place they had rented in the country and to which Fritz commuted on weekends.

Fritz had created a most successful housewares retail business. He was, like my father, an expert merchandiser. Fritz sought out new and unusual products all over the world and thereby attracted a wide clientele for his store.

We did not have much contact with Fritz's family, the Backenroths, or with that of his stepmother, the Kammermanns. I remember the Kammermanns chiefly for their tricking Fritz into co-signing notes for large sums and then subsequently defaulting and leaving Fritz to pay off their business debts.

Fritz's father and the family of his second wife were some of the few Orthodox Jews I knew personally—twice daily prayer, kosher observance, and all the rest. The fact that some of them managed to be both religiously observant and totally unscrupulous in business had a profound impact on me in the long run. I simply did not understand how one could be devout before God and yet cheat one's fellow human beings, especially members of one's own family, as the Kammermanns had done with Fritz, whom I admired very much.

The Vienna of my day had a six-day workweek that was nearly universal, bankers excepted, so family social gatherings were limited to Sundays. Given the several overlapping circles I have described, socializing even within these limits took up all the time adults had for such activities. As a result, as a family we did not interact with people other than the ones I have tried to bring to life here. To be sure, I spent time with friends from school, but that never included our parents. Thus, I moved in a Jewish milieu, though mostly a milieu of assimilated Jews.

Summer vacations

The summer break in the school year in Austria was somewhat shorter than it is currently in the United States. These vacations were occasions for travel and family visits.

I will reserve the story of the summers I spent with my maternal grandmother for later; these summers have remained vivid memories for me to the present day. I have already mentioned the two summers I spent with Valli and Erwin. They are less vivid in my memory, except for the summer we spent in Vöslau near Vienna, where there was a rather grand outdoor swimming pool fed by mineral springs. Vöslau is a neighbor of the much better known spa Baden bei Wien.

In 1931 and 1934 I went to a summer camp in Italy, the same one described by George Clare in his remarkable book of reminiscences *Last Waltz in Vienna*. All participants were of high school age and from Vienna. We were taken to Cesenatico on the northern Adriatic coast in special railroad cars attached to regular trains.

The camp season ran for two months, but in the years I was there, I stayed only one month. I had to return home to be tutored in subjects I had failed, so that I could be promoted to the next grade (more about that later). I am sure my enduring love for the ocean and the beach stems from these summers.

The entire summer camp enterprise was Viennese (even the cooks came with us). It seems that Italian food was not considered fit for Viennese tastes and stomachs. The only part of the local scene that was considered acceptable was the Italian ice cream parlor.

Although Italian cooking was not considered fit for us, Italian culture was. Our day trips included Florence, Ravenna, and Venice. We were also offered a chance to go overnight fishing on some of the commercial fishing vessels in the harbor. The smell of these vessels was enough to convince me that this was not something my stomach could manage when combined with even the slight chop of Adriatic waters.

The camp was coeducational, a fact that had not stayed with me but looms large in George Clare's reminiscences, in which "the girls" play a significant role. My strongest impression from this time involves my 1934 roommate, a Sephardic Jew, the only member of his people I had ever met. He was far more mature than I was. He was well-read and had a wide range of interests, including architecture. It was he, in fact, who introduced me to the work of Le Corbusier, the French planner and architect.

While I was at the camp in 1934, Austrian Nazis attempted to overthrow the dictatorial Dollfuss government. The attempt, which was orchestrated from Germany, nearly succeeded when the Nazis gained control of the chancellery by assassinating Chancellor Dollfuss. What forced Germany to terminate the venture was Mussolini's ultimatum that Italian troops would enter Austria unless Hitler called back the so-called Austrian Legion and permitted the restoration of the Austrian government under Chancellor Schuschnigg (Dollfuss' successor).

I do not recall how much we learned about all this while in Italy. But when the train that carried me back to Vienna crossed the Austrian-Italian border, we could see Italian troops in position along the border as far as the eye could see.

I spent part of one summer with Mama at one of the Austrian lakes, and still another summer on the island of Rab on the Adriatic coast of Yugoslavia. Still more saltwater!

What I cannot recall is any vacation with my father or with both of my parents together. Most years my father went to visit Badgastein in the Austrian Alps for a month to take the waters. He always went alone and stayed at the same hotel. Many years later, in 1949, when Oscar visited Badgastein, some of the hotel personnel identified him instantly as the son of their former regular visitor Ignatz Diamant. I found this very puzzling because I never thought that there was much resemblance at all between my father and either of his sons.

Freddy's paternal grandfather

One of Freddy's paternal uncles

Both my parents grew up in small Slovakian villages, but I never visited my father's native village, Dolná Krupá, even though he visited there regularly. So I never met any of my father's family, except for his two brothers who also lived in Vienna. However, over the years I gathered that my father had a number of brothers and sisters, and that there were numerous uncles, aunts, and cousins about whom I knew nothing.

Grandmother Herzog and Vrbové

Some of the most vivid and happy memories of my preteen and early teen years were the summers spent with my maternal grandmother, Kathi Herzog, in the Slovakian village of Vrbové. I came to know and enjoy greatly many members of Mama's family, both those living in Vrbové and elsewhere. When I first visited Grandmother Herzog in the mid-1920s, she was already a widow. Much later I was told about the tragic death of her husband.

My grandfather's fate sadly reflects the precarious conditions under which Jews lived in the rural countryside of Central and Eastern Europe. As World War I drew to a close, the Empire's authority disintegrated, and the various nationalities began to form their own states and state authorities. This transition period was one of chaos and disorder, exacerbated by food shortages that were caused, at least in part, by the Allied blockade of the Central Powers.

In the absence of stable authority, bands of peasants roamed the countryside plundering food supplies and commercial establishments, many of them operated by Jewish merchants. One such band not only plundered Grandfather Herzog's store, but killed him in the process. There seems to be some universality to the fate of minority entrepreneurs the world over, especially in times of trouble when they become the most visible victims of the disgruntled majority community.

What was so fascinating about my stay with Grandmother Herzog was the stark contrast between life in Vienna, a city of two million, and life in this small rural village in which the daily routines resembled those of the medieval villages about which I had read, or was soon to read, in my history books.

Vrbové was a village along a single dirt road, though I seem to remember paved sidewalks here and there. Along this one road were all the farming establishments (complete with stables, big dung heaps, horses, and so on), and also the churches, a synagogue, a number of pubs, and a variety of stores, such as hardware and dry goods.

In the morning, the cowherder would trudge down the street and with suitable noises call the farmers to let out their cows to be taken for their daily grazing. Then later on a little boy would lead a string of geese for their daily constitutional.

Once or twice a week, the town crier would parade down the street, stopping from time to time. He would beat his drum insistently to collect an audience and would then read official announcements.

Yet, by that time, radio had arrived in the village, and newspapers came via trains. In fact three trains came each day, traveling on the branchline that connected with the main rail line to Bratislava (the administrative capital of the Slovakian segment of Czechoslovakia) and ultimately to Vienna, bringing me back to the twentieth century!

Vrbové not only provided me with a sense of rural and agricultural life, it also gave me a strong sense of what a truly observant Jewish community was like. Because I was there only during the summer, I never had a chance to participate in the observance of the High Holidays. But I certainly participated in the regular observance of the Sabbath, from preparing the household on Friday to the ceremony ending the Sabbath. These were all faithfully observed, not only by Mama's family, but by virtually all the Jewish families of the village.

I was also frequently able to observe the ritual slaughterer at work dispatching chickens and geese, which were a major part of the daily fare. The only modern two-story structure in the village was the religious school run by the local rabbi. He had collected the funds for this highly visible modern building from pious Jews in the United States!

Still other events helped sharpen the contrast between life at home and life with Grandmother Herzog. There was the weekly bath in soft rainwater, which was collected in barrels from downspouts.

Perhaps most fascinating was the routine of fattening geese, which were kept in stalls that made it impossible for them to move around. At least once a day, one of the housemaids would appear with a great supply of soaked kernel corn. She would immobilize a goose by holding it tightly under her bent knees, force open the goose's mouth, and stuff it full of corn. Holding the goose's beak tightly shut, she would work the corn down the goose's long neck as if stuffing a sausage.

When ready for slaughter, these animals would have endless layers of fat, which would be rendered and then used as a principal cooking ingredient, taking the place of butter or shortening. Even more importantly, this method of feeding left the poor animals with hugely enlarged livers—the legendary goose livers, the foie gras of Strasbourg fame! These livers were highly prized delicacies. How highly prized, I can best illustrate as follows.

Mama was one of five children: four sisters and a brother, Max, an international merchant. Max left his native village early in life and eventually made his way to Cairo, which became the principal seat of his business and his residence. He was greatly admired by the entire family and much beloved by his four sisters. At one time, Max had expressed a longing for the goose livers of his youth, so his four sisters took turns preparing a liver and having a tinsmith make a tin for it. The liver was placed in the tin, which was soldered tight and shipped airfreight to Cairo!

By the time of my visit, only one of Mama's five siblings still lived in Vrbové, my aunt Jeanette Blum and her family. They looked after Grandmother Herzog. I want to single out my cousin Max Blum because of his quirks of luck as a survivor. Max was very much in love with a girl and wanted to marry her—and she him! But his parents and the young woman's parents had already made arrangements with marriage brokers to find spouses for their offspring.

It was not that Max's beloved was truly unsuitable, but that both she and Max had gone against the expressed wishes of their families. In the face of this resistance, the two sought out relatives in the United States, secured affidavits of support, married, and departed for the United States in the late 1930s. As a consequence, Max was one of only two members of his family to escape the Holocaust.

As it turned out, the Slovak puppet regime, which was created under Nazi auspices and presided over by prelates of the Roman

Catholic Church, became the most ruthless and avid persecutor of its Jewish population. They relentlessly rounded up Jews under their control and handed them over to German authorities for "transportation to the East."

The other survivor of the Blum family was my cousin Margit, who together with her husband and two teenage sons, all reached their destination in the "East." Yet, miraculously all four members of that family survived and returned to Bratislava where they had lived. Although Margit's husband resumed his profitable lumber business, they lost the business in 1948 at the communist take-over. Despairing completely over their future in Czechoslovakia, they immigrated to Israel.

Life in Vrbové was influenced in significant ways by its proximity to the famous spa Piešťany. The spa attracted people seeking its healing products from around the world—even Americans, as it was always said with some awe! Piešťany traded most effectively on its medicinal springs and hot mud, which were supposed to heal crippling diseases such as arthritis, gout, and rheumatism. A patient arriving by train would immediately see Piešťany's logo on the railway station roof: a figure breaking a set of crutches over his knees, a visible promise that whatever crippling diseases one brought, they would surely be cured before departure!

The presence of wealthy visitors only a few miles away stimulated the economy in the surrounding countryside, a clear example of what we now call trickle-down economics. I observed, for instance, a trade in peasant handicrafts that was engendered by this lucrative market. The peasant craftswomen (no male embroiderers as far as I could tell!) were in no position to deal directly with potential customers in the spa or even with the retailers there. They needed intermediaries with the necessary cash, language, and merchandising abilities. That was the service that my aunt Jeanette Blum provided, among many others like her.

I remember a great variety of needlework designs and techniques for tablecloths, napkins, and other fine linens. I can only hope that the profits made by intermediaries such as Aunt Jeanette were not such as would make me wince today—but I cannot be sure. What I have retained from my exposure to these handicrafts is an inordinate fondness for richly embroidered table linen. I still think that these are just about the height of elegance, surpassing even the damask table linens and the damask bedding and toweling that were part of Mama's trousseau. When we broke up our household in 1938, her trousseau still contained sheets, towels, and pillowcases that had never been used.

In Vrbové as in Vienna I had few if any playmates. Yet I do not remember being lonely or at a loss for what to do, even if it was only scavenging for and eating fruit from the orchard behind the Blum-Herzog establishment. Occasionally I hiked across the fields and watched harvesting activities or gazed at the foothills of the Carpathian Mountains in the distance.

What suddenly came into view as I tried to recall these days is the 10 a.m. morning snack that Grandmother Herzog prepared: garlic bread toasted on top of a coal stove! I remember these summer months in Vrbové with great fondness.

My schooling

I have spent nearly half a century preparing to be and being a professional educator, yet my recollections of my own school years are quite meager. I remember hardly any of my teachers. I did not find learning easy or exciting, with the notable exception of history. My annual grade reports reflect a most uneven performance over the years, near honors some years, near failure in others.

When Mama went to consult my teachers during one of my lower secondary school years, she brought back their judgment of my performance: "He is a nice boy, but he tends to daydream." I hope this will not provide an epitaph for the rest of my life, but I would not disagree with my teachers' succinct evaluation of me then.

I attended one year of kindergarten at age five. It was operated as part of a Roman Catholic girls' school, but the kindergarten was open to anyone. (I believe there was no public school kindergarten, even though the city of Vienna provided generously for expectant mothers and infants.) I have only two bits of memory from kindergarten. One is the teacher, "Aunt Bertha," who was a loving, embracing mother figure.

The other bit of memory is represented by a studio photograph in a sterling silver frame. In the photo, I am wearing a Biedermeier costume, looking for all the world like a young, chubby Franz Schubert with a swallowtail coat and a stovepipe hat. The entire outfit was made of crepe paper. I wish that photo had been preserved, if only to entertain our grandchildren, but in the stress of breaking up a household and of impending emigration, a kindergarten costume party photo did not enjoy a high priority for preservation.

Vienna's post-1918 public schools, like those elsewhere in Austria, were an ideological battleground between the city government (controlled by the Social Democratic Party from 1918-34) and the federal government (dominated by the Catholic-conservative Christian Social Party). Schooling for the primary grades (1 to 4) and the vocational-terminal grades (5 to 8) was under local control, Social Democratic in the case of Vienna. However, the academic preparatory system and all higher education were controlled by the federal government and under Catholic-clerical control.

Thus, during my school years, Vienna's public schools were a proving ground for philosophy and practices of progressive education. However, because the all-male teaching staff was a career corps, many of them recruited under the monarchy, the actual classroom practices were probably much less progressive than the blueprints handed down by the city's educational mandarins.

I attended the neighborhood grade school, which had a predominantly poor and working-class student body. There were no PTAs or other organized community involvement in the schools, but I recall that from time to time, my father would contribute clothing for my poorest schoolmates.

On the intellectual side, I recall the first-grade readers, which were based on syllable and word recognition principles. Instead of Dick, Jane, and "See Spot run," Ma-ma and Mi-mi were major actors. If Mi-mi had a brother, I do not recall!

The great dramatic incident of my grade school years occurred in the fourth grade when I had an accident that required the removal of my spleen. It was a truly life-threatening incident, and we were fortunate to obtain the services of the country's leading surgeon. I was away from school nearly a month at the very beginning of the year, but I seem to have made up all the work without great difficulty. As children do, I recuperated quickly and easily.

In the later stages of recovery, I found it all great fun, for I harvested presents of all kinds. I recall mostly the books. Of these, two stand out in my memory: Mark Twain's *Tom Sawyer* (in translation) and a juvenile version of *Don Quixote*. I kept rereading *Tom Sawyer* for years, enjoying the adventures of Tom and Huck but with little sense of the time and place of Hannibal, Missouri. In my ignorance, I was in good and noble company with such as Franz Kafka, who located his "great circus" in Oklahoma, and the opera composer who placed a scene in his work "in the desert north of New Orleans"!

Like most European countries before World War II, Austria operated a two-track school system, in which a fateful sorting out took place after fourth grade. The perniciousness of these systems was not the sorting out, but in the actual basis for the process—social class. Typically, working-class children were funneled into the terminal prevocational track, while middle-class children entered the university-preparatory *Gymnasium* (or *lycée*, or whatever it might be called).

In my case, there apparently was some hesitation about where I should be sent. After my four years of *Volksschule*, I attended one year of the *Hauptschule*, the terminal track school, but then I was transferred to a *Realgymnasium*, an academic-type secondary school. There I completed my secondary education with the *Matura*.

Thus, I spent the seven years of secondary school in the company of other "nice" and often poorly motivated middle- and lower-class children, both male and female. In secondary schools located in more affluent parts of the city, the student body would have been middle or upper class in composition, with a heavy contingent being the children of professionals, intellectuals, and business people. In some of the elite secondary schools and those located in essentially upper middle-class districts, there might well have been a sizeable Jewish contingent. But in the school I attended, I was often the only Jewish pupil in the class.

I should add that the other minority representatives, when there were any, were children of working-class families. Several of them began the course of study, but not one of them lasted through graduation. Almost invariably, they had to drop out and go to work to help their families. This was increasingly the case as the effects of the Great Depression took their toll on the Austrian economy.

So it was then that the majority of my classmates were sons and daughters of civil servants, craftsmen, and shopkeepers rather than offspring of bankers, doctors, and lawyers.

The school year ran from mid-September to early July. The school week was six days, and the school day went from 8 a.m. to 1 p.m., with only one ten-minute break for a mid-morning snack. Saturday classes usually ended at noon. There was a mid-year and a final reporting of grades. The grading scale ran from 1 to 4 (Very Good, Good, Sufficient, and Not Sufficient) with 1, 2, and 3 being passing grades. The entire school day was devoted to classes in the various subjects. There was no time out for study hall or anything like it.

My grade reports show that in any given year I received grades in ten, eleven, or twelve subjects. The grades in these subjects had equal weight, though some subjects were offered daily while others took up only one or two hours per week. Religion and physical education were required every year, as were German language and literature, Latin, history, geography, and mathematics. One foreign language was required during the last four years (French in my case). Biology was required for five years, chemistry for three, and physics for five. In the lower three grades, music and shop (as it might be called) were required. I also have a year of shorthand on my record.

In the last two years, there were also required courses in philosophy and architectural drawing, *Darstellende Geometrie,* for which I have never found an equivalent in an American secondary school. The curriculum at the *Realgymnasium* I attended was revised after World War I with the intention of loosening up the academic tracks, which had previously made a sharp distinction between those aiming at arts and sciences and those preparing for engineering and applied science studies. The revised curriculum was designed to enable a student to enter either of these two tracks. So then, Greek was eliminated and architectural drawing was added.

Although students could choose between the different types of secondary schools, once they had made that decision no further choices existed. All subjects were required, and passing grades had to be obtained in each. Admittedly nobody ever failed physical education or religion, but for all other subjects a failing grade at the end of the year meant having to repeat the entire grade, including all the subjects in which the student had earned passing grades. Twice in the seven years, I was in danger of being left behind, but more about that later.

Throughout the seven years, my favorite subjects were history and geography, while my nemeses were mathematics and *Darstellende Geometrie*. I had a failing grade in mathematics at the end of the fourth grade (US eighth) and in *Darstellende Geometrie* at the end of the seventh grade (US eleventh). The system provided one last reprieve: a comprehensive examination in the failing subject at the end of summer, just before school opening. Success in that exam permitted the student to be promoted to the next grade. Failure at that time was fatal. It meant repeating all the subjects and falling behind an entire year.

My near-failures were accompanied by much recrimination at home, mostly from Mama and Oscar, and repeated suggestions that I ought to be apprenticed to learn a trade. For some reason unknown to me, Mama thought I should be apprenticed to a furrier! But these threats were never carried out.

Instead, arrangements were made for me to be tutored during the summer. In both instances, the tutoring was successful and I moved on to the next grade. However, because of the tutoring, I had to be content with only one month at summer camp in Italy. Perhaps it was these abbreviated stays that kept me from becoming involved with girls, an experience George Clare recalls so fondly in *Last Waltz in Vienna*.

The academic secondary schools had a high attrition rate. When I started in the second grade (US sixth), there were three parallel classes in our grade, each consisting of about thirty students. When I graduated, there were only two parallel classes of about twenty-five each, an attrition rate of nearly fifty percent. Yet with all this company in my own and parallel grade classes, I can recall only the one friend that I mentioned earlier, Walter, with whom I shared an interest in music, especially opera. I cannot recall spending time outside classes with any other classmates.

My being the only Jewish student in the class was surely a factor, but I should honestly admit those personal qualities that also contributed: I was not a gregarious person, and by my teen years I had become accustomed to being pretty much a loner. Not seeking out others and not being sought out by them are, after all, two sides of the same coin.

Learning foreign languages was an important part of my teenage education. In school I had seven years of Latin and four years of French, both required subjects. I started French in the fifth grade (US ninth). At that time, Mama decided that I should also learn English, a testimony not so much to her prescience as her genuinely cosmopolitan outlook. Perhaps she also had the image of her beloved brother, Max, the international businessman, in mind.

For English I had a number of private tutors, beginning with my cousin Fritzi, whose choice of reading materials I treasure to this day: Oscar Wilde's fairy tales and Kipling's *Just So Stories*. Subsequently I received conversation lessons from two English women, who introduced their pupils to English culture in a variety of ways, including recruiting us to help stir the Christmas pudding!

Then shortly before emigration, I was tutored by an American medical student who prepared me for life in the United States by having me read articles from the *Reader's Digest*. What is more American than that? In subsequent years though, I tended to take a less favorable view of the *Digest's* right-wing nationalism.

In all these cases, the instruction I received was one-on-one or at most in very small groups. As a result, I arrived first in England and then in the United States with a reasonable command of the spoken language. My written expression, however, remained a form of transliterated German for quite some time, until my teachers in English 101 and 103 at Indiana University began to make serious inroads into the imperfections.

Somewhat the same pattern held true for French, though in that case the foundation for my command of the language was laid by four years of language instruction in school (an unrelenting grammar drill). Private conversation lessons came only later from a French woman who helped me prepare for the oral portion of my comprehensive examinations for the *Matura*.

Physical education was also a required subject for all seven years of *Gymnasium*. The passing grades of 3 (or C) that I received were largely unearned. I was not much good at calisthenics. I could not run well. I was no good at soccer. When it came time to choose teams, I was always the last one to be chosen. Still, I learned to swim. I had a season's pass for Vienna's oldest outdoor artificial ice-skating rink. I took tennis lessons. I went skiing in the Alps. In retrospect, I would say that the program served me well because it was aimed at universal participation and individual excellence, rather than team competition.

Still, considering such inauspicious beginnings, one might wonder how I survived, and even succeeded, first in basic training and then in Officer Candidate School in the army. Having depicted myself here as having no great physical aptitude, I will have to explain later how and why I volunteered for airborne service in World War II.

As secondary schooling came to a close, the question of life beyond *Gymnasium* became ever more urgent. This was especially so because my desire was to go to university and study history, with the intention of teaching and doing research in history in secondary school. I had no delusions of grandeur about a university appointment!

Although university study had been open to Jews as early as 1848, and even though the university medical school had some Jewish faculty members by the 1930s, the conservative governments that controlled Austria both before and after World War I rigidly excluded Jews from teaching at most levels. The prospect of exposing children to Jewish teachers was viewed with even greater horror than a Jewish presence in the university faculties.

It was simply unrealistic for a Jew to expect a teaching appointment in the foreseeable future. Thus, my career aspirations reinforced my family's judgment that I was indeed an impractical, hopeless dreamer.

Because I was a very undecided, accommodating teenager, I did not push hard, if at all, for my desired future. What made me accommodate myself to the advice of Mama and Oscar was that I genuinely wanted to do whatever Mama wanted me to do, especially after the death of my father in September 1934, shortly before my final year in secondary school. Just as I faithfully observed the religious requirements for the year of mourning, so I accommodated myself, probably quite unconsciously, to Mama's suggestions about my future.

Oscar lent his business experience to strengthen the argument that I should seek a future not in the retail end of the textile business but in the manufacturing side. I eventually complied with their suggestions by enrolling at Vienna's Textile Institute for a one-year intensive course designed for academic secondary school graduates, the *Abiturientenkurs*.

The trauma of secondary school graduation has been a frequent subject in German literature; however, I seem to have sailed through it without any great upheaval or angst. I easily passed all four written examinations in the required subjects: German, Latin, mathematics, and history. For the oral portion of the exam, one could choose the fields in which one was sure to shine. To take account of possible weaknesses in the four required written subjects, if one failed any written exam, one would then have to be reexamined orally.

All the exams, written as well as oral, were conducted by a team of teachers and ministry of education officials from outside the school. Thus, the teachers who had shepherded us through the years could, at the end, only stand by and cross their fingers. The only other place where I have encountered a comparable arrangement was at Swarthmore College, where in the honors program, outside examiners had the final voice on graduation and on the level of honors to be awarded each graduating student.

It seems to me that the truly profound influences on my development occurred *outside* my formal schooling. This does not mean that I consider my *Gymnasium* education irrelevant or insignificant. Quite the contrary. The very thorough grounding I received in foreign languages, literature, mathematics, history, and geography provided the foundation on which I have built much of my subsequent intellectual life.

In the textile industry

In the Vienna of 1935, in the midst of the Great Depression, Textilschule Wien was a thriving institution taking up a whole city block in Vienna's fifth district (a considerable distance from my home in the sixteenth district). I cannot truthfully say that Mama and Oscar sent me there. At least I have no recollection of foot stamping, pouting, or any other form of resistance. In the last years of *Gymnasium*, my interest in history had only deepened, but you can well imagine the reactions of members of the various families with whom we socialized when they asked me, "And what do you want to be?" and I answered, "I want to study history."

For a Jew to want to study history and to teach (after all, what can you do with history except teach?) was so outlandish that it qualified as an idle dream. It only confirmed their judgment of me as a "nice" but obviously totally impractical person.

As it turned out, my year at the *Textilschule* profoundly affected my life in ways I could not foresee. It changed the pattern of my academic performance in a very positive way. As well, through the institute, I made friends among Jewish people of my own age and social background. In turn this produced my first great romantic attachment. Although I was eighteen, I had had no meaningful contact with young women, in spite of having spent most of my school years in coeducational classes. Then too, as a result of my training, I was, at age nineteen, given a chance to manage a small textile mill in Yugoslavia.

Most importantly, my textile training and experience served as a means to make contact with people in the United States who assisted me in my immigration efforts, and who gave me employment from my arrival in New York until I volunteered for the army the day after the Japanese attack on Pearl Harbor. This war service enabled me ultimately to do that which I had always wanted to do—study history. Thus, the unfolding of these events constitutes a most powerful illustration of serendipity.

My grades at the *Textilschule* give evidence of a strong steady performance: half As, half Bs. I believe that this is a remarkable record. The *Abiturientenkurs* was a course for graduates of academic secondary schools. It compressed into just one year most of the material from the four-year course that was designed for fourteen- to eighteen-year-olds coming directly from their eight years of terminal secondary education. The *Abiturientenkurs* had intensive instruction in all aspects of textile production (from spinning to weaving to textile finishing), with additional courses in areas such as fiber technology, textile design, the chemistry of textile fibers, accounting, and principles of management.

In contrast to my roller coaster performance in my seven years of *Gymnasium*, my year at the *Textilschule* reflected my steady application to academic requirements. Although I continued lusting for history, I took my year at the institute seriously, with very good results. That performance pattern has persisted throughout my career. One might, of course, suggest that I was, as always, an obedient child who did what he was told to do; however, my secondary school record would not bear out this contention. I might have been docile, but I certainly did not perform as I was expected to.

Then too, those who are critical of formal education could suggest that I was simply very proficient at regurgitating what my instructors taught. Surely there was much of that during my life in the armed forces, especially in the academic component of Officer Candidate School. However, I hope that I can show from my later career that more than rote learning was at work. I would argue that the intellectual equipment was there in the earlier years, but neither the incentive nor the maturity to use it to the fullest.

Nevertheless, having embarked on an occupation that required a fair amount of manual dexterity and technical savvy, neither of which I had much of, it is not surprising that I scored no great successes during my years in the textile industry. That my heart was not in the textile business, I can hardly deny.

Ralph and Gretl

It was in the *Textilschule* that I met Ralph Schwarz, a fellow student who became the closest, most influential friend of my younger years. We spent most of our spare time together. My admiration for him knew no bounds. He was more intellectually profound, more widely read, and simply more mature. I cannot now recall the substance of his influence on me in detail, but bits and pieces remain, such as his admiration for the poetry of Rainer Maria Rilke and the music of Gustav Mahler.

Ralph had a quick mind and was interested in many things. To top it off, he was a well-trained and serious athlete. He specialized in what was then still considered middle distances, such as 400 and 800 meters. Yet I do not think that it was simply a one-way admiration society. If it had been, our friendship would not have survived our year together in school. I also believe that Ralph's honesty would not have permitted such a relationship to continue.

Ralph was the only Jewish friend of my early years. He was my only social link outside the various family circles in which my family socialized. Yet religion as such did not really enter into our relationship. His family like mine was essentially a secular one and in fact, observed much less Jewish ritual than my family did. We were both products of Viennese bourgeois Jewry: well educated, devoted to the arts, and leftist in politics. That is to say, our affinity was cultural rather than religious or ethnic. To the extent that we were the offspring of a well-defined minority, we clearly shared outlooks and interests.

There was probably some contrast between our two families, not necessarily in wealth but in lifestyle. Ralph's father had a university degree and was the chief financial officer of a mid-sized textile-related company, and his family seemed to lead a life more strongly oriented to intellectual pursuits than mine. That was reflected in Ralph's greater sophistication and in his range of knowledge in literature and the arts.

Our friendship had many characteristics of a teenage relationship. It so happened that we lived at opposite ends of Vienna, I in the west, he in the southeast in a middle- to upper-class bourgeois neighborhood. At the end of one evening's memorable discussion (memorable *not* for the content of our conversation!), we discovered that I had missed the last streetcar home from Ralph's apartment. So Ralph offered to walk me home (a walk of about one and a half hours) so that we could continue the discussion. I should note, in passing, that in the 1930s there was no part of Vienna where it was not safe to walk any time of the day or night.

Arriving at my apartment house and finding that whatever problem we were attempting to solve still eluded us, there was nothing to do but walk back with Ralph to his house! By then it was 3 a.m., and fortunately I was able to catch a night bus that operated at infrequent intervals during the darkest hours until the regular streetcars resumed operation at 5 a.m. Who but eighteen-year-olds absorbed in a "profound" discussion would engage in such a ridiculous enterprise?

It was Ralph who introduced me to Gretl Wertheimer, a classmate from his *Gymnasium* days. Gretl was the grande affaire of my late teens and early twenties. In retrospect, I see my relationship with Gretl as a form of being in love with love, but some aspects of our relationship did not become clear to me until much later. Without having any direct evidence, I began to suspect that Gretl really was very much in love with Ralph, whose attention was centered entirely on Edith, a girl he had met long before our *Textilschule* days.

As a result, Gretl and I were more often part of a foursome than we were a twosome. Contact with Gretl was suspended during 1936-37 while I worked in Yugoslavia, but resumed when I returned to Vienna in the spring of 1937. From then on, our meetings were infrequent because of the long hours (work plus travel) at the textile mill in which I worked after my return to Vienna.

In March 1938, the *Anschluss* brought all Jews closer together but also tended to preoccupy us, as individuals and families, with finding our own emigration possibilities. Apparently the Wertheimer family had better contacts in the United States than my family, for Gretl reached New York long before I did. Having found well-paying employment—quite a feat for a recent immigrant in New York City—Gretl was also able to help her parents emigrate.

Gretl was very intelligent, well organized, and driven, quite the opposite of my own makeup in those years. If I began later to display some of those qualities, I certainly did not display them then, at least that is what even the most loving members of my family told me.

After I settled in New England and was working in a textile mill there, I spent many weekends commuting to New York to see Gretl. By then it was clear that whatever interest or love Gretl once had for me had cooled considerably, if not completely. The outbreak of World War II put an end to these visits. We did stay in touch, and Gretl later visited us in New Haven while I was in graduate school working on my doctorate.

Work and emigration also began to separate me from Ralph, whose emigration shaped up quite differently than for most of us. The reason for Ralph's somewhat unusual path of emigration was his father's membership in the Masonic Order, in the one grand lodge that had exclusively Jewish members.

It is difficult to make clear to an American audience that Europe's Masonic Lodges were centers of great influence and profound significance in European societies. Although by 1938 European Masonry had declined in significance, the bonds within the order easily crossed even national boundaries.

As a result of his father's Masonic ties, Ralph was able to obtain the necessary visas and employment in a French textile mill. Eventually he was transferred to a mill in Colombia. Ralph married Edith and they emigrated together, but their marriage did not last. Following his divorce, Ralph married a French woman.

After many years in responsible positions in Colombian mills, Ralph was again moved, this time to one of the largest textile mills in the United States, located in Danville, Virginia. However, our contacts became ever more attenuated, and they ended when I realized that responses to my Christmas cards and other seasonal messages always came from Ralph's wife. Apparently Ralph did not want to respond to me directly, for reasons I have never fully understood.

I have seen Ralph only once since we separated in Vienna after the *Anschluss*. In 1949 in the course of one of his frequent business trips to the United States for his Colombian employer, Ralph visited us in New Haven. The timing of the visit made it possible for him to sit in on a discussion section that I conducted as a graduate assistant for the beginning political science course at Yale.

What I remember about his comments was his wonderment at the informal way students talked to me, their "professor." He noted in particular that while talking to me after class, one of the students had his hands in his trouser pockets. Ralph clearly took this to be a sign of disrespect.

I am sure Ralph had hoped for university study and an academic or intellectual career, even though our religion and the world's economic conditions required us to pursue more practical careers. Perhaps he regretted more than I could fathom that he had been unable to escape the textile mill. Perhaps he envied my good fortune in having been able to do so. Ralph had a keen mind and strong personality. He might have felt that rewards had not been apportioned fairly between the two of us.

The textile mill in Beška

Toward the end of my one-year course at the *Textilschule*, an employment opportunity arose to which I responded with much excitement. It came through a family connection, but that made it no less substantial or exciting, especially given the continuously depressed state of the European economies. The German economy had gone into high gear, fueled by the accelerating war preparation of the Third Reich. (Hitler had solved Germany's unemployment problem!) However, there was as yet no spillover into the rest of Europe. The position I was offered was as manager of a small textile mill in the village of Beška in Yugoslavia.

The family connection that resulted in this job offer came from a brother of Grandmother Herzog, Leopold Weiss. Uncle Leopold had been most successful in business in a variety of enterprises and had amassed a considerable fortune, much of it in prime farmland in Slovakia. However, he had a reputation for being irascible. He was not on good terms with his children, and his son Paul had left home to create his own world. Paul had built up a textile mill into a most successful enterprise but then had died unexpectedly in 1934, still unmarried. Thus his father was left with the task of disposing of his son's estate.

I do not know how Uncle Leopold had learned about my textile schooling. In any case, he contacted me and offered me the position of manager of that mill. This meant that at the age of nineteen, I would have the chance to be my own boss, both professionally and in my life in general. The prospect of all that was almost overwhelming, and it detracted little from my excitement that I would have to live in a small village in a country whose language I did not understand. There was simply no doubt in my mind that I wanted to go and see what I could do.

I was so excited and so preoccupied with my own feelings that I did not give much thought to Mama's feelings in the matter. She was sufficiently business-oriented to appreciate the opportunity offered me. But she must have been very reluctant to let go of her only child, especially since the death of her husband was so recent. As it turned out, I returned to Vienna in mid-1937 in good part because by then, she had openly asked me to, and because I realized that I simply had to respond to that manifestation of her loneliness.

I should mention that beneath the surface of the whole affair, there was an element of family politics that nobody ever fully expressed. Uncle Leopold was the wealthiest member of Mama's family, so it would have been considered most impolitic for me not to respond positively to his job offer. I was aware of this, but I was so full of excitement about being the manager of a textile mill, no matter how small it might be, that I really paid no attention to the family politics.

Beška was then a small village of several hundred inhabitants, located in the part of Yugoslavia that had been detached from Hungary by peace treaties and awarded to the then brand-new Kingdom of the Serbs, Croats, and Slovenes. Under Hungarian rule, the region was called Vojvodina, but under Yugoslavian authority, it was referred to as the administrative district of Srem, and its administrative center was Sremski Karlovci. Beška is on the main railway line that runs south from Budapest through Novi Sad to Belgrade. It was about an hour's train ride from the capital.

To me the most remarkable aspect of Beška was that most of the population were descendants of Svabian settlers who had been brought in by the Habsburg Empire in the late seventeenth and eighteenth centuries to clear the forests and farm the land. The Schwaben who worked for me were a most diligent and friendly people who had maintained their Svabian dialect and German culture in this foreign environment. So as it turned out, I was able to direct the work of a small mill in Yugoslavia by using my native language, German, after all!

The one road in Beška was unpaved, but there were paved sidewalks in some places. The village had a complement of stores and pubs, though I did not frequent them much. The government reflected the multi-ethnic character of this then quite young kingdom. The postmaster was a Croat who mercifully was willing to speak German with me. The stationmaster was a Serb who either did not speak German or did not care to admit that he did. My contacts with the stationmaster were extensive, for we shipped all the mill's products by rail to a network of wholesalers. Thus one of my first tasks was to master enough of the Cyrillic script to be able to make out bills of lading for our shipments and to deal with arriving goods, principally the yarn we used in the mill.

Uncle Leopold was in Beška when I arrived. He provided me with a thorough briefing of my duties. Interestingly I have absolutely no recollection of my pay. Likely this is a reflection of my thoroughly noncommercial frame of reference and of the financial security in which I grew up.

After a few days, Uncle Leopold departed, and I was on my own. Fortunately, Paul Weiss had established the mill on a most solid footing. He had created a product much in demand and had recruited and trained a reliable workforce. He had identified reliable suppliers, and most importantly, he had created an effective network of wholesalers. All I had to do was maintain an ongoing operation and hope that changes in market conditions would not require innovative managerial action, at least for a while.

The mill was located only a short distance from the railway station. It included an owner/manager's house, which was cleaned by a maid, who also cooked my meals. The residence building fronted on the street such as it was, and the mill itself was clustered around an interior courtyard. One of the weavers also served as a live-in guard and maintenance man, and we became good friends. He provided me with a window on the local Schwaben in a variety of ways.

One might think that an urban and reasonably well-educated Austrian Jew whose principal tastes were intellectual would suffer severe culture shock from such a transplantation. However, perhaps because of the summers I spent in Vrbové, the shock was not too severe, even though Vrbové was considerably more modern in many ways than was Beška. Generally I viewed it all as a great adventure, in good part because it provided me with an opportunity to be on my own and to be my own boss.

That there was a considerable cultural gap between Vienna and Beška was driven home to me early in my stay. I grew up on a breakfast of cocoa and *Kipferln*, the Viennese croissant (or is the croissant the Parisian *Kipferl?*). So my stomach turned over when by chance, I saw our live-in guard consume his breakfast of cold sliced meat washed down with large gulps of the prize product of the region: plum brandy, Slivovitz!!

Otherwise, the contrast in food was not as great as one might think. Mama had brought her cooking repertoire and skills to Vienna from her native village. Her style of cooking was not all that different from that of Beška. After all, even the most patriotic Viennese now agree that Viennese cooking is actually an amalgam of cuisines of various parts of the empire, from whence came the young women who staffed the households of the Viennese bourgeoisie.

The question of suitable footwear soon arose. But it was resolved without trauma. I gave up my city shoes in short order for a pair of wooden clogs that proved much superior for navigating the dirt roads and paths of Beška.

During my year in Beška, I made several trips to Belgrade to deal with wholesalers and suppliers and to indulge in the one big-city pleasure I missed very much: coffeehouses and their newspapers. Belgrade provided my introduction to the tiny cups of hot mud called Turkish coffee that I began to prefer to the Viennese product, which in my days was half coffee, half chicory or other stretcher. (The price of coffee was very high as a result of high import duty. I certainly marveled when I arrived in the United States to find that even the poorest could afford the unmixed product.) In Belgrade I caught up on newspapers and magazines, and I always took an armful back with me to Beška.

My most frequent travels, however, took me no further than the region's administrative center, Sremski Karlovci, about a half hour away by train. I had received detailed instructions from Uncle Leopold about our fiscal obligations to the Yugoslav government, particularly in light of the foreign ownership of our enterprise. My recollection is that we owed the central government a form of value-added tax. We were required to keep detailed sales records and remit the tax owed every calendar quarter to the tax collector in Sremski Karlovci. Mind you, we could not just mail in the amount owed, but rather we had to take it to the tax collector's office in person and in cash, together with our tax records.

According to Uncle Leopold's instructions, I was to hand our records to the tax collector, and he would check them, acknowledge our payment of the tax, and return our record books to us. To carry out this transaction, I was to put the amount owed inside the tax record, along with a plain envelope containing a certain sum, in large-denomination dinar notes, above and beyond the amount of the tax owed. As Uncle Leopold predicted, the record book was duly returned to me, minus the amount we owed legally and also minus the envelope!

I do not remember being shocked by these instructions. I had begun to understand the prickly national pride of these newly created nation-states and their desire to protect their newly found sovereignties against all kinds of foreigners, especially those from the former dominant imperial nations. I fully understood that as a foreign enterprise, we had to be particularly scrupulous in our record-keeping and not try to lighten our tax load by doing business off the books.

Furthermore, the payment of what Anglo-Saxons might crudely call a bribe, I simply saw as the common practice of smoothing one's way by greasing the appropriate wheels. These were not bribes, but tips or transactions for which the Austrian *Trinkgeld* or the widely used *baksheesh* are considerably more euphonious and probably more honest, too. Thus, we were not bribing the tax-man; the money in that special envelope constituted a legitimate cost of doing business.

These visits to Sremski Karlovci had another side to them, one that was rather more social. After I had done business with the head of the tax office, he and three or four of his junior administrators invited me for drinks. In my case that was an invitation to disaster, for I had grown up in a household with very little alcohol in evidence, except for an occasional glass of beer for my father and the obligatory wine used for Seder celebrations.

My one binge had come during the *Fasching* (Mardi Gras) season of 1936 when Ralph, Edith, Gretl, and I made up a foursome to attend some balls. I ended up losing my cookies at five in the morning. Given this record of a capacity, or rather incapacity, to hold alcohol, my being plied with drink after drink of Slivovitz could only lead to catastrophe.

I had come to Sremski Karlovci by train early in the afternoon and counted on returning to Beška for dinner. Our formal business was completed speedily and then it was off to the inn. I fought them off as well as I could, daring not to offend these government officials.

I looked at my watch and said, "Time to go to catch the next train." I was greeted with a chorus of, "There's another train soon." This was repeated several times until I desperately pointed to my watch yet again and noted that the last train of the day was not far off. That finally did the trick. It was about 8 p.m. by then, and my hosts certainly did not want to have to look after me for the rest of the night!

So they all escorted me to the railway station, accompanied by much merriment, and carefully installed me in a vacant compartment. Fortunately, I retained enough competence to get off at the right stop.

Equally fortunately, our live-in guard and caretaker had suspected what might be happening to me and had met every one of the afternoon trains until I finally stumbled into his arms from the last train of the day. Thus I had some solid support for the short walk from the station to the mill. I am sure that I fell into bed without delay, and I am equally sure that I had a hangover of considerable proportions the next morning. During subsequent tax visits, I was more successful in fending off all this Serbian hospitality.

Most other aspects of my managerial duties were less colorful and also less disruptive of my daily existence. As I noted earlier, my cousin Paul had created a product with a steady market: woolen shawls about a yard square, with fringes about ten inches long on all four sides. Women usually folded the shawls triangularly and wore them draped over their heads or their shoulders, depending on the weather. These shawls sold well all year round. Interestingly, there seemed to be no great demand for a choice of colors. Henry Ford would have loved it—all colors as long as they are black!

We purchased the yarn from a variety of spinners, both in Yugoslavia and abroad. It was in connection with our yarn purchases that I became aware of the Third Reich's aggressive economic foreign policies, especially in the context of German efforts to penetrate and dominate the smaller countries of Central and Southeastern Europe, from Austria through Bulgaria.

I learned that German spinners sent buyers into Yugoslav wool-producing regions and offered higher prices for the raw wool than Yugoslav spinners could offer simply because they did not receive government subsidies as did the German spinners. The raw wool was shipped to Germany and spun into yarn, which was then offered to Yugoslav weavers like us at prices well below those of Yugoslav spinners!

All this was a well-coordinated effort to "peacefully" penetrate Yugoslavia, with the military follow-up coming in 1941. As it turned out, however, we were not tempted by the German offers because the German spinners did not offer the type and quality of yarn we needed.

Vienna and new pursuits

By the spring of 1937, the allure of my managerial experience had worn off, I wanted to see Gretl again, and most importantly, Mama was increasingly lonely in the apartment that had once housed a large lively family. I returned to Vienna, so ending all my contacts with Beška. Emigration and World War II effectively pulled the curtain down over this episode. Within a year of my return from Beška, the *Anschluss* came, and in another year, I was en route to England and ultimately, to the United States.

On my return to Vienna, I discovered that jobs in the textile industry were scarce indeed. It was largely through Oscar's strenuous efforts that I was taken on as a management trainee by a large Vienna textile mill, Hermann Pollack & Sohn. It was an unpaid position, but there was promise of eventual advancement and salary. That my family was able to sustain my taking an unpaid position only underlines my earlier observations about the continued success of our retail enterprise throughout the Depression years of the 1930s.

Not only that, but when Mama asked me what I wanted for my birthday, I asked for a season ticket to the Sunday morning subscription series of the Vienna Philharmonic! These concerts were held on Sundays at 11:30 a.m., a most unusual time by American standards! I suppose that in a Roman Catholic country like Austria, one could easily manage both attendance at mass and an 11:30 a.m. concert on a Sunday. Since my hours at the mill together with a streetcar commute of at least one hour each way made my weekday opera-going all but impossible, these Sunday concerts were the true highlights of the 1937-38 musical season. So it was that the year after my return from Beška was like a period of calm before a great storm.

It was in this last year before the *Anschluss* that I began what turned out to be a much-abbreviated program of university studies. Once again the prevailing climate of the time dictated practicality. I enrolled at the Hochschule für Welthandel. This might be translated as the "College of Business Administration of the University of Vienna," but that would be a considerable simplification of the Austrian-German system of higher education, which draws very sharp distinctions between a *Universität* and a *Hochschule* (which is never translated as "high school" without causing apoplexy among a sizeable portion of the middle class, or at least among those who know what an American high school is).

I enrolled in a full-time program of studies that would lead to the *Diplomkaufmann* degree. To translate this term as "diploma merchant" would devastate an even larger number of burghers. This was, in fact, a sort of MBA degree, long before these three letters took on the magical qualities that Europeans now associate with this wonderful American invention.

I was assured that there was no problem with enrolling in full-time study while working full-time. An elaborate network of professional tutors was available, working out of various coffeehouses (only in Vienna!). These tutors had notes for all the courses and could offer tutoring at any time convenient to the student. The program was built around comprehensive exams at stated intervals, but had no quizzes, progress tests, or the like. Attendance at classes was only for those not otherwise occupied.

An enrollment book listed all the courses one would take. In the book were spaces for each instructor to sign on the first and last day of class. For a small fee, a *pedell* (a low-level administrative employee of the university) would take the book around to the appropriate instructors for their signatures. Most instructors had little rubber stamps to speed up the process and conserve their valuable time.

The *pedell* was really a combination janitor and clerk. Many were former military, mostly senior noncommissioned officers, who had done their "thirty years" and were collecting pensions. These men had clearly mastered complex organizations and knew how to handle raw recruits, that is to say, first-year students. Without them, the universities would probably have collapsed into utter chaos. Jacques Barzun, in his autobiographical *Teacher in America*, reminisces about his student days in Paris and recalls how a comparable corps of such officials actively ran the university, including providing the most reliable information to students about degree requirements and idiosyncrasies of the faculty.

My career as a future *Diplomkaufmann* was cut short in March 1938 when Jewish students were expelled from all institutions of higher learning within days of the *Anschluss*. I had already signed up for second-semester courses, but the registration of all Jewish students was canceled in short order. Austria had "come home" into the Reich.

Other dimensions: music and politics

Family, friends, school, and work all combined to shape my life during the preemigration years. Perhaps it is misleading to label all these years as preemigration. Hardly anyone in our extended family circles or among Vienna's nearly 200,000 Jews very seriously considered the possibility of emigration before 1938—not even after January 30, 1933, when Hitler took power in Germany. Perhaps facing total disruption of one's established life is so monstrously difficult that one simply does not want to face up to it.

At that time, the only Jews who seriously considered emigration were Zionists, whose religious or political vision of Eretz Israel was not shared by many. Given the strong assimilationist forces at work in Vienna's Jewish community, it was not surprising, alas, to hear Zionists belittled as Jews who collect money from a second Jew to send a third Jew to Palestine.

This strong assimilationist sentiment is particularly noteworthy because the number of Jews who could trace their family back to Viennese roots over several generations was quite small. Many Viennese Jews in the years of my youth were fairly recent arrivals, my own parents among them. Yet the influence of Jews on Vienna, its life, and its culture was profound. An exhibit entitled Vienna's Popular Favorites in Sound and Picture (*Die Zeit*, March 27, 1992), mounted first in Vienna and scheduled to travel to other cities, demonstrates the influence that Jewish artists and performers had on popular culture. It reminds us that songs that have come to symbolize Vienna, such as "Wien, Wien nur du allein" and the "Fiakerlied," which contain lines such as "My pride is to be a true child of Vienna," were written and composed by Jews.

It was this culture that helped shape my childhood and young adulthood. For me, the two most significant elements of this culture were music and politics. Both have been equally potent influences in my life, especially during my first twenty years.

Music

In my recollections about Mama, I have already pointed to the one great musical influence in my earlier years. But I should mention, too, the presence of a grand piano in our living room and the violin lessons to which I was subjected from age seven or eight on. That my love for music survived six or seven years of violin lessons is testimony to a strong devotion to that particular Muse.

On the other hand, a thorough exposure to literature at school produced no more than routine responses. However, I should acknowledge that the years of *Gymnasium* lessons in mostly German literature did give me a reasonably solid foundation in the written and spoken word.

This foundation was reinforced by frequent theater visits, especially to the Burgtheater, the premier state theater, which offered a classical and occasionally modern repertoire. There I saw works of Goethe, including *Faust* (both parts and also a production that condensed both parts into a single evening!), as well as works of Schiller and Lessing. I also saw productions of translated works that had become a regular part of the literature taught in schools and performed on stage. There were productions of classics by Shakespeare, Molière, and others, but also productions by near contemporaries, such as Ibsen and Strindberg. I vividly remember a *Peer Gynt* production in which all the Grieg incidental music was sung, played, and danced by performers from the Vienna State Opera.

This cosmopolitan approach to literature was fostered in German-speaking areas by a literary tradition that valued translations and translators. It was a tradition that did not treat translators as drudges to be paid as little as possible. The cavalier treatment of translators in much of the English-speaking world was brought home to me while I was a graduate student after World War II. I was asked to translate into English and prepare for publication an as-yet untranslated work by the great Austrian constitutional lawyer Hans Kelsen. I refused when I discovered that on a per-page basis, I would be paid only a small fraction of what the typist would be paid for transcribing my translation!

To resume my recollections about music, I remember my weekly violin lessons as a series of ordeals to be avoided as much as possible by faking headaches or even an occasional vomiting. Yet for six or seven years I trudged to my teacher's apartment for lessons. My recollection is a rather Victorian vision: a strict disciplinarian teacher, an apartment filled with big pieces of dark wood furniture, his wife and possibly some children dressed in severe fashions and dark colors.

Although my lessons were an ordeal, I made progress from year to year as a consequence of my talent and/or my teacher's ability to teach me. When I was fourteen or fifteen, I graduated to the easy Viotti concerti, which I certainly could not have done if he had not been able to elicit appropriate skills and performances from me. Could the same regime produce comparable success in a culture that does not expect and enforce a certain level of respect of, and obedience to, authority? Or was I simply a particularly obedient child?

During the upper grades of *Gymnasium*, I finally rebelled, not against music lessons, but against the violin and that particular teacher. I had begun to tinker with our grand piano, playing tunes and even trying to compose music. I announced that I wanted to shift to the piano and found no resistance to my wish. Had I been running up against an open door?

My new teacher was a youngish member of the Unger clan with a lively approach to teaching the piano. I made rapid progress because I had been thoroughly trained in music theory, could read music, and felt at home with the piano. I derived great enjoyment from the piano and independently sought out sheet music and albums for more music to play.

By then I had lost touch with Franzl and his love of the theater, but my friendship with Walter was beginning to develop, and my interest in opera, especially in the work of Richard Wagner, was growing rapidly. In fact I became the victim of a full-scale Wagner craze. I bought piano scores of his operas, and I attended as many performances of his operas as I could squeeze into my schedule. It was an inexpensive craze at that. It involved only the cost of tickets for fourth balcony standing room at one Austrian Schilling (about 20¢ at the then-current rate of exchange) and the cost of piano scores, which were available as second-hand or remaindered items in music stores.

One had to line up for the limited number of standing-room tickets early in the afternoon (especially if one had a particular standing place in mind). Sometimes I would go directly to the opera house from school, equipped with my dinner in a bag, a folding stool that would fit into my briefcase, the piano score, and whatever homework needed to be done. Once the box office opened, we raced up four steep flights (no elevators!) as fast as we could to secure our favorite locations. Mine was a set of steps under an exit light, where I could sit down and have enough light to follow the score. I had little interest in seeing the stage. Much of it would have been obscured, even if I had tried to see something. The opera house had many visually-obstructed seats but really no hearing-obstructed spots. The acoustics of that old lady were nearly perfect.

Not being able to see was no great deprivation in those days. The theater's budget had already become severely limited and permitted neither the mounting of new productions nor the engagement of great star singers. The truly great Austrian actors, singers, and directors had quickly migrated to Berlin, London, or New York (and that long before 1938 when there was still another exodus).

I recall a production of *The Magic Flute*, which had been one of Gustav Mahler's great achievements as musical director of the opera before he left Vienna for the Met in 1905. When I saw it, the sets had become threadbare, the production stale, and the singers average. What saved it was the playing of the pit orchestra, the Vienna Philharmonic. Given these conditions, who needed to see anything?

The zenith (or nadir) of my Wagner craze came in 1935 during my graduation exams for *Gymnasium*. The written and oral exams coincided roughly with the last full Ring Cycle of the opera season, before everything was packed up for the move to Salzburg for the festival period. I can no longer remember the exact sequence of events, but I recall sitting for a written examination in the morning, spending most of the afternoon queuing up, attending the performance of whatever part of the Ring Cycle was being presented, and getting home by midnight. Next morning I was up at seven to get to school for the next part of the written examination!

Attending the Ring Cycle in the midst of final exams was just mindless adulation. Still, persistence of my Wagner devotion can be judged by my decision to take all my Wagner piano scores with me into emigration. At that time and even later, I was not prepared to hold Wagner responsible for either the crimes or the inanities of the Third Reich.

I can understand that many, especially in Israel, object most strongly to the performance of his music. I would not do so myself, mostly because I believe that political censorship of the arts, even though it has a long and even respectable paternity going back to Plato, is incompatible with my basic premises about a free democratic society. To say that the state can prescribe artistic standards is to subordinate art to politics; rather, the two are a seamless whole, in dialogue with one another, without one being subordinate to the other.

It might sound hyperbolic to say that I lived surrounded by music, but that was indeed the case. Several symphony orchestras held special concert series for high school students. Sunday morning mass was sung in the old Imperial Chapel by soloists from the State Opera and the Vienna Boys Choir. Music in a variety of forms came from the state radio. Live music enlivened Sunday afternoon walks or visits to outdoor cafés. Operettas were performed in numerous theaters. Film musicals, which I found most enchanting, were increasingly imported, chiefly from the United States.

My musical tastes were not as limited as my Wagner craze might suggest. I began to be drawn to the music of Mozart, who was considered passé and lightweight when compared with Wagner, Brahms, Bruckner, and others. I recall, too, that in spite of my Wagner craze, for me the most powerful operatic performance of those years was Alban Berg's *Wozzeck*. It was exactly the sort of *Gesamtkunstwerk* that Wagnerians should have admired, but they did not, in good part, because so many of them found in Wagner added justification for their anti-Semitism.

I also began to take an interest (how and why I do not know) in the work of J. S. Bach, whose music was rarely played in the concert halls of a Roman Catholic country such as Austria, since Bach seemed to be the epitome of the Reformation. I remember a concert of Bach's organ works attended by a handful of people in the Musikvereinsaal, an auditorium that could hold over a thousand.

I doubt whether I had more than an inkling of the fugal and contrapuntal elements of Bach's music. I also doubt whether I had any significant understanding of the profound religious inspiration of Bach's music. Yet given my later religious conversion, I must assume either that something was present then that made me respond, or that I simply stumbled into a musical experience that would have consequences unfathomable to me at that time.

Evidence that art and politics have indeed been intertwined in my life can be found in the last public concert performance I attended before March 13, 1938. After that, Jews were not permitted to attend public performances of any sort. The concert was devoted entirely to Mahler's *Symphony of a Thousand*. It was conducted by Bruno Walter, who had fled Germany in 1933 and was soon forced to flee again, as were many in the audience that evening. What more dramatic linkage between art and politics could there be? The works of the composer were banned, the conductor expelled, and a good part of the audience destined for "shipment to the East."

The next public music performance I was able to attend was a concert of the Boston Symphony conducted by Serge Koussevitzky sometime in 1941 or 1942. By then I was, of course, free to attend as many concerts as I wished, but my factory pay at the federal minimum wage of 37.5¢ an hour did not permit many such luxuries.

Politics

The family is assumed to be the principal instrument of political socialization, the transmitter of political culture. However, my family served only in a minimal way in such a capacity. Mama seemed to have no political interests, or at least did not express any to me that I can recall. I remember my father to be a man of business whose politics was solidly middle-of-the-road, as was shown by his long-standing devotion to Vienna's centrist daily, *Neues Wiener Tageblatt*.

The strongest political impulses within my family came from Oscar, who was an active member of an organization of Social Democratic merchants. Oscar took a lively and direct interest in the political currents of the first Austrian Republic. Some manifestations of his interest will appear later on.

The lifelong evolution of my views as a democratic socialist was rooted in the Red Vienna in which I grew up. The people of Vienna did not attain universal suffrage in local elections until the overthrow of the Empire, when republican institutions were established during a change of regime. This change was championed by the working class and its principal institutions: the Social Democratic Party, the trade unions, and a variety of affiliated organizations, such as youth organizations, book clubs, and gymnastic societies.

The change of regime was accepted, though reluctantly, by the parties of the center and right. With the first election by universal suffrage, the Social Democrats gained control of the Vienna municipal government. Subsequently they gained control of the Vienna *Land* administration under a federal constitution, which made Vienna a city as well as a constituent federal state (such as Hamburg and Bremen have been in post-World War II Germany).

To this red influence should be added the immediate physical environment in which our family enterprise and residence were situated. I spent the first twenty years of my life in an apartment located above our store. Vienna's western districts were heavily industrialized and thus constituted part of the city's Red Belt, none more red than the sixteenth district *(Ottakring)*, in which we were located.

Until this Red Vienna was destroyed in a civil war in February 1934, the Social Democratic Party was engaged in a massive effort to create a socialist environment in which workers would be immune to being enticed by bourgeois media into adopting bourgeois lifestyles and values.

More importantly, through its control of the Vienna city and *Land* governments, the Social Democratic Party constructed a modern welfare state, literally a cradle-to-grave system. Expectant mothers received free prenatal care in the municipal clinics. Every expectant mother was presented by the city with a complete outfit for the baby's first year. At the end of life, those loyal Socialists who wanted no part of religious burial rites could choose to be cremated (elsewhere in Austria, Roman Catholic-dominated *Land* and local governments barred cremation because it was unacceptable to the Roman Catholic Church on doctrinal grounds).

One can truly say that Red Vienna tried to practice what Antonio Gramsci later preached: the working class must create its own world if it were ever to escape bourgeois "hegemony." Thus, from early on I was strongly influenced by Social Democratic ideas and the movement that they inspired.

There is at least one other element of my attachment to democratic socialism: the position of Jews in the emerging democratic politics in the late nineteenth and early twentieth centuries. The one political movement that accepted everyone under a banner of democracy and equal rights was the socialist International Party. In Austria, there existed a strongly entrenched Roman Catholic party that clearly had no place and no appeal for Jews. Other bourgeois parties tended to be more or less nativist, that is to say, they were the European equivalent of what one might call the WASP-ish Republican Party in the United States, at least as that party existed in the late nineteenth and early twentieth centuries. As a result, Jews flocked to the one political movement that seemed committed to equal access for all, and they rose to positions of leadership in the myriad party organizations.

My own identification with social democracy in a country rife with virulent anti-Semitism must be seen in light of these political and social forces at work in a city that can be considered the birthplace of modern anti-Semitism. Ideas of race and racism might have originated elsewhere, but anti-Semitism as a political program may well be credited to late nineteenth century Vienna. In *Mein Kampf*, Hitler praises Karl Lueger and Georg Ritter von Schönerer, Vienna's two great anti-Semitic leaders, for having taught him the principles of racial anti-Semitism and the technique of charismatic mass leadership.

While I was in first grade (1923-1924), Austria conducted a general election. I cannot say that I learned to read from the huge, voluminous election manifestos plastered all over the city (these were days without electronic media). But I could say that my reading about politics got an early start and has not really abated in all the years since then. Now, of course, it is no longer election wall posters but C-SPAN and CNN, not to mention the *New York Times*. Yet in spite of my commitment to social democratic programs, I was not much of an activist—nor has that changed.

However, I must have belonged to some party youth organizations, for one of my persistent memories is a party-sponsored showing of Eisenstein's *Potemkin*, which brought the entire youthful audience to its feet and which ended in the singing of the "Internationale." I remember, too, watching Vienna's May Day parades in the 1920s and early 1930s. These parades impressively displayed the reach of the Social Democratic movement—from the trade unions to the Red Falcons (the Socialist sponsored alternative to the Boy Scouts). They also reflected the scope of Socialist alternatives to bourgeois organizations by featuring gymnasts, mountaineers, nature lovers, and the like.

I joined a socialist book club, the Gutenberg Guild, which distributed books that were meant to reflect the movement's aims and ideas. The English-language works that were made available in translation, such as those by Jack London and Upton Sinclair, constitute what might be called protest literature. These works exposed the "true" nature of capitalism in America. Also included were some of the works of Mark Twain, a choice somewhat more difficult to explain, except that the thoroughly dyspeptic view Mark Twain took of American life must have struck the book selectors as yet more criticism of American capitalism.

Then, too, there was the ideological fiction, which told of brave proletarian maidens being seduced by bloated capitalists. Others had plots built around historical events, such as the one centered on the communist uprising in Shanghai in 1926, in which sexually explicit scenes alternated with street fighting and ideological rhetoric. But the Guild also included one of the great mystery authors of the twentieth century, B. Traven. I remember reading *The Treasure of the Sierra Madre* in a German translation.

The Socialist movement tried to wean workers away from the bourgeois press, especially the tabloids. It also sought to redirect their interest in football (soccer) from professional (bourgeois) league sports to amateur (Socialist-organized) club sports. It is pretty clear that these attempts failed, for the workers wanted their sports section in the Monday morning tabloids along with everybody else.

Only the most devoted believers could tolerate the *Arbeiter Zeitung*, the official party organ, in which everything, including the daily installments of serialized novels, was ideologically correct. Still more proletarian maidens being deflowered by bloated capitalists. These must have been the times before capitalists discovered health spas and began pumping iron!

Civil war

After World War I, Austrian politics was polarized along ideological lines. There were three camps: the Catholic conservative camp on the right, the Socialist camp on the left (these two usually constituted close to ninety percent of the votes cast in general elections), and at center-right the small camp of Pan-German Nationalists and the Peasant Party. The latter joined the Christian Social Party in a coalition that governed Austria for most of the years of constitutional government, which ended in 1931 or 1934, depending on how the term is defined.

Tensions were held in check during the relatively prosperous 1920s. However, the onset of the Depression (which in Austria can be dated from the bank crash of 1926) increased the tensions steadily. The situation was exacerbated by the rise of the Austrian branch of the Nazi Party and of the proto-fascist militia, the Heimwehren.

The Social Democratic Party was supported by armed worker brigades and had created a paramilitary organization, the Schutzbund, which stockpiled weapons and carried out continuous military training. With all sides fielding paramilitary formations, civil war seemed inevitable. It came finally in February 1934. There was intense fighting in our district, with much of the action centered around the district party headquarters, the Arbeiterheim.

I knew nothing about the conflict until it was over. Along with a group of fellow students from the *Gymnasium*, I was learning to ski in the Alps as part of the school physical education program (all while being excused from classes for a whole week!). We returned to Vienna to find that Social Democratic control of the city had been eliminated by force of arms.

By the following May, a corporativist constitution had been imposed on Austria by a Catholic-conservative government. In effect, a native fascist regime had come into being in Austria. That regime was nearly toppled the following July by a German-supported Nazi coup that assassinated the Austrian chancellor. However, this effort ultimately collapsed: Hitler was under pressure from Mussolini (then still the senior Axis leader), who did not want Italy to have to confront an expanding Germany at the Brenner Pass.

Again, with uncanny timing, I managed to be away from Vienna, this time at summer camp in Italy. After that, Austria's clerical-conservative regime managed to muddle through for nearly four years before being brought down by Hitler, who by then had become the dominant partner of the German-Italian alliance.

The Socialist defeat in the 1934 civil war had direct consequences for our family enterprise, in particular for our sales force of about six, plus the usual one or two apprentices. It was quite evident to me that just about all our employees had strong socialist leanings. I was told, when I returned to Vienna from the week of skiing, that on the Monday when the civil war started, two of our salesmen had disappeared.

Oscar knew the reasons for their disappearance. These two were members of the *Schutzbund*, the Socialist paramilitary formation. Both had responded to a call for action and both had been involved in the fighting. One of them, sensing the collapse of the Socialist forces early on, slipped away from the combat and returned to work several days later without having been identified and/or captured by the government forces.

The other one was indeed captured and imprisoned for several months but released under an amnesty. He, too, returned to the store and resumed his duties. It would never have occurred to my family to do anything but give them back their jobs, no questions asked.

Subsequently we came under considerable pressure from officials of the Vaterländische Front, the government-sponsored single political movement, to dismiss these two employees. Since my father had died in September of that year, pressure was brought to bear on Oscar as head of the firm. However, Oscar held his ground, and eventually the authorities ceased to pursue the issue.

The general political culture of Vienna was strongly socialist, and our store and residence were located in one of Vienna's reddest districts, but the political climate in my seven years in *Realgymnasium* was anything but leftist. Academic secondary and higher education were under federal (Catholic-conservative) control. Furthermore, academic secondary education was essentially a middle-class preserve. Thus, I was often both the only Jew and the only socialist in a class of thirty.

After 1933, the Austrian middle class and especially its young succumbed to Nazi influences. Although this must have affected my school life in the last two years, I truly have no recollection of anti-Semitic harassment, either verbal or physical. I am sure many of my teachers (all from good middle-class families) had been drawn into the Nazi camp. But again, I cannot recall any of my teachers acting in a biased manner. Given my very mixed academic performance, I would have to say that all my low grades were earned—I deserved just what I got!

What I do remember from these last two or three years of *Realgymnasium* were numerous political debates with my classmates. None of them led to estrangement or physical violence. We argued endlessly, but that was hardly a peculiar characteristic of teenagers in the 1930s. We were all reasonably well-to-do, middle-class youngsters, and we shared the preoccupations of teenagers in other times and places.

I think I was more politicized than many of my classmates, and more politicized I have remained for most of my life. But I was never a radical egalitarian, either in politics or in economics. Had I known about the Fabians in the mid-1930s or about the "model" Swedish welfare state after World War II, I might well have subscribed to such visions.

Although I detested Austria's Catholic clerical establishment, I have come to have profound appreciation for the notions of social justice enunciated in a series of papal encyclicals and lay Catholic writings.

I have never been able to equate freedom with free market, a concept exported from Vienna by the intellectual forebears of the present-day neo-conservative worshippers of the free market, Friedrich von Hayek and Ludwig von Mises. If I represent any sort of Austrian school, it is not the one associated with Hayek and Mises.

Many of the brightest of my own and subsequent generations succumbed to a god that eventually failed. Not having succumbed in the first place, I can say, perhaps somewhat smugly, that I had no need to replace that particular god with one labeled free market. Perhaps my social democratic vision will disappear with me. So be it.

Chapter 3

Freddy's Story: America

(1938-1942)

In the nearly fifty years since the end of World War II, the history of the Jews under the Third Reich has been examined at length in scholarly treatises, popularized accounts, fiction, film, and other media. As these events recede in time, and as the survivors reach biblical age and beyond, the questions continue: *Didn't you know what was coming? Why didn't you leave? Why didn't they (those who survived) leave?*

All I can do here is give one person's answer to such questions and try to explain, to myself as much as to anyone, how it all happened to me. But there will be no grand explanations, for an individual fate does not, after all, permit grand generalizations.

Antecedents and consequences (Vienna, 1938)

Austria nearly succumbed to Third Reich aggression in 1934, as I recorded earlier. Since I was so interested in history and politics, I found the events unfolding in Germany to be overwhelmingly significant. I was, of course, familiar with anti-Semitism in Vienna and the rising popularity of the Austrian Nazi Party even before 1933, so I had no doubt about the seriousness of a right-wing extremist threat against the Jewish people.

Given my strong social democratic convictions, I was appalled by the rise of an Austrian fascism, which presented itself as the only possible defense against German Nazism and expansionism. I cannot pinpoint exactly when, but I became convinced that the world was moving inexorably toward a general world war, even though appeasement was rampant in France and Britain, and the German-American Bund impeded any US involvement in Europe.

Yet it was not until well after the annexation of Austria in March 1938 that I began to explore possible avenues of emigration. How is it possible to be at the same time convinced of the inevitability of world war and yet continue one's daily round of activities—go to work, attend concerts, be in love, plan to obtain a university degree—as I did until the very day when German troops triumphantly crossed the border into Austria?

There is no easy answer—nor even a difficult one—although I have been asked this question countless times. However, any answer I could give would contain some of the following elements.

Before 1938, my life and that of my family evolved in an orderly manner. What needed to be done and what was enjoyable to do commanded my attention most of the time. It was easy for me to lose myself in the world of the present moment and the immediate task, and that is what I did. Yes, I knew "it was coming," but no, I did not do anything about it until the threat was aimed directly at me. Even then, it took almost a full year before I could manage to leave Germany, which I did in April of 1939.

The second element of my answer involves the degree of willingness of other countries to receive those wanting to emigrate. In the midst of the Great Depression and for almost a decade afterward, few countries were prepared to accept refugees for fear that they would deprive citizens of the few jobs that might open up in a depressed economy. There was also the fear that refugees desperately seeking a safe haven would accept any sort of wage and thus contribute to the miserable condition of the resident population.

Furthermore, most countries had then, and still have today, strict laws about the number and types of immigrants they are willing to accept. So it is not enough for one to be brave and determined to immigrate to a country whose language and culture are foreign. The country in question must be willing to receive the immigrant. In too many cases, the determination to escape was more than matched by the reluctance of potential recipient countries to open their gates to the immigrants fleeing the Third Reich.

The year 1934 marks the beginning of the end of an independent Austria. The civil war of February 1934 strengthened the hold of an increasingly authoritarian Catholic-conservative government over Austrian life. In the end, all but a small segment of the Austrian people were alienated. The Austrian patriotism of the pre-1938 period that was depicted in such glorious Technicolor in *The Sound of Music* gives a misleading impression of the extent of pro-Austrian sentiment in the overall population.

The July 1934 Nazi coup had failed because Mussolini forced Hitler to withdraw his protective cover from the so-called Austrian Legion. However, eventually Italy accepted Germany's insistence that Austria be incorporated into the greater Reich. Even before 1938, Hitler forced the Austrian government to include in the cabinet men who could only be termed crypto-Nazis. The entry of German troops put an end to the government's desperate last-minute efforts to rally anti-Nazi sentiments against the German troops. By that time, independent Austria was doomed. With the *Anschluss* in March 1938, Austria became a part of Germany.

But to come more directly to my own fate and that of my family, it is necessary to draw a picture of what the *Anschluss* meant directly to Austrian Jews. After January 1933, Nazi control of the German government was accompanied by many brutal acts against Jews and others considered enemies of the new Reich, including the opening of the first concentration camps.

However, it did not immediately bring Jewish life and business to a halt. For some time, Jewish students continued to attend schools and universities as before. Jews were able to sell their businesses and transfer wealth abroad. They could leave the country for an exploratory visit and return. In short, the Third Reich's consistently hostile policy toward the Jews was instituted gradually.

In sharp contrast, after the *Anschluss* in March 1938, this pattern of gradualism disappeared in Austria. Jewish businesses in Vienna lost their non-Jewish customers virtually overnight. For quite a while I assumed that what happened to us in Austria was simply a repetition of what happened to other Jews in the Reich after 1933. Only much later did I discover that the swift and ruthless cruelty, not only of the Nazi Party itself, but of Austrians in general, was sui generis.

For instance, in Germany, Jewish businesses continued to have non-Jewish customers in spite of occasional boycotts. In his memoirs *Last Waltz in Vienna*, George Clare describes his surprise about the leeway Jews had in Berlin when he visited there after the *Anschluss* in the summer of 1938 (by then there had been five years of increasingly sharper constraints on the Jews). From other memoirs, I have learned that as late as 1937 Jews in Germany could still obtain university degrees, whereas in Austria, Jews were expelled from all institutions of higher learning within days of the *Anschluss*.

In puzzling over this contrast, I had always ascribed it to a sort of learning process by the Nazi regime. I assumed that by the *Anschluss*, the regime had learned how to crack down on the Jews, based on the lessons learned in the Reich between 1933 and 1938. However, this explanation does not account for the differences George Clare and others observed. There is an alternative and probably more convincing explanation for the contrast between Berlin and Vienna: the deep-seated anti-Semitism endemic in Vienna and in Austria as a whole, as well as the sources from which Austrian Nazis drew their leadership.

Although some roots of Viennese anti-Semitism reach back to the Reformation, others can be found in the nineteenth century, such as Karl Lueger's long term as mayor of Vienna. Lueger created the Christian Social Party, a movement that helped focus the resentment of Vienna's middle classes against new methods of mass marketing and mass production—forces that genuinely threatened the economic and social survival of the middle classes. Because Jews played a prominent role in developing these new forms of economic activity, they became a flashpoint for Lueger's charismatic leadership of the middle classes.

Sadly, this record of anti-Semitism continues unbroken to the present day. It is reflected in recent public opinion polls which reveal that many Austrians still believe that "Jews have too much power," and that they would not want to have Jews as neighbors, or even shake their hands. Such views are still being expressed at a time when Austria's Jewish population could at most be called miniscule.

It should be noted that the leadership of the Austrian Nazi Party came disproportionately from German communities in Bohemia and Moravia. These Germans felt marginalized by the establishment of the post-1918 Czechoslovak republic, and therefore, had gravitated to German-speaking Austria, where their intense nationalist fervor (often characteristic of an ethnic minority) set the tone for the Austrian Nazi Party. So then, given the anti-Semitism endemic to Austria and the radical nationalism of the Austrian Nazis, I was not surprised to learn much later that Austrian Nazis had held a great many top command positions in the major concentration and extermination camps.

Whatever the explanations (or their validity), the full fury of the Nazi state descended on us within days of the *Anschluss*. I was dismissed from my management intern position at Hermann Pollack & Sohn, which immediately came under Nazi administration. My enrollment at the Hochschule für Welthandel was canceled. Most importantly, not a single customer entered our store—there was a nearly total boycott of Jewish enterprises that was effective within the first day or at most two days of the Nazi takeover.

This was a disastrous moment for the main source of our livelihood. Into this scene stepped Rudolf Fuchs, one of our longtime salesmen who had disappeared in February 1934 and had fought on the side of the Socialist uprising. He was also the one whom Oscar had protected when the government pressed for his dismissal. It turned out that after fighting with the Socialists and having been protected against dismissal by his Jewish employers, Rudolf Fuchs had become a member of the illegal Nazi Party. Now he proceeded to take over our store.

The term used for this process was *Aryanization*. I was never fully cognizant of the details of the arrangement, and it might well be that we would have fared worse if the store had been taken over by another member of the illegal Nazi Party who claimed this particular Jewish booty for his services to the Nazi movement during its period of illegality and persecution. However, the settlement was such that there were sufficient funds for Mama and me, as well as for Oscar, to continue to live in some comfort until we should be able to emigrate. But no matter how favorable the settlement, the business my father had created and built and into which Mama and Oscar had poured their talents and energies was lost to us.

After World War II, we could have reclaimed control of the premises, but neither Oscar nor I had any intention of returning to the Brunnengasse to operate a retail business. No other form of restitution was offered to us.

It has been suggested that I ought to be thankful to Adolf Hitler for having liberated me from the confines of the Brunnengasse and for having opened an entire new world to me. I accept that proposition readily, but I wish that some less painful way could have achieved that result. Yet this can be viewed in the light of what I said earlier about the difficulties of forcing humans out of their accustomed grooves. It takes something like an earthquake on a Richter scale of 6.0 or above to achieve such a result.

Let me add a final observation about the confiscation of our family enterprise. The same Rudolf Fuchs who had first been a militant Socialist and then an equally militant Nazi (or who at least gave a splendid imitation of one) sought to ingratiate himself with Oscar when Oscar visited Vienna in 1949 to look after our family properties. He offered Oscar his services for all kinds of deals. But Oscar steadfastly refused. Fuchs also asked Oscar for my address so he could send me a picture of my father. Oscar refused since he did not want Fuchs to try to work his schemes on me. Oscar probably thought me still sufficiently unworldly and feared that I might succumb to Fuchs' blandishments.

What happened to our family enterprise happened to virtually all Jewish business establishments. My sister Valli's husband, Fritz, lost a thriving housewares retail business. Liesl, my sister-in-law, lost her position as a buyer for a luxury store. After World War II, Liesl attempted to claim a pension to which she was entitled on the basis of years of service before 1938, but Austrian government authorities rejected her claims!

Just about all the members of our various extended family circles suffered comparable fates. In the case of more sizable enterprises, such as the Unger retail menswear empire, more could be salvaged than from a corner grocery. Large enterprises with international connections could transfer wealth abroad—at least for the first few months after the *Anschluss.*

Thus, Jewish enterprises were ruthlessly Aryanized in very short order, and the former owners were left without any means of earning a livelihood. I believe that we were able to salvage more than many other Jewish families, but our ultimate fates—emigration or extermination—differed not at all from that of the vast majority of Vienna's Jewish community, which numbered around 200,000 in 1938.

Where to escape? Where to go?

Having been deprived of our livelihood, having been expelled from the universities, having been prohibited from attending concerts, movies, or any form of public entertainment or event, we were left with only one thing on which to focus our attention: emigration. In Germany, it might have been possible to entertain the thought of continuing life under the Nazi regime in the earlier years after 1933, but I know of no one in Vienna clinging to such a possibility. One's entire energy was devoted to finding the answer to one dominant question: *Where to go?*

Since the late nineteenth century, the United States had been the Promised Land for European Jews whenever they were threatened by anti-Semitic violence—be it the pogroms of czarist Russia or the more systematic persecution in the Third Reich after 1933. Migration was made easier for later generations by the help of family and friends who had gone before. Other countries hardly figured in emigration plans, partly because they offered no systematic immigration possibilities and partly because they were thought to be so foreign in culture, climate, and so forth that survival in such a hostile environment seemed hardly possible.

As it happened, in neither my mother's nor my father's family had there been any sizeable migration to the United States. So then, for us the usual procedure of asking a relative for help simply did not exist.

Almost all the members of both my parental families perished in the Holocaust. Among the exceptions were two cousins from my father's family who made it to the United States, two cousins who reached South America, and one cousin from my mother's family who also made it to the United States. By what must be accounted a miracle, one family among those who were unable to emigrate survived at the end of the war: my cousin Margit (from my mother's family), her husband, and two teenage sons were found alive in different extermination camps at the end of the war. They returned to Bratislava, where they reestablished the lumber business they had operated before the German takeover. However, in 1948 the Communist coup deprived them of their possessions again, and they finally despaired of life in Central Europe and immigrated to Israel.

It is no coincidence that most of those who safely reached the New World came from Vienna, while only two cousins survived from among the large families on both my father's and my mother's side in Czechoslovakia. The Slovak puppet regime of Monsignor Tiso, a prelate of the Roman Catholic Church, was one of the most ruthless persecutors of Jews, rounding them up mercilessly and handing them over to the Germans for "transportation to the East." Also, it is likely that Jews living in the small villages of Central and Eastern Europe (as was the case with most of my relatives) simply had less access to the information necessary to emigrate because they were less in touch with the outside world than were the Jews of Vienna.

It might be helpful for understanding the complexity of Jewish life under multiple threats if I recount an episode involving Arthur Fürst, the husband of my cousin Margit (the one nonemigrant survivor). Some months after the *Anschluss*, during the summer of 1938, Arthur visited Vienna to find out what life was like for us in the Third Reich. Traveling with a Czechoslovak passport, such a visit presented no dangers to him at that time (the abandonment of Czechoslovakia which began with Munich and Peace in Our Time was still some months ahead).

I remember vividly how we pleaded with Arthur to liquidate all his assets at home in Bratislava, obtain hard currency, and emigrate as quickly as possible. At that time, we all thought that France or England were absolutely safe places, even if he did not want to venture as far as the United States. Since his assets were still under his control, such a move would assure his family's safety.

Arthur simply did not understand our concern for their safety in Czechoslovakia. After all, he pointed out, his country was protected through nonaggression pacts with France and Britain, who would surely come to his country's defense. Besides, Czechoslovakia had the region's best armaments industry and could field a first-rate army.

There was no way we could make our fears comprehensible to him. All we could do was lament his shortsightedness, without necessarily admitting that we might have been equally blind to possible dangers if someone had confronted us with the shape of things to come one year before the *Anschluss*.

Since we had no links to the United States, Oscar and Valli and their families looked elsewhere for opportunities. They were successful, at least in part, and they illustrate the sort of efforts made by emigrants to establish bases for their future in other countries.

In Oscar's case, it was his wife, Liesl, who very imaginatively used her international connections in the luxury retail trade to lay a solid foundation for business in Australia. Oscar eventually developed an export-import business there as well. They coordinated their move with the family of one of Liesl's sister's, the Lazars, who operated Vienna's premier sporting goods store and thus had international connections as well. To lay this groundwork took over a year.

Oscar and Liesl finally left Vienna in August 1939. They stopped in London to see me, a visit that stands out sharply in my memory, for it was the day that Germany and Russia announced the signing of the Hitler-Stalin pact, which triggered the dismemberment of Poland and with it, the beginning of World War II. By the time war was declared, Oscar and Liesl were on the high seas. As it turned out, they safely reached Sydney on schedule, but their household goods were trapped by the war on a dock in Genoa and never reached them.

Oscar & Liesl
At their Home
Sydney, Australia, c. 1951

Both were highly successful in Australia, and they enjoyed a most comfortable life. Their success was aided by the relatively relaxed pace of life and business in Australia, which stood in sharp contrast to the pace of life in the United States—especially on the East Coast and in New York, where so many Austrian and German refugees settled.

The *Anschluss* also put an end to the successful housewares business developed by my brother-in-law, Fritz, with the help of Valli, who proved to be a first-rate businessperson like most of the Diamants (present company excepted). Fritz had scoured Europe for items not usually obtainable in Vienna, so he had extensive business connections, as Liesl did. Some of these connections enabled Fritz to obtain French visas.

They planned to establish in Paris a business much like the one they had built up in Vienna. They were planning an orderly departure late in 1938. But instead, they took flight on the day and night of *Kristallnacht* (November 9, 1938). Having valid visas, they were able to catch the next train west and to make it safely to Paris.

In Paris, they were indeed successful in recreating a thriving commercial enterprise within a short time. However, with the blitzkrieg in May 1940, they once again were confronted with a total loss of what they had built up in such a short time with their hard work and imagination. They fled south from Paris into unoccupied France. There they made efforts to immigrate to Colombia, where some members of Fritz's family had established themselves.

Anyone familiar with the fate of refugee Jews in France will know the eventual fate of Fritz's family. They were rounded up by the Vichy authorities and handed over to the Germans for "transportation to the East," where they perished along with the vast majority of European Jews. My nephew, Erwin, was about fifteen years old at that time.

Obviously, Mama and I had none of the resources that Oscar and Valli could call on. For us the United States was the obvious and the only target of emigration. However, we did not have the proverbial uncle to summon for help.

I have learned since that in the months after the *Anschluss*, many Jews engaged in retraining programs. In particular, intellectuals, lawyers, and businesspeople, who feared that they would be unable to pursue their original profession in their new home, sought to equip themselves with marketable skills. I was not aware of these activities. I assumed that eventually I would find employment in textile production, for which I had respectable credentials.

I was also confident that I was ahead of most potential emigrants with regard to language skills: I had passed a stringent test of spoken French in secondary school, and I had at least four years of English conversation lessons. Yet with all that confidence in what I might be able to do once I got there, the question of getting there had yet to be answered.

We begin the immigration process

The first step in the American immigration process was to register at the nearest consulate as a quota immigrant and to receive a quota number that would indicate one's place in the annual quota of immigrants from one's particular country of origin. Mama and I did this in July 1938 after what might seem a considerable delay from the events of March. What took us so long? I cannot either recall or explain, but I imagine the delay was a sign of our general puzzlement over how we ought to go about it all.

In registering, we came face-to-face with the intricacies (some would say the inanities) of the then-current American immigration laws. Those laws had been enacted in the early 1920s in the wake of the country's first "Red Scare" and in the belief that it was time to halt the immigrant flood from Europe, which had peaked just before World War I. The laws specified quotas of "national origin," that is to say, the number of immigrants per year that would be permitted to enter the United States from any given "nation."

It has been charged again and again (and denied by defenders of the law) that the size of the annual national quotas reflected ethnic, perhaps racist, prejudices—that the size of quotas indicated the degree of desirability of immigrants from various nations. Large quotas were assigned to Anglo-Germanic countries, much smaller quotas for Latin and Slavic countries, and total bars to immigration from others.

To complicate matters, a potential immigrant was assigned to a given national quota based on her or his birthplace and the national territory in which that birthplace was located. That determination was not based on conditions at the time of the potential immigrant's birth, but on the status of the territory as defined in the various peace treaties marking the end of World War I.

For our family this meant that although Mama and I both were born in the Austro-Hungarian Empire, she in 1885 and I in 1917, the post-1918 peace treaties put her birthplace in Czechoslovakia and mine in Austria (merged with Germany and the German quota in 1938). As a result of my having been placed on the German quota list and she on the Czechoslovak quota list, there was no hope that we could emigrate together. My number would come up much sooner than hers would.

So we decided (or were forced to decide) that I should emigrate as soon as the German quota would permit, and that Mama would then be able to follow as a dependent without too much difficulty. I never bothered to find out exactly how that would work. We simply concentrated on my getting out as soon as possible. Subsequent events proved us correct, but they also demonstrated that Mama, as always, focused her attention and her efforts on the *Fredikind* and that I took the arrangement for granted. It took quite a while for me to understand fully the magnitude of her love.

Becoming registered as quota immigrants was relatively easy. The truly monstrous problem for us was the total lack of family or other connections in the United States who could execute the necessary affidavit of support, which assured the US government that the person executing the affidavit had the necessary financial resources to keep the potential immigrant from becoming a public charge. Where could we find such a benefactor?

During the spring of 1938, someone suggested to me that as a skilled technician, I should have no trouble getting jobs in textile mills, and that I should consult trade directories available at the various consulates for possible employers, offer my services to them, and ask them for the necessary affidavits. Neither I nor the Good Samaritan who made this suggestion realized that under immigration law, jobs could not be offered to quota immigrants prior to their arrival in the United States.

It was probably just as well that ignorance was bliss in this case. I did as was recommended to me and copied names and addresses of about a dozen textile mills from the directories available at the consulate. I must have consulted a regional directory, for all the addresses were on the East Coast. Or perhaps like most immigrants, I thought that the country ended at the Hudson River or the Allegheny Mountains, with only wild Indians occupying the distant reaches of the West.

I composed and typed a rather nonidiomatic but reasonably correctly spelled letter, describing my training and my experience and offering to work at any job that might be available. I asked the recipients of my letters for help by executing an affidavit of support, and I assured them that I would never take advantage of the obligation represented by the affidavit. As might be expected, most of the letters went unanswered. A very few replied that they could not undertake the responsibility of executing an affidavit but encouraged me to contact them for employment once I reached the United States.

Among the mills I had picked out as promising targets was a natural for my SOS letter: Diamond Textile Mills, Inc., in Taunton, Massachusetts. I learned subsequently that I had misspelled Taunton as "Tamiton" when copying addresses at the consulate. This is not surprising given the idiosyncrasies of my handwriting: my letters *m*, *n*, and *u* generally come out as a series of pothooks, and so what I copied as *aun* in Taunton, I subsequently transcribed as *ami*. But just the same, my letter reached its desired destination. Perhaps in those days the Post Office took greater care with poorly addressed letters than simply consigning them to the circular file.

It turned out that the Diamond family had escaped from Russia at the time of the pogroms in the early 1900s. Eventually they succeeded as silk weavers in New Jersey, but after World War I when the bottom fell out of silk weaving due to the creation of synthetic fibers, they switched to rayon weaving. Eventually they sought to escape the unionization drive among weavers in New Jersey and moved to New England, where they had mills operating in New Bedford and Fall River, as well as the one in Taunton. There were several brothers, and each of them managed one of the mills.

It was Abe Diamond, the head of the Taunton mill, who received my letter. He responded promptly and positively about a future job, but indicated that because of family obligations, he could not execute an affidavit. He promised to find someone who could do so. In due course, he persuaded a young lawyer in Taunton, Frank P. Cohen, to serve as a guarantor for me. With the affidavit assured, a path to the United States had been cleared for me and ultimately for Mama, who could enter the country as a family member of a resident alien without any need of further affidavits.

The American government did little, if anything, to open the door to those fleeing the Third Reich beyond what was provided for in existing legislation. However, individual members of the country's Jewish community obviously felt a strong obligation to help those reaching out to them for assistance.

The next months were far from tranquil or easy. Along with everyone else, I feverishly sought for avenues of escape. There were many cases of outright fraud, in which large sums of money were extracted from Jews for nonexistent emigration schemes. At one time word got around that it was possible to immigrate to the Dominican Republic with visas issued by the Dominican Consulate in Vienna. Hardly any of us knew much about the Dominican Republic, but in the absence of any hope for immediate emigration, the Dominican Republic, or Haiti, or Madagascar (where Nazi authorities at one time hoped to send all the Jews) was clearly preferable to our present situation.

Such an option would enable us to wait for the eventual American visa *outside* the Third Reich. We could not know that our conditions then, in the summer and fall of 1938, were relatively benign compared to the ever-tightening net of restrictions that the Third Reich drew around us after the events of *Kristallnacht* (November 9, 1938), even before it proceeded to the "Final Solution" in 1941.

Kristallnacht: the mounting dangers

I have depicted my life in the Third Reich as difficult but not impossible or personally threatening. This might well be the result of an unconscious effort to screen from my memory (and thus, also from this account) the truly cruel and frightening aspects of that life. I am confident, however, that I have not lost very much, if anything, in an Orwellian "memory hole." This confidence rests in an understanding of my own makeup. My repeated reflection on my emigration years leads me to affirm that I accepted the events in my life during those years with relative equanimity.

The one time this placidity was totally disrupted was during the events of November 9 and 10, 1938: *Kristallnacht*. During these twenty-four hours, I felt total fear for my life. But the outcome for me was unlike that for most Jewish males throughout Germany. I should note at this point that histories of *Kristallnacht* in Vienna report that *all* Jewish males between the ages of eighteen and sixty-five were rounded up and transported to concentration camps. I was not. I do not know whether I was the only exception. Probably not.

On that day Mama and I were listening to the radio with mounting fear about the events that were unfolding throughout Germany. There were just the two of us in our apartment above the store that was no longer ours. We received phone calls warning us that it would not be safe to stay in the apartment.

For reasons I cannot recall, Mama and I decided that we should spend the rest of the day with Aunt Hedwig, the widow of my father's brother Adolf, and her daughters Terri and Helli. Their apartment was located in the ninth district, some distance away from ours in the sixteenth, but we decided to walk there, thinking it might not be safe to take the streetcar.

It was late in the afternoon when the doorbell rang. We all stiffened in total fright. It would be the SA or SS to arrest us all. All five of us went to answer the door. We were confronted not with young SA or SS troops, but with a middle-aged Viennese police inspector who informed us that he had orders to lock up the apartment and arrest any males present.

At this moment, I was not looking at Mama, but she must have turned chalk white when she heard the arrest order. It must have been such a stark expression of terror that the police inspector asked quite kindly whether she was unwell.

Mama pleaded for the life of her only child. Apparently she appealed successfully to the basic feelings of a middle-aged police inspector (likely with a wife and children at home) who had been doing police work long before the advent of the Third Reich.

He told Mama and me that we could leave, but he insisted on turning my aunt and cousins out of their apartment. (They managed to regain possession of their apartment later, and my two cousins successfully immigrated to South America. I do not know whether Aunt Hedwig was able to go with them.) Mama and I, spent by this experience, returned to our apartment. Thus, I survived the terrors of *Kristallnacht*.

In the months following *Kristallnacht*, we felt the tightening grip of the Third Reich. The Reich imposed a whole series of punitive measures on its Jewish population, supposedly in retaliation for the attack by a young Polish emigrant on an official of the German embassy in Paris. Jews were ordered to surrender all precious metals in their possession, with the exception of wedding rings and gold teeth, and they were limited to DM10 in the amount of currency they could carry with them on leaving the country. The Third Reich also imposed a collective fine on the Jewish communities as a *Sühnegeld* for the criminal attack on an official of the German government.

I believe that it was at this juncture that passports of Jews were marked with a big red *J* on the first page. Later all Jews had to take Israel or Sarah as part of their first names and were so listed in passports.

Although these were clearly extraordinary measures, they constituted but another step in the tightening of the noose before the Final Solution. In a most cold-blooded manner, the policies of the Third Reich were meant to impoverish and denigrate Jews in successive steps that ended with their physical elimination in the gas ovens of Auschwitz and Bergen-Belsen.

I realize that by conceptualizing Third Reich policies in this manner, I seem to be taking sides in a continuing controversy over the place of the "Jewish question" in the Third Reich. I am strongly ideologically inclined, that is to say, I give great weight to the ideas people carry around with them. Thus, I have no problem with the proposition that the Jewish question was the lynch pin of Hitler's ideas from early on, and that it became a central element of government and party policy after 1933.

From that perspective, the Final Solution becomes the ultimate step in an "intentionalist" policy process, and not simply a wartime expedient arrived at from more or less circumstantial premises, that is, once it was clear that the Third Reich could not export its Jews, the Final Solution followed as the most appropriate policy given these particular circumstances.

Hope on the horizon

One consequence of *Kristallnacht* was a radical change in situation for me and for all other Jewish males aged eighteen to sixty-five. From then on, the majority of Jewish males were in greater danger in a way they had not been before. Eventually, of course, the Final Solution exempted no one, regardless of sex and age. But with *Kristallnacht*, the Jewish community was confronted with the task of finding ways for a speedy emigration of a group of individuals in imminent danger.

Fortunately, as a result of negotiations among world Jewish organizations, a scheme was devised within which males who could produce evidence of eventual emigration elsewhere could be admitted to Britain under a transit visa to wait there until they could go on to their destination. I believe this was a significant achievement for the Jewish community in Britain, which had to contend with the Peace in Our Time Chamberlain government and England's nearly watertight immigration laws.

These immigration laws, it would seem, had a soft spot for English middle- and upper-class housewives who complained about an insufficient supply of suitable native domestic help. It became possible for foreign females to obtain work permits in England for domestic positions. (I never heard of any comparable efforts to recruit males.)

This became known in Vienna, and soon English households had well-educated Viennese housemaids, cooks, and nannies, whose English might be less than perfect but who were sure not to walk out at the first scolding from their mistresses. After all, their stay in England was tied to a specific employer, and they faced expulsion and return to their country of origin if their employment was terminated.

All this may sound somewhat cynical and as if to impugn the good intentions of British employers. That would really be unjust, for under this program quite a number of women (mostly widows) and their children were able to leave Germany, assured of a roof over their heads on arrival.

Ironically, most of these newly minted domestics from Vienna probably had enjoyed the services of their own household help, so their first attempts at dusting, sweeping, and silver-polishing might well not have won the approval of their new employers. Yet there is evidence that ultimately the human and humane benefits of these arrangements were considerable.

The program for males, who were in more imminent danger, took a more organized form. Jewish organizations obtained the use of Kitchener Camp near Sandwich in Kent, an abandoned British army camp last used in World War I. It had been a transshipment point for British troops heading for the continent, so rail lines led into the camp and from there to embarkation points on the beaches. At full capacity, the camp was able to house 4,000 male refugees.

Jewish organizations renovated the camp, furnished it for its new inhabitants, and provided an English staff and financing for the continued care and feeding of the camp inhabitants. The British government issued visas to individuals who had been carefully screened by the Kultusgemeinde in Vienna as to having presented evidence that they would eventually leave for a destination in another country.

The British visa in my passport clearly specified "Transit" and ordered the holder to proceed directly to Kitchener Camp on arrival and to remain there until departing from the United Kingdom. This was a strictly limited generosity.

Having received the affidavit of support from my sponsor, Frank Cohen, and having registered as a quota immigrant with the US Consulate in Vienna, I squarely met the requirements of the Kitchener Camp program. The application process was tedious. It required standing in line after line. But the result was my acceptance into the program. I was left to wait for notification of my departure date on one of the weekly trains. Eventually I was scheduled to leave for Kitchener Camp in late April 1939.

The *Anschluss* had deprived all Jews, sooner or later, of all sources of current income. Wealthier families had more of a cushion than poorer ones, and they could also outfit themselves more adequately for the first stage of life in another country. At the time I left, one was still permitted to take clothing, books, and other personal items, without any limit being imposed by the German authorities.

However, as I was going through the Kitchener Camp application process, Mama and I found our resources shrinking steadily. We decided to give up the apartment above our former store and move in with Aunt Gisa. What I remember most vividly about the breakup of our household was the size and condition of what had been Mama's trousseau. There were stacks of linen—sheets, towels, pillowcases, and so on—that had never been used! Mama had indeed conserved her treasures carefully.

Thus, I spent the last few months in Vienna not in the familiar surroundings of my youth, but in a strange place made comfortable only by Mama's presence and by the close ties I had with Aunt Gisa. Of the two sisters, Gisa was in some ways the livelier one. Her late husband had been a pious, stolid man who shared few of Gisa's interests and seemed not to appreciate her human qualities. Like Mama, Gisa had devoted all her energies to her husband's business. Neither she nor Mama really fit the stereotype of a bourgeois *Hausfrau*.

Preparations for Kitchener Camp

All Third Reich policies regarding the Jews were persecutory and cruel. The Reich's loudly proclaimed desire to have Jews emigrate as quickly as possible was combined with a set of administrative procedures calculated to make the emigration process as difficult and humiliating as possible.

By the time I made my final preparations for Kitchener Camp, the procedures for gaining permission(!) to emigrate had been centralized in one place and orchestrated, as I learned much later, by an obscure SS officer named Kurt Eichmann. One might say he earned his spurs for promotion to more important tasks with his achievements in Vienna.

The SS, which had control over the emigration process, chose to locate the emigration center in one of Vienna's grand city palaces. I no longer remember all the details of this charade of degradation. One had to line up early in the morning and make innumerable stops at tables where papers were scrutinized and stamped, all this accompanied by a steady stream of invective, though without physical abuse as far as I could observe. It became obvious very quickly that the purpose of Eichmann's design was not administrative efficiency but a final humiliation before emigration.

With that behind me, I was faced with the considerable task of deciding how to fill the ship's trunk I would take with me. (That trunk has survived not only the transatlantic voyage but also countless moves within the United States since my arrival in 1940. It still serves as a convenient storage place.) Obviously, what I would take should be useful for my life in a strange country where I would probably earn very small wages.

"Useful" for me were several volumes of Wagner, Mozart, and Bach scores, a copy of Goethe's *Faust*, two volumes of the Viennese comedies of Johann Nestroy and Ferdinand Raymund, and a German translation of Rostand's *Cyrano de Bergerac*—not to mention a volume of Beethoven piano sonatas, piano transcriptions of his symphonies, a volume of Mozart piano sonatas, assorted J. S. Bach suites, and Bach's Italian concerto.

"Useful" for Mama (as Ann recollects more fully than I can) included sheets, pillowcases, towels, napkins, and a sewing kit with big spools of cotton thread (which have been used for nearly fifty years now to sew up Thanksgiving and Christmas turkeys, with enough thread left for another half century). Most importantly, I had a wardrobe of suits, shirts, shoes, and so forth that was ample enough to last my first two years in the New World, until Uncle Sam provided standard issue OD (olive drab) clothing and equipment.

Freddy
Vienna, Austria, 1938

Some of my Viennese wardrobe was still usable when I started my university studies at Indiana University in 1945. One overcoat, which lasted into the 1950s, probably expired from the heat in Florida where I was then teaching. A bespoke black double-breasted suit made for me in 1935 by the Unger establishment's custom tailors (no off-the-rack suit for me) survives to this day for an occasional evening at the opera at Indiana University, provided the thermometer falls below freezing.

Included in this wardrobe was a green Irish tweed sports suit consisting of a jacket, knickerbockers, and a matching visor cap. A formidable outfit, but what would I do with it while working in a New England textile mill? I might possibly have gotten away with it at Yale, but in my first years in the New World, New Haven was only a train stop en route from Providence to New York. Mama also insisted that I should wear a hat, so after much remonstrating, I bought one and wore it on the train. That I left it "accidentally" on the train as we got off to board a cross-channel steamer, I can hardly admit to myself.

I saw my departure from Vienna not only as an escape from an ever more threatening environment, but also as an adventure. I really had no conception of what life would be like in Kitchener Camp or eventually in the United States, but I looked forward to it all with excitement and pleasure. Mama must have felt tremendous relief in the knowledge that I would be safe, even if she would have to wait for some time before she could join me. We saw the separation as a temporary one and looked forward with confidence to our eventual reunion.

Such a level of confidence suggests that neither of us then fully grasped the total depravity of the regime we confronted. Even though I have always considered "race" to be the central driving force of the Hitler regime, I did not really understand that the regime would not be satisfied with expelling the members of the inferior race but would ultimately proceed to total extermination. Eventually I faced that reality, but I cannot pinpoint now when this happened.

Departure for England

The weekly transport for Kitchener Camp to which I was assigned left Vienna in late April 1939. I do not recall whether it was an entire train or simply additional coaches hooked onto regularly scheduled trains. The accommodations were third-class coaches with every seat filled, but I doubt that anyone minded. I do not even recall how we were fed, even though the trip from Vienna to the Channel coast takes nearly a full day.

We crossed the German-Belgian border near Aachen during the night. Tension clearly grew as we approached the German border, fed by unspecified fears that something might happen in the last minute to prevent our exodus.

Yet I cannot recall that the realization of having escaped from the Third Reich produced any great "free at last!" outbursts. We had been beaten down in various ways during the preceding year since the *Anschluss*, and we were too tired from sitting up in third-class coaches to be capable of any exuberance. Even at that, how much more advantaged we were in 1939 traveling in relative comfort, taking many of our belongings with us, than those who in subsequent years were "transported to the East" and to death in the gas ovens.

From the beginning, the Third Reich had taken command of all communications media in Vienna and promulgated strict penalties for those trying to obtain information from foreign sources such as radio broadcasts. I remember a very few occasions of listening with some others to Radio Strasbourg, so that we might get a sense of what went on in the outside world and get another perspective on events inside Germany.

The foreign news was free from the pervasive official bias of the German media. Yet it left us wondering whether the outside world had a realistic sense of what was happening in Germany. We wondered even more why the rest of the world did not attempt to combat all the evils of the Third Reich. We placed most of our hope on the American president. "Why doesn't Franklin Roosevelt help us?" we asked again and again.

Except for these rare occasions of listening to foreign broadcasts, we had to take our news from the government-controlled media. As a result, the longer we were exposed to only the official version of events, the more we began to feel the impact of the central message of anti-Semitic racism—at least, I certainly felt it.

At first I listened to speeches by Hitler and other major Nazi leaders because I thought it necessary to understand their message and the possible impact of that message. Reflecting on all this much later, I realize that it is impossible or at least very difficult for a captive to withstand the denigration of her or his jailer. Perhaps we were indeed some form of "lower life" that had no right to exist.

So then, it might have been that our lack of enthusiasm and relief on crossing into Belgium was part of this experience. It would take a while to be able to breathe freely again and to accept our freedom joyfully and in more expressive ways. It would take a while to regain our self-confidence and an assurance of our true worth.

Kitchener Camp, England (1939-1940)

Kitchener Camp was a collection of one-story military barracks, plus the necessary storehouses, kitchen/mess hall, bathhouse, and administrative buildings. Each barracks was a single squad room (in US Army terms) with double-decker bunks, two small pot-bellied stoves, and washroom/latrines at each end of the building.

Each man kept a few belongings in a suitcase under the bed. The rest were kept in common storerooms to which we had access at stated times. There was a bathhouse where we could take weekly showers, all the men from one hut at the same time. Hot showers were strictly limited to a very few minutes; more time was allowed for cold showering.

Freddy
Kitchener Camp
England, 1939

There were a small English camp staff and English cooks, but the refugees were expected to do all other work around the camp. Given the socioeconomic composition of this refugee group, work requiring skilled craftsmen had to be done by outsiders. Our group of lawyers, doctors, and businessmen was not much help when skilled plumbers and electricians were needed, as they often were for that somewhat ancient barracks.

I cannot remember what recreational facilities if any were provided for us, or if there was a store or canteen, as the British would call it, that sold items of everyday use. Certainly we must have had access to newspapers, for I cannot imagine managing for ten months without newspapers. By the terms of our visas we were restricted to the camp, and we could travel or visit elsewhere in Britain only if we obtained permission from the camp administrator, specifying the times and places of our visits. We were free to leave during daylight hours, and many did so, but I do not know whether gates were locked at specified times. In any case, I do not think that bed checks were made at any time during my stay there.

I remember three specific occasions when I was absent from the camp. The last was in December 1939 when I traveled to London to receive my United States immigration visa.

The first occasion was a trip to London to see Oscar and Liesl, who were en route to Australia. I suppose that makes me one of a small number of my own and later generations who can remember London before the Blitz. I thought it a beautiful, glorious city. The fact that its grandeur and wealth were the result of imperial conquest did not prevent my being overwhelmed by Hyde Park, Regent's Park, Piccadilly, Marble Arch, and so forth. That there was unbroken sunshine during my stay was simply the frosting on the cake. This visit also provided my first experience with an English bed and breakfast, still more to admire. Not even the news of the Hitler-Stalin Pact and what it might well bring in its wake diminished my enjoyment of this visit.

The second occasion I was absent from camp was really a series of occasions that provided me with an introduction to that great English tradition of tea. It was not high tea in its full panoply, but it was certainly most enjoyable. Apparently, residents of the area around the camp wanted to extend a welcome to the refugees. I do not know how contact was made for me, but I received an invitation to tea from two elderly women (now that I am seventy-five I probably would not call them that) who lived in a cottage in Deal, about ten miles from the camp.

I am rather certain that I was suggested to them because I spoke English fairly well. At least my command of spoken English was far stronger than that of most of my campmates (thanks to Mama's insistence on my learning English and taking extensive conversation lessons).

The problem of transportation was solved by a camp bicycle. There were several bikes that we could borrow for trips to Sandwich or other nearby places. So one Sunday afternoon, I set out on a camp bike for my first tea. As it turned out, it was the first of several invitations that provided a wonderful break from the camp routine and allowed me a look at the English people in their native habitat. Not very far from the camp were Margate and Ramsgate, which are very popular seaside places. I wish I had visited them. My images of Ramsgate, Margate, and Blackpool are today indelibly colored by Orwell's *Wigan Pier*.

By referring to my excursions to Deal as a break from camp routine, I do not want to imply a negative picture of our life at Kitchener Camp. After all, we had been safely brought out of the clutches of the Third Reich while members of our families and the majority of Jews in Germany were still subject to its fury. I have several snapshots taken while I was at Kitchener Camp. They show a smiling Freddy in sport shorts and tee shirt—and that was not just a pose for the camera.

Freddy
Kitchener Camp, England, 1939

Kitchener's populace

When I arrived on one of the earlier transports, the camp population was still small, but it grew week by week until it reached about 4,000 at the outbreak of World War II, after which all further transports stopped, England and Germany being at war. The average age of inhabitants in the all-male camp was forty. I believe that I was among the younger camp residents. We had come from all parts of Germany, Austria, and the Sudetenland. Later transports brought people from the rest of Czechoslovakia, which the Germans overran in March 1939. The group reflected the social composition of the Jewish communities of Central Europe: well-educated and professional.

I remember no cleavage lines among the inhabitants except one. From time to time, former Austrians (mostly from Vienna) would become involved in arguments with former Germans (mostly from Berlin) about the essential nature of the Third Reich and German people. However, I do not remember any such exchanges after the war broke out in September.

As I mentioned earlier, the Kitchener Camp program was established on an understanding between the British government and the Jewish community that only those with bona fide reemigration possibilities would be admitted to the program. I discovered soon after I arrived that the program was also used, though only to a modest degree, to rescue prisoners from concentration camps.

At that time, an inmate could gain release from a camp if his family could submit proof of immediate departure from Germany and admission to another country. As a result, a number of prisoners were released from concentration camps after showing that the Kitchener Camp program had accepted them. Often the proof that a prisoner would ultimately be admitted to a third country was flimsy or even nonexistent. Whether the SS knew of this sort of subterfuge I never learned. For a while at least, the Kitchener Camp route provided an escape from concentration camps.

It was at Kitchener Camp that I met for the first time men who had spent varying amounts of time at camps like Dachau. Before releasing them, the SS had extracted their promises not to disclose to anyone what camp life was like, accompanied by dire threats of what would happen to those who broke that promise. However, the former inmates seemed not to consider themselves bound once they were beyond the reach of the SS. It was as if they felt compelled to tell the rest of us what had happened to them in the concentration camp system. I am sure that the absolute horror of that experience created a need for catharsis to purge themselves of the memories, in part by sharing them with the rest of us.

Consequently, for me the concentration camp system became an indelible reality at a time when Hitler was still assuring the world—much of which believed him—that after the takeover of Czechoslovakia, he had "no further territorial demands." Because I knew that the *Judenfrage* (that is to say, racial anti-Semitism) was the central core of Hitler's program, I regarded the Final Solution and the extermination camp system as the inevitable culmination of the Nazi program.

Each weekly transport brought more former concentration camp inmates whose needs to share their miserable fate with the world were as great as those who had preceded them in earlier transports. They talked and we listened and became further convinced, if that was possible, of the profound evil that confronted the world.

Camp routine

As I mentioned, most camp maintenance tasks fell to the inmates. On the whole, these tasks were not arduous and did not require long hours of work, especially as the camp population increased week by week. Among the least desirable jobs was what the US military called KP, dishwashing and related tasks. The increasing camp population had to be fed three times a day—at the peak that meant 12,000 meals a day!

Because KP was among the least desirable jobs, the administration sweetened the pot by making each meal a separate shift, so that those in the breakfast shift had most of the day free from then on, while the evening meal shift did not have to report until late in the afternoon. The noon meal shift was the least convenient; it tended to mess up one's day. If I remember correctly, shifts changed weekly.

Before going further, I should point out that I had grown up in a household with a live-in maid, and in a society in which males had no responsibility for any housework. I had never washed a pot or dish, washed out a pair of socks, or even shined my shoes. Yet I willingly joined the dishwashing crew and stuck with it for several months. It was a hot assignment, even during the usually cool English spring and especially during the summer months. I

Freddy (far right)
On kitchen duty at Kitchener Camp, 1939

have a snapshot of the dishwashing crew, bare except for shorts and big oilcloth aprons.

There was great camaraderie among us. We always tackled our jobs with much joking and laughter. The work was hard and messy, but it was over quickly, and we then had the rest of the day free.

Another fringe benefit for the dishwashing crew was easy access to food, especially to those items for which one had special preferences. I had developed a taste for tinned fish, and I used my tours of dishwashing duty to appropriate as many cans (usually served as part of a cold supper) as I could without appearing too greedy. My family, especially Ann, has never shared this peculiar taste (though Alice acquired the same strange preference while in boarding school in France, probably because all the alternatives offered were worse!).

The dining hall was arranged like the army mess hall it had been during World War I. It was star-shaped, with the kitchen in the center. At the head of each wing, there were steam tables with cast-aluminum containers from which food was served. These containers constitute the horror stories of my dishwashing days, especially during the breakfast shift.

The British camp administration had made few if any concessions to the Central European palate, with the result that much of the food was wasted—as it was even when Tommies populated the mess hall. Because the containers were in the steam tables for some time, the food became baked on, and cleaning the pans became an arduous task.

Nothing was as resistant to our valiant cleaning efforts as porridge pans at breakfast. At first we were absolutely baffled by the gray-white stuff served as breakfast. After a while we found out what it was but did not like it any better. As a result, most porridge pans came back to the kitchen three-fourths full, with the cold porridge adhered to the pans like glue. It was enough to make one avoid the breakfast shift, even though it meant surrendering an uninterrupted day thereafter.

As it turned out, I did not have to spend all my time at Kitchener Camp wrestling with sticky porridge pans. I do not remember how the change came about, but some time in late summer or early fall, I was transferred to the camp administration office as a clerk. I can only guess that my above average (for the camp) command of written and spoken English was a factor in the transfer. I did a variety of jobs, only the last of which I remember: preparing leave permits for the signature of the camp director, a procedure that came to be a government requirement after the war started. I still have the permit that I issued to myself to leave the camp permanently for immigration to the United States.

Having to talk with English camp administrators on a daily basis probably did much to improve my spoken English. In retrospect, it seems that Kitchener Camp was a most appropriate preparation for a life in which I had to look after myself, and still later a life of sharing tasks and chores in a married household. After the Kitchener Camp porridge pans, helping Ann, before the days of dishwashers, to dispose of the remains of a dinner for ten after the last guests had left well after midnight was no more than a routine exercise. Perhaps the traditional wisdom about never knowing what skills will come in handy also applies to porridge pan scouring.

World War II begins

Kitchener Camp was a sizeable enterprise by late summer in 1939, when the outbreak of World War II interrupted many of our routines. To begin with, the British government suddenly considered us not simply refugees but "enemy aliens." After all, we had entered the country carrying German passports marked with the letter *J*. For a while we were restricted to the camp without any exceptions.

After some time, the British government faced the situation realistically. We were after all as much enemies of the Third Reich as the British people. In light of the appeasement policies of the Chamberlain government, we might have been excused for pointing out that *we* had been enemies of the Third Reich long before HM Government came to realize that Hitler simply could not be appeased, that there was really no end to his territorial demands.

The British government proceeded to set up a number of tribunals, each consisting of a group of senior lawyers who acted as hearing officers. They screened the camp population one by one and were authorized to change our status from "enemy alien" to "friendly alien" if they were assured of our credentials as bona fide refugees from the Third Reich and thus supporters of the British in the war against Germany. I know of no case in which this reclassification was not authorized. With that done, we could move freely within a five-mile radius of the camp, but we had to obtain permission to travel further or stay overnight elsewhere.

Another major war-related development affecting Kitchener Camp was the British government's decision to accept émigrés as volunteers in the British armed forces. However, the government apparently continued to have reservations about us, because these volunteers were not integrated into regular units of the armed forces. Instead they were placed in separate units called the Auxiliary Pioneer Corps (RAPC), a combination of the American engineering and quartermaster branches. They were not to be armed and would be limited to Kitchener Camp.

A small Regular Army detachment came to Kitchener Camp to screen applicants for this corps. Along with many others, I stepped forward. When they examined my records and found that I would soon immigrate to the United States, they rejected my application. The examining officer smiled and said, "You go on to America. You'll be back here before long." The RAPC continued to function throughout the war, and eventually many if not most of its members found their way into regular units of the armed forces.

Kitchener Camp came to an end amid the hysteria that gripped England with Hitler's May 1940 assault on Western Europe. The

British disaster at Dunkirk brought down the Chamberlain government and led to Winston Churchill's great coalition wartime government. With the German army on the Channel coast, the German refugees became a "potential fifth column," no matter how fervently they proclaimed their hatred of the Third Reich and their loyalty to the Allied cause.

The British government resorted to measures that found an echo in the United States after Pearl Harbor in the internment of Japanese Americans (in which case the internees were not aliens carrying Japanese passports, but native American citizens for the most part). German refugees were interned on the Isle of Man, and some were shipped forcibly to distant parts of the Empire, such as Canada and Australia.

Yet the British government came to its senses much more quickly than the American government did—and while German troops were entrenched much closer to British soil than Japanese forces were to California! The internees were released and permitted to resume normal lives. They were not kept in internment for the duration, as were America's Nisei.

I cross the Atlantic

A good part of my contentment with life in the camp rested in the knowledge that my immigration to the United States was imminent. During the summer of 1939, I was informed that my place on the quota list had reached the top and I could expect my visa in September. But with the coming of the war and fearful anticipation of German air attacks, a mass evacuation of London began almost immediately after war was declared. The consulate in London became fully occupied with repatriating American citizens and suspended visa operations.

Fortunately, when the reality of what came to be called the phony war set in, evacuees returned to London (somewhat prematurely, as it turned out) and the consulate resumed issuing immigration visas. I was informed that I should appear at the consulate on December 5 to receive my immigration visa. The final stage of my emigration was at hand.

In the meantime, the outbreak of war disrupted another aspect of my emigration plans. Before leaving Vienna, I had used local currency to book a passage on a German liner from an English port to New York, but once war was declared, no German passenger liners crossed the Atlantic—before long they were replaced by German submarines! Cunard Lines, which continued to provide transatlantic passenger service, demanded payment in pound sterling.

This was an unexpected hurdle. I could only throw myself once again upon the good will of Abe Diamond. I explained the situation to him and promised to repay the loan. Again Abe Diamond came to the rescue, thus enabling me to book passage from Liverpool to New York for January 1940.

Travel to Liverpool from Kitchener Camp required an overnight stay in London. There Jewish aid organizations provided me with a space in one of their shelters in London's East End. It was a clean, friendly place in which I had a small cubicle to myself. The next morning I continued by train to Liverpool to start my voyage across the Atlantic.

It has been my fate to cross the Atlantic three times at the *worst* possible time of the year: January 1940, 1944, and 1945, the last two courtesy of the US Army. The January 1940 crossing should have been a joyous event—lots of food, good company, and a comfortable cabin—if only I had not been so susceptible to seasickness. I should have known what was coming, for I could get raging headaches just traveling by train!

Arrival in New York

We entered New York harbor on a clear, mild January day. I watched the harbor pilot come aboard and noted in particular that he was *not* wearing a uniform, an aspect of the United States that I came to appreciate greatly. I had really had my fill of uniforms and militarism! Unfortunately, as a result of World War II and a steady process of change for which I have no better term than Europeanization, there are now many more uniforms all around us. In particular, motorcycle policemen in their black leather jackets and black boots bear a resemblance to some members of the Third Reich, a reminder that I could do without!

My first look at the New York skyline was almost a moment of déjà vu. I had seen so many pictures in prints and movies of the Manhattan silhouette that I experienced little surprise or awe. Rather, it was as if I were arriving in a country I already knew well, not an uncommon feeling among middle-class European immigrants who had devoured American literature, movies, and popular music as I had. Of course, in reality I did not have much of a picture of what actually awaited me in this vast and often strange land.

Our ship docked at one of the mid-town Manhattan piers on January 20, 1940. We went through immigration procedures on-board ship, and then waited for our luggage to be unloaded and taken through customs. The pier had a fenced-off section where persons waiting for immigrants to complete the process could be near them, separated only by a knee-high movable fence. Gretl was waiting for me, and we stood close together, one on either side of the fence.

After an early breakfast onboard ship, I had put an apple from the fruit bowl in my pocket, not knowing how long the customs process would take. I took out the apple and offered Gretl a bite, which she accepted. Almost immediately, a US customs official swooped down on us and demanded to know, in very stern tones, what I had passed on to my friend.

I was absolutely terrified. I saw the doors of the Promised Land closing before my eyes. Gretl and I earnestly explained that bites of apple were the only "goods" that had passed between us. Apparently we convinced him. He even let us keep the apple. Those must indeed have been simple and innocent days. In a comparable scenario today, we would both have been strip-searched at least, if we did not have to submit to having our stomachs pumped.

After that adventure, the rest of my stay in New York (only a long weekend) left much less of an impression on me. My arrival was monitored by Jewish refugee organizations. I was housed for these few days in a shelter of HIAS, the Hebrew Aid and Sheltering Society, in accommodations that were a little more elegant than those in London's East End. The shelter was located near Union Square, if I recall correctly.

I had been instructed by Abe Diamond to call him after I arrived, and I did. His instructions were simple: "Take a train to Providence, Rhode Island, and I will meet you there." I did as I was instructed, having called him once more to tell him when I would arrive. I had landed in New York on a Thursday and the following Monday I was en route to Providence.

That was the first of many trips to and from Grand Central Station, which in those days still deserved the adjective "Grand." I got off the train at Providence, and before I could even look around, a short man in his fifties greeted me enthusiastically. Later I asked him how he knew whom to greet. He said he had only to look for someone in European-style clothes!

Taunton, Massachusetts (1940-1942)

Abe Diamond and I got along well together from the very beginning. He drove us the twenty miles from Providence to Taunton and put me up in his own house for the first few nights. The rest of the family, Mrs. Diamond and their daughter, were equally hospitable. Abe had arranged for me to board with the Frank Freedmans, a Jewish family who had fled Russia during the great pogroms, as had the Diamond family. I lived with the Freedmans for two years, until I entered the armed forces in January 1942.

My integration into a new life continued at a rapid pace. I arrived in Taunton late Monday evening. By the next Thursday morning (only one week after landing in New York), I was at work at Diamond Textile Mills, Inc., the center of my work life for the next two years. Considering that in 1940 the United States was still struggling to overcome the effects of the Great Depression, it was remarkable that I was able to walk into a job one week after landing in the country. That I had a job awaiting me was the consequence of Abe Diamond's determination to help someone who had suffered much the same fate as he had.

At the same time, he in no way tried to dominate or direct my life. Having put me on my feet, so to speak, he let me find my own way. Just the same, when I needed help later with a loan to provide travel for Mama, he again went to work and found a friend who would cosign the loan for me. When I entered the armed forces, I stored my trunk with him, and when I reclaimed it after the war, he sent it on promptly and wished me good luck in my new venture into academic life.

It is not an exaggeration to say that I would not have known where to turn if Abe had not taken on the task of helping me. I was a stranger, but he took me in. What greater testimony can there be to his kindness and selflessness?

It seems to me that during my two years in Taunton, I led two lives, or perhaps one life in two separate compartments. My world at work was quite distinct from my life outside the workplace. I did not think that one was in any way better than the other. It was just that my life outside the mill was very different from that of most if not all of my fellow workers. At the same time, I came to be very friendly with those with whom I worked closely. I never sensed any sort of hostility from them, even though I must have seemed to them a rather strange creature in their midst.

Although I had advanced academic training in various aspects of the textile industry, the jobs available to me required manual dexterity and familiarity with machinery. I possessed neither to any great degree, nor was I able to acquire them in my two years at the mill. I had never tinkered with machinery, I had used tools only rarely, and I was simply not very adept with my hands. As a result, I became a sort of jack-of-all-trades, doing a variety of jobs requiring not much skill.

I was paid accordingly, the federal minimum wage of 37.5¢ per hour, or $15 for a forty-hour week. Eventually, I received 42.5¢ per hour, or $18 per week. I do not recall whether that constituted a raise or whether a change in the federal minimum wage law required the upward adjustment.

My co-workers were European white ethnics, Polish, French, Portuguese, and so on, who lived in contrasting worlds based on their ethnic backgrounds. The French went to the French Roman Catholic church, the Poles to the Polish Roman Catholic church, and so on. Their English was unlike anything I had ever heard, making communication at times problematic.

My greatest difficulty was communicating with John, a Portuguese from Cape Verde. His imaginative use of the English language defies description. I was assigned to him from time to time when an extra heavy workload required overtime. (My weekly paycheck would then balloon to $20 or $22!) I can still see him at his machine: slight, nimble, good-natured, helpful, all the while massacring the King's English.

The Poles formed one of the largest ethnic contingents in the mill, in particular several members of one family who seemed to be Abe Diamond's favorites. The father was a shift foreman and two of the sons, about my age, were mechanics. (I do not recall what the other members of the family did in the mill.) I was invited to their house several times, and we often talked during lunch breaks.

My most memorable time with them was at the wedding of one of the sons. The wedding ceremony was held late on a Saturday morning but the festivities lasted until Sunday morning! For the occasion, the Polish Hall was rented and decorated, and a Polish band from nearby Fall River was engaged. Food and drink were laid up in enormous and seemingly endless quantities.

The bride and groom stood at the door in their wedding finery to greet the guests and receive their congratulations. After a while, I noted that the groom had a drink not only with me, but also with every male guest that came through the receiving line. How he stayed on his feet, I have never been able to figure out. In fact, as it turned out, I was off my feet long before the bridegroom was! Perhaps he just faked it.

The remainder of the celebration consisted of eating, drinking, and dancing the polka. I never found out whether the band could play any other dance music, or if they had, whether anybody would have danced to it. In my innocence about the possible effect of all this hard liquor on a near teetotaler, I ate and drank along with the rest, at least for a short while.

I can only report that for me Slivovitz (plum brandy) and Polish sausages constitute a deadly combination. I lasted about two hours and then tottered home to my room and was sick for the rest of the day. The rest of the party, I later learned, ate and drank until the wee hours of Sunday morning. I found out later that this was a fairly typical sort of wedding among Polish families, and not just in Taunton.

Life beyond the mill

My life outside the mill reflected the cultural setting from which I had come, as well as the sort of interests that determined what went into my ship's trunk. The Freedman family remained my landlords for my entire two years in Taunton. Mr. and Mrs. Freedman had come or been brought from Russia in the early 1900s. They had two sons about my age, who no longer lived at home. Mr. Freedman was retired and not in good health most of the time I knew him.

Both were always kind and helpful. I cannot imagine that they did more than break even with their charge for room and board. They charged me $8 per week when I first arrived. Some time later, they raised it with many apologies to $9. It remained at that rate until I left them in 1942. In return they provided me with a comfortable, clean room, simply furnished, and with three meals a day, including lunch to take with me to the mill.

Mr. and Mrs. Freedman spoke Yiddish to each other, and Mr. Freedman was a faithful reader of the New York Yiddish daily newspaper, which still flourished in those years. They expected me to speak Yiddish as well and seemed puzzled when they discovered that I did not. My ignorance of Yiddish was not surprising, because my parents, though trilingual (German, Slovak, and Magyar), disdained Yiddish as the language of the Jews of Eastern Europe. *Ostjuden* was a derogatory term used, it is sad to say, by Jews as well as anti-Semites.

What I discovered in my years with the Freedmans was that Yiddish is a German dialect. Once that dawned on me, and I began to draw on my twelve years of Hebrew instruction, I came to understand a fair amount of spoken Yiddish, but I certainly could not produce any of it myself.

That I was able to live comfortably though frugally on $15 per week was due chiefly to Mrs. Freedman's modest room and board charge and to the contents of my ship's trunk. I did not spend a penny on clothing until late in the 1940s while at Indiana University, when I invested in a double-breasted suit on the occasion of having been appointed as a teaching assistant and put in charge of teaching two independent sections of the beginning political science course.

I could not imagine that anything else would do for such an occasion. All professors wore suits in those days; I could certainly not do less. I must also have been deeply impressed with the white shirts that most American males seemed to favor then, for I allowed myself the luxury of an Arrow shirt at the cost of $1.98!

My clothes were, of course, recognizably European, as Abe Diamond had pointed out when he met me at the Providence railroad station, but that did not bother me. My being recognizably non-American showed in other ways, too. For example, though I took my lunch with me to the mill every working day, I never bought a regular lunch bucket. I had brought with me the leather briefcase that had held my schoolbooks during secondary school, and I decided that my lunch would fit there quite adequately. So I walked to work every day carrying my lunch in a leather briefcase. Clearly one of a kind!

More difficult was the problem of my work clothes. I solved that by wearing the oldest items in the trunk. I did get a certain amount of attention and even some ribbing, but it was always good-natured, at least to my face. I scored the biggest hit when I tried to pretend the knickerbockers from my green Irish tweed suit were regular trousers by not buckling them below the knees and letting them hang loose. It was the sensation of the day at Diamond Textile. I did not repeat the experiment!

My expenditures and general living costs must be seen in the context of 1940 prices, for example: 12¢ for a gallon of gasoline, 50¢ for a haircut, and 50¢ for putting rubber heels on a pair of men's shoes. I was able to buy a small portable typewriter for $30. During all my years in Vienna, I had always had whatever money I needed or wanted for both necessities and pleasures, except for the last few months before emigration. Yet during my Taunton years, I never felt poor or deprived.

I was able to repay Abe Diamond the money he had loaned me for my own transatlantic travel. I also repaid the loan that would have financed Mama's transatlantic passage, had she been able to get out. Thus, when Ann and I were married, the money set aside for that purpose (about $300) was my contribution to our joint wealth—not counting, of course, a trunk full of clothing, books, and music. Ann still remembers the green Irish tweed suit, which she admired only for the quality of the material.

I spent much of my time listening to the small radio provided by the Freedmans. American radio programs were, of course, a far cry from the stodgy, state-controlled radio programs in Vienna, and I sampled just about all of them. I listened to all sorts of musical programs, not only the concerts of the New York Philharmonic, *The Firestone Hour*, and *The Telephone Hour*, but also weekly to *The Hit Parade*. After all, I had seen just about all the American-made movie musicals in Vienna and was much taken by the popular favorites of those days. I cannot say the same for current Top 40 hits.

I went to the movies regularly and became a great fan of Hop-along Cassidy. My tastes were never purely highbrow. I continued to enjoy popular movies and music for quite some time. It was only with the appearance of *Hair* and the rise of rock and roll that the generation gap caught up with me.

Having grown up on newspapers in Vienna, I simply contin-ued my habit of reading more than one newspaper to get more than one political perspective on current happenings. It took me a while to figure out that reading more than one American mass-circulation newspaper was no help in broadening one's political awareness. American newspapers were *business* enterprises, and politics were not necessarily the primary concern of the majority of their readers.

I also made a great discovery: the comics, especially the Sun-day funnies of the Hearst papers, which were always out on the streets on Saturday night. I am not sure whether *Little Orphan An-nie* and *Dick Tracy* go back to the early 1940s, but *Prince Valiant* and *Gasoline Alley* certainly do. The comic strip that intrigued me most was *Katzenjammer Kids*. I recognized its intellectual origins immediately—the work of the German satirist Wilhelm Busch, in particular his Max and Moritz cartoon stories.

I was hooked on the comics almost immediately. Over time my addiction has become permanent, especially to comic strips such as *Doonesbury* and *Tank McNamara*, which comment upon yester-day's headlines in franker, more incisive ways than many editorial comments.

I was fortunate to witness the birth of *PM*, that noble experi-ment of a newspaper without advertising, which was financed from the coffers of the Marshall Field fortune and edited by a bona fide American (non-Marxist) radical. I had no doubt that *PM* was a newspaper par excellence. I followed it avidly.

I also tried to make sense of another major component of the American newspaper, the sports pages. I read enough to become a Red Sox fan, which made me the 1940s equivalent of a yuppie and disgusted those of my fellow mill workers who rooted for the Boston Braves, a true workingman's team. These were the glory days of Ted Williams and Jimmy Foxx. There is, I admit, a remnant of Red Sox sympathy left in me even today.

Perhaps this allegiance is why I thought the late Bart Giammatti to be such a fine Yale president, and why I understood fully that being baseball commissioner clearly outranked the Yale presidency! Still, I find baseball a boring game, as I do football. Only cricket is more boring. None of them can hold a candle to soccer, which was then virtually unknown in America.

I was particularly intrigued by the sports pages of the local Taunton newspaper, with its endless reports on local amateur sports, adult, adolescent, and small fry. I have learned, from reading small-town newspapers, that nothing is more important to locals than their homegrown teams. I believed then, and still do, that reading the sports pages of an American newspaper, whether metropolitan or local, is essential to understanding important aspects of American life.

Soon after my arrival in Taunton, Abe Diamond took me to a meeting at the B'nai B'rith lodge and introduced me to the membership. As a result, I was adopted by a group of younger members more or less my age, who invited me to their homes and took me on weekend outings.

I particularly remember a day trip to Cape Cod in an open convertible. A day on the beach in the sun followed by a drive home in an open car gave me a humongous crop of fever blisters, identified since then as herpes simplex. I needed medical attention, and it took weeks for the blisters to heal. I have been troubled with fever blisters on my lips ever since.

I also made contacts with other newly arrived immigrants. One was a dentist from Berlin, who had immigrated with sufficient funds to be able to take time to learn the language and study for the medical exams that would allow him to practice in the United States. Later emigrants from Germany were unable to pursue such a course, and thus many highly qualified medical men and women were unable to practice their profession in America.

My Taunton friend had established a good practice by the time I met him in early 1940. He lived quite comfortably with his wife and child in a house that also contained his dental practice. We had a standing date for Friday evenings to play piano four hands. We enjoyed our music-making so very much that we hardly missed a week. Apparently we were good enough to please his wife, our captive audience of one.

A steady companionship also developed with a family from Vienna who had a little girl named Lillian. I grew fond enough of Lillian to suggest the name to Ann for our daughter. Ann, with more family sensitivity, proposed that we name our baby Alice after my by-then widowed sister-in-law. But Lillian was used as the middle name. Very early on in life Alice made it quite clear that she thought Lillian to be a "perfectly yukkie" name and was glad that I had not prevailed.

Another friend, Charles Rodgers, had come to Taunton to work in one of its oldest industries as a silversmith. He had studied at the Wiener Werkstätten, Vienna's famous art and crafts institute, and easily found work at Reed and Barton's as a designer. This small group of companions might not seem to constitute a wide circle of friends, but it was not out of character with my social life in Vienna, and it satisfied me completely.

The country and I prepare for war

If I ever had any doubts about Hitler's plans for world conquest, they were certainly dispelled by the events of May and June 1940, and ultimately by the German assault on Russia in June 1941. Yet in the United States, Franklin Roosevelt was running for a third term and promising to "keep the country out of war." A powerful antiwar movement arose in the form of America First, an organization supported by leading members of Congress and most importantly by the charismatic figure of Charles Lindbergh.

This antiwar movement included some thinly disguised pro-German elements, which were grouped together in the German-American Bund. As we learned later, they were supported and inspired by agencies of the Third Reich, including, more or less openly, German consulates in the United States.

This resistance against what seemed still another American entanglement in European conflicts received much of its impetus from the disillusionment that followed World War I, which had been touted as the war "to make the world safe for democracy." With war threatening the world yet again, many Americans were determined that this time the country would not be lured into the distant conflict.

Eventually Congress and the American people began to realize the inevitable need for building up American armed forces against the fascist powers extending their influence in the world. The military draft was established so the armed forces could begin to expand beyond its small core of regulars. When the draft legislation came up for renewal in 1941, it passed the House of Representatives by a margin of one vote!

During 1941, I became increasingly convinced that in the coming conflict, my place would be in the armed forces. But as a resident alien, I could not enlist, even though I was subject to the draft. I had received a regular draft number and had passed a physical examination, making me 1A, fit for service when called.

The deepening conflict in the United States over the country's role in the war had direct and very sad consequences for Mama. During the summer of 1941, the American government found increasing evidence of the Third Reich's direct involvement in the antiwar, isolationist movement. Given the basic sympathy of the Roosevelt administration for the Western Allies, it was not surprising when Washington ordered all German consulates in the country closed except the Embassy in Washington. Germany retaliated by closing all American consulates in Germany. As a result, all issuance of immigration visas stopped within the territory of the Third Reich.

Mama was, in effect, trapped, and we lost touch with her. Once war was declared between the United States and Germany, no further communication of any sort was possible. If Mama had been able to reach a country in which American consulates still functioned, she could have eventually obtained her visa, but she was also further handicapped by the small size of the Czech quota to which she had been assigned.

After the war, Oscar and I initiated a search for her. Gretl helped by contacting some possible locations in Europe. Eventually we learned that late in 1941, Mama had been deported together with Aunt Gisa to Theresienstadt, a detention facility of a special kind. Theresienstadt was a show place, a sort of Potemkin village to which German authorities sent both older Jews and prominent Jews about whose fate there was a lively interest in the West.

Germany even admitted some foreign inspection teams to Theresienstadt, whose supposedly humane style and comfortable accommodations were intended to assure the outside world of the bona fides of the Third Reich. What the outside world did not learn until after the war was that eventually just about all Theresienstadt inmates ended up "in the East," where the Jewish communities of Europe perished in gas ovens.

All of this we did not learn fully until well after the war. But long before Pearl Harbor, I felt extreme anger at the German effort to drive a wedge into American society. This effort had direct and fatal consequences for the dearest human being of my early life.

On Sunday, December 7, 1941, the attack on Pearl Harbor changed everything. Historians have commented repeatedly on the dramatic turnaround in American society following the attack on Pearl Harbor. While on the day *before*, there was a vocal and sizeable minority if not a majority clamoring to keep the country neutral, the day *after* found the country united in the face of the attack on Pearl Harbor and clamoring for all-out efforts to defeat the country's enemies, East and West. I have never before or since experienced as electric an atmosphere and as strong a sense of unity among people as I did during the days immediately following Pearl Harbor.

I had been to a meeting of young B'nai B'rith members that Sunday evening. As soon as we heard the news about Pearl Harbor, and without waiting for the formal declaration of war, which followed in another day or two, I knew what my next step would be. On Monday morning, I went to my local draft board and asked to be called ahead of my regular draft number. I could take that step, even though I could not enlist in the regular forces.

Since I had been classified 1A, it took the draft board only a few days to produce the famous Greetings letter ordering me to report for induction at Fort Devens, Massachusetts, on January 14, 1942. I told Abe Diamond what I had done, and he fully understood what had moved me to act.

I have often been told, mostly in jest, that I am a great one for volunteering. I agree that there have been times in my life when remaining silent rather than stepping forward would have been the better part of wisdom. Yet on December 7, 1941, there was no doubt in my mind that I had an immediate and personal stake in the evolving conflict, and that I should contribute to the resolution of that conflict directly and not just on the home front.

If I did not contribute directly to fighting the Third Reich, why should others with much less at stake? The action was not in any sense heroic. I saw it as an act of duty. However, I simply could but imagine, on that December 7, 1941, how that single act would transform my life forever.

Part II

Our Paths Cross

Chapter 4

A Wartime Courtship & Marriage

Ann's Account
(1942-1944)

My life continued in more or less the same fashion in the weeks following my illness. We were all greatly affected by the dismal events taking place in Europe. It was all very grim. The Nazis were still making inroads into Russia, and they had gone south into Greece, and the German General Rommel continued to battle English troops in North Africa.

Certainly all these events impinged on our thoughts and lives, but they had no real immediacy for us. Many of the men with whom I had worked in the quartermaster's office were now in the theater of operations, but I had not retained ties with any of them. Indeed, we were kept so very busy that we had little time or energy left for musing or philosophizing. We were coping with new conditions both at work and at home. Outside of work, we were coping with a lack of supplies.

Indianapolis (1942)

Three of my brothers were in the armed services. My brother Joe and my brother-in-law Glenn (Mae's husband) were farming with almost no help, so their hours were unbelievably long. Uncle Bill was working with carpentry units engaged by contractors who were building for the military. A large unit was being built between Indianapolis and Columbus, Camp Atterbury. Uncle Bill did not commute home—his hours were long, and he even worked on Saturdays and Sundays.

After the long period of little or no work during the 1930s, here we were all racing around like mad with war work. The hectic pace continued from 1939 through 1944. America, very literally, was not prepared for war, and what was accomplished in those years was almost unbelievable.

My cousin Ruth graduated from high school in June and took a job in downtown Indianapolis. Uncle Bill was away much of the time working with the carpentry units. My dear aunt Mabel was not in good health. She was in fact dying, though I was only dimly aware of it.

Aunt Mabel had run many errands for me and had always taken care of the household laundry, the grocery shopping, and the cooking. Now these tasks were becoming increasingly hard for her. They were especially difficult without Uncle Bill and the car, for we lived several blocks from either a trolley line or a grocery store.

We had almost no time for any kind of entertainment. We worked away from home, and then we came home and worked some more. So although I talked with Alfred Diamant at the office and found our talks interesting, I am sure I gave no more thought to him than just that. I had neither the time nor the energy.

However, he did provide me with firsthand information and expert opinions on affairs in Europe. Then as now he read newspapers. I think there is an expertise in acquiring knowledge from newspapers that he has always had. It is a singular skill acquired by very few. Certainly I have never known his equal. In later years I have been known to say that he can't live unless he has sniffs of printer's ink every day!

The Halloween party

Time passed very quickly, and in October we decided to have a Halloween party at my aunt's house for all the supply sergeants I dealt with. Ruth's boyfriend, a young man from the Hope-Columbus area, had enlisted in the navy only recently and was away in training. We civilians were always being asked to entertain these young men in military training in our homes. Because Aunt Mabel was so unwell, we were very limited in what we could do. We could not have a dinner, but we decided that we could have a Halloween party.

So we planned simple party games with silly prizes and for refreshments, popcorn and cider. We may have had some other things to eat, but I doubt it because butter, flour, and sugar were strictly rationed. (When I could see at Fort Harrison how military cooks wasted these things, I felt very angry and wanted to give them a good scolding!) I issued my invitations to the military, and Ruth asked her female friends. I believe I asked only one female, a young woman in my own office.

The day of the party came, and the phone began to ring. It soon looked as though our party was fast disappearing. The phone calls were all from young men at Fort Harrison whose units were being alerted or moved about. Then Ruth's female friends also dropped away for various reasons.

However, to our sur- prise, my mother called and said she was on her way to visit, accompanied by my two younger sisters. Mother was worried about her sister's health, so when she had an opportunity to come to Indianapolis, she seized it. Of course, Betty and Martha were delighted that there was to be a Hal- loween party.

As it turned out, that evening the only military personnel that appeared were Corporal Brophy and Sergeant Diamant from the headquarters company and my co-worker Eleanor Met- calf. None of Ruth's friends

Ann (front), Louetta,
Betty, & Martha
Hope, Indiana, 1940s

appeared. We had to change our planned entertainment rapidly. The games and refreshments were all very familiar to Corporal Bro- phy, but to Sergeant Diamant, it was all very new and, I had the impression, not particularly interesting or appetizing.

He told us, not at all tactfully, that he did not like popcorn, but we all noted that he ate quite a lot of it. Perhaps because there was nothing else to eat. The party was not a brilliant success, but it had a pleasant aftermath, as you will see if you read on.

Courtship

Some days later, Sergeant Diamant came to my desk and said that he had bought two tickets for a concert at the Murat Temple in downtown Indianapolis, and that one of them was for me. It was a concert outside the season ticket concerts, at which the India-napolis Symphony was to play a special program with the concert pianist Rudolf Serkin. I agreed to go.

They played Beethoven's Fifth Piano Concerto, *the Emperor Concerto*. For me, it was like being transported into another world—the beauty of it flowed over me, around me, and into me. It was an indescribable experience, and it changed my life. It changed Sergeant Diamant's life as well. From then on, we both knew our lives were to be together—even though there might be some corners to turn first.

Both of us being practical and sober people, we went back to our workplaces and performed our usual tasks. But we spent every possible evening together from then until Freddy, as I began to call him at his request, left for Officer Candidate School (OCS).

Aunt Mabel approved of him because he took me to enter-tainments other than movies—things such as the theater, musi-cal events, and Sunday afternoon string ensemble concerts. These were all things I loved most to do, but I never before had a male friend who initiated them and who enjoyed attending them as much as I did. At his invitation, I went to Thanksgiving dinner with his headquarters company. It was a workday—no holidays for the military when at war!

Soon after, on December 13, Freddy left for Officer Candidate School. While he was away, he wrote me every day, and he com-plained that I did not do likewise. At Christmas time he phoned, and we tried to arrange getting together but it did not work out, so I went to spend Christmas with Mother, Betty, and Martha. How-ever, I did not once mention this new dimension in my life to my family. I do not know why I did not. I do know that our lives and our nation were in such flux that I had not yet had a chance to come to terms with my remarkable experience myself.

Besides that, I was more than a little scornful of all those fluttering young females who went on endlessly about their young men or swooned over public idols. Genuine feelings I sincerely respect, but I have never been able to suffer fools gladly. It takes a great deal of self-discipline even today to be courteous to those I consider pompous. For whatever reason, I did not discuss Freddy or my feelings for him with anyone else.

Finally the time for Freddy's graduation from OCS approached. I was importuned to come to Fort Knox to pin the bars on the very excited second-lieutenant-to-be. It did not occur to Freddy that I might have more than a little trouble getting there and finding a place to stay and a way to afford it! As salaries went in those days, I was doing very well, but less than a year before, I had had all those tremendous medical bills, and I had not yet paid back all the money I had borrowed.

In our early days, this was one of our greatest differences. I was very, very cautious about spending money, and Freddy was disdainful about allowing such considerations to restrain his impulses. Time and Freddy have changed me. In fact I sometimes think we may have reversed our roles!

My cousin Dorothy and her husband, Sherman, were then living in Jeffersonville, Indiana, up across the Ohio River from Fort Knox, Kentucky. (Because Sherman was an auditor in the Army Finance Corps, they moved frequently.) I phoned Dorothy, told her all about it, and she immediately said that I should come to them in Jeffersonville, and they would be happy to take me over to Fort Knox for the ceremonies.

So I managed to attend Freddy's graduation from Officer Candidate School. However, Sherman pinned on the bars for me because my hands seemed unable to perform the task. On Sunday afternoon, Freddy and I went back to Indianapolis by train. As it turned out, it was a fateful train ride.

If I were telling this tale in terms of Greek mythology, I would say that Pan must have been playing his pipes, and Eros must have summoned a corps of minions to pull me forward with golden ropes. By this time the Fates had taken over. I was walking directly into what I thought of as The Marriage Trap, and with only faint objections! By the time we detrained in Indianapolis, I had agreed to marry Freddy, right away.

Wedding preparations

My leave had been for only one day, so I was obliged to return to work at Fort Harrison on Monday morning. In fact, I worked until the day we went together to the Marion County Court House to get our marriage license. Freddy seems to remember that I did all the organizing and arranging, and that he was only an innocent bystander throughout. I expect that is correct, but by way of exoneration I must say that I was the birthright Hoosier, so I knew the laws. I simply did what needed to be done.

Indiana law required marrying couples to prove themselves free of venereal diseases before issuing a marriage license. I found a physician in Irvington who kept evening hours and made an appointment with him to administer the blood tests. Then I talked to the minister of the Irvington Methodist Church about performing the ceremony. To him, I think, the marriage did not sound as routine as I had assumed it was, but he said he would talk to us, so I made an appointment with him directly following our doctor's appointment.

What I recognize now, and what people with more education and worldly experience saw at once, was that there might well be many pitfalls in a marriage between a European Jew and a parochial American Protestant. It never occurred to me that this was a problem. Freddy says now that he had some fleeting thoughts on the subject, but he wanted very much to get married so he pushed them away.

Perhaps I was more of an innocent than I thought I was. For my part, I had consented to marry Freddy, and I was going about it in the ways I knew. And I was setting up a home, just as Freddy wanted me to. His chief weapon in persuading me to marry him was that he was very alone, and he wanted to feel that he had a home to return to.

So we went to the rectory to talk with the minister. He must have decided that we passed the marriage test, for he set a time for the ceremony. He may have expressed some doubts, but if he did, it all flew over my head, for I do not recall any. I have heard it said that memory is selective (we remember only what we wish to remember), and I agree there is some truth in that. What I remember most clearly about our conversation with the minister is almost the most trivial part of it.

The minister and other Protestant clergymen in the city were feuding with the Marion County clerk. They claimed he was lining his pockets by adding an illegal fee for marriage licenses. The minister said that the legal fee for a license was $2.50, but the clerk was charging $5.

In the Depression years of the 1930s, marriages were much less frequent. After the country went to war and the manpower draft was instituted, young couples were marrying in droves. It was the minister's thought that the clerk was taking unfair advantage of these young military men. And so he was.

Despite the minister's sage warning, we also contributed to the clerk's well-lined pockets. At the clerk's office, we too were told that the fee was $5. He brought out a neat little folder containing two forms—one was the actual government form, the license, and the other was a form for the official performing the rite.

I said that we wanted only the license, and that our minister would provide his own form. Well, that brought a scowl and a frown! He put the folder away quickly and brought out another form. It was an exact replica of my parents' marriage license. It was about twenty-four inches by sixteen inches and embellished completely around with cupids bearing garlands of roses, ribbons, and hearts. In fact it looked like a huge valentine in rather poor taste.

I told him that it was not what we wanted! We wanted only the small legal certificate, like the one in the folder. He replied that it was either one or the other—$5 for the first folder or $2.50 for the valentine.

"Well," I said, "in that case, I guess it's no marriage. I'll have neither!" And I walked out.

But Freddy paid the $5 for the folder! He said later, what else could he do? He had already bought the rings, and he did not want to lose his investment! Besides that, he was afraid I would buy the valentine, and under no circumstances was he going to present that to his captain when he reported back to duty. He was required to take the actual license with him to change his status from single to married.

During those three days, we also found and moved ourselves into a small apartment. That was another miracle. The advertisement for it was in the small Irvington community newspaper. A woman, Mrs. Ryker, was offering two furnished rooms with shared bath and kitchen. It was a long walk from Aunt Mabel's house and a long walk to the shops and the trolley, but it was quite satisfactory, so we took it most happily.

Our wedding

Our wedding took place on March 18, 1943, on a lovely Thursday morning. The weather was especially nice, almost warm. I wore a new dark blue serge suit with a white blouse, and Freddy wore his full dress uniform. The ceremony took place at Irvington Methodist Church in the church parlor, since Freddy was not a Christian. We had planned a simple wedding, but it did not come off quite as we planned.

We had unexpected guests! They even brought a dinner, including the all-important cake. I would never have asked any of my relatives to spend their precious ration coupons on me, but on her own, Aunt Mabel had called Mother and

Ann & Freddy
Their Wedding Portrait
Indianapolis, March 1943

told her of our plans. Mae drove herself, Mother, Martha, and Betty to Indianapolis for the wedding. So as it turned out, my mother and all my sisters were there with me when I got married.

My family brought a roasted chicken, delicious noodles made in Mae's special way, other things I cannot remember, and the cake. We had to throw away the concert tickets that Freddy had bought for our wedding evening, but I was very happy indeed to have my family around me, to know they loved me and wished me well.

I expect Freddy was, too. Before he went back to his post, he expressed satisfaction that he now had a family. Indeed he did. Mother came to love him very much, for he was always very loving, kind, and thoughtful to her.

We had only one week together until Freddy's leave was up and he had to report for duty at Camp Polk. It was an extremely happy week for me. Having succumbed to love and marriage, I did it with my whole heart, and I was rewarded with a truly adoring husband! He made me feel sweet, kind, pretty, and all those gracious traits never attributed to me before.

Most of all, I somehow felt complete. I had a true soul mate. I had never before felt that I needed one, but now I realized I had. Indeed, life took on a new, most satisfying dimension. I still think I was right, even though now it is almost fifty years later and there have been many heights and depths between. We are still soul mates.

356 Arlington Avenue North

Freddy went to Camp Polk in Louisiana, and I continued to work at Fort Harrison and keep the apartment. Mrs. Ryker was very good to me and very helpful. She was a widow with one son, a very well-known one at that. Stanley Ryker played a wind instrument in a famous jazz band. It always struck me as slightly incongruous that someone as straight-laced and WCTU (Women's Christian Temperance Union) as Mrs. Ryker had a son who was a jazz musician and played in the nation's top jazz bands and in world-famous ballrooms. But she did, and she loved him more than anything else in the world.

I remember that when Freddy and I went to inquire about the apartment, she made her opposition to alcohol quite clear. Because we readily agreed that we would not bring any liquor into the house and that we would not drink, she welcomed us as newlyweds with open arms and friendly interest.

Betty graduated from high school that same spring and came to share the apartment with me. She found work at a fairly large naval ordnance plant, which had been built on Arlington Avenue, the same street on which we lived. Our address was 356 Arlington

Avenue North and the Naval Plant was about 1400-1500 North. It was a fairly long walk. But then we were all accustomed to walking.

Freddy wrote me nearly every day from Louisiana, where he was finding Camp Polk very uncomfortable. I became a nagging wife almost immediately when he told me that he was not going to evening mess because as an officer he had to wear full dress uniform in the dining room. Instead, he bought two chocolate bars and a soda pop from the canteen and ate them in his room, wearing only his underwear and with a fan on him.

I was appalled. I could just see all his teeth falling out from too many sweets as he became ill from malnourishment. Anyone who knows me well understands that I have always taken care to ensure that my family eats good nutritious meals at stated times. It is impossible for me to behave otherwise.

Vacation in Brown County

Toward the end of August, Freddy was scheduled for a leave and I for a vacation. I longed to get away from the city. I was able to obtain a room for us at Indiana's Brown County State Park, one of the products of President Roosevelt's make-work programs of his New Deal in the early 1930s. As soon as it opened, it became one of my favorite spots for swimming and picnicking.

When Freddy arrived in Indianapolis, he was very reluctant to go any farther. He just wanted to stay where he was. It was cooler than Louisiana. We traveled by bus from Indianapolis to Nashville, and then the park service took us by car to the inn. Even in the bus, the trees and green scenery of Brown County (the altitude of which is among the highest in Indiana) created a sense of coolness that the city lacked. We were relaxed and happy even before we jumped into the pool.

Our compatibility was again apparent. We both loved swimming and hiking the trails. It was a wonderful interlude. The food was good, and we did not have to use our coupons or walk to the grocery and carry our purchases back. We even enjoyed the square dancing on Saturday night. On Sunday my relatives from Hope came with a picnic lunch to enjoy with us. Mae and Joe each had a daughter by then, Julie and Becky, the two most beautiful and clever little girls in the world. We had a lovely day together.

It seemed to me that Freddy was pleased to be a part of my family. He had met both George and Roy by arrangement in Louisiana, where they all were stationed. And he clearly enjoyed our family picnic day. In fact he told me then, and wrote me from Camp Polk after his return, how wonderful it was not to feel so alone in the world and to be able to feel he had a family again.

Freddy returned to Camp Polk at the end of our too-short vacation. Soon after that, he was transferred to a special intelligence unit at Camp Ritchie, Maryland, near Hagerstown. I resumed my usual work routine at Fort Harrison, living with Betty in our apartment.

It was a quiet, almost dull time for me and lots of others even though we were busy as bees. At Fort Harrison, each day held a different and new event. The newly built Billings General Hospital was fully staffed and operating. Units changed and were added every day. Goods were checked in and checked out of the warehouses almost without pause. And bewildering changes in army regulations issued forth every week.

It was about this time that I wrote to Freddy's brother and his wife. I had learned about his family before we married. I knew that Freddy's mother was his father's second wife. I knew about his father's first wife and about Freddy's half-brother, Oscar, and half-sister, Valerie. They had been long married, and Valerie's son was only a few years younger than Freddy. I was passionately interested in these people, very concerned for them, and greatly upset with the horrible events that had changed their lives. For many years I had been reading about what was happening in Europe, and now I was personally involved with those who had experienced it.

Oscar and his wife, Liesl, had established themselves in Australia, where Liesl's sister, brother-in-law, and their two sons had gone a few months before they did. After our vacation in August, I sat down and wrote to them, introducing myself. I told them how Freddy and I had met, and something about my family, my religion, and my American background. Oscar answered and seemed overjoyed with my news. He welcomed me in the sweetest, kindliest manner possible and thanked me profusely for having written and given them news of Freddy.

Liesl's mother lived in New York with her daughter Mary and her family. After the war I met them all, including Liesl's sister from the West Coast and Freddy's Diamant cousins from New Jersey. Without exception, everyone accepted me with great friendliness and cordiality. Neither of our families ever questioned our marriage. That contributed to our happiness and to the stability of our life together.

Adele

I must relate one happening in particular since it had interesting international overtones. I had become good friends with Adele Panzer, a woman who worked in our office. She was from one of Indianapolis' most respected and prominent families. Her father had been one of its first surgeons and the founder of its first hospital, on the spot where the Murat Temple now stands.

He was of German origin and had been educated in Germany. After establishing himself in Indianapolis, he had gone back to Germany to acquire a wife from one of the princely families. Adele was one of six children, all of whom were raised in strict German family style right there in Indianapolis in a big house in Woodruff Place. Her father had even brought over all their household staff from Germany.

Adele was perhaps forty years old or so and was working for the first time in her life, with me as her supervisor. She was not unfriendly, but at first she was reserved and aloof. After a while we became quite good friends, and I spent more than one weekend with her. She unbent to me when she learned that I had a season ticket for the Indianapolis Symphony concerts. Her brother Kurt Panzer chaired the committee that made the symphony possible.

I had dinner twice with Adele's aunt, the widow of a very famous Swiss obstetrician and gynecologist. Her aunt was beautiful and gracious. She had come from Germany to visit her older sister in Woodruff Place, and Dr. Panzer had brought home the Swiss doctor whom he had recruited for his new Indianapolis hospital. Likely his sister-in-law's beauty helped Dr. Panzer retain his colleague, for they married and lived in Indianapolis for the rest of their lives. It was in her home that I had dinner with Adele and her sister.

Adele had so much character, perhaps because she had undergone so much unhappiness. She and her sister had been tutored at home by governesses and then had gone to New England to Vassar College. Soon after her debut, she had visited in Germany, where she met and married a prince in one of the small kingdoms. As it turned out, he was a sadist. She was terrified of him, and her life became a veritable hell.

Escaping was both difficult and dangerous! Finally she convinced her brother and his wife of the kind of man he was, and they helped her to escape. She was not able to take anything with her—not even a change of clothing. She had been entirely dependent upon her brother for everything, including a course at a local business college so she could get a job.

When a military company of refugee Austrians was formed at Camp Atterbury, the former Austrian Archduke Otto came to Indianapolis to bless the new company. Adele was asked through her brother to be the archduke's dinner and dancing partner. She was not flattered; in fact, she was angry. But she felt obliged to her brother, so she accepted for at least one dinner. She told me in her restrained way that she never wanted to see or be with any titled German men again. So much of her life had been wasted by her truly terrible marriage.

Yet Adele was one person at Fort Harrison who approved and was truly happy for me when I married Freddy. She told me later that she had observed Freddy and me walking and talking together before Freddy went to Officer Candidate School. When she saw us, she said, she was struck by the thought that we *belonged* together.

Camp Ritchie

In September Freddy was transferred out of Camp Polk. When I next heard from him, he was happier and in the Military Intelligence Service at Camp Ritchie in Maryland. In my position at Fort Harrison, I read a lot of army communications and new regulations, so I knew about Camp Ritchie, but I did not fully understand the role of the Military Intelligence Service (MIS) in the conduct of the war. However, I was soon aware that my husband was much happier in the MIS than he had been in his previous military unit.

Freddy's letters from Ritchie were a bit less frequent, no longer one each day. He explained that he generally had evening classes and sometimes night exercises. Since I did not write daily, I felt a little less guilty about not doing so. It seems to me that Freddy never really appreciated the time and effort that women had to give to shopping, laundering, and even grooming. Just to get a haircut took an appointment. We did not have wash-and-wear garments, and laundry services were extremely limited and expensive. Keeping clean and well groomed consumed a lot of our time and effort.

Christmas 1943

At Christmas Freddy surprised me by arriving in Indianapolis while I was at work. One of his colleagues had given him a lift home in his car. Usually Freddy thought only in terms of roses, but this time he had bought a pot of poinsettias, the first I had ever been given. Poinsettias are so common now that it is hard to remember how rare they were then. It was typical of Freddy to buy them for me. It explains in a way why I came to love him so very much. What they cost did not bother him at all. He just wanted to bring me a beautiful gift.

Freddy brought me another expensive and beautiful gift, which I still treasure. My under-the-tree gift was a set of sterling silver dessert plates. They are still museum lovely. (Kirk Silversmiths, where he bought them, are still in Hagerstown.) As usual he bought tickets for everything available in music and dance, including Sonja Henie and her skating troupe.

Unfortunately, he was called back to Ritchie early when his team was put on alert. He left behind another gift, of which I was unaware until some weeks later, and for which I did not thank him until many, many weeks later than that.

As usual they had been called early only to hurry-and-wait. So over a long weekend, I went to Ritchie. We visited Waynesboro, Pennsylvania. Unfortunately we were caught in a snowstorm and had to wait until we were plowed out so that I could take a taxi to Harrisburg to catch a train back to Indianapolis. My leave from work had been granted most reluctantly, so I was terrified at the thought of not getting back in time.

Expectations

A few days later Freddy called to say goodbye. They really were leaving. I was overwhelmed. I cried hard, so hard I could not speak. Betty took the phone to tell him "goodbye" and "God bless" for me. Dissolving into tears was completely out of character for me. I had always been able to school my emotions very well. That I was not in control of my emotions was the first indication of my pregnancy.

From then on, I was sick, sick, and sick again, and not just in the morning. Some days I could not even tolerate water. My boss, a captain, laughed at my plight, but not in a nasty way. He kept saying that I should not resign, that it would pass eventually.

As I look back at this time in a historical sense, I can see that in Indiana, at least, we were still emerging from the Victorian Age, in spite of the changes that had come about following World War I. One of the Victorian taboos to which I was sensitive concerned an evidently pregnant woman appearing in a public or prominent place.

In my position at Fort Harrison, I dealt far more with men than women, and as my pregnant condition was apparent almost at once, I knew instantly when someone was looking at me with aversion rather than admiration. I was not very happy about that either. So I resigned and moved back to Hope.

There was also the very practical need to see a doctor, which I had not yet done. The military had taken so many doctors that the ones who remained were few in number and overworked. There was only one still practicing in Hope. Although he was a general practitioner, he had cared for Mae and others I knew during their pregnancies.

My cousin Dorothy had by this time moved to Columbus, Ohio, and she begged me to come stay with her and put myself in the care of an obstetrician. Later I wished heartily that I had done so. But during 1944 I was definitely not functioning in my usual way. My actions were instinctive and not necessarily reasonable.

Aunt Mabel died that spring. She had been an active force in our family life for so long that her passing can only be viewed as another turning point. My mother, who had been the least strong in her family, was now the only surviving member. She had two sons in the Pacific theater of war and one in the European theater.

And I had a husband in England. So all our lives were being disturbed and changed in ways over which we had no control.

Ruth married Alvin Ping, who was in the submarine branch of the navy. Betty met the man she later married at the naval ordnance plant where she worked. Martha, now a senior in high school, had a steady friend who would soon be inducted and who was begging her to marry him. I suppose she must have felt very doubtful, for she refused and married someone else some years later.

Indianapolis had undergone change and so had Columbus. Noblitt-Sparks (later called Arvin Industries) prospered but only minimally. Cummins Engine Company, which for about ten years had been small and given to research and experimentation with diesel engines, grew to giant size by producing diesel engines for military tanks. Soon it became an international company. The capital used to start the company came from the same company that Uncle Hal had been vice-president and general manager of only a few years earlier.

After leaving Fort Harrison, I had few contacts there. In fact living in Hope isolated me from the world I knew in Columbus and Indianapolis. I was in an almost semi-conscious state all the months I was pregnant, so even Columbus, its activities, and its people seemed only distant entities.

I remained ill and uncomfortable much of the time, and as I grew larger, I had a great deal of trouble walking, for I developed severe sciatic pain. The doctor gave me pills for the nausea and pills for the sciatica, but they helped not at all, for I vomited back most things that I put down my throat.

It has been suggested to me, both then and since, that all my sickness and pain came about because I was under such great stress. However, I was with my mother, and I had no money worries. I had saved all Freddy had sent me in the months after our marriage, and the allowance from the US Army was more than I needed. In addition, when Freddy became attached to the 82nd Airborne Division, he was paid an additional $100 a month, which he sent to me and I put promptly into war savings bonds. I am sure we were as prosperous as we had ever been.

During 1944, communication with Freddy was not very satisfactory. Letters from me got to him intermittently but sometimes not serially, and I received letters from him in the same manner. I think it was March when he finally learned he would be a father before the year was out, and he learned of Aunt Mabel's death before then.

By the time Freddy learned of my condition and replied, I was no longer at Fort Harrison. Surely no one was ever more jubilant. Every letter he wrote to me was filled with his joy and protestations of his love. He was just as sure that I was as pleased and happy as he was.

At times when I could hardly hold my head upright because I was so sick, reading this kind of missive almost made me angry. But usually I concluded that if he could be so happy thinking of the family he would have when he returned, then I could be happy he had this to think about, instead of the very chilling and daunting prospect of taking part in the impending European invasion.

I think neither of us admitted to ourselves that he might not come back. Then, too, my miserable condition kept me so occupied with trying to cope with everyday living that I had little energy for worrying. I followed events overseas as closely as possible. When reports of the invasion started coming through on the radio, I stayed glued to it for hours.

Freddy's letters from England written before the invasion did not actually start to arrive until after D-day. The US Army processed no mail for about a month before, lest any invasion news leak out inadvertently to the enemy. The first letter I received (near the end of June) described that chilling night and the subsequent two weeks or so. Receiving the last letter first was terribly confusing and upsetting. From it I learned that Freddy had been wounded, but that he was alive. He was feeling fairly well and being cared for in a hospital in England.

By then, I needed to give my attention to preparing for the baby, who was due on September 10th. So many people contributed so kindly to these preparations. I was very grateful. Baby clothes and furniture were not for sale in the stores. All one could do was put one's name on a list to be notified if goods should come in. So my friends and relations were scouting for used clothing wherever they could.

Diapers were the greatest problem, even secondhand ones. They were the hardest item to find. When Steve arrived, he had less than three dozen secondhand diapers, and no new ones until he was six months old. We had to wash diapers every day until he was potty-trained. He probably holds the world record for the youngest child ever potty-trained.

Yet there never was a more docile, quiet, and cooperative child than Steve. I truly thanked God for him and his sweet disposition. With Steve, I discovered that taking care of one's own child differs greatly from caring for siblings.

My birth certificate

That summer I acquired a birth certificate, something that has created minor complications for me through the years. In the early days in the United States, birth records were not carefully kept. Countless families had no family Bible, nor a fixed church affiliation, and they seldom baptized babies. I doubt that either my parents or any of their parents could have produced a birth certificate.

All my mother's babies were born at home and delivered by Dr. Norton. He was supposed to have sent a record of each birth with the date and the baby's name to the county clerk's office, which in turn was to send it on to the state. As you may guess, his birth records were not always sent, and those sent were not always accurate. In later years, such incidents were regarded as highly suspicious by Frances Knight, that most zealous anticommunist, and the director of the State Department Passport Office during the McCarthy era.

While I was at Arvin (Noblitt-Sparks) in Columbus, they began to receive contracts from the military establishment. The company was asked to be very careful about the political reliability of their employees and to get birth certificates from everyone. Our office gathered the relevant information and sent requests to state offices for copies of our birth certificates.

I assumed they had received mine since I never heard anything further. When I resigned to go to Fort Harrison, I asked if I might have my birth certificate, for Sherman Stevens had told me that I would need one to work for the military. To my surprise, Arvin said they had never received one for me. They had not taken the birth certificate requirement seriously, particularly for someone like me, so they had never followed up on it. I was not by any means the only one unregistered, and none of my bosses ever thought I might be a spy.

Even Mr. Locke at Fort Harrison was not very concerned that I did not have a birth certificate, but he did say that I should go to the state office as soon as was convenient and talk with the personnel there. When I did so, they dug out the record of a child born to Hugh and Louetta Redmon on my birth date, but the child's name was *Mary Ann*. I had, of course, gone through all my life with the name *Annabelle Redmon*. It upset me greatly, but I could not undo the past, so I took my *Mary Ann* certificate to Fort Harrison and the US military establishment.

During that summer in 1944, I did my best to rectify the mistake made so long ago. Mother, Joe, and I went to the County Court House in Columbus. There Earl Finkel, our old friend and former neighbor, went before a judge and swore that Annabelle Redmon and Mary A. Diamant were one and the same person. I was then issued a court certificate bearing the name *Mary Annabelle Redmon Diamant* in place of the birth certificate.

I really wanted to leave the *Mary* off altogether. But since I was *Mary A.* to the military, and my husband was in a military hospital in England, and who knew how and where we would be when he came home, I decided not to create greater complications than those I already had to cope with.

Besides all that, I was physically so very uncomfortable, so big, and walking only with sciatic pain, I just could not be bothered. Once in a while, a relative or friend from years past asks me why I changed my name, and I really wish I did not have to explain. Nobody ever understands.

Twice in later years, I have been treated with great discourtesy and skepticism because of this mix-up. I have felt exceedingly angry both times. About twenty years ago, the Social Security agency wrote me a nasty letter accusing me of many things, among them that I was claiming a false social security number, because I had not notified them when I changed my name in 1944.

They were right. I had not. It had never occurred to me to do so, for when I worked in the federal civil service, we were not covered by social security. At that time, civil servants had their own retirement plan. I retired before I had been with them for ten years, so the amount deducted was refunded to me. It was such a small amount that I had put it into our joint savings account and forgotten all about the whole business.

The second time was in 1966, while we were living in Haverford, Pennsylvania. I used my court-issued birth certificate to apply for a passport. My application for a passport was refused because they did not regard my court-issued certificate as valid. Again I was exceedingly angry and upset. My husband and my children received their passports without question—and only I *with all my American background* was refused because I was probably a Russian spy with faked documents!

I talked with our Pennsylvania senator's office staff in Philadelphia, and Freddy talked with Frances Knight's office in Washington. Finally, he found out what I should do to satisfy the passport office. I was asked to send a notarized statement from Joe that he had a sister Mary Annabelle Redmon Diamant, that he had been living and present when she was born to Hugh and Louetta Redmon, and so forth.

I could never understand why this was more valid than the court document that Joe and my mother had signed before the judge in 1944. It was all so silly! I had made such an effort in 1944 to set it straight, and yet it seemed to be all in vain.

Steven's birth

To return to 1944, as September 10 approached I became more and more eager for my baby to be born. By that time I was so large that though I was not nauseous any more, eating was troublesome. Finally the doctor reported that dilation had begun and that it would be only a few hours or days. However, only after many false alarms and an attempt to induce labor was Steven Roy Diamant born on October 1, 1944, in the Bartholomew County Hospital.

He weighed eight pounds and seven ounces. He was not fat, but he had a very large head, which must have accounted for much of his weight. That poor head did not look so good when I first saw it, for his had been an assisted birth, and the marks of the forceps were clearly visible.

Steve's mama did not feel very good either, I might add. I could not have had more careful and loving attention than I received during my two weeks in the hospital. It was wartime, and there were too few doctors and too few nurses, and they were all overworked, and supplies were limited. But I lived only because of the care and concern of the staff.

I was badly torn, so I bled excessively and I needed lots of internal stitching. The day following Steve's birth, I began to have a fever. My temperature became so high that I was totally unconscious at least forty-eight hours. Because sulfa and penicillin were needed by the military abroad, civilian supplies were limited—but they gave me sulfa, and I gradually improved. I had become anemic. They debated about a transfusion but decided against it. I finally went back to Hope in an ambulance.

At home I hemorrhaged once more, and with that effusion I passed a cotton surgical pad that had been left inside after the stitching. My cousin Dorothy had been right. I should have gone to her in Columbus, Ohio, and had a specialist's care. Just another example of hindsight being better than foresight.

When I was able to get up and move about again, I found that I had difficulty walking. The hip that had given me so much trouble throughout my pregnancy was still painful.

The hospital had given me a footprint of Steve, which had been used as his identification. I sent it to Freddy. When he received it, he was ecstatic.

Ann & Steven
Columbus, Indiana
November 24, 1944

My mother was utterly delighted to have a baby to bathe and dress again. There could not ever have been an easier child to care for than Steve. As long as he had my milk, he was happy. In fact he would go for long hours and never fret to be fed. But he grew slowly, and everyone worried about it except me. Steve and I were compatible then, and we still are. Caring for him was as natural as breathing. Of course, I adored him.

I had not wanted to have children in my young life, and I had certainly hoped to be established in a home with my husband when I did. However, I accepted the turn of events philosophically. I was happy to be with my mother. And I was more than happy with my *superior* baby!

Fortunately, we were able to get a woman to come in twice a week to help with the washing, ironing, and cleaning. Martha and her school friends helped, too. One of them in particular loved to trundle Steve around in his baby carriage. Steve always went to sleep when taken for a ride, a habit that persisted even when we acquired a car a few years later.

Freddy comes home

We led a bucolic kind of life for weeks. Of course, none of us could be free of worry. The war still raged in both Europe and the Pacific. There were sad reports daily in the newspaper about people from families we knew. I expected to hear soon that Freddy had been sent back to the combat zone, but that did not happen. As our military hospitals in England began to fill up with wounded from the European front, patients such as Freddy, who only needed time to heal, were using valuable space. So he was sent home.

It was purely coincidence that the headquarters hospital for orthopedic patients was in Louisville, Kentucky. Freddy was brought from England to Fort Devens, Massachusetts, but he was unable to phone me because Mother did not have a phone. She had moved to the house we were in, a rental, after the war began, and home phones were not available. (The woman who owned the house had moved in with her son and his family, and we were able to use their phone or the pay phone at the post office.) Freddy wrote me at once from Fort Devens, and then again from Louisville after he arrived at Nicholas General Hospital. Being ambulatory, he was granted home leave, and in a matter of days, our little family was together.

Now it seems incredible that it should have taken so much planning and maneuvering for him to get from Louisville to Hope, but it did. When it finally came about, Freddy was so happy and excited that even though Steve was asleep, he just had to wake him. He seemed overwhelmed that he had a son.

Life took on a much rosier glow even though he was still in the army and we had no idea what his superiors would decide. We assumed he would be given an office job that used his language skills in some way. But those inflexible army regulations held that in his position, still a first lieutenant infantry, and with the physical impairment he now had, he would have to be retired.

Freddy's Account
(1942-1944)

ountless books, movies, TV shows, and comic strips have depicted, in both serious and comic veins, the trials of a draftee being inducted into the armed forces and the weeks of basic training that are to transform the supposedly hapless civilian into a trained fighting machine. There is not much that I can add to this from my own experience. However, what might have been different for me was that I had a sense of personal involvement and a personal commitment to the task of defeating the Axis powers.

Through the next three and a half years, I approached my tasks, even the seemingly simple-minded ones, with this commitment in mind. If anyone had a personal stake in the war, I had one. Whatever happened to me from basic training to D-day and beyond, I accepted as part of the price that had to be paid to bring down the evil regimes that confronted the United States in World War II.

What I did *not* foresee in early 1942 was that my service in the armed forces would be rewarded with the truly great love of my life and permission to pursue the university studies from which I had been barred in Vienna. There is, indeed, much to be said for serendipity.

Induction, Fort Devens (1942)

My induction center days at Fort Devens in January 1942 continue to remain a blur. I had never shared a bedroom with another person, and yet there I was in a squad room with over one hundred other recruits, all equally confused and too excited to sleep, except for the few who, almost without exception, let the rest of us know how well and deeply they slept by snoring loudly and with gusto. During the days, there were endless rounds of tests, physical examinations, and shots, and more shots. Based on the results of these tests, we were sorted out for basic training. Together with a sizeable group, I ended up at Fort Knox, Kentucky, the armored force training center.

By what mysterious logic would the army send the one recruit who could not even drive a car to receive basic training in tanks, trucks, and half-tracks? I found out that I had scored exceedingly high on all sorts of mechanical aptitude tests, so I was considered a natural for training as a tank mechanic. What the army did not seem to understand was that demonstrating mechanical aptitude with pencil on paper is not necessarily a good predictor of being able to drive a nail straight.

Basic training, Fort Knox

My eight weeks of basic training at Fort Knox during the chilly Kentucky winter days were filled with numerous events, ranging from lectures and films on sex education (complete with graphic pictures of diseased sex organs) to days on the firing range.

In early 1942 the armed forces had not yet developed many new weapons with which to fight the war. So we practiced firing with the old Springfield single-shot bolt-action rifle. It had quite a kick, especially for unsuspecting recruits. It knocked you back two counties and left you totally baffled in spite of the drill sergeant's explanation about adjusting the rifle sight to account for such magical forces as windage. I collected more Maggie's Drawers (a red flag indicating that the target was missed) than anybody else on the firing range. I might well have been the "champion" of that recruit class.

Most of our drill instructors were Regular Army sergeants, and many were southerners because the American armed forces drew its regulars from the most economically disadvantaged part of the country. I have especially fond memories of my platoon sergeant, a thin, tall, blond Kentuckian whose dialect and inflections remained endlessly puzzling to me, especially when he talked about the "calvary." It turned out that he was not referring to a religious experience—he was just recalling his days in the US *cavalry*.

When it was discovered that I could not drive anything and so, could not be entrusted with any truly valuable piece of equipment, such as a tank or even a truck, I was classified as a motorcycle dispatch rider (these were pre-jeep days) and sent to learn to ride the biggest Harley-Davidson then in existence. Much later this earned me a lot of respect from my teenage son, whose ultimate dream was to own a Harley-Davidson. We were taught to ride these monsters in a muddy field.

I must have done well enough. Eventually I was sent out on US 31 (then a two-lane highway) to accompany sixty-truck convoys on practice runs. Several riders were assigned to each convoy. We would stop at intersections to block off cross traffic until the entire convoy had passed, and then we would catch up with the convoy, pass it until we reached its head, and repeat our intersection duties. That often meant passing a convoy traveling at 45 mph on a cold February day with sleet nearly blinding you. Still more work for my fairy godperson!

Because part of basic training was clearly *indoctrination,* we were shown a series of War Department films entitled, *Why We Fight.* A good part of the footage was from German newsreels and captured German army films, all devoted to demonstrating the awesome power of the German war machine. These were scary all right.

Having discovered the Louisville *Courier-Journal* and its first-rate coverage of the war, I read it daily, cut out stories about the war, and posted them on the company bulletin board. This caught the attention of the training cadre and probably got me labeled as slightly nutty by my fellow recruits. I have been cutting, posting, and passing on to others ever since, as my colleagues will testify only too readily.

I also caught the attention of the training cadre because I could march in time in close order drill, I could tell my left foot from my right foot, and I could do about-face without getting my feet hopelessly entangled. With my musical training, keeping time was easy for me. Even with my minimal physical dexterity, I made up for what I otherwise lacked in early morning calisthenics with enthusiasm and diligence.

Fort Benjamin Harrison

At the end of the training cycle, when orders came for the recruits to be shipped out to regular units, no orders came for me. So it was decided that I should be retained as part of the training cadre, and I was promoted to corporal. I still have a vivid memory of sitting on my bunk, sewing corporal's stripes on my uniform shirt and blouse.

Within a few days, the next group of recruits arrived, and there I was along with my old "calvary" sergeant putting them through close order drill, and despairing about getting them to tell their right feet from their left. All this came to an end within a short time with the arrival of an order transferring me to Fort Benjamin Harrison, outside Indianapolis. Not only that, but I was to be transferred as *Private* Alfred Diamant! What had happened?

I found out subsequently from my Fort Knox company commander that the US Army began to have cold feet about all the "enemy aliens" in its ranks, just as the British government had had in 1939 about the Kitchener Camp inhabitants. Quite a few resident aliens subject to the draft had been called for service either because their number had come up in the lottery or because they had volunteered for induction as I had done right after Pearl Harbor. Apparently we were not considered sufficiently alien to be discharged from the military, but with our German passports, we were suspect enough that we should not serve in any part of the armed forces where we would ultimately become involved in frontline combat.

Again note the parallel to the British decision to place refugees in service units such as engineering and quartermaster. We were safe enough for the proverbial water carrying but not for fighting. There was also the legitimate concern about the fate of people like me if we should ever become prisoners of the German armed forces. We would bear the double stigma of being Jewish and of having fought for the enemy.

So then it came about that all "enemy aliens" serving in the Fifth Corps area were removed from combat-related units and transferred to Headquarters Company, Station Complement, Fort Benjamin Harrison. That was the origin of my transfer order.

My company commander assured me that the transfer order had been issued before my promotion had proceeded far enough through channels to reach the area headquarters, and that when it did, a correction order would eventually reach Fort Harrison. In the meantime, I had the heartbreaking task of removing my corporal's chevrons. If I did not cry, I certainly felt like doing so, in spite of my company commander's assurance about the efficiency of army channels. His confidence in the rationality of army procedures was much greater than mine, and he proved to be correct in the end.

When I arrived at Fort Harrison, I found myself joining several dozen enlisted men who had been sent there from a variety of army posts for the same reason I had been. The headquarters company to which we had been assigned furnished all sorts of services, administrative and physical, for the post command. This post command presided over a collection of specialized units, ranging from a reception center like the one I had passed through in Fort Devens, to military police battalions, a school for cooks and bakers, a school for army chaplains, and later on an early detachment of WACs (Women's Army Corps).

During my first weeks there, my life was not very pleasant. The officer and NCO (noncommissioned officer) personnel of the company were older Regular Army people who seemed to enjoy making life difficult for the enlisted personnel under their control. Our being foreigners and speaking with strange accents did not help the matter. All this seemed to pile insult on my already-injured ego.

Perhaps the most unpleasant assignment one could get at HQ (Headquarters) Company was prisoner-chasing. The military prison on the post held a small number of army prisoners convicted by court martial and serving short sentences for various infractions. There also was a large floating population of AWOLs, soldiers (especially draftees) who had decided to "go home." They were reported as AWOL (absent without leave) to civilian police or sheriffs who found them in short order and delivered them to the nearest military prison for eventual transfer to their unit for trial and sentencing. The prison population was almost without exception a foul-mouthed and sometimes violent lot. They frightened me no end.

Prisoner-chasing as an assignment meant guarding prisoners while they were outside the prison carrying out menial tasks such as garbage collection and picking up litter, all seemingly useful but really just make-work exercises. The guards were armed with shotguns and were responsible for keeping prisoners under control. It was impressed upon us (an empty threat, I am sure) that if a prisoner escaped and could not be quickly recaptured, we would be incarcerated in his place.

To make all this even more of a charade, I was never given instructions on how to use the shotgun or given a chance to practice firing it. Perhaps it was expected that every red-blooded American would know how to use a shotgun. Nobody bothered to find out that except for a little firing at Fort Knox, I had never held any sort of weapon in my hands!

Prisoner-chasers would report to the post prison at 8 a.m., take charge of their prisoners, and proceed on the appointed round of tasks. Prisoners were entitled to a mid-morning break, so back we went to the post prison. All prisoners were strip-searched before entering and again before they left, which cumulatively took at least an hour. Then it was back to work until lunchtime and the same time-consuming procedures. The routines were repeated again in the afternoon.

I wonder if an efficiency engineer ever calculated the output per man-hour to determine the cost of the whole enterprise. But then it was just make-work anyway. More importantly for me, I detested the whole assignment. I loathed the foul-mouthed atmosphere that enveloped both guards and prisoners, and I longed for the satisfaction I had felt with my tasks during my weeks at Fort Knox.

All this came to an end after about a month when the first sergeant called me into the office and showed me a copy of the corrected transfer order. In retrospect it seems that the scene was a take-off on Carl Zuckmeyer's *The Captain from Köpenick*, where an old out-of-work tailor finds a package containing a Prussian army captain's uniform, puts it on in a railway station washroom, and emerges a commanding figure who proceeds to take over the town hall, and for a while at least, leads the life of Riley.

I suppose that in the Regular Army, which had been stingy with promotions during the years between the two World Wars, a deep gulf divided enlisted personnel not only from commissioned officers but also from noncommissioned officers. Now that the corrected transfer order had transformed this foreign creature into a corporal, the first sergeant bestowed some friendly words on me for the first time.

From then on, life at Headquarters Company became much more bearable. I was taken off the prisoner-chasing roster and assigned to other duties. Eventually I was assigned to the company supply room, where I was appointed company supply sergeant and promoted to staff sergeant.

Miss Redmon enters my life

The supply room assignment turned out to be most fateful. It included the task of requesting supplies for our company from the office of the post quartermaster. I had to fill out the appropriate request forms, which had to conform to the appropriate ARs (army regulations). I then presented them to a civilian clerk, the property clerk, who would scrutinize my requests. When she found them accurate and conforming to the relevant ARs, she would authorize me to draw the supplies from the warehouse.

That crucial center of power who regulated, and at times made miserable, the lives of all supply officers and supply sergeants at Fort Harrison was Ann Redmon, or more precisely, Mary A. Redmon.

Although HQ Company contained many people with backgrounds and personal histories similar to mine, I made few close friends, and hardly any of those friendships lasted beyond the Fort Harrison days. My supply sergeant was a Hoosier from Crown Point who was a good, kindly superior. One weekend he took me home with him to Crown Point, and we spent part of a Sunday at Dunes State Park. When he was transferred, I succeeded him and was promoted to staff sergeant.

I also got along well with the first sergeant who succeeded the older Regular Army man I mentioned earlier. He was a younger wartime draftee who shared some of my interests and very importantly, offered me rides into town on my first dates with Ann.

In light of my later research interests, it is perhaps not surprising that I took readily to army administration. I considered it a challenge to puzzle out the army regulations and get the requisitions filled out correctly. I suppose that for Ann, the quality of my work overcame the handicaps of my appearance and my accent.

Ann had then, as she has sustained throughout her life, a profound regard for the quality of execution of any task that she has undertaken—from furnishing a home or planting trees to carrying out studies for the League of Women Voters or serving on a state commission examining public school financing. I was not an observant enough person in these or even later years to apprehend and appreciate fully Ann's striving for excellence.

Yet how can I explain my transformation from an average academic performer in Vienna in the 1930s to a magna cum laude degree from Indiana University in 1947? Certainly emigration, the challenge of life in a different country, and World War II all shaped me in crucial ways. Perhaps I should be "thankful" to Adolf Hitler for having forced me out of my comfortable shell. Or should the credit for this transformation be accorded to the woman whose standards and striving for excellence moved me in ways and directions I had only vaguely dreamed about?

Unexpected opportunities
I had been at Fort Harrison only a few months when I received two unexpected opportunities that changed the direction of my army career. In June all the non-citizen personnel in the company were called together and informed that under recent laws passed by Congress, all resident aliens who had served at least ninety days in the armed forces were eligible for immediate naturalization, with all requirements such as residency being waived.

Clerks from the federal district court in Indianapolis came to Fort Harrison to process the necessary papers for us. On July 15, 1942, an army truck took us to Indianapolis, and we took our oaths as citizens of the United States. It was all done in such a routine manner that it almost robbed the event of its tremendous significance.

Soon after that, my company commander called me in and pointed out that as a naturalized citizen, I had become eligible to attend Officer Candidate School and receive appointment as a commissioned officer. I believe I was the only one of the newly naturalized group singled out in this way.

It should be pointed out that in 1942, as the armed forces expanded rapidly with increasingly larger numbers of draftees called to duty, there was a severe shortage of commissioned officers to oversee training and command all the newly formed units. Unit commanders were instructed to identify promising candidates and encourage them to apply to the Officer Candidate School course, which lead to a commission as a second lieutenant. "Ninety-day wonders," they were called, for they emerged from a three-month course that was supposed to be equivalent to the four-year course at military academies.

I was terribly pleased and excited about the captain's suggestion. I proceeded to file the necessary papers, which were accompanied by strong recommendations from my company commander. Eventually I was ordered to report to the armored force Officer Candidate School (OCS) at Fort Knox on December 13, 1942. So it would be back to Fort Knox to see whether the ugly duckling of January 1942 could be transformed into an officer and gentleman by March 1943.

Daily routine at Fort Harrison

Until my departure for OCS, my life continued with its daily rounds of supply room activities. Being a dispenser of items that both officers and enlisted men wanted, I was treated well. Perhaps one episode will illustrate what the supply room business was all about.

To prevent the spread of athlete's foot infection, the army required a basin with an antiseptic solution to be placed at the entry of every shower room and replenished at least once a week. During the summer, we exhausted our supply of disinfectant, so I produced the necessary requisition to draw what I thought would be a box or bag of the chemical—one needed a tablespoonful per basin each week, and there were only four basins for the company shower rooms.

The requisition was duly approved by the quartermaster and presented to the warehouse. There was a long delay during which people scurried back and forth. Finally the warehousemen produced a barrel (the fifty-five-gallon size at least) and said, "Here's your order."

It took two of us to wrestle this monster from the warehouse to our supply room. When we opened it, the chemical fumes just about felled my poor supply room PFC (private first class). We had to put on gas masks to ladle some into a smaller container. At our rate of usage, we calculated that the barrel would surely last out the century.

When I told Ann about this adventure, with many snide remarks about the incompetence of the QMC, she coldly rejected any responsibility and blamed it all on the lazy warehousemen, who knew what opening that particular Pandora's box would mean.

With the onset of summer 1942, I began to work evenings as a projectionist in the post outdoor movie house. Our machines would be considered museum pieces today: their light came from arcs produced by carbon rods, which had to be adjusted manually from time to time. Generally I enjoyed seeing all the movies, but there was one exception, *Gone with the Wind*, which was excessively long. At the end of the summer, I moved to the indoor theater and continued to work there until I left Fort Harrison in December.

Courtship

Clearly Miss Redmon, as I called her, was a good person to work with. But beyond that, she was both interested in and well informed about art, music, and events in the world—those things that I cared so much about. There was no doubt about her absolute condemnation of fascism. She was also a lot more skeptical about the Soviet Union than I was, in a period well before we came to grasp the nature of the god that failed. Ann was, and is today, a genuine libertarian who suspects the often-good intentions of even the most benevolent dictator.

We had many conversations that strayed beyond ARs and company supplies. I noticed that she was generally eager to talk about events in Europe, an eagerness that led me to tell my company commander, only in jest, that if he wanted something from the QM not in the company's table of organization, he should let me know. I would go and tell Miss Redmon some more stories about the Blue Danube. It continues to irritate her to this day that I would have said such a thing, even in jest.

It should be apparent from my earlier chapters that my contacts with women of my own age had been very limited. My grande affaire with Gretl had come to an end, and I had had only the most casual contacts with young women in Taunton and during my few months in the army. So it is perhaps not surprising that it was Ann who took the first step. In October she invited the supply sergeants who dealt with her to a Halloween party at her aunt Mabel's house, where she was living.

As it turned out, the other invited supply sergeants were in units that had been alerted for overseas service or were restricted to the post for some other reason. So only Corporal Brophy, my supply clerk, and I attended. Ann's younger sisters, Betty and Martha, also came, as did her Mama and her cousin Ruth.

So there we were, the only two males surrounded by Redmon females. I must confess that I have very little recollection of what we did that evening, but I certainly felt that I was the recipient of a most friendly gesture, and I wanted to reciprocate this kindness.

It so happened that the next concert scheduled by the Indianapolis Symphony in early November included a guest appearance by the pianist Rudolf Serkin, who would play Beethoven's Fifth Piano Concerto. If I had had any sense of what was appropriate, I would have asked Ann whether she was interested and also free on the day of the concert.

Instead I simply purchased two tickets, marched into her office, and said, "I have two tickets and want you to go with me," or words to that effect.

Fortunately she accepted my invitation. I very much fear that if she had told me that she had a previous engagement or had pretended to have one, I would have crept away and not made another move. On such contingencies hang our lives.

I do not know what Ann expected would flow from such a conventional date. And I do not know what I expected. I certainly loved music and looked forward to the performance, but little beyond that. Although I was surely a very normal twenty-something male with regards to sexual appetites, I was also a very shy and lonely foreigner with very little experience in relationships with women.

Our encounters would probably have led to no more than a casual friendship if it had not been for what happened on our first date as we listened to Serkin playing the Beethoven concerto. As a result of the musical experience we shared, a bond developed between us. As if by magic. I believe that we both sat through it as if transfixed by an emotional upsurge that we shared without any advance warning.

From that moment on, I knew that I would not want any other companion in my life, for I had found a person with whom I could share the most profound moments of a lifetime. That I am able to articulate it now should not be dismissed as mere hindsight. It is, rather, a way of clarifying what were probably then somewhat inchoate but nevertheless very genuine feelings. If love means a bond that unites a man and a woman with regard to their profound feelings, then certainly I was in love, and I could only hope that Ann shared my feelings.

In the weeks that followed, we were together again and again. We would meet in downtown Indianapolis, I coming from Fort Harrison and Ann coming by bus from her home on the city's east side, quite a distance away. I still remember standing on the corner of Market and Pennsylvania, watching for the East Tenth Street bus or trolley. When I saw Ann alighting, I always admired her shapely ankles silhouetted against the vehicle from which she descended.

The more often we went out together, the more I discovered aspects of her to admire, especially her eyes, round and clear and looking at me (not necessarily on the very first date) in a way that made me feel like melting away. She seemed to become more lovely and desirable with each successive date, and all in a period of no more than six weeks, from early November until December 13 when I left for Fort Knox.

Our dates included a range of events, from a performance of the *Messiah* to the Ice Capades at the Indianapolis Coliseum. I mention the latter occasion not so much from personal recollection but from Ann's recounting, with a mischievous twinkle, that I tried very tentatively to kiss her during one of the taxi rides, but I got no further than planting what she called a very chaste kiss on the top of her head!

A somewhat unusual date was on Thanksgiving Day, which during the war was a working day in the army. HQ Company had mounted a turkey dinner with all the trimmings, to which we were allowed to invite guests. There was even a printed program with the menu and a list of the participants and their guests. I picked up Ann from her office and walked her back there after the meal when everybody returned to work.

December 13 arrived with snow on the ground. Ann came over to HQ Company to see me off. She walked with me to catch the bus that would start me on my way to becoming, or so I hoped, an officer and a gentleman in the army of the United States. I saw OCS as still another phase in my great adventure in the US Army and my determination to play a significant part in the war against the fascist dictatorships.

In recounting our wartime romance, I have quite unintentionally failed to reflect on what must seem to others to be profound differences in our backgrounds—ethnic, religious, socioeconomic, and so on. However, our different backgrounds were never an issue in our relationship, brief as it was, though concentrated in a very few weeks. Although questions of marriage did not arise at any time during that period, I felt profoundly at ease in our relationship.

If I had then been asked whether I could foresee a lifelong bond between us, I would have responded affirmatively without hesitation. Why? I will not essay an answer, but I will simply point to the record of half a century. During those fifty years, we have created a union that surely reflects a profound convergence of values, temperaments (mostly?), positions on political, economic, and social issues, and most significantly, religion. Our convergence on religious matters meant an abandonment of my familial religious traditions, but it came to be a vital center of our lives and of our children's lives.

Officer Candidate School, Fort Knox

When I applied to OCS, I had indicated QM as my first choice for officer training, thinking that I was well prepared for such work and recalling my rather inglorious days in armored force basic training. But they saw only my high mechanical aptitude test scores and my Fort Knox training, and they decided against my first preference. I believe that I would have been of more use to the QM corps, but in the end my armored force officer career was mercifully short, and I spent the rest of my active duty with the Military Intelligence Service.

After fifty years it is impossible to give more than a cursory account of the thirteen weeks of officer training. It consisted mostly of classroom work in subjects ranging from mess management to military tactics and strategy. There was also a goodly amount of close order drill to give future officers a chance to learn how to command troops in formation.

The classroom work was highly formalized lecturing with frequent tests, in which one was required to reproduce the information previously provided. The procedure reflected the often-ridiculed nature of the armed forces: for everything there is a right way and an army way. On the exams the only correct answers were those of the latter kind.

I still remember the utter fury of a member of my squad who ran head-on into this nightmare. He was a GM factory-trained mechanic from Elizabeth, New Jersey, who had a well-paying job in an automobile dealership. Now he was confronted with the OCS course in automotive maintenance, and he tended to answer test questions in the right way based on his GM training. His result: grades in the 70s or below. On the other hand, I had no independent knowledge of the internal combustion engine, and I answered the questions the army way. My result: grades in the 90s.

My friend saw this discrepancy of grades, and knowing full well that I could not even find the slot in which to put the key to start an engine, he erupted in anger and cursed a blue streak in his inimitable New Jersey patois, with more four-letter words than I had ever heard even after a full year in the army. I began to realize that it was one of my talents to learn things from a book and give the desired answer without fail, a useful skill in some circumstances, especially in highly structured bureaucratic organizations. So I sailed through that part of OCS training with the proverbial flying colors!

However, I came close to being dropped from the OCS course for my shortcomings in close order drill. This was not because I failed to master all the mindless formalities of that regimen, but because the troops I commanded, my fellow OCS candidates, could not understand my heavily accented commands. There was also the problem that under tension my voice tends to rise into higher registers, thus becoming even more difficult to comprehend.

The tactical officer took a few of us aside to tell us bluntly that we would be washed out of the course in short order if we did not improve our performance on the drill field. So I and my comrades in misery took ourselves out to the drill field on Saturday after inspection and for a good part of Sunday, and there we practiced projecting our voices and issuing and executing commands. The extra effort paid off, for we all graduated in good order.

What private life I had consisted of writing to Ann frequently, nearly every day according to her recollection. She preserved those letters, as well as later correspondence, but most of it was destroyed under circumstances that I leave to her to recount, simply reciting several mea culpa mantras. I also observed Valentine's Day with a gift of handkerchiefs.

Freddy
Officer Candidate School
Fort Knox, 1943

As graduation day, March 13, 1943, grew closer, our excitement mounted. Every day we survived without being washed out brought us closer to our gold bars. Finally the day came to be measured for uniforms, a definite sign that we had made it.

Ann says I urged her to attend the graduation exercises, which were scheduled for a Saturday morning. I guess my invitation became persistent enough, because Ann consented to attend and to pin the second lieutenant bars on my uniform. She arranged to be driven to the exercises by Dorothy and Sherman Stevens, her cousins who lived in Jeffersonville, Indiana, up across the Ohio River from Louisville and Fort Knox.

Saturday was a clear, pleasant day, and the ceremonies went smoothly. Afterwards the Stevenses drove Ann and me to their house, where I met Aunt Bertha (Dorothy's mother) and the Stevens children. We stayed there overnight. Ann had to return to work at Fort Harrison on Monday morning, so she planned to take the train back to Indianapolis on Sunday afternoon. What I would be doing was less clear.

When the graduation orders for my class appeared, we learned that most of us had been assigned to the 8th Armored Division at Camp (now Fort) Polk, Louisiana, a training division that could take in 12,000 draftees for a basic training cycle. We were granted a ten days delay en route and ordered to report in Louisiana on March 24.

So on that Saturday, I knew where I had to be in ten days time, but I had no clear notion of what I would be doing in the meantime. I thought vaguely about visiting the Diamonds and my other friends in Taunton, but with Ann scheduled to return to Indianapolis on Sunday, I decided I would go with her.

Memories are very tricky. Much of what we remember is not the original event but mostly the later retellings, suitably embellished, corrected, or even bowdlerized. This is especially true if the later retelling is not based on one's own recollection but on that of another person. Under these conditions, we can never really be sure that we are recalling the events exactly as they happened. With that said, I will go on with my narrative.

About halfway to Indianapolis, probably near Columbus, a significance that escaped me at that time, I ventured very timidly to say, "I would like to get married."

Ann responded, "Do you have anybody in mind?"

I must have indicated that she was, indeed, the object of these intentions, for we then argued the pros and cons of immediate marriage versus waiting for the end of the war.

In any case, Ann indicated that she needed some time to think it over. I agreed that she should take all the time she needed, provided she came to closure by the time we reached Indianapolis!!

Marriage

Ann consented to marry me—and right away. This was the beginning of a most hectic ten-day period, which included Indiana's three-day waiting period for blood tests, finding an apartment, buying rings, getting our marriage license, engaging a church and minister, and announcing our plans to Ann's family.

I remember the trance-like quality of these ten days. Although I clearly participated in all these activities, there was also an air of unreality in which it was all suffused.

In all this, as in much of our later life, Ann was the realist. Unlike most newly married soldiers' wives, she kept her well-paying job. And she was the supreme realist in that she resisted my sexual advances, even in the last days before our marriage. She was true to her basic values, and she was determined to act on them, the highest form of realism.

One of the immediate questions was that of the marriage ceremony. I probably had vague thoughts about a civil ceremony rather than one in a synagogue. However, Ann's profound roots in Protestantism gave her no other thought but the Methodist Church she attended. It was probably a clear sign of my drift away from institutional Judaism that the church wedding made me only minimally uncomfortable. One has to have been a Jew growing up under the oppressive Austrian Roman Catholic Church-state union to understand how a Christian ceremony of any kind would cause discomfort.

The unexpected appearance of Ann's family at our wedding on that March 18, 1943, turned what was intended to be a simple ceremony into a festive and especially joyous occasion. Nine days later when I departed for Camp Polk, my own feelings were those of fulfillment. I was no longer a lone individual in a strange country. There were now two of us who seemed to think and feel in accord about the most basic values, in spite of our differences in native language, religion, ethnicity, and family background.

At the time of our marriage, the New Testament passage "I was a stranger and you took me in" was not anywhere in my realm of understanding. If anything, Jews in most of Europe were indeed strangers, and the hostility of the native people was unending and often violent. Yet I came to experience the reality of this central Christian tenet when members of Ann's family—her Mama, her older sister, Mae, and her younger sisters, Betty and Martha—came to our wedding.

I experienced it when Ann and I visited at her Mama's house the following Sunday, and I met most of the other family members living in and around Hope. Not an eyebrow was raised about the strange-sounding creature (although in a genuine US Army uniform) who had become a member of the Redmon family.

Year after year, in annual family gatherings, at weddings, high school graduations, and other occasions, I was simply another member of the clan. Even if I could not speak with authority about crops and fertilizers, I could talk about politics, something dear to just about all Hoosiers. I had eagerly married Ann. That I would also marry a whole new family (now that mine was scattered by emigration or murdered in the Holocaust) was truly a joyful and unexpected premium in my life.

Camp Polk

I spent six months at Camp Polk with the 8th Armored Division. This was probably the least satisfactory segment of my army life, partly because I was clearly a square peg in the round hole of an armored division, and partly because I was totally unprepared for the near-tropical climate of Louisiana.

What made it even more unsatisfactory was my separation from Ann, to whom I was linked only by correspondence and by my extravagant gesture of having an Indianapolis florist deliver a dozen red roses to her on the eighteenth day of each month! I suppose I took the separation to be an inevitable part of our wartime existence. But I was helped in part by my continued strong personal commitment to the war against Hitler.

Clearly I was not much use to the tank and truck companies of the division. So after a while I was sent to the division's medical battalion to teach the fledgling corpsmen such vital subjects as close order drill and map reading. I probably should not read too much into this, my first encounter with teaching. Yet there was a sense in which I welcomed this chance to do something that related to teaching, which I had been proclaiming for years was my desired lifework.

From the very first days of our marriage, Ann and I had talked about what we wanted to do after the war. In all the years since her graduation from high school, Ann had held fast to her determination to continue her education. By contrast I was much less sure about my own postwar goals. In good part, my indecisiveness was the result of my unfamiliarity with the country's educational system. But Ann persisted in asking me, "What would you want to do *best?*" to which I could only answer truthfully, "Study and teach history."

What turned this from a mere wish into reality was the GI Bill of Rights, which offered veterans as much as four years of post-secondary education with all expenses paid and a living allowance geared to family status. Perhaps not just then at Camp Polk, but throughout the rest of the war, it was Ann who helped firm up my desire and ultimately my determination to devote my life to study and teaching. As a result when my participation in the war came to an end in early 1945, we lost no time in making contact with Indiana University to take the first steps in a direction that would determine not just the next four years, but the rest of our lives.

My military duties at Camp Polk were humdrum but tolerable. On the other hand, physical conditions were downright miserable—from hot, poorly ventilated living quarters to attacks by forms of life I had not even imagined. Chiggers were the persistent, itch-inflicting enemies of anyone who insisted on spending days on end in the piney woods of Louisiana.

I had only two breaks from this daily routine of heat and bugs. Ann's two youngest brothers, George and Roy, had been called into federal service with the Indiana National Guard in 1941 and were stationed at a camp nearby. I arranged to meet them on a Sunday afternoon. We spent several hours together. It was an easy and comfortable get-together just as it had been

Freddy with Roy (left)
& George (right)
Alexandria, Louisiana
May 31, 1943

with all the other Redmons. They embraced me without question or reservation. There has never been a single member of that family, including in-laws, who has treated me otherwise.

The other break came later in July, with my only home leave during my Camp Polk days. When I reached Indianapolis, it was quite hot there as well. So I wanted only to sit quietly in the backyard of the little house where we had rented an apartment. Ann had other ideas, to which I objected with much griping. In the end I consented, and I was rewarded with the rural charms of southern Indiana.

Ann had arranged for a long weekend in a cabin at the Abe Martin Lodge in Brown County State Park near Nashville, Indiana, and an exposure to the folk wisdom of Abe Martin. We had a few glorious days of hiking and swimming, an evening of square dancing, and even a visit from some of the Redmon family with their small children. Our harmony during these days was unbroken. I continued to luxuriate in the warmth and security of our marriage.

Camp Ritchie

During the summer of 1943, war planners must have decided that there would eventually be a need for people with a command of major European languages when Allied troops invaded the European continent to conquer Germany. Early in the fall I received secret orders to report to the Military Intelligence Service training center at what the secret part of the order identified as Camp Ritchie, Maryland, for training as an interrogator of prisoners of war. With that began the last and most interesting and satisfying phase of my army life.

Camp Ritchie's pleasures were many. Indeed part of Camp Ritchie is now Camp David, and the location of the camp in Maryland's Catoctin Mountains appealed to me just as much as it does to the presidents who have spent much of their "free" time at Camp David.

One particularly memorable feature of Camp Ritchie was the food in the officers' mess. It was prepared by carefully selected Italian POW cooks, so it featured antipasto and other delights of Italian cooking. What a contrast all this was to Camp Polk, its heat, its chiggers, and the general dull routines of army duty.

The three-month course that was to train me as an interrogator of prisoners of war (IPW) was a fascinating exposure to the organization and functioning of the armed forces of the Third Reich. For the first time, I felt that I was being taught something truly *useful*, and that I was being prepared to make a genuine contribution to the conduct of the war. There was also the pleasure of working with many highly educated people who had backgrounds similar to mine. Many had been rescued from inane army duties and were now put to work in a more meaningful way given their background and past training.

This group included Karl Mautner, a poor relation of a prominent Austrian family. Karl became my good friend and airborne buddy and has remained so to this day. He is a devout Roman Catholic. Though he was not married, he wanted very much to be. However, he demanded not only love, but also full religious compatibility from his intended spouse. He did not find this ideal mate until after the war. The news of his marriage showed up promptly in Karl's Christmas card, which reflected his profession of animal photography. Soon successive Mautner children replaced the dachshund and terriers on Karl's Christmas cards.

In October the Catoctin Mountains are decked out in their best fall foliage colors. Ann visited me one weekend, which we treasured for every minute. In a rather comic way, while dining at a local restaurant, we found we were the only couple conversing in English. It seemed that the other nonnative-born GIs from Ritchie had equally nonnative-born spouses or girlfriends, and that I was the only Ritchie soldier with a native-born American wife! All this linguistic activity made rather a joke of the effort to keep secret what was going on at Camp Ritchie, what with all these GIs speaking heavily accented English or conversing in a variety of European languages.

Both Ann and I thoroughly enjoyed our Catoctin Mountains weekend. Yet we also found great satisfaction in our work and were prepared to continue this arrangement as long as the war required it of us.

My training course was scheduled to end shortly before Christmas, but early in December my graduating class was alerted for overseas movement. It was no great surprise to us. We saw our work and training as important for the attack on Hitler's Europe, for which only the date needed to be fixed.

We were given two weeks of home leave. I departed happily for Indianapolis, looking forward to my first Christmas and New Year's celebration with Ann. I can remember little if anything from these days except that well before December 31, the scheduled end of my leave, I was ordered back to Camp Ritchie.

Once we got back to Camp Ritchie, we found ourselves playing the old army game of hurry-up-and-wait. I called Ann to tell her that there would be no overseas movement anytime soon and urged her to come for another visit. She took an overnight train, traveling in mid-winter. We spent a long weekend at Waynesboro, Pennsylvania, where we discovered that on Sunday evenings, the only entertainment permitted by the then Pennsylvania blue laws was church service, so we added a Sunday evening service to the morning service we had attended.

We woke up Monday morning in a winter wonderland, with enough snow on the ground to threaten the bus service to Harrisburg, where Ann was to catch the train. Fortunately she made it home safely.

It would be another year before we would see each other again. At that time I would get my first glimpse of Steven, who was born on October 1, while I was still in a hospital in England.

Parachute training

I was in Europe all of 1944. I sailed from New York with the Military Intelligence Service (MIS) detachment in January and returned home on December 31, sailing from Swansea. I spent the year in Europe involved in preparations for D-day, participating in the D-day invasion, and suffering the consequences of my participation in the assault—first in a German hospital and then for the rest of the year in American army hospitals. The story of that year deserves to be told in full, but in some other place.

The MIS detachment of interrogator of prisoners of war specialists, photo interpreters, and order of battle specialists landed in England in early February. Nobody seemed to know what to do with us. When that happens, the army decides that further training is necessary, so we were sent to school.

The various intelligence short courses were conducted in London. We were housed in comfortable hotels, and the central London officers' mess was in the Grosvenor Hotel on Park Lane. I feasted on British newspapers and magazines, having begun my career of clipping stories for Ann and sending them back with my letters and theater programs.

Soon after we arrived in England, our detachment of intelligence specialists was visited by recruiters from the airborne division. They were seeking volunteers to take parachute training, be rated as parachutists, and accompany the airborne troops on their D-day action. This was a chance to practice our trade in quite extraordinary conditions. How we would do this in the heat and confusion of an airdrop, nobody had figured out.

Without hesitation, I stepped forward. It seems that I persuaded Karl Mautner to come along. I "volunteered him," as he put it later.

I did not tell Ann what I had done until after I had successfully completed the training course, including five practice jumps over an airfield in England, and received my parachute rating. With the rating went hazard pay of an extra $100 per month, not a small amount in those days. Ann saved it all and used it to pay for her pregnancy and delivery.

Freddy (far right)
Receiving his Parachute Wings
Leicester, England, 1944

Without ever saying so, Ann succeeded in indicating that she saw this action of mine as evidence that I had not fully grasped the responsibilities I had assumed, especially when she was expecting our first child.

Ann had hoped to be able to work during most of the months of pregnancy and then to return to work soon after delivery. However, her hopes were totally thwarted by her continued sickness during pregnancy and the medical consequences of a most difficult and long, drawn out delivery. She was incapacitated for weeks on end after giving birth.

Volunteering for parachute training might seem the epitome of a macho attitude. Yet anybody who knew me then and has known me since will testify that physical bravery and male strutting are not part of my makeup. I did it because I considered the war to be a personal responsibility to which everything else was subordinated. At the same time I must admit that I did not understand the anxiety it would cause Ann, especially given the difficulties she experienced because of the pregnancy.

After resigning her job at Fort Harrison, Ann moved to Hope to live with her Mama and younger sisters. That move essentially isolated her in a small town of 1,100 inhabitants, which did not even have a movie theater. Ann did not have an automobile to get to Columbus or Indianapolis. All this time I was in London, then in Leicester and Nottingham, and then later in an army rehabilitation hospital near Birmingham as an ambulatory patient. The hospital was looked after by the Red Cross, which provided tickets and transportation to concerts in Birmingham and to the Shakespeare Festival in Stratford.

When the story of my D-day participation, POW experience, and long hospital stay became known, there were many expressions of "Poor Freddy!" To these Ann would retort indignantly, and rightly, "What about 'Poor Ann' stuck here in Hope, Indiana?"

It was a complaint well taken. I can only respond that I tried to share my experiences with her through letters, newspapers, and programs of various events I was able to attend. Ann had been most insistent that she did not want children, and I had promised to do my part. Obviously I had failed her. The resultant pain, suffering, and discomfort were visited upon her, the female, while I, the male, pursued my macho activities with less than proper concern for our joint responsibilities.

D-day

After completion of parachute school in late March, those of us in the MIS contingent enjoyed a truly bucolic interlude before receiving our D-day assignments. Our unit was stationed in the lovely Cotswold town of Broadway in Worcestershire, where we were quartered in private homes.

My D-day assignment took me to the 508th Parachute Infantry Regiment of the 82nd Airborne Division, then stationed near Nottingham. I was placed in command of a six-person interrogation team, two officers and four enlisted men. Some of us were parachutists; the others were to come in with the glider elements of the division. After seeing some of the Normandy battle sites, I think jumping was safer than entrusting one's life to the overgrown cigar boxes called gliders.

The official war history of the Normandy airborne landings indicates that although the 101st Airborne Division was able to execute its landings fairly successfully, bringing its units down pretty much where planned, the units of the 82nd Airborne Division were scattered far and wide. Our plane dropped its troops nearly *twenty miles* from the designated drop zone, far from any element of the division.

Of the eighteen men in our plane, thirteen were killed soon after landing, four were taken prisoner, and only one man (the T-5 of my interrogation team) escaped the Germans entirely. He was hidden by a French farmer and led back to American lines by the French underground. The four who were taken prisoner were not in German hands for long. After the Allied forces sealed off the Normandy peninsula, the Germans seemed to abandon their American prisoners as they retreated north toward Cherbourg.

Not only did we land far from any other group of Americans, we also landed far apart from each other. I landed about 3 a.m. and I did not see any other Americans, only German patrols out combing the countryside for us. They seemed to see no need to maintain security, which made it possible for me to hide easily from them while it was dark. But when daylight came, the cat-and-mouse game was over. A German patrol flushed me out from behind a hedgerow, and I was shot and captured.

From then until my early release from the army in April 1945, I lived in a variety of hospitals. My medical history also deserves a separate account. Here it is enough to say that I suffered a lumbar fracture as a result of the bullet that entered my body in front but did not penetrate completely. The bullet lodged in some soft tissue where it remains to this day.

That the bullet traversed my body without injuring an internal organ amazed the doctors greatly. Even more so did the x-rays of my lumbar spine, which showed a fracture of the third lumbar vertebra with the bullet having missed the spinal cord by the smallest distance imaginable. That was as much a miracle as my escaping arrest in Vienna during *Kristallnacht*. I am glad that fairy godpersons are prepared to work overtime for me.

Back to England

I was a prisoner in a German field hospital along with 150 other GIs for ten days. The Germans abandoned the hospital after evacuating their own wounded and personnel to Cherbourg, where they all were eventually taken prisoner at the successful end of the Normandy campaign. We were liberated by the advancing American forces and taken back to hospitals in England. I was in a body cast for six months, but ambulatory most of the time.

Once in England, I was able to write Ann my first post-D-Day letter, telling her as much as I could and trying to reassure her about my condition: I was not in pain, I could walk around and eat normally, and the doctors expected to send me back to duty before long.

I hoped fervently that my letter would reach Ann before she got one of those infamous War Department telegrams with its supposedly comforting, but actually very ominous, phrases about injuries and the good care being given to the wounded warrior! I succeeded in that, so Ann was able to face the local Western Union man with the assurance that she had already heard from me.

After several weeks at a general hospital, I was transferred to a rehabilitation hospital. I assume the expectation was that I would be rehabilitated through various therapies and then sent back to my unit on the continent, where Patton was pushing his tank columns across France. But autumn came, the Allied armies reached the Rhine, the airborne assault on Holland failed, and I was still in rehabilitation.

Eventually the medical people decided that I could not be returned to my regular duties but could perform the limited service duties of a desk jockey. At the same time, army hospitals in England were filling up with war casualties, so a decision was made to return home those for whom continued hospitalization did not seem to promise continued improvement. In early December I received orders for return to the ZI (zone of the interior) for final disposition.

Home Again

Once again I crossed the Atlantic in mid-winter and suffered from seasickness every inch of the way. I was sent to an army hospital in Louisville and immediately given thirty days of home leave, followed by another leave in short order. Quite obviously the army had little use for me. I offered to return to Europe to assist during the German occupation, but my offer was not taken up.

On paper I was a first lieutenant infantry fit for only limited service. By early 1945 the army apparently had quite a number of people like me. I was ordered to appear before a medical board, which retired me for "combat incurred disability." This entitled me to a pension of eighty percent of my pay at retirement, which I have continued to receive to this day.

For most of my extended home leaves, I moved in with Ann, Steve, Mama, and Martha in their small house in Hope. However, for my first leave the three of us had the run of the lovely old Bartholomew County farmhouse that belonged to Stanley and Ruth Baker. Ruth had gone to visit her sister for a month, so Ann was cooking and keeping house for Stanley, who continued with his job at Cummins Engine Company. We had the house to ourselves for most of the day. It was a generous gesture on the part of the Bakers.

Ann and I had our longest uninterrupted period together in the nearly two years of our marriage. The Baker house was situated in the middle of fields with woods on one side of the property. It was the most peaceful, serene setting I could imagine. It was wonderful to share it as a family! I finally had an opportunity to learn what it means to bring up a child, a novelty for an only child like me.

There was the additional pleasure of a piano in the house, and before long I accompanied Stanley's fine baritone in a variety of vocal music. We even recorded some of our joint efforts, including Figaro's "Non piu andrai" aria, which ends the first act of Mozart's *The Marriage of Figaro*.

Even before I learned that I would be discharged, Ann and I resumed our deliberations about our postwar plans. I had gone to technical school in Vienna and worked in textile mills not because that was what I desired to do, but because the career to which I aspired was closed to me.

Yet I doubt whether I would have pursued my dream of university studies if it had not been for Ann's steadfast urging that if studying history was what I wanted to do most, then I should go and study history. Financially this would be feasible. I could count on my army pension check and the GI Bill that was now available to me. I had served long enough to complete my first academic degree.

I felt that Ann's own ambitions would be fulfilled, at least in some form, if she could share an academic life and experiences with me. I did not fully comprehend the depth of her devotion and determination until years later, when I observed how many academic careers were cut short when a wife could no longer suffer the deprivations of graduate student existence or maintain sympathy with academic intellectual pursuits.

It was Ann who made the contacts that led to our visiting Bloomington to talk to Wendell Wright, then dean of the Junior Division. I was one of the first veterans to use the GI Bill, so I was something of a novelty in the wartime university, which then had six thousand female students and a number of army training programs.

I was allowed advanced credits for my foreign language competence (German), for my officer status (ROTC credits), and from my Vienna *Gymnasium* credentials. What was truly overwhelming to me was the friendliness and personal concern of all the Indiana University officials with whom I dealt.

I was admitted as a freshman and started academic work in June 1945 in the second summer session. In my first-year courses in history and government, I again encountered people who took a profound intellectual and personal interest in me and my studies. F. Lee Beens and John Stoner remained my friends for the rest of their lives.

Yet in spite of all this solicitous attention, I was totally petrified about the academic work that confronted me. I told Ann again and again that I would probably fail all my courses or at best would eke out grades of C. She believed me implicitly at first, but later threatened to strangle me when I completed the AB degree in two years, summa cum laude! I had started down a road from which I was not to be deterred, though there were formidable hurdles yet to overcome.

Of the two questions asked us again and again, one has now been answered. We have told how and where we met. We have suggested in our separate ways what this encounter was like, and the course it took in the midst of World War II. We have described the values and interests we shared, and how we thus felt encouraged to marry and look forward to a life together after the war. I have also described how my postwar career choice was made and demonstrated the harmony of our ideas about our future life.

The second question will be more difficult to answer. What has sustained that initial harmony over half a century, in spite of the *disharmony* in our backgrounds, origins, religions, and so forth? A wartime romance might well produce the proverbial rosy glow for a while, but what about the dissimilarities that must eventually arise during the routine of daily life and in making crucial decisions about career, child-rearing, and religion, not to mention politics and the day-to-day allocation of the often quite meager academic salary?

Would not these realities dispel the rosy glow quickly and lead to disagreement, conflict, and eventual breakup? For us they did not, but why they did not is less easily answered. Even as we write this, we are not sure that we will be able to produce answers that will be coherent and persuasive to ourselves and to our readers.

Part III

Our Life Together:
Ann's Story

Ann writing her memoirs
Treasure Cay, Abaco Island
The Bahamas, 1988

Chapter 5

Bloomington & New Haven

(1945-1950)

With Freddy retiring from the army, our life together stretched out before us full of possibilities. We resumed our discussions about the future. Freddy had long ago confided to me that what he wanted most to do in life was teach history. He had not changed his mind about this, but he was extremely doubtful whether he should or even could do it. I set about making plans and finding out how best to implement them.

Bloomington, Indiana (1945)

First we went to see my friend and teacher Otto Hughes, who was now the principal of Columbus High School. Life has so many coincidences! Just at that time Mr. Hughes was considering the position of principal of Indiana University's School of Education's experimental school. We had gone to see him at a most opportune time, for he was planning a trip to Indiana University to talk to the dean of the School of Education. He arranged for us to go with him, so that Freddy could talk to the people at the Indiana University admissions office.

As it turned out, arranging for Freddy's admission to Indiana University went smoothly. Everyone there was so friendly, so helpful, and so welcoming in every way. What was difficult was finding a place to live, and then getting us and our belongings moved into it. We had to wait until Freddy's discharge papers were processed before we could know just how we stood financially. I had of course been saving money. In fact we both thought we were unbelievably rich, for we had about $2,000! Even so, my experiences had taught me to be careful.

About this time Betty became engaged to Harold Hustedt, whom she had met at the naval ordnance plant. They were planning a quiet wedding at a Methodist church in Indianapolis. Betty wanted me to go to Indianapolis to shop with her for clothes for the wedding. I left Steve with Mother, along with bottles of formula from the doctor, who thought Steve should have something in addition to my milk.

Betty and I spent a long day shopping and with good success. When I arrived home, however, Mother was greatly upset. Steve had eaten nothing during the sixteen hours I was away. He had not cried or complained; he just had not eaten. He was fine and very glad to see his mama and be fed her milk. But his grandmother declared she absolutely would not keep him again. So from then until we fed him from spoon and glass, Steve and I were not apart for long periods of time.

This situation put quite a strain on our plans to move to Bloomington. Freddy was absolutely petrified at the thought of going alone to look for a place to live. Yet carrying Steve around was a real burden for both of us. It was our good fortune that we went into a furniture store in Bloomington to ask whether they had any baby strollers.

The salesman stared at us. The strangest look came over his face as he said, "I haven't had anything of the kind for more than five years. Just this minute, I was unpacking one of two that I received less than an hour ago."

We went to the back of the store to look at the stroller. There were still bits of packing on it, but I set Steve down into it and he liked it, too. No one can know how happy we were, or how lucky we felt. The stroller was heaven-sent.

Steve
Hope, Indiana, 1945

The salesman must have had friends or relatives waiting for a stroller, for he was reluctant to sell it to us. But Freddy was still in uniform and we were so radiant over our find that I guess he could not refuse. So we went back to Hope in the little jitney bus carrying Steve's first brand new piece of equipment bought by both his parents.

504 South Washington Street

We almost despaired at finding a place to live. Once again we were fortunate. We were able to rent the main floor of a nice house on South Washington Street. The house belonged to Mrs. Hattery, a widow who was going to stay with her daughter for three months while her daughter's husband was away. The daughter had one child and was expecting another, so Mrs. Hattery would be needed there for an extended time. We felt remarkably lucky!

Freddy, Steve, & Ann
South Washington Street
Bloomington, 1945

Mrs. Hattery was a member of one of those families (we have come to know several) who moved to Bloomington so that their children could attend university while living at home. Two of her sisters were just then retiring and returning to Bloomington to live. Both became good and helpful friends to us. Mr. Hattery had been in the construction business (we can still point out houses in Bloomington that he built). During the Depression years when he would otherwise have been idle, these two sisters commissioned him to build houses for them for their retirement years.

After Mr. Hattery's death, Alice Hattery divided her house into two apartments. She lived in the one on the main floor and rented the one above to two women, one a high school Latin teacher and the other a bookkeeper for the local Dodge-Plymouth dealer. Mrs. Hattery was a little doubtful about renting to us because of Steve. She was afraid that he would bother the older of the two women, Dora Oliphant (the bookkeeper). But in fact, the opposite was true.

Dora became Steve's great love. His very first words were "See Dora," meaning that he wanted to go to see Dora. She adored him, petted him, and fed him bits of Hershey bars. (He had never had candy from me!) If he were sick, injured, or in need of comfort, she could always soothe him. We remained friends with Dora all her life. We are still friends with Alene Caplinger, who later married and moved to Columbus, Indiana.

Establishing a family life

It is Freddy's task to write about the great friendliness and many kindnesses of so many people at Indiana University and mine to relate the more prosaic details of establishing a family life. Like the university, the Bloomington community welcomed us with open arms. From our earliest days there, Freddy and I have always thought of Bloomington as a wonderful place to live.

In spite of physical problems and the wartime dearth of goods and services, our first year in Bloomington was an almost idyllically happy one. It was such a peaceful place. Freddy and I needed that stability and slow pace to establish the roots of our marriage. We enjoyed doing so many things together, such as attending lectures, hearing good music, and seeing good films.

There were many material things we needed, but neither of us wanted to complain. One need was laundry facilities. We had no washing machine, and laundry services were limited because of a lack of workers. Though Steve was a most superior child, we still had diapers to wash nearly every day. Because I had to wash them in tepid suds, I also boiled them for sanitary reasons. The basement at Mrs. Hattery's house was excellent, and the copper boiler, fixed laundry tubs, hot water tank, and furnace it contained were the best. Even so, wringing out sheets and towels was difficult, so I had to enlist Freddy's help.

Camp Kitchener and the army had been good teachers for someone who had grown up seldom having to do anything for himself. In Europe there had always been a supply of household service people. There had been a smaller supply in the United States, but they were well nigh nonexistent during this war.

In fact these years were a turning point for American women. They entered the factories in great numbers and remained there—never paid as well as men, and seldom attaining supervisory positions. But they performed their jobs well and demonstrated diverse abilities, and the workforce grew to need them. Unfortunately women are still fighting for equality, both legal and actual, in the workplace.

Laundry became less of a problem for us when very early on the local Home Laundry agreed to do our flat work. That lightened my workload enormously. I was learning more about shopping for food and cooking nutritious, tasty meals economically. Over the years I have been helped greatly by a legion of grocers and butchers.

Even when everyone else began to shop only at supermarkets, I continued to seek out the home-owned markets. In those early days, they could usually come up with an unusual small cut of meat or a different fruit or vegetable and suggest ways of cooking and serving it. I also became adept at rerunning leftovers. It was all an enjoyable game for me.

Just as it was when our two neighbor women asked me if I would cook their dinner, too. If I would simply make enough for them, they would bring their dishes down and take the food upstairs to eat in their own quarters. They would be happy just to have their dinner planned and cooked. So that was what I did for the remainder of our time in Mrs. Hattery's house. The money they paid me pretty well covered the cost of our food.

Up until that time, desserts had never been a part of my menu planning. At home dessert had been a rare thing. In our large family, cakes, pies, and cookies were never prepared in a routine fashion, and they always disappeared quickly. However, this husband of mine did not feel that a meal was complete unless we had dessert. When I had not prepared one, Freddy went to a little sweet shop just back of us, which existed by the patronage of students from the high school across the street from it. He brought back the thickest, most luscious milkshakes ever created, and we greedily drank them.

I suppose I should not have been surprised that I gained weight. But I was shocked when I did. After all, I had been admonished and stuffed for years to no effect, and now here I was gaining weight! It was amusing in an ironic way.

We were both very active. We walked everywhere and never even considered buying a car. Steve's stroller had a bit of space behind the seat where we stowed purchases. Most stores were nearby on the Square or on Kirkwood (the street connecting the Square and the university). There was a small jitney bus that traveled through Brown County to Columbus, which was adequate though not fast or particularly comfortable. That we both gained weight, I attribute not to a lack of exercise, but to our peaceful, happy existence after a critical and stressful year.

Of course, there were some flies in the ointment. Aren't there always? One problem was my health. I continued to have sciatic pain in my right hip and leg. It had begun to affect my back as well since I favored my painful hip when standing and walking. I consulted a female doctor. I suppose she was in Bloomington and available because she was female and not subject to the draft.

She seemed far less interested in my pain than my weight. She lectured me severely about gaining weight. She also fitted me with a diaphragm for birth control and gave me a better understanding of the whole physical process of conception than I had ever had before. After completing these projects, she sent me to Indianapolis to an orthopedic specialist.

The specialist was overworked and not very interested in a complaining woman with pain. After examining me, he determined that my hip had not returned to normal position after childbirth. He sent me to be fitted with a corrective corset. How I hated wearing it! But I did wear it because it relieved the pain quite a lot. Freddy called it my armored plate. The whole back was a series of steel stays secured in place like a Victorian corset by laces.

In it, I could not bend, but I became very good at kneeling! There was another disconcerting aftermath which was never medically explained: I fainted fairly often and for no discernible reason. Both these nuisances disappeared after Alice was born, but that did not happen until 1952.

Another problem during this peaceful happy time was that Freddy was very tense and uneasy about his courses and his performance as a student. Usually he would vomit his breakfast before an exam and go to take it looking as if he were facing the guillotine. When he returned, he would moan and groan until I would start to believe him and wonder if it had been wise to start this enterprise. But then invariably he would come home with an A!

It was years later and after I came to know Liesl and Oscar Diamant that I grew to understand some of Freddy's doubts and fears about his ability to succeed at what he wanted to do. However, in 1945 in Bloomington, I had no doubts about his abilities. From those first days at Fort Harrison when he had presented those perfectly prepared requisitions to me, through his schooling in OCS and the stream of well-written letters I had received from him, I *knew* he had great intelligence and mental capacity.

By attending university, Freddy was doing exactly what I had always wanted to do. I have always considered myself an equal partner in his learning process. Is that the answer to our years of happy marriage? We both always have loved learning; we still do. And we both have given much of our lives to those students of his who loved learning, too. In that way, we have always acted as one.

One of Freddy's courses was in English composition. It was a course that he greatly needed. His writing was actually a literal translation of German composition, as if he thought in German and translated into English. I found his compositions awful and said so. He was very proud of his writing, so he felt hurt and angry at my plain speaking, and we quarreled about it.

I tend to be quick-tempered and speak hastily, and Freddy tends to pout and be disagreeable. But neither of us wants to live in disharmony, so our quarrels have seldom lasted long, though on rare occasions, it has taken us a long while to laugh about them.

In retrospect, I realize that Freddy's writing improved only when he ceased to think in German. One day Alene, one of our upstairs friends, brought down a German textbook because she and I wanted Freddy to teach us German. He refused to do so. It was then that I began to understand that he was really intent on cutting himself off from his past and beginning a new life as an American. He seems to have succeeded very well. Years later when we lived in Germany for a year, the Germans said he spoke German like an American. Even the Viennese did not recognize his German speech as being that of a native speaker!

Housing woes

We had expected to stay in Mrs. Hattery's house only until the end of August. In late July she wrote to say that her daughter wanted her to stay longer. She asked if we would like to continue renting her apartment. We were overjoyed to do so. We had been constantly alert for another apartment and had followed every lead we heard about, but we had found nothing else.

The war in Europe had ended in May, and in August the war in the Pacific ended. I am not sure how Freddy now feels about the use of the atomic bomb in Japan, but I must confess that I rejoiced that we had it and that we used it. I am still glad we did. For years we had been reading of the atrocities practiced by the Japanese in every area they conquered. To my knowledge, they had never shown mercy or compassion to anyone. I thought it high time they were conquered. While today I am willing to concede that the unleashing of atomic forces was not an altogether happy event in the affairs of men, I still recall how thankful we were to hear that Japan had surrendered.

As young men came home, they began flocking to the universities on the wings of the GI Bill. Bloomington was even smaller and less prosperous than Columbus. Now suddenly Bloomington was called upon to supply and support more people than it ever had. So there was even less opportunity for married students to find housing. Under the wise guidance of the president, Herman B Wells, Indiana University employed many stratagems for accommodating all of us.

Freddy put his name on the housing list, and whether it was his fault or the fault of the housing office, headed by a most formidable dragon-lady, we were not given a trailer in the trailer park. Instead we were to have an apartment in the converted barracks buildings that were being erected.

Dear Mrs. Hattery let us stay on in her apartment for three additional months while she helped her sisters, who were retiring from academic jobs, to get settled in their Bloomington homes. But then the time came for us to move, and we had no place to go because our barracks apartment was *still* not ready for us!

Betty had married Harold while we were still in Hope, and they had a baby boy that summer. She offered us a room in their house in Indianapolis, so Steve and I went there, while Freddy was given a bed in the attic of the Moores' house (one of Mrs. Hattery's sisters) in Bloomington. It was not an ideal arrangement, but we survived. There was a positive side to it all. Since I could leave Steve with Betty, I was able to shop more easily in Indianapolis for the household-type furnishings we would need for our barracks apartment.

Hoosier Courts

We had been given a move-in date in early December for our apartment in what came to be called Hoosier Courts. The date arrived and our apartment was still not finished. To make matters worse, a carpenter strike was beginning. We decided to move in anyway. At least we would be able to celebrate Christmas together and in our new home.

By the time we settled in, Christmas was around the corner. Freddy had not yet bought our tree. Not having been in the habit of decorating trees or even celebrating Christmas in his growing-up years, it was not as important to him as it was to me or our children (though I think he loves having a tree now). I had bought a box of Christmas tree ornaments in Indianapolis and was eager to use them.

Freddy went to the Square by bus to buy a tree. He bought a tree but then found he could not get it onto the bus. He carried it home, and as he walked, needles fell off the tree. The poor guy arrived at the door not in a happy humor—and bearing an almost naked tree! We decorated it anyway. Steve was happy with it, but it was not a tree we kept until Epiphany. It came down right after Christmas.

Until the next semester, we and one other couple with two children were the only occupants of the building. We quickly became acquainted with the Bards, who were Italian and from New York City. Rita Bard thought she had moved to the end of the earth. I guess it did look that way.

The university had purchased a farm and then imported on flatbed trucks a disassembled military training camp from Illinois. When we looked out our windows, we saw mud and ruts and dried corn stalks. The buildings had been set up on blocks in a cornfield, so they had no basements, and because of the carpenter strike, no skirts.

**Ann & Steve (standing)
with cousin Chuck
Hoosier Courts, c. 1947**

The interior was almost as bleak. Each building contained eight apartments. The door to our apartment was near the main entrance of the building. Our apartment consisted of a living room with a kitchen area, a bath, and two bedrooms. The living room was just a long bare room with one window at the front and one at the back. The kitchen area was at the far end of it. One bedroom was quite small and had an army bunk in it. The other bedroom was larger and contained side-by-side bunk beds. There were no curtains and no shades. And because of the carpenter strike, we had only subflooring.

Gas-burning space heaters provided our heat, and we had ice-boxes for perishables. For all of us in Hoosier Courts, those ice-boxes were the worst aggravation. The young man who delivered the ice seemed to delight in walking through the hallways and down the full length of the living room to the kitchen carrying as much sticky red clay on his boots as he could manage and still move his legs! This continued even after we had chipped stone streets and walkways.

We made many delightful friends in Hoosier Courts. We were all happy to be there after the stress and privations of the war. Our children played together both stormily and happily, and about the time we left, there was even a cooperative nursery playgroup being formed. We developed strong friendships with the Bards, as well as with Beth and Byrum Carter, Earl and Marjorie Hoff, Fred and Barbie Burgess, and Betty and Howard Brumfield.

I admired Rita Bard tremendously. She was efficient and hard-working. Rita, her mother, and her sister taught me about Italian cooking. I still make lasagna and meatballs as they taught me to all those years ago. The cheese and pasta needed for their Italian dishes could not be found in Bloomington, so Rita's mother sent her packages of supplies from New York every so often. Rita's father was a professional musician who had been recruited by Sousa and brought to this country to play in his band. For a long while he played in a band directed by Toscanini in New York City.

One day a very welcome surprise arrived at our apartment at Hoosier Courts. During my years at Arvin (Noblitt-Sparks), I had come to know the man in Indianapolis who sold Royal typewriters and serviced the ones in our office. While Steve and I were in Indianapolis staying with Betty, I had looked him up. He remembered me very well. I talked with him about acquiring a typewriter. He had none available then, of course. The war years were difficult for him and his business, as they were for many others.

I put my name down on his list for a typewriter as soon as he had some for sale again. So it happened that when I answered my door that day, whom should I find but my friend with a very new upright standard Royal typewriter. What a wonderful sight!

That typewriter must have been one of the first produced for domestic sales, and he had brought it to me. How lucky I felt! The price was a big chunk of money for us in a way, but it was a very good investment. I typed Freddy's notes, papers, and theses. I also typed these things for others. I used it for writing letters, addressing Christmas cards, and various other things until the late 1980s when my arthritic fingers could no longer hit the keys hard enough to print.

In June 1947 Freddy graduated from Indiana University. I was not able to attend the graduation ceremony because Steve had chicken pox. Some of my family drove to Bloomington with my mother, but alas not one of them wanted to stay with Steve while I witnessed the ceremony!

I could understand why those with small children would not want to carry Steve's germs back home, but I had thought Mother would babysit. Instead she said that this was her first opportunity to see one of her children graduate from university, and she did not want to miss it. So she went, and I stayed home with Steve. I found it ironic, but Freddy was pleased to be regarded as Mother's child.

A car trip to the southwest

That summer Freddy began work on a master's degree in government (his AB was in history). In August, we went on a long car trip with the Reeves family. Lucille Hudson Reeves and I had been friends since my early days at Arvin, where we both worked. We had many things in common, most pertinently that we were entirely without parental support and dependent upon our own work for our livelihood. Lucille left Arvin to work as a civil servant in Washington, DC.

Alton Reeves was the postmaster in Hope. He was several years older than Lucille and a childless widower. I cannot remember how long Lucille worked in Washington, but one day she reappeared at Arvin as Lucille Reeves. They had married in Washington and returned to live in Hope.

I liked them both very much indeed. We were all enthusiastic supporters of the New Deal and of Franklin and Eleanor Roosevelt. Lucille and Alton had included me in many of their weekend car trips to state parks and historical monuments as well as to American Legion meetings, for Alton was active in the legion.

When I left Arvin to go to Fort Harrison, I had their enthusiastic support. At about the time of my marriage, they had their only child, a boy named Alton C., Jr.—A. C. for short. They were wonderful friends to me when I was pregnant, and when Freddy came home, we all became very good friends.

Our trip to the southwest was most congenial and pleasant. Our little boys played together so very well. We all thought we were probably very superior parents. It was Freddy's first trip west of the Mississippi and the first for me by car. (Some years earlier I had visited Denver and Evergreen for a month, traveling by train from Chicago.) This trip was a wonderful vacation! We went across country to Denver, Colorado, south to Santa Fe, New Mexico, and then across northern Texas on our way back home.

Steve
Bloomington, c. 1947

We stayed nearly a week in Evergreen, Colorado, where my aunt Lily still spent her summers. I had been almost certain Aunt Lily would dislike my choice of a husband, but she had been pleased from the first announcement. From time to time she sent me useful things for our home. The quilt she pieced and quilted for my main wedding present remains in my small collection of handmade quilts.

Cultural activities

Life continued through the next year very pleasantly indeed. Freddy and I both realized that we liked living in an academic community. We especially appreciated the Indiana University Auditorium (which had been built by the Work Projects Administration during the 1930s). There we were able to enjoy wonderful entertainment at prices we could afford. I heard my first full opera there when the Metropolitan Opera performed two different operas on successive nights during their spring tour. We also enjoyed drama, ballet, symphony orchestras, and musical shows.

Sometimes a speaker would give a short talk a day or so before a performance to anyone interested in hearing about the composer and/or writer. I always tried to go to these talks. One time the speaker was Fritz Busch. I believe the opera was a Verdi, and someone asked him if it would be sung in Italian or English.

He replied that of course it would be sung in Italian. He spoke at great length about how operas should always be sung in the language in which they are written and was almost contemptuous that such a question should be asked.

Then the persistent questioner said, "But I thought in Germany they were always sung in German."

The surprising reply was, "But of course they are. How else could the Germans understand it?" We all laughed, and I wondered if he had any idea why.

Then there was the premier performance of a Kurt Weill opera, *Down in the Valley*. Kurt Weill himself came to oversee the production. And it was Kurt Weill who was the preperformance speaker. Weill was Viennese, and Freddy had told me about him. I usually went to the preperformance talk, needing it most, and then Freddy and I took turns attending the performance itself while the other stayed home with Steve. Babysitting was only then coming into use, and we had no car to transport a babysitter. Once in a while couples exchanged sittings, but this was rather rare, so more often than not we each went alone.

When the work on Freddy's master's degree was near completion, his mentors at Indiana University advised him to go to a more prestigious school to study for his doctoral degree. He had two big decisions to make: where to go and what to study—history or political science.

By then I had come to realize that my earlier role was being modified. Freddy and I still talked things over, but I was no longer his chief consultant. Only his professors knew how to guide him toward his goals, so I played a very small part in his career decisions. And how Freddy agonized over decisions! So much so that I have often wondered how he came to such a quick and emphatic decision about me and our marriage.

New Haven, Connecticut (1948)

Eventually Freddy decided to go to Yale University. In the spring of 1948, we started planning our move to New Haven, Connecticut. Our first task was to visit New Haven to find a place to live.

With Steve being such a pill about changes in his routine, we did not want to take him on our scouting trip. We asked my brother George's wife, Thelma, if she would bring her little girl and stay with Steve in our apartment until we returned (she had her own car). God bless her; she agreed to this, so our minds were relieved about Steve.

Our trip took on some aspects of a pleasurable vacation as we traveled to New York and New Haven unencumbered. It was our first journey sans Steve since Freddy had returned from Europe, and Steve was already three and a half years old! However, our introduction to Yale and New Haven was less auspicious than our introduction to Indiana University and Bloomington had been.

This was late May and early summer had already begun in Bloomington. But in New Haven, it was still early spring. I had only lightweight clothing with me, so I spent much of the time chilly, if not cold. Amidst all the tweeds, I felt rather like a country cousin. To Freddy this was a nonsensical notion. Perhaps so, but it did color my first impression of New Haven.

Yale had put up Quonset huts for its married students, but again we were at the end of a waiting list. We were given a list of private rentals, and I nearly went into shock when I saw them. I knew our housing at Indiana University was subsidized, but these rents were more than twice the rent we had paid Mrs. Hattery, or even any other private rentals in Bloomington.

Nevertheless, we went to inspect everything on the list. Only one rental was located where I could put Steve outside to play unattended. All the others looked like slums to me. What one sees in a new place, I suppose, depends on one's past experience and one's hopes and expectations. I had always been poor, but I had never lived in the slum-like conditions of old filth that we saw in New Haven. Although the apartments we viewed were newly cleaned and painted, I just could not think of living in those surroundings.

In the end Freddy persuaded me to put our money down on the most expensive one. As a place to live, it had its drawbacks, but overall it turned out to be a good decision. Having transacted our business, we went to New York City. We had enough time for me to see my first Broadway musical, *Carousel*, before we entrained for Indianapolis and Bloomington. On our way back, I concluded that I could bear New Haven if I could sometimes go to New York for entertainment. Of course, I did not know then about all the wonderful entertainment I would see and hear in New Haven itself!

All was well when we returned home to Bloomington. I think Thelma may even have enjoyed her experience. But she was confounded by Steve's choice of music. One of our first purchases had been a record player and a few records. Although we had bought a few children's records for Steve, he seldom wanted to play them. His and his father's tastes were one and the same long before he could articulate them.

When the summer semester ended, we set about moving ourselves and our belongings to New Haven. We shipped our belongings by truck, leaving behind what we could bear to part with. We flew to New York. This was Steve's and my first flying experience. By then one of my good friends from high school was a seasoned flight attendant for American Airlines. She had even been a cover story for *Life* magazine. But in 1948, it was *my* first flying experience. We had two lovely days in New York City and arrived at our new home with the moving truck at the door, a good omen for our two wonderful years in New Haven.

Orange Street

Our apartment was on Orange Street, which ran from East Rock to the harbor. Freddy discovered very quickly that there was a public beach near the end of our bus line. Soon Steve and I had our first dip in salt water and we were jumping waves. We loved the beach just as Freddy did!

That same bus took us to an open-air market where local growers sold a variety of fruits and vegetables. We shopped there for most of our food while we lived on Orange Street. At first we all went, but Steve did not enjoy it much. So Freddy, who had gained confidence in his ability to shop, went alone. He bought a folding wheeled cart and every Saturday morning went to the market to buy our needs for the week with $10.

Ann, Freddy, & Steve
Orange Street,
New Haven, c. 1948

In New Haven we had no trouble obtaining cheeses and pastas for Italian dishes. The ethnic groups dominant there in 1948 were Irish, Italian, and Polish. Although they were all Roman Catholic, one would not have known that they had a common faith by their attendance pattern. The Polish went only to the Polish Catholic Church, Italians to the Italian Catholic Church, and Irish to the Irish Catholic Church. Being from the Midwest, I found this ethnicity puzzling but interesting to observe.

Pauline Haas

Just before we moved from Bloomington, a memorable event occurred concerning Gus and Pauline (Polly) Haas, our neighbors in Hoosier Courts. Gus was a graduate student in government like Freddy. He and Polly had a baby just a few months old. I knew Polly was a painter. She had painted a large portrait of the Stoner children, which the Stoners had over the fireplace in their living room. (John Stoner had been one of Freddy's professors at Indiana University.)

One day Polly came to see me with a proposal. She told me she was from Cincinnati, where she had studied at the Cincinnati Arts Academy before she and Gus were married. She was working on an MFA at Indiana University and finishing her equivalency to a thesis. She needed to submit four portraits to her committee for approval. She had completed three and had to paint a fourth rather quickly, because Gus, like Freddy, was leaving at the end of the summer semester.

Polly had been unable to paint as much as she had hoped because of her baby, and she had been puzzling over how to manage the fourth portrait. She told me that she had heard from the Stoners how much I admired her work, and that she had a proposition for me. She would paint Steve's portrait if I would assist. She would give the portrait to us after her committee had viewed it and given her a grade. This would be her very first painting of a young child. My job was to keep Steve quiet while she painted, and I was to make absolutely no comment on her work.

We managed this all with very little fuss. We worked while her baby napped. Steve would always be quiet if I read to him, so my task was easy. It was more difficult for Steve and Polly. Polly had to work swiftly because her baby was restless and did not sleep for long periods. Steve was not happy with his perch. Polly needed him at a certain angle and height for her eye, so she set a kitchen stool on top of her baby's feeding chair table, and Steve was perched on that. Polly caught his uneasy look with his slightly thrust-out lower lip very well.

I admired Polly and her work tremendously. In all the years and all the galleries, I have seen very few artists living or dead that I thought might be better—and by now I have seen a very great number! One of the first things we unpacked and hung on the wall in our New Haven apartment was Polly's portrait of Steve.

Steve
Portrait by Pauline Haas

The Dunns

In New Haven, Steve was the first to make friends with Ann and Jim Dunn, a recently married couple who were subletting the top floor apartment for the summer. I always knew that if I could not hear or see Steve, he had gone upstairs to see the Dunns. Ann stopped by one day, and she had barely entered the room when the portrait of Steve caught her eye. She walked over to it, read the signature, and said, "Pauline Anderson Haas! I *thought* it looked like Polly's work."

Ann and Polly had been students together at the Cincinnati Art Academy and knew each other very well. They were both dedicated to painting, and both extraordinarily good, though their styles were quite distinct.

Likely it was Ann and Jim who introduced us to the beauty of the Connecticut countryside. At that time, Ann was painting scenic watercolors, and she was very, very good. I treasure two of her watercolors of that area, a painting of East Rock in the park, and one of the valley near the Sleeping Giant.

The first New Haven settlement was established between West Rock and East Rock. From the harbor, these great rocks appear as two ancient castles guarding the land and the Quinipiac River, which runs between and empties into the sound, creating a natural harbor. The city built parks on both rocks. Steve and I could easily walk or take the bus to East Rock, and we often did.

We were all enchanted with the first snowfall in New Haven. I had never known any snowfall like it in Indiana. It came one Sunday afternoon

Steve
New Haven, c. 1948

when Freddy and I had gone to have dinner with another graduate couple, who were living in a summer shore cottage outside the city. We started home early, but we had at least two transfers to make, so it took hours to get to the Green (the center of New Haven). Then we had to walk the rest of the way home.

The snow was *so* very beautiful! Somewhere along the way, we phoned our apartment to say we were on our way. It was a comfort to have such a pleasant young man (an undergraduate) with Steve. He assured us that they were fine and it did not matter how long he had to stay.

How Steve loved playing in the snow! We adults soon grew tired of it. It could be such an inconvenience, and the great, dirty-gray piles of snow on the Green remained an eyesore until they disappeared in spring.

Judy

It was also through Steve and in New Haven that we started to become a family with a common church. On one side of us on Orange Street lived the owners of our apartment, the Squeglias, an Italian family. The parents, the son (and his wife and son), and the daughter (and her husband and son) were all engaged in running a family grocery. On the other side of us lived an older Italian family, relatives of the Squeglias.

Just beyond them lived a family named Spose. The Sposes had a daughter Judy, who was ten or eleven. Judy was a very bright, friendly little girl who "adopted" Steve. She would come over to get him and take him back to her house so he could listen while she practiced the piano. She was an extraordinarily good pianist. She had a teacher in New Haven, and every second week her mother took her to New York City to the Mannes School for a class with a master teacher.

Judy also took Steve another block over to her church, St. John's Episcopal Church, which had fairly spacious grounds where a small playground had been set up for the benefit of the neighborhood children. Here she supervised his play. She also introduced him to the rector, Mr. Gummere, whom we all came to love.

Culture and academics

Freddy was very excited and happy with his classes at Yale. He was stimulated by the discussions with his fellow graduate students, most of whom have remained friends to this day. They have stayed in touch through the national meetings of the American Political Science Association and an annual exchange of news letters at Christmas. Since Freddy was one of the few who were married, and since our apartment was nearby and fairly spacious, our place became a favorite spot for Freddy and his fellow students to meet and talk, and also to eat my homemade goodies and meals.

Many well-known people came to Yale to lecture, conduct seminars, exhibit art, and perform musically. I in particular devoured it all. I enjoyed these delights alone for the most part because Freddy was usually engaged in study. He always had papers to prepare and long reading lists to wade through.

I remember when Eleanor Roosevelt came to lecture. Her speaking voice was high-pitched and thin, but I liked what she had to say. I also went to hear Edith Sitwell, who read her poetry. She was even harder to hear, so I had to be content with reading her poetry and the books and articles about her and her brothers.

It was in Yale's Woolsey Hall that I heard Jascha Heifetz play the violin with a piano accompaniment. I was forever after his enthralled admirer. Though I have heard many world-famous violinists since, for me he remains *number one*. Sometimes Freddy went with me to these events; sometimes I went alone. Finding a sitter for Steve was easy because the male graduate students were glad to stay with him. They had made quite a pet of him, and he adored having them for sitters.

Yale drama students were excellent, and we bought season tickets for the performances. Helen Lane often came in her car to take me to the plays. Bob Lane was finishing his degree at Harvard and had to return there often. Helen and I did many things together while he was away.

I not only typed many of Freddy's class notes, but I also typed his papers and read a great many of the books on his reading list. When Dr. Driver, one of his professors, learned I was doing this, he started suggesting things for me to read. It was then that I read the books of Sidney and Beatrice Webb and many others of the

Fabian group. My favorite reading has always been biographies, and he loved giving me suggestions.

Oscar and Liesl visit us

That summer was our only time ever to be with Freddy's half-brother, Oscar. Oscar and Liesl made a fairly leisurely trip from Sydney, stopping in Honolulu for a few days, and then on the West Coast to visit Liesl's sister Margret and her two daughters. After they arrived in New York, they phoned us to arrange their visit.

Freddy went to New York alone the next day and returned in the evening. A few days later, Oscar and Liesl came to New Haven to visit with us for a few days. They brought presents for all of us. Steve was ecstatic about his, a red fire engine that he could ride. Needless to say, it was admired by every little child who saw it. We went to the beach with them one day, and Freddy was delighted to show them around the university.

Later we went to New York to stay in a hotel with Oscar and Liesl. This gave us an opportunity to spend time with other relatives, too, including Liesl's moth-

Freddy, Liesl, Oscar,
Ann, & Steve
New Haven, 1949

er, Sophia Hartmann, and Liesl's sister Mary Hirschkron, as well as Mary's husband, Richard, and son, Robert. We also visited with Oscar's cousin Willy Unger and his wife, Grete, who lived in New York.

In Vienna Willy had been quite wealthy, and he had been able to bring some of his wealth out. With his international connections, he was able to establish himself very comfortably in New

York. His daughters, Marianne and Lilly, went to the University of Chicago.

Marianne had married an engineer and was living in Bridgeport, Connecticut, with her husband and two sons. We visited them one Sunday with Grete, Oscar, and Liesl. Lilly, I did not meet until some years later, for she was married to John Kautsky, then a graduate student in political science at Harvard.

Oscar and Liesl had always been loving and supportive in their letters and phone calls, but I learned then of their amazement and doubts about Freddy's choice of profession and his ability to pursue it. Freddy had told me that he had been an indifferent student. I had come to regard these reports with the same suspicion as I did his assurances to me after every exam that he had failed.

Now I began to understand that either he had managed to misrepresent himself to his family, or his family had misunderstood him, for they regarded him as a sweet boy who did not cause trouble, and who would need to be pushed along because he would never push himself hard enough to accomplish anything! I am sure his family had never categorized Freddy with Willy Unger's daughters or John Kautsky (Lilly Unger's husband and the grandson of Karl Kautsky, the foremost socialist theorist in Austria).

Freddy, I came to perceive, is as unlike his family as I am unlike mine. Yet each of us loves our relatives and feels great loyalty to them. In this again we are alike. Freddy differs greatly from others I have met with whom there could be a natural comparison. He is never pompous; quite the contrary, he is far more likely to be self-effacing than boastful. Sometimes I have wished he would take a firmer stand in a controversy. Usually he is willing to concede there are two sides to every question.

Kindergarten

One of the first books Freddy purchased after Steve's birth was Dr. Arnold Gesell's account of his observations of young children. Gesell's school and research facilities were in New Haven. In fact Gesell's work was one of the main conversational topics among the graduate students. Soon after our arrival, we visited his school, and we seriously considered putting our child on the list.

The main reason we did not was that getting him there and then back home was very inconvenient. It involved taking the Orange Street bus to the Green and transferring to a city bus to the school. Then I would have to return two hours later to pick him up. That meant that I would spend about the same amount of time on buses as he spent in school. So Steve stayed home with me for the first year we were in New Haven. The second year, he went to kindergarten.

Because the public kindergarten was several blocks away, too far for Steve to walk alone, we placed him in a private school near us that he could walk to alone. Steve loved to be read to, and both Freddy and I loved to read to him, especially A. A. Milne's Pooh Books. But how and when Steve learned to read, I do not really know.

When we decided to send him to Miss Gailor's school, it was for my own convenience, so I would not have to escort him there and back. But it turned out to be a very good place for him. His classroom was divided into sections in which instructors directed various activities. The children could move about from section to section as their interests dictated.

Evidently Steve identified himself with the more advanced students in reading, and he was reading with them from the beginning. This is not to say that he was writing and doing arithmetic as well, for he was not. When Steve began bringing workbooks home with little notes attached suggesting that we help with his homework, I was dumbfounded. I went to the school to observe what was being done so that I could be better informed to help him. Freddy and I did not discuss this phase of Steve's early schooling very seriously, nor did we worry about his "tilted" start in school.

Aunt Lily visits

During the fall, Aunt Lily came to visit. She was so happy that I had married someone who was going to school and aiming for an academic career. She and I went to New York to visit art museums. I think she tired easily and was unable to see some of the pictures very well, but she seemed pleased we went. She was definitely interested in Steve and his kindergarten. We had long discussions about education and how learning began, how it was nurtured, and so on.

She had been a primary school teacher and was still very interested professionally. Freddy gave her Dr. Gesell's book to read, and we took her to see the Gesell school and research facility. She thoroughly enjoyed it all, so much so that after she returned home, she sent me a rather nice check to contribute to Steve's tuition. I was grateful, of course, and I was very happy to know she had enjoyed her visit.

During her visit, Aunt Lily told me how she had occupied her time during the war. She had lived in Denver, where she had become reconciled with her daughter, Helen. At the beginning of the war, Helen and her husband had moved to Los Angeles. Her husband had just passed his bar exam in 1940, and he had become an attorney there for the airplane manufacturer, the McDonnell Douglas Corporation. The company grew by leaps and bounds, so he had prospered.

Perhaps Aunt Lily wanted to show him that she did not need his help to take care of her money, for she had spent her time very agreeably in increasing her dollars several times over. She bought houses in Denver, remodeled them in whatever way seemed appropriate for the area, and then sold them at a profit. She was very set-up over her accomplishments. I did not blame her a bit. Indeed I admired her very much.

Having enjoyed her visit so much, Aunt Lily wrote that she was coming for another visit. She wanted to see New Haven in the spring and spend more time in the museums in New York. As it turned out, neither of us enjoyed her second visit quite as much. It was a stressful time for Freddy and me. Freddy was frantically preparing for his exams. He had already accepted a job in Florida, and I was preoccupied with getting us there, and more than a little stressed with it all.

As well, Freddy had been notified that not only had he exhausted his tuition benefits under the GI Bill, but we would have to pay the tuition for the present semester. This was a rather sizeable amount. Fortunately we were able to do it. We had been quite comfortable in New Haven and had not stinted ourselves in any way on entertainment, clothing, or food. Freddy had been paid though not munificently, and we had lived on less than our income, so we managed to save a bit.

Gainesville on the horizon

Freddy took his exams in May and fortunately, passed them. Even I had been concerned because I knew that very few students pass the first time. We then turned our attention to moving to Gainesville. We decided that we would give up our apartment, and that Steve and I would go to Gainesville to find a place to live. Freddy would remain in New Haven until September and then join us. Freddy did not want to leave Yale yet. He wanted time to work on his dissertation. In a way, the decision to go to Gainesville was made for us. Freddy is writing about that, so I will simply say how we did it.

Our plan was that Freddy would remain in the apartment until the end of June and then get a room in a university dorm. Meanwhile Steve and I would take a first-class compartment on the train to Bradenton, Florida. We had contacted our neighbors from Hoosier Courts, Betty and Howard Brumfiel, to tell them of Freddy's appointment at the University of Florida. They had suggested that Steve and I come to Bradenton first, and then Howard would drive us to Gainesville.

Freddy accompanied us to New York and helped us into our little room on the train. Steve was unhappy about leaving his good friends, Judy Spose and Billy Rodman (his playmate from school), but he was very excited about sleeping on the train, so he was cooperative, good-humored, and looking forward to a new adventure.

Freddy said goodbye to us and got off the train. I went to the window to wave as the train started to move. Then it dawned on Steve that only he and I were going away! He started to protest, cry, and carry on in a way that surprised me very much. I had to hold him tightly, for he was trying to open the door and get off the train. He kept sobbing, "Why isn't Daddy coming? I don't want to go without Daddy!"

I had not been happy about doing this all on my own, and I did not care for the separation either, but I was kept so busy comforting Steve and trying to distract him that I did not have time for introspection or even sadness. I had to be cheerful. It was too bad that I could not have brought the record player along and soothed Steve with music, our usual method. However, as a going-away present, Billy had given Steve *The Wind in the Willows*, so we read most of it on our journey to Florida. Neither of us had ever read it before, so we enjoyed it together. It was a wonderful present, and we both still think it is a great book—timeless!

In New Haven June is a very beautiful month. It is cool, but so many trees and shrubs bloom in June. The rhododendrons, azaleas, and roses are beautiful almost beyond belief. Because winter is long and gray, this great blossoming is quite a restorative to the spirits. So it was in this restored spirit and with some excitement that I had started off to Florida.

Then, too, I thought I was looking very well, almost modish! Freddy had encouraged me to buy some very nice clothing in New Haven's excellent shops. I had purchased a summer suit that gladdened my heart. In New Haven I could wear it all summer, even on trips to New York. It was this suit I wore on the train trip to Florida. I also had a truly chic hat for the first time in my life. It was made by Therese Fleming, whose husband Ted was one of Freddy's colleagues at Yale.

Ted Fleming had entered Paris with the American liberation forces on that first day. He was with the first company to enter Paris. Most of the French were so jubilant; they embraced their liberators with great joy and emotion. Ted was one of those lucky ones! Therese, who would become Ted's wife, not only embraced him, she took him home with her, and her whole family overwhelmed him with their joy and wishes to please. They fed him the best French dinner they could contrive. Before long, Ted and Therese married, and Ted brought Therese back to the United States.

They had a house in New Haven, where they lived while Ted was in graduate school. Therese, who had trained to be a milliner in Paris, decided to practice her trade in New Haven. She made up a range of hat styles and arranged for a showing. I was so enchanted, as I always am with remarkably well-done work of any kind. I wanted to buy the one she called the Cardinal's Hat. It was made of a very soft, red straw and had a round crown and wide brim shaped like the ones the cardinals of the Church of Rome wear. She had sewn a navy blue tasseled cord around the crown. I love red, and I loved that hat!

Therese said it was not the hat for my suit. She made a hat specially for me, an abbreviated sailor of navy blue, which she cut and shaped right on my head. She added a fairly wide white ribbon tied round the crown with a very perky, largish bow in the back and a half-veil in the front. I really did look elegant in it, perhaps for the first and last time in my life. Whenever I wore that hat and suit, I attracted attention. People turned and looked at me with admiration.

Too bad that I could not have had Therese's advice earlier, and for a longer period in my life! The Flemings moved to Detroit when we moved to Gainesville, and it was nearly twenty years before I saw Therese again. However, she did sell me the red hat as well just before we left New Haven, though she was reluctant to do so. She had wanted to make me a red hat with a narrower brim, which would have better fit my small, narrow face, but she hadn't the time.

So when Steve and I stepped off the train in Bradenton, Florida, that was the outfit I wore, the summer suit of lightweight, unlined wool, and the chic French hat. Howard met us wearing short shorts and sandals, and in less than two breaths, I understood why!

It was so suffocatingly hot on that platform that I very literally wanted to emulate the man in the parable and "rend my garments" off right there. Looking chic was utter nonsense. Florida's climate was so very different from what we were used to! Both Steve and I had considerable trouble adjusting to the extreme heat.

Howard had put off making a business trip to Tallahassee until we came. He and Betty had the extremely thoughtful idea that it would be best if he took us to Gainesville in his car and helped us find a place to stay.

It was very wise of them. I do not know what we would have done without his help, because the train did not actually go into Gainesville. It stopped at Waldo, about fifteen miles northeast of Gainesville, which we in our ignorance had not anticipated!

So we stayed with Howard and Betty a few days, and then Howard took us to Gainesville. There we found a room in a private house, cooled only with ceiling fans. In 1950 there was virtually *no* air-conditioning in Gainesville. Howard went on to Tallahassee but said that on his way home, he would stop by to see how we were. We have never been able to repay the Brumfiels for their thoughtful, unselfish help, but I have never forgotten it and have tried to do for others as they did for us!

Chapter 6

Gainesville & New Haven Again

(1950-1960)

S teve and I were busy over the next few days as we began our search for housing. Like Bloomington, Gainesville was a small, sleepy town that was the home of a state university and the many students brought to it by the GI Bill. Again there were many helpful, friendly people, and again there were scarce supplies.

In Gainesville the realtors had gotten off their marks with much greater speed and ingenuity than had their counterparts in Bloomington. I was fortunate in my choice of realtors. Mr. Kirkpatrick was both kind and competent as he guided me around the city.

I was quite appalled at the rental houses, which were dark and musty-smelling—as repelled as I had been two years earlier in New Haven. Then the realtor showed me the new houses being built in his company's housing project, and I really liked what I saw there.

Gainesville, Florida (1950)

The housing project was located about three miles from the University of Florida. The university was in the southwest, and the housing project was in the northeast. Freddy wanted us to live near the university, within walking distance, so that is where I first looked. The old houses, I simply did not like. There were new houses nearer it, but they were still not within walking distance, and they were higher in price than the new ones in our realtor's housing project.

I loved the little houses in that housing project! They were being built on an old airfield that was absolutely barren, but the site had the important advantage of being at a higher altitude. Altitude was important because when Steve and I arrived in Gainesville, we were treated to some torrential rainfalls. The natives were happy about it, but we found it a terrible nuisance. The sewers were inadequate, and after a few minutes of downpour, we had to remove our shoes and wade about in our bare feet.

I wanted to live in as high a spot as possible, so I decided to take one of the new houses that were set on the relatively high airfield. Best of all was the down payment—only $50! Yes, just $50. Of course, nothing could be finalized without Freddy, but for $50 I could reserve the house.

Our real estate agency also owned some small one-story apartment houses, which were built for military families during the war. I decided to rent one of those apartments until our house was ready. The apartment had one bedroom, a bath, a kitchen, and an adequate living-dining area. It was totally unfurnished, except for a cook stove and refrigerator.

I called Freddy to tell him of my arrangements and that we would have to buy a car. He was flabbergasted! However, I must say that though he may have doubted my wisdom, he accepted all that I had obligated him for with no arguments and no hesitation.

He must have known that I was pleased and excited, and he must have felt some relief. When I had talked to him from Bradenton just after our arrival, I had thought I could not bear to live in such a climate. That I had bought a house was a good indication that I was prepared to stay!

Freddy had asked me to call at the university and introduce myself to Manning Dauer, the chair of his department. This I did a day or two after our arrival. I must have met others around the department as well, but I remember only Fred Hartmann, probably because Fred and Reggie have been such dear friends all through the years. We have spent a great deal of time together including countless holidays because they, like us, were rather much on their own. Neither of them had a parent. When I told Manning and the Hartmanns about my plans, they endorsed the reliability of my realtors and offered no concerns about buying the house. I think they even regarded it as the best thing to do.

Steve chooses a church

One evening Fred and Reggie invited Steve and me to their house for dinner, and another evening we went with them to a potluck at their church, University Methodist. Thus far, I have said very little about religion because up until this time, it had not been a subject that Freddy and I discussed very much. Before we were married, our discussions about religion had not been very deep or conclusive. When we agreed to marry, religion was not an issue. Differences in religion did not seem to trouble us.

I was always very clear about what I was and what I would remain. Freddy had always seemed doubtful. I must explain that my actions and behavior are simply me being me. There is no part of me that accepts subterfuge. I loathe shoddiness, both spiritual and physical, and I will not lie. What I most often do is try to find the kind thing to do or say while not compromising my principles.

I am very much a child of my mother and of a long, ethical Protestant faith that allows one to think and worship as one sees fit, and that brings comfort and a closeness to God and His Love. For me, God is Love. There is no place in His Love for hate. How can there be *religious* wars? They are a contradiction in terms, for they are a supreme expression of hate.

Thus I was intent on doing what was right for me. At the same time, I wanted never to hurt Freddy in any way, or to persuade him to do something he did not believe in. Nor did I want to direct Steve in ways that might be repugnant to his father. As a result, for a time there was a shadowy unfilled dimension in our life together.

When we first moved to Bloomington, I insisted that we try going to First Methodist Church. We went but it did not work out well and did not develop into a regular habit. For one thing, Steve burned a good-sized blister on his hand in the nursery his first time there. After that, he resisted going and Freddy was obviously uncomfortable. When we moved to Hoosier Courts, where the buses did not run on Sundays, going was no longer feasible.

In New Haven there were only two Methodist Churches within a rather large region. The one nearest us was a large one just off the Green. Our visit there was not a happy one. Steve refused to go to the nursery. He stayed with us and as was his habit, quickly fell fast asleep. Freddy again was uncomfortable. I gave up, and again for a while, no one went to church. Then just before we moved, we began going with Judy Spose to St. John's Episcopal Church, where Mr. Gummere was the rector. I was less content than Freddy and Steve, but I was glad to be going to church as a family.

When Steve and I were in Gainesville those first two weeks in the summer and the Hartmanns befriended us, we went with them to University Methodist for a potluck, to a worship service on a weekday evening, and to church with them the next Sunday. Steve was happy enough, and I found the Reverend Springfield to be an acceptable minister.

Then one day Steve and I were walking down a street in downtown Gainesville. We went by a stone church with a red door. Holy Trinity, it was called. Steve stopped me right there. He said with some excitement, "There's *my* church. We must go in and say a prayer."

In some wonder, I complied, and we went in. It was a very lovely church. It was not huge, but a fair size, and it had lots of beautiful, carved light wood. Steve moved in hops, skips, and jumps in those days, and he hopped right in between the pews, pulled down the kneeler, and when I knelt next to him, he said a little prayer, which I suppose he learned from Judy or Mr. Gummere. I was very moved.

That evening I asked Steve why he had been sure that church was *his* church. I do not remember that I had a complete answer. But when I asked him about the Methodist church where we had gone with the Hartmanns, he said that it was not a "real" church, that it was a place where you go to have a good time.

Sometime before our first Christmas in Gainesville, both Steve and Freddy were baptized. Freddy and I took classes with Mr. Hauser, the rector of Holy Trinity, and we were then both confirmed in the Episcopal Church. I was extremely happy to be a family together in one church.

Some of my happiest memories of Gainesville center around activities at Holy Trinity. It was there that I first taught Sunday school (to the four-year-olds) with Laura Smith as my instructor, supervisor, and friend. Laura and her husband, Beanie, had two children, Ronnie, a boy Steve's age, and Frances, a girl Alice's age. They became our dear friends.

Chiggers

But let us return to the summer of 1950. When Howard Brumfiel came back through Gainesville to check on us, he was amazed at all the decisions I had made, but he approved. He suggested that Steve and I go back to Bradenton with him. However, we had to stay in Gainesville. Freddy had already packed up our possessions and shipped them to Gainesville, so I had to be in our apartment to receive them.

I really would have preferred to go back to Bradenton with Howard. Living in our one room and eating out had begun to tell on both Steve and me. I was also a little worried about Steve because of my ignorance about the climate and how to live in it.

Gainesville was full of trees with Spanish moss hanging from their limbs. We walked everywhere, and Steve was always jumping up to catch onto the moss and pull it down. We were totally unaware, though not for long, that tiny, red bugs (called chiggers in Indiana) abounded in the moss. Before long, Steve's head, face, and shoulders were covered, really covered thickly, with chigger welts.

Steve had an allergic reaction to the bites, just as I always did. He became a pitiable sight, and the itching was driving him crazy. Fortunately a friendly doctor, who ate breakfast where Steve and I did, noticed Steve's welts and told me that I should dunk Steve in salt water several times. Nothing else was half as good. He was quite right! Nothing from the drugstore helped, but the salt water cured him in a day or two.

Freddy joins us

As soon as the movers unloaded our possessions at our apartment, we left for Bradenton to stay with the Brumfiels. Freddy joined us there at the end of August. We took quite a long trip with the Brumfiels across the Everglades to Miami and then on to Key West. There we stayed a few days more before returning to Bradenton, and then going on to Gainesville, where we had much to do.

In New Haven, when we had moved into our furnished apartment, there had been twin beds for us, and we had bought Steve a youth bed. Our small apartment in Gainesville had no furnishings at all. We settled on buying a small convertible couch for us to sleep on but little else. For a while our card table and its matching chairs were our only other furniture.

Manning Dauer, the chair of Freddy's department, lived with his mother, and they had a tradition of calling on new families in the department. I shall never forget the Sunday afternoon they called on us. We could never have looked as bad as I felt we did. I was acutely aware of our untidiness, and I was embarrassed the whole time.

Mrs. Dauer was committed to the customs of the Old South. Since this was a Sunday afternoon call, Manning wore a suit and tie, and his mother wore a dress, stockings, a hat, and white gloves. In our scantily furnished apartment, there was only the convertible couch and folding chairs on which to sit. The only other chairs we owned were Steve's small rocker and his high chair. We managed to survive the call. During our years in Gainesville, I came to have a great deal of respect and admiration for Mrs. Dauer.

Steve begins school at Kirby-Smith

The time soon came to enroll Steve in first grade. We were told his school would be Kirby-Smith, the oldest of the white schools in town. It was 1950, and the schools were still segregated. This was a concept I had to come to terms with.

Segregation had never been a subject for much discussion in my parents' home, but we had *never* been allowed to speak slightingly or disparagingly about anyone for reason of race, color, or poverty. My father was much less adamant than my mother, but he was always there to enforce her views. They both truly believed in human rights for everyone. They would never tolerate it if we mocked a foreign speech or boasted of our abilities as compared to those of our peers. So seeing black people stand back until white people had boarded the bus was offensive to my sense of proper behavior, as were countless other things.

Be that as it may, I could not change the customs that existed. Like most women, I concerned myself with my child and my husband, providing them with creature comforts insofar as I was able and to the extent of my still limited energy. We bought a car, a very stripped-down Ford, and we bought and ordered furniture for the house that was being built. We also had to buy cooler clothing. Needless to say, we were very busy, and we spent most of our savings.

On the first day of school, Kirby-Smith was a madhouse. Steve and I were disappointed by the disorderly manner in which enrollment was conducted. I had in hand a report from Miss Gailor about Steve's kindergarten year, noting his accomplishments and lack of accomplishments. I had hoped to talk with the teacher, but that was a forlorn hope.

Since enrollment was such a disagreeable experience, Steve did not enjoy school at first, and it was quite a while before he went alone without persuasion. He was very advanced in reading, but he needed to learn to write more legibly and to take arithmetic seriously. Luckily he had a lovely, dedicated young woman for his teacher. She guided him along very well.

My mother's death

In the spring of 1945 my youngest sister, Martha, had graduated from high school. Not long after she had started working in the accounting office of Cummins Engine Company in Columbus. Mother and Martha had then moved to an apartment in Columbus.

When we were in New Haven, Martha had visited us. She and I had spent a day or two in New York seeing shows and having a good time. Martha was thinking of marrying Albert Horn, a young man from Columbus near my age, and eventually did so.

In 1945 about the time that Freddy first enrolled at Indiana University and we moved to Bloomington, my mother's health took a very serious turn. Mother had always had what Dr. Norton called a rheumatic heart, a result of the rheumatic fever she had as a small child. In 1945 her body began retaining fluids, and her heart was not strong enough to eliminate them. She was put on diuretics and told to eat no salt.

Mother had a very limited range of tastes, and even at the best of times, she had never cared much about eating. When she was advised to stop eating salt, she nearly quit eating altogether! During the summer before we left Bloomington, she came and stayed two weeks with us. I worked hard at getting her to eat, and I succeeded rather well. I gave her lots of the fresh fruits and vegetables that she liked without salt, and I cooked dishes with lemon juice substituted for salt. She did very well with that but she was very weak.

More recently, Mother had been making visits to each of her children in turn, a stay of two weeks with each. I think she liked that because she could enjoy her growing number of grandchildren. How she loved them all!

I had been hearing from my family in Indiana that Mother was steadily growing weaker and dwindling away. Then one day, Betty called me in Gainesville and said she had just taken Mother to Joe's house after having her visit for two weeks. It was her considered opinion that if I wanted to see and talk with Mother, I should come without delay, for she was sure the end was near.

Freddy was very dismayed that I should leave at such a crucial time for him, but I wanted very much to see Mother. So with Steve in school and our house not yet ready, I went back to Indiana. Betty was right. Mother was in the hospital when I arrived in Indianapolis.

When I went to see her, she was lucid but very weak, and so shrunken and small. I was able to spend two days and nights with her in the hospital. We had lovely talks together. She was very aware and loving, and she wished that she could see Steve and Freddy, too. About five days after I arrived, she died. I could hardly bear it. It is forty-some years ago now, and I still miss her. So many times I think to myself, I wish I could see and talk to Mama.

Louetta Quick Redmon
In her later years

I was in Indiana for almost two weeks. Freddy found that far too long for me to be away. However, it had been two years since my last visit, so I had a lot of catching up to do. There were nieces and nephews born during my absence whom I wanted to meet. I needed to see all my sisters and brothers, and some cousins as well. Though there are decided differences among us, still we are a close, loving family. At this time when Mother had left us, only we could comfort each other.

When I returned to Florida in late October, the weather was much more bearable. The Hartmanns had introduced Freddy and Steve to a new place to swim. Magnesia Springs was one of those amazing places where pure, clear water bubbles up out of the ground in a seemingly never-ending stream. The water was at the unvarying temperature of 72°F all year round. Water from the spring was bottled and sold commercially. The company operating that business had also put in a beautiful tiled pool into which they diverted spring water. We found it a wonderful place to swim and cool off!

The pool was set in the middle of north Florida's jungle-like growth, enclosed by a chainlink fence and reached by a sandy, un-paved track. At times we could hear or see wild hogs rooting around beyond the fence. We were told that occasionally, a snake found its way into the pool during the night and had to be fished out in the morning.

Hopes and expectations

We spent our first Christmas in Florida in our apartment. In late February we moved into our new home. I remember the tremendous joy I felt about that. I began to think about enrolling at the university to get a degree. Before I go on to describe the events that happened next, I must go back about two years to relate a decision I made then.

When Freddy first enrolled at Yale, the registrar, noting that he was

Freddy, Ann, & Steve
Northeast Seventh Street
Gainesville, 1951

retired from the army with a permanent disability, said they would like one of their orthopedists to examine him and give the university his opinion on the condition of Freddy's spine. Freddy was very impressed by this doctor and his examination. He told the doctor about my sciatic pain and the corrective corset I had to wear, and asked him if he would examine me.

I was impressed by the orthopedist, too. After he examined me, he said he wanted me to see one of his colleagues on the faculty for a complete physical. Both doctors took a great deal of time and care with their examinations and asked many questions about me, my pregnancy, and the delivery.

It was their opinion that my hips were still in the position they would be in if I were preparing to give birth. They said that as a woman's body prepares for birth, the position of her hips changes, and that after childbirth, her hips resume their normal position. According to these physicians, my body had never returned to normalcy. For what reason, they simply did not know.

Both physicians agreed that having another child in a normal way, not a C-section, would very likely correct my problem. The orthopedist, in particular, said that I should not regard this as anything more than a possibility. Most of his experience had been repairing the broken bones that male students acquired in skiing accidents, and that was why he had wanted the second opinion.

My problem was unique in their experience, and they wanted me to understand their hesitancy in giving advice. The orthopedist said the brace I was wearing was probably helpful for the pain, but it did not correct my basic problem. He said nothing at all about seeing an obstetrician.

I went home to Freddy with a great deal to think about. What the doctors said made a great deal of sense to me. Freddy was less impressed. Since he had not been present during my pregnancy and Steve's birth, he seemed unable to understand how awful it had really been.

At any rate, his first year at Yale was not a good time to test the doctors' theory, so I went on using the diaphragm, even though at that time in Connecticut, it was unlawful to practice birth control. Early on in the second year, I used no preventatives whatsoever, but nothing happened.

When we moved into our house in Gainesville, I was still not pregnant. I was no longer able to wear my body brace. I had been in Florida no time at all before I found that wearing my body brace in the tropical heat and humidity was next to impossible. I developed a body rash that was almost worse to bear than the sciatic pain!

It was about this time that I decided to enroll at the university and get a degree. I had no more than started that ball rolling when I discovered that I was pregnant! I was just as sick and uncomfortable as I had been the first time. Again I lost more weight than I gained. But this time I wondered if it might not be an eel I was gestating. The life beginning within me never stopped moving, or so it seemed. I spent most nights on a lounge chair on our screened-in patio.

My friend Reggie Hartmann was also pregnant. The contrast between us could hardly have been greater. Reggie felt very well, and it was not apparent that she was pregnant until a few weeks before her baby was born. I again was looking very large at four months. Reggie and I went to the same doctor, and even though he set our delivery time within the same month, Vicki Hartmann was past two months old when Alice was born. She was a month early, and Alice was a month late.

Alice is born

Alice was born on January 29, 1952, in the Alachua County Hospital. I will never forget awakening and hearing a voice say, "Aren't you ever going to wake up and see your beautiful little girl with Alice-blue eyes?"

There was a nurse beside me holding a baby. I sat up, and she handed the baby to me. Sure enough, there were two big blue eyes staring at me out of a darling little heart-shaped face. I felt so well, and I was ready for a meal.

When Freddy came, I hopped out of bed, and we walked down the corridor and looked in the nursery to find our infant. She was indeed a miracle. My sciatic pain was gone for the first time in more than eight years! I had some problems, but they were comparatively minor. No one can know what it meant to be without that sciatic pain. Again I failed to get an AB, but I gained a child!

Before Steve was born, Freddy and I had discussed names by correspondence. He had said that if we should have a daughter, he wanted her to be called Lillian. He loved that name. That was not a name I particularly cared for, but I agreed. I chose the name Steven for a boy. My cousin Dorothy Stevens had been so very good to me, and she had made so many beautiful things for my baby.

Now here we were in 1952 with this lovely little girl with great blue eyes, and I said to Freddy that she just had to be called Alice, Alice Lillian if he liked. She was the epitome of Alice in Wonderland as she was forever looking about, and it had been a *wonder* that we had her! So our baby girl was baptized Alice Lillian at Holy Trinity in Gainesville, Florida.

Friends and neighbors

It was such a joy for me to have a house of our own, especially such a clean, pleasant little house as the one we bought in Gainesville. A part of that pleasure was in our congenial neighbors.

On one side were the Tilleys: Barbara, Wes, and their children, Susan and John. On the other side was a middle-aged couple, Ethel and William Merrill, who had two grown sons no longer at home. Immediately behind us were Charles (Gene) and Jane Cutts, who had no children. Beside them on one side were the Pettys with one little boy, Tommy, and on the other side were Harold and Mary Jean Hansen, whose little boy, Steven, was younger than our Steve.

All but two of the husbands were just beginning their teaching careers at the University of Florida. Kirkpatrick and Pearson's housing project there on the old airfield could not have had more than about three hundred houses, but most of them were bought by people very like us. The men were war veterans, whatever their present occupation. These were the first houses they had ever bought, and most were financed through the government and the Veterans Affairs GI Bill.

It was a very congenial, happy group of families. The children walked to school together and played together. This is not to say that there were no quarrels, disputes, tears, and angry stompings-home, but the mothers were generally in accord, and there were never any great disputes among the parents.

Perhaps a sociologist should conduct a study about why there was such accord among this fairly diverse set of people, whereas today it seems there is so little tolerance for differences. If children quarrel, adults take it up. The quarrel becomes major and is followed by gunplay, injuries, deaths, or lawsuits. Or is it just that now that I am no longer a participant, I am relying too much on news reports?

As much a feminist as I am, I must say that a great deal of the harmony we experienced had to be because most of the mothers were at home, cooking the meals, cleaning the house, washing and ironing the clothes, gardening, and very often sewing clothes. Only two of the families I knew directly during those first few years had mothers working at jobs while grandmothers looked after the house and children. Neither of those were academic families.

When I came to know more people whose parents or grandparents had lived in Florida, I learned that many of them had grown up in families where several black people had been employed as gardeners, cooks, laundry maids, cleaning maids, and so on. However, in Gainesville in 1950, few families had more than a daily maid and sometimes a weekly gardener.

The black people generally lived in small clusters scattered throughout the city. They had their own schools, churches, library, and funeral director (the richest black man in the city). There was one black medical doctor but no black hospital. Medical care came mostly from white doctors, and the white hospital served both black and white patients. A few black nurses cared for the black patients.

At first I was upset and annoyed at the patronizing way this was done. Later I came to recognize that more than patronizing was involved. There was a familiarity and a personal liking and understanding—maybe even love—existing between blacks and whites that I did not understand or even know anything about. In a few instances, I found that when I tried to do a kind act, it was not understood and was resented.

But I have wandered! I wanted to relate how so many of my neighbors became friends and the contributions those friendships made to my life—both to a more mature wisdom and to a greater happiness than I might have otherwise known.

Barbara Tilley and I became especially close, partially because our families were so compatible. Susan was younger but bigger than Steve. They were great friends. She was very intelligent, and sometimes drove him mad because she argued about everything, mostly the books they both read.

There was no child matching John Tilley's age at our house or nearby. He spent a lot of time with me. In fact he was at our house so much that more than one casual caller thought we had three children. I loved him very much. He was very intelligent, sweet, and peaceable. John and I enjoyed things together. He liked the music I listened to, and after he learned to read, he read our children's books, of which we had a rather great number.

When Alice was about two years old, the Tilleys had a third child, a delightful little girl, Virginia. Virginia and Alice played together endlessly. They had such wonderful imaginations. During one period they became horses and would only whinny and kick rather than speak. It could be exasperating!

Both Barbara and I were caught up in the McCarthy hearings. We listened all the time and updated each other if one of us missed anything. Wes taught in humanities at the university college, which was patterned after the University of Chicago program designed by Robert M. Hutchins. Wes himself had been a graduate student at Chicago.

Many of his colleagues had been recruited without doctorates specifically because of their writings and creative ideas. One colleague was cited by McCarthy as belonging to a communist cell while a student at Harvard and was called to testify. Barb and Wes knew the man and his family very well and were highly indignant and very involved.

Barbara's family lived in Kansas City, Missouri, where her father, a lawyer, was a judge and her mother was a concert pianist. Judge Dew was a stalwart Republican and a confirmed foe of the Pendergast machine. Wes' family was not at all political but were very musical. His parents had played piano and organ in movie houses in the days of silent films. His father had worked in Hollywood in the early days of filmmaking as a cameraman and had filmed for Pathé News in Mexico during the raids of Pancho Villa.

Later they had a studio in Austin, Texas, where they taught music. Once or twice the older Tilleys visited in Gainesville, making our children very envious because they had no grandparents to visit and bring delightful presents.

I also became very close friends with Jane Cutts, our neighbor just behind us. Our link was the League of Women Voters, which was my chief intellectual interest for many years. Neither Jane nor I were avid political party workers. We were issue-oriented. I was better at organizing and setting up study programs, doing research and investigation, and writing papers, whereas Jane was better at presenting, speaking, presiding, and lobbying. She was very gifted at moderating debates and remained reasonable and calm during controversy.

The Cuttses were the first of our group to leave Gainesville. They adopted a beautiful little boy a year before they left. Charlie, who was an engineer, went to Washington, DC, to head the engineering division of the National Science Foundation. Steve, Alice, and I spent a week with them a few years later during a spring break when we were living in New Haven. What wonderful friends they have been!

Tommy Petty's family I never knew very well, in spite of the fact that Alice regarded Tommy as her own personal property, so he was in our house a great deal. His grandmother took care of him and did the housework. His mother worked in an office. Tommy's father, who was a regional salesman for a food company, was away from home during weekdays. I should not have been surprised, and yet I was, when Tommy Petty became a very well-known singer and leader of a rock band.

We had erected a swing set in our backyard and put an immense sandbox near it where the children could swing and jump into the sand. Often Tommy used to swing wearing one of those coonskin hats that were popular during the time of the Disney film *Davy Crockett*.

We usually ate our evening meal later than the Pettys. After his meal Tommy would come over to our yard wearing his coonskin cap and swing while singing "Davy Crockett" at the top of his voice until Alice came out to join him. The only words he knew were "Davy Crockett, King of the Wild Frontier," and he sang them over and over again until even Freddy was glad to excuse Alice early from the table to go out to silence her friend.

Allergies and academics

Today one might wonder why I did not get someone to look after Alice or put her in a nursery school so that I could enroll at the university to finish my degree. The answer to that question is involved and complex, for it involves reasons of place, society, finances, and my own limited health and energy.

First of all, there were no nursery schools or cooperative play-groups. Then, too, both Steve and Alice were plagued with allergies and often ill, so they needed my attention. They were affected differently, but they were both extremely sensitive.

Steve always had a stuffy nose, headaches, and many colds. From the day he was born, he had an erratic appetite and was seldom excited about eating. During our first years in Florida, he ate so little that he hardly grew at all and was often sick. So I felt the need to give him my care and attention.

One of our first acquaintances in Gainesville was Dr. Marvin Kokomoor (Koke), a pediatrician. His father taught mathematics at the university, and Koke and his wife, Mabel, had just returned to Gainesville to open his practice in the summer of 1950. Steve was one of his very first patients. We met him at that very first potluck at University Methodist Church. It was a lucky coincidence because he and Steve got along very well together. It was Dr. Kokomoor who first tested Steve for allergies and gave him allergy shots.

When Alice was born, she nursed greedily and was always hungry. She slept very well, and very early in her life, she would sleep through the night without crying (as did Steve). But when she was only a few weeks old, I discovered blisters on her hands and arms where she had sucked on them during the night. We found that she was not gaining weight. Yet she did not want a bottle, and whatever formula she took from a bottle, she would vomit up within minutes. It did not seem to perturb her at all. She cried very little and retained her alertness and activity.

Then one day I found that I was bleeding after she nursed. So my doctor had some tests done and found a growth in that breast. How could I have the growth removed when my baby could digest only my milk? That was forty years ago, and medical science has advanced greatly since then. In 1952 the doctors did not have ready answers.

We had to find *something* to give Alice besides milk. We tried orange juice, which she loved, but it was difficult to strain it sufficiently so she could take it from a bottle. Then, too, I suspected that when that much substance was taken from the orange juice, there was not much nourishment left, so I spooned it into her mouth. It was a tedious task. She could not be still for very long and would frequently knock aside the spoon and spill the juice.

We finally tried powdered skim milk dissolved in sterile water. Neither Freddy nor I will ever forget her taking that first bottle of milk. She drank the whole bottleful down, hardly stopping to catch her breath. She then lay back on his arm with the most beautiful yet silly grin on her face, and promptly went to sleep. Eureka! We had found something she could take. I went into the hospital and had a cluster of cysts removed from one breast.

We later found that Alice was allergic to fats. For years I had to watch her diet closely and be alert for food reactions. She also had asthma. We called her our little seal because she barked so much. As a result I never felt that I could leave Alice safely with a maid for any length of time, for that was the only way that babysitting was done in Florida in 1952 and 1953.

There was also the problem of our limited finances. Freddy's salary was so small that it barely covered our basic needs. We had spent all our savings buying a car, a house, and furniture. And we soon found that there are a lot of expenses involved in taking care of a house, a car, and children! There really was nothing left over to pay tuition or hire a maid.

Perhaps I could have borrowed money, but that would have been the height of selfishness, for it would have increased our financial burden. That was the last thing Freddy needed. He was already very troubled. He needed to complete his doctorate, and for that he needed leisure for research and writing, not more financial worries. I did what I could to be most helpful. So although I very much wanted to finish my degree, I decided that this was not the time or the place.

The League of Women Voters

I have no clear recollection of my first League of Women Voters (LWV) meetings. My first memory of real involvement is my participation in a study of the newly formed United Nations. I think it was Rachi Marshall in Gainesville who asked me to work on her committee.

Rachi asked Reggie Hartmann, too. Reggie had been a political science major at the University of California at Berkeley (where she had met and married Fred), but she was not really all that interested in political science any more. She has a creative spirit— she was wonderful at designing and making clothes for herself and her children. She did a lot of work in children's activities and later in literature, writing, and translating from German. The LWV had no lasting appeal for her, as it did for me.

While I was involved with the LWV in Gainesville, I did a great deal of work on two national studies. One concerned the relationship between the United States and Latin America. The other concerned water, its sources, and uses. I still feel a sense of satisfaction about how much I learned about these subjects. I gave talks to clubs and interested groups and even visited other leagues within the state to talk on these subjects.

It should be noted that I had many good, reliable sources for both subjects right there at the University of Florida. Some of the best scholars in the nation on Latin America and Latin American affairs were there, and the books and periodicals in the university library reflected these interests. The material for the water study came largely from the schools of engineering and agriculture.

I always loved working with the local LWV group wherever I was, because they were such a wonderful group of women. I suppose there must have been some fanatical members now and then, but I doubt that they remained very long in the league. For one thing, they would not like the way the LWV worked. Each issue was always first studied, and then both pros and cons were presented and a consensus taken *before* a stand was acted upon (typically as a lobbying effort). This balance of study and action would not appeal to those who had already made up their minds.

Dinners and cookie parties

In spite of my preoccupation with my children and house, I have always been very interested in Freddy's career, both the learning and teaching aspects of it. Freddy had been teaching since he first started at Indiana and at Yale, but his position at Florida was his first independent appointment. He was a member of the faculty even though his title was still instructor because he was without his PhD.

After we moved to Gainesville, I do not recall discussing Freddy's classes and students very much. That is not too surprising. I had a lot to do and a lot to learn about living in a very different climate. And of course, the months of nausea and vomiting while I was pregnant with Alice did not leave me much time for conversing with Freddy either.

Then, too, because of his allergies, Steve's health was worrisome and he required a lot of attention. To be truthful, I must say that I enjoyed Steve. We were always very good companions. He loved being read to, even long after he could and did read alone. Reading him a story after his bath and before bed and saying evening prayers with him were rituals.

It must have been the Christmas before Alice's first birthday that we first decided to have Freddy's students come to our house for a drink (coffee, milk, or orange juice) and Christmas cookies. Right after Thanksgiving, I started to bake and store cookies for the event.

Every place we have lived, we have given this party on the same day—the last day of classes before Christmas break. And every year, more than half the students have already left town. To give the remaining students a treat, Freddy brought them to the house at class time, one group in the morning and one in the afternoon. They loved it! One shy young man told me that he never supposed he would ever be invited to a professor's home. This was during the early fifties, and it startled me to think that we could be seen as an exclusive class.

In later years and other places, our cookie party changed, but Christmas and cookies have always been synonymous in the Diamant household. It was in Florida that we started using pecans, and that I first baked our family's most-loved cookie, nut balls. The recipe came from Irma Rombauer's *Joy of Cooking* (she calls them Pecan Puffs). Steve especially loves nut balls.

For a very long time now, I have bought packages of shelled pecans from Koinonia Partners in Americus, Georgia. But in those early years in Florida, we bought pecans in the shell unsorted, from a little old man who preferred going fishing to selling (and he often did!). Freddy spent many a Saturday afternoon listening to the Metropolitan Opera broadcast, cracking pecans, and picking out nutmeats.

The very earliest orange groves in Florida were in the southeast section of Alachua County between the lakes. One of our cookie-eating students brought us oranges from the old groves. His father, a retired military officer, had also planted newer varieties of oranges, and later we also had some of those. It was there in Florida that we began our long tradition of fresh orange juice for breakfast and fresh grapefruit for dinner, at least during the Florida citrus season.

In addition to our cookie parties, we also had student dinners. This was long before the Danforth Foundation encouraged and sponsored faculty entertaining students in their homes. We did it simply because we enjoyed it. I had two different menus that I developed just for such groups. I tried to keep it simple, something I could prepare and serve alone but also something that tasted good and was a satisfying meal.

For one menu, lasagna was the main dish. I had to make my own pasta and use substitutes for the ricotta and mozzarella cheeses. Crusty bread was not always available, but I usually found something with which to make garlic bread. I also made fresh tossed salad in a big dishpan. For dessert I often served ambrosia, a southern dessert I first ate at a church dinner. Ambrosia is simple, just orange sections mixed with grated coconut. But made with fresh ingredients, it is light and tasty after a filling entree. Sometimes I made cookies, too.

The other menu was a local favorite unknown to me before I lived in Florida. It was a rice and chicken dish known as perloo. Marjorie Kinnan Rawlings, a resident of Alachua County, says it began as a dish cooked by hunters over an open fire. Perloo consists just of boiled rice with any kind of meat tossed in, and for seasoning only salt and lots of black pepper. It is unbelievably good when made by southern cooks. In Gainesville, perloo suppers were the equivalent of the chili suppers of my own elementary school days in Indiana.

Dollie Parris

It was Dollie Parris who taught me how to make perloo, though mine never tasted as good as hers did. Dollie was such a good friend and a sweet, loving person. She came into our lives shortly after Alice was born. When we were preparing for the birth of our new baby, one of our needs was someone to take care of Steve after school. Freddy could not always be home that early, and Steve, who was seven years old, could not, of course, come home to an empty house.

When a young black girl named Vergerie was recommended to us as capable and trustworthy, we had her start coming to get acquainted with us and our ways early in January 1952. Vergerie came in mid-afternoon and stayed until evening two or three hours a day. She was lively and entertaining.

I was most happy to have her around during those long days of waiting for Alice to arrive. Being so short of money, we had to dispense with her services soon after Alice and I came home from the hospital. I cannot remember how much we paid her, but I am sure it was less than it should have been, while also being more than we could really afford.

A year or so later, a black woman came to our door and introduced herself as Dollie Parris. She asked if I could use a maid. She said she was in need of work and had heard from Vergerie that I was a very nice woman. Dollie told me that she had been working as a full-time maid for Billy Matthews, who had recently been elected to Congress. The Matthews family was moving to Washington, DC, so she had to find other employment. When I talked to Mrs. Matthews, I found that she had been teaching school and Dollie had been her housekeeper. She said her children adored Dollie, and they hated to leave her behind.

Freddy and I talked it over and decided it would be a great help to have someone at least half a day each week. I knew I would welcome even a half-day of relief. So we decided to try to squeeze out enough money to pay her. Dollie came one afternoon each week, and we came to love her very much, especially Alice. When angry with me, Alice would tell me she would rather live with Dollie.

On her afternoon with us, Dollie took care of Alice and did our ironing. Reggie Hartmann made all the clothes for her two little girls and little boy. She designed them, made the patterns, and sewed them by hand, until she could afford to buy a sewing machine. She passed on all the girls' clothes to Alice, and so Alice was beautifully dressed for a very long time. However, these lovely dresses had to be ironed, as did Freddy's shirts. Of course, for play Alice wore shorts and sleeveless T-shirts most of the year. She hated wearing long pants and long sleeves, even on cooler days.

Whatever we may have thought we had learned about raising a child from having cared for Steve, we quickly had to discard with Alice. Steve seemed to understand what we asked him to do. I was always careful to explain why. I explained things in the same way to Alice. However, even when she was quiet long enough to listen, she never remembered for long—or else she could not resist doing things in her own way.

Before Alice was strong enough to crawl on all fours, she would wiggle off beds and chairs and then move on her belly across rooms. She took all the books off shelves. She stuffed things in the toilet. She played in the gar-bage can. No drawer of clean clothing was safe from her grubby hands. When she was not rearranging the house, and while in her bed, play-pen, or chair, she sucked her thumb and twisted her front hair. Washing or combing her hair was a major battle. The playpen never held her very long. She climbed out of it. It did not matter to her that the last time she had tried it, she had pinched her fingers or fallen on her head.

Alice
Gainesville, c. 1954

At the same time, she was the joy of my heart and I adored her. Just when I thought I absolutely could not tidy another room she had just upset or give her one more bath, she would do some-thing I thought so sweet or so clever that it erased my anger and restored my soul! But with Alice life was not tranquil. She seemed destined to learn by trial and error. So I greatly needed the af-ternoon break that Dollie gave me. What a blessing that she ever came to our door!

Perloo dinners with Freddy's students

I have wandered from my theme of working with Freddy and his students. During those years I have little recollection of shar-ing Freddy's intellectual life. If it had not been for the League of Women Voters and my friendship and discussions with Barbara Tilley, I might well have fallen into mental lethargy. In some ways I may have done just that anyway, but I was happy in my life, and I especially enjoyed having students in our home.

I remember two East Asian students in particular. One was Japanese and one Korean. I had been interested in China and read a great deal about it before our marriage. I assumed too easily that no great cultural differences separate Korea, Japan, and other Asian countries. However, these two students had very different characters, and they revealed to me that East Asians differ as much from one society to another as do peoples of the western world.

Kobayashi, who was from Japan, told me about how he and his classmates had felt when they learned that the emperor was not a god but just another human being. Although his English was good, it was not quite adequate to communicate how that event had affected his life. But it was obvious that it had affected him profoundly. Kobayashi was a pleasant, polite young man, but for as long as I knew him, he remained skeptical and cynical.

It was my perloo menu that I served when I knew that East Asian students would join us. I remember the evening I met Hwai-Yol Jung, who was from Korea. Hwai-Yol was so very intelligent. He had such a sweet, pleasant manner, and seemed so compassionate. That evening he came into the kitchen to ask if he might have a second serving of perloo.

I had cooked the perloo the day before and put it in my turkey roaster to reheat in the oven just before serving, and there was lots left. Later I took my own plate of food into the living-dining room where the students were sitting about, many on the floor, and I sat down beside Hwai-Yol. He had eaten his second plateful and had the half-smile of a satisfied puppy.

As I sat there and ate, Hwai-Yol told me what he had been thinking. In Korea he had been near starving, as had all the others he knew. Rice had come as a relief supply, and he went every day to stand in line for his day's ration, which was just as much as he could carry in his two cupped hands. At that time, he said, he never thought he would ever be full of rice again. He patted his tummy as he smiled and said, "I'm full. And it was so good!" These are the kinds of things that have made me feel pleased with being a part of Freddy's life. We keep having similar experiences, even now!

Thinking of Kobayashi reminds me of two other dear friends we came to know in Gainesville and with whom we still keep in touch, Ivan and Esther Putnam. Ivan was the first director of foreign student affairs to be appointed at the University of Florida. Ivan and Esther were also members of our church and sang in the choir. They had a little girl, Cindy, who was a bit older than Alice, and two little boys.

Esther and Ivan were tireless in their attention to our foreign-born students. When Jack Kobayashi married, it was Ivan and Esther who took the bride-to-be, a lovely Japanese girl, into their home. They arranged for a wedding and reception there (on a very hot Sunday afternoon!). These particular students stand out in my memory, but Freddy had a great many others through the years, and many of them visited our home.

Freddy's dissertation

When we had been in Gainesville two years, Freddy had a summer free of teaching. He wanted to arrange a stay in Washington to use the Library of Congress to work on his dissertation. He kept insisting that he could not pursue his dissertation work until he had some uninterrupted time in a library. Fred Hartmann, his colleague and friend, served in the navy as a reservist. He was required to do two weeks of active service each year, and he planned to drive to Washington, DC, that summer for this duty. So it was arranged that Freddy would go with him to spend time in the congressional library.

After Freddy was home again, the dissertation remained almost untouched. Manning phoned me now and then to discuss the need for Freddy to finish this work. I could tell him little. Freddy would not discuss it with me either. The whole business had become rather wearing on me, to say the least!

This particular time in our married life was a testing time. Surviving it strengthened our ties greatly. For my part, I was not unhappy. Having our own pretty little house, two children whom I loved passionately, and congenial friends and neighbors kept me busy and reasonably content. I was quite sure in my own mind that Freddy would come about in his own time, and all would be well!

The Diamant Family
Gainesville, Florida
c. 1955

The tornado incident

At both Indiana and Yale, we had enjoyed lots of music and theater, but in Gainesville, we hadn't much of either. There were no cultural centers very near us. For entertainment, we went to movies more than ever before. In those years, there were many good ones. We also went to the beach quite often. Our family has always loved ocean beaches! And then, too, we spent many evenings having friends in for dinner and going to friends' homes for dinner.

In 1954 the Hartmanns went to Bonn, Germany, for the year. Fred was one of the very first to receive a Fulbright grant. That same year Sylvia and Bill Havard and their daughter Deborah came to Gainesville. Freddy and I really enjoyed Sylvia and Bill. Bill had grown up in Baton Rouge, Louisiana, and Sylvia in England.

Sylvia was the typical lovely English female. Her coloring was so beautiful it was startling. She had golden blonde hair, deep blue eyes with lovely long dark lashes, and glowing white skin touched with rose. She was as sweet and pleasant as she was beautiful. Bill was a marvelous raconteur. An evening with him was always an evening of laughter. Their daughter Debbie and our Alice were the same age. Sometimes they played well together, but too often they disagreed loudly. I have never been able to decide how much of it we should blame on Alice.

Our Alice and Steve liked to sleep, and in this, we were fortunate. We could always take them with us to friends' homes in the evening and put them on a bed or couch where they would fall asleep. We could pick them up and take them home to their own beds without trouble. Debbie Havard was not like that. When put to bed, she howled, screamed, and wanted drinks of water.

One evening the Havards came over to listen to election returns with us, for we were all four avid about politics. We put the girls to bed—Debbie in Alice's room, which was her choice, and Alice in our bedroom. Debbie would not be quiet and go to sleep, so we closed the doors to listen to the radio. A bit later Freddy went into our bedroom. He came back with a strange look on his face and beckoned me to the room.

Our room was a mess, an absolute mess. A tornado could hardly have made it look worse. Alice had gone through the closets and drawers, and she had upset, spilled, mangled, or scattered everything on which she could lay her little hands. There was broken glass from smashed containers and mirrors, and so many red globs around the room that we snatched up Alice to examine her for cuts and bleeding. But she was fine. The red globs were lipstick and rouge. Instead of going to sleep, Alice had amused herself by wrecking our room.

Bill had a strange reaction. When he and Sylvia saw what happened, he immediately said, "It's Debbie's fault." He snatched Debbie out of Alice's bed, gave her some slaps on her bottom, and said to Sylvia, "Let's take her home."

In vain Freddy and I kept saying, "Debbie didn't do anything. It was Alice who made this mess." But Bill said that Alice would have gone to sleep if Debbie had not screamed so long and so loudly. That might well have been true, but Freddy and I felt it did not excuse Alice. We well knew that Alice loved being destructively busy.

New Haven, Connecticut (1955)

With the passing months, Freddy's unfinished doctoral dissertation became an ever greater concern for us. Manning Dauer was instrumental in solving that problem when he showed Freddy an announcement from the Danforth Foundation about teacher-study grants and urged Freddy to apply.

Freddy did so and received a grant that enabled us to return to New Haven in 1955 for one year. During that time Freddy would have no other obligation but to concentrate on completing the last requirement for his doctorate. So that August we rented our house furnished, packed up our personal belongings, and went back to New Haven.

We had asked friends in New Haven to send us a list of faculty who were going away and wanted to rent their homes furnished for the year. After correspondence and phone calls, we rented sight unseen a house in Hamden, Connecticut from a Professor May in the French Department. Unfortunately the house had only two bedrooms, but since the bedrooms were large, Alice and Steve were able to share a bedroom with only minimal difficulty. Alice had to sleep in a crib again, which she was physically small enough to do without discomfort. She did not like the idea, but we were able to persuade her, and it worked well enough.

There were adjustments for everyone to make. For Alice it was hard to get used to wearing more and heavier clothing, and to learn that she could not just run outside in indoors wear. Nor did she immediately find someone to play with. Appointments had to be made to play with another child. So she learned to play alone. For Alice playtime was different, inside and outside.

Steve had a difficult adjustment to make at school. The Hamden school system was like the system under which I had been taught; however, it had a far more rigid pattern than even I had known. It had a female principal who had been in the Connecticut public school system all her career, and I rather doubt she had gotten as far as Columbia Teachers College in New York to upgrade her theories or her skills. There was one way to do things, and that was her way.

In Gainesville Steve's teachers had been young, enthusiastic, and trained in the philosophy of readiness to learn. Evidently, Steve had not been ready for math, for we soon found that he was failing in it. Freddy took over helping Steve adapt to the conformities of learning math by rote. After all it was the way Freddy had been taught.

I had to listen to all that ensued. I am sure it bothered Steve much less than it did me. Although I, too, had learned multiplication tables, it had been presented to me more as a learning game, with multiplication as a tool I would always need. Steve knew how to multiply. He knew concepts and use. He just could not answer quickly.

This particular episode probably illustrates better than anything else one of the very real differences between Freddy and me—our attitudes toward our children and their training. I had grown up in an unstructured way, so it was hard for me to let Freddy shout and shove his children into rote learning.

When I interfered, he would get very angry with me and say that I was undermining him in the eyes of his children. I would acknowledge the fairness of his argument, and I really did try not to interfere. But I often forgot, and in the heat of the moment, I kept on interfering. I concede that I am a very stubborn sort. I still believe in my concepts rather than his.

That year was tough in many ways, but it brought many pleasures as well. We were able to renew our friendship with Ann and Jim Dunn, and we came to love Christopher and Jennifer, their charming, talented children. We also renewed our acquaintance with the Reverend John Gummere at St. John's Episcopal Church. There we acquired two new friends, Alice and Marit Helland, who taught in the Sunday school and whose nephew, Frank, was Steve's age. They planned many trips and excursions for Frank and Steve and sometimes Alice.

Judy Spose, Steve's old friend, was in her last year in high school. She was still a friendly, charming person, but she was very busy and had less time for Steve. However, one of Steve's friends was in a nature conservation club. The club headquarters was in West Rock Park, so we spent a lot of time there. I think it was Steve's greatest interest during that year.

One of the first things I did in New Haven was start driving a car again. In Gainesville Freddy had been urging me to get a license, for he found it onerous to be the only driver in the family. I took some lessons from the same teacher he had practiced with five years before and got my license. Because of my earlier years of driving on the farm, it was a much easier task for me than it has ever been for Freddy.

Ann, Snoopy, Alice, Steve, & Freddy
New Haven, 1955

In New Haven we were once again able to hear great music and musicians and to go to plays and musicals. The Yale glee club remains in my mind as presenting the very best of the many Christmas programs I have heard, except for the oratorios we heard in Germany and France.

We also went to New York to see the wonderful decorations at Rockefeller Center. We saw the New York City Ballet perform *The Nutcracker Suite*. Alice especially loved it! It was her first ballet, and she moved out into the aisle to sit on the steps, enthralled throughout. For a little girl who found it hard to sit still for very long, this act speaks for itself. She was enchanted. To have children who love the kind of things you love is so very wonderful!

This was also the winter we first visited Freddy's cousins in Newark on New Year's Day. This was always Eric and Herta Diment's day to give a party. After living in Sweden for several years, Herta had acquired a taste for Swedish cooking, and for this occasion, she served many Swedish dishes. This was the first time they saw Alice. Alice fell in love with Aunt Judith (Eric's mother) and Fritzi (his sister). The rapport between Alice and Aunt Judith remained even in later years.

We all stayed very healthy that year. Steve's allergies, which dominated his life so much of the year in Florida, became quiescent soon after the first frost in September in Connecticut. He had no colds. He ate well and grew. It was a pleasure to have to buy clothes in a larger size by mid-year.

That lovely state of affairs ended in June, however. June was such a beautiful month in Hamden. The roses were so lovely, and there were so many of them. But poor Steve had one of the worst attacks of hay fever I ever knew him to have. His eyes were swollen and running, and so was his nose. His face became swollen and covered with cold sores. Fortunately it abated somewhat before the Fourth of July.

That was also the year Alice became tractable, except for washing her hair. She really was a treasure the whole year through. She was healthy, no colds and no coughing, and she began to practice her tidying ways. She kept the room she and Steve shared very tidy and scolded him when he was untidy.

Early in the new year, I became more than a little concerned that Freddy had not yet put very much down on paper, at least as far as I knew. I do not remember that we discussed it very much. I cannot bear to be nagged, so I avoid doing it myself. But I recall one incident in the early weeks of the fall semester. Freddy decided to learn Russian, so he hired a tutor. This gave me cause for concern. I had no qualms about his learning Russian. I just wanted him to finish his dissertation! I must have brought the subject up, for he dropped the tutoring.

Eventually Freddy wrote his first chapters and showed them to Dr. Driver. Dr. Driver criticized them so harshly that we both were in despair. I must have forgotten those early days at Indiana University when Freddy would despair to me that he had failed each time he took an exam. Just when I would be trying to prepare myself for a change in his occupation, he would come forth bright and smiling, having produced whatever was needed in first-class style. It is no wonder that later in life I required a pacemaker for my heart!

As it turned out, it was not until April that I was required to do much typing. Then for another month, I did a great deal of typing and retyping. I could have recited that first chapter. I am not patient, and monotony drives me mad, so those next three or so months were terrible for me. After the usual rounds of housekeeping and childcare, every other possible minute was given to typing.

Most of the footnotes and a great many words in the text were in German, a language I did not know. It soon became apparent that I was making many typing errors by misspelling the German words, so Freddy suggested that I have my eyes examined. For some reason, it has always been hard for me to believe that anything could be physically wrong with me. I always resist such thoughts. So it was Freddy who made an appointment with an ophthalmologist for me. I was fitted with reading glasses, which I wore on a cord around my neck, and I began to type the German words correctly.

As I sit here recalling the tediousness of typing that manuscript, I think of how much easier it would be to produce a dissertation manuscript today using a computer. I had to make *seven* perfect copies of each page. It had to be typed on special white bond paper and show *no* erasures. That was hard enough. But every time Freddy showed the manuscript to Dr. Driver, he would change a word or phrase or the placement of something. I began to stomp off angrily and swear I would not retype another thing!

The simple change of a word or phrase was not so simple to change in the manuscript. Most often it did not involve retyping just one page. Usually a page would end with words left over or not enough words to finish the last line, so I would have to redo any number of pages until they all came out neatly and evenly. That was a time that tried my soul!

For some time, we had been trying to persuade my niece Julia Klipsch (Mae's daughter) to visit us. I felt guilty about how we were always imposing ourselves upon them when we visited in Indiana during the summer. I would have loved to show return hospitality to any of my family, but rarely did anyone visit us. So we were very glad when at last Julie came.

It was unfortunate that Julie came for a visit while I was still so busy with the typing. But as it turned out, Julie's coming became a most fortunate event for all of us. The whole family had always loved Julie very much, and this visit made us love her even more. She was an agreeable companion for Steve, and she loved playing with Alice. The two Helland sisters took Steve and Julie on a trip to Sturbridge, Massachusetts, and the Dunns took them all to the beach.

Although Freddy was finished writing, I still had typing to do, and we had to get ourselves and the house ready for our departure. Freddy took Steve and Julie to New York City for a few days, while I continued to type. When all the work on the dissertation was finally completed, we both felt a relieved sense of accomplishment. It had not been ready in time for Freddy to be awarded his degree in June, but having fulfilled the requirements, Freddy had the assurance of his doctorate in hand. We were ready to go home to Florida.

Gainesville, Florida (1956)

We took Julie home via Niagara Falls, and after a brief visit in Indiana went back to Gainesville. There we had a rude awakening as to how other people live. Our house and lawn were a near disaster.

The couple who had rented our house for the year had no children. He taught in the School of Education, and he and his wife were both native Floridians. I knew that they had a cleaning maid, so I had assumed everything would be in order. Perhaps they thought it was. Looking back from a greater perspective, I can understand their point of view a bit better now. But I know that I could not ever endure living with as much filth as they left in our house.

They must have had a problem with the space heater, because oily cobwebs were everywhere. We had venetian blinds throughout, and this oily dirt was on every slat. Many cords on the blinds were broken, too. All the furniture was dirty and sticky.

The curtains and upholstery were in shreds. Most of our bedding, pillows, and blankets had been left outside in the rain. All our pillows smelled moldy. Our cooking utensils were ruined. They all were out of shape or had burned-on food clinging to the rims.

The rug in the breezeway, which I had bought new during the summer before we left, was totally ruined. It smelled so greatly of cat urine that it almost made us ill. The rug even had holes in it. They had three cats, which were often left locked in the breezeway for hours. Evidently the cats were also responsible for shredding the cushions and the curtains.

We all had to work many hours to clean and renew our house and everything in it. I believe we ate out for several evenings. I know we threw out every cooking utensil and every pillow. One of the legs on the dining table had been broken, so we had to cart the table off to have it refinished and the leg repaired. Even the lawn had to be replanted!

I came to understand that there are quite a few people living in the south who live in this very casual fashion, to put it kindly. Probably I should not say "living in the south," because there are people everywhere who do not regard cleanliness as being as important as I do.

I expect that some of my fervor is related to my allergies. For some years, I have suffered from chronic asthma. I have come to realize that much of my ill health throughout my life has resulted from my allergies. The chief irritants for me are house dust and molds. Even before I was tested, I suppose I acted by instinct. I have always worked hard to keep my surroundings clean.

With this experience behind us, we were once again comfortable in our home. We very happily took up our old friends and acquaintances in church, school, and neighborhood. Some changes had come about, but none of great significance except that we saw the Hartmanns less because Reggie was having problems with her health.

During the next two years, our lives changed very little but our schedule became busier as our children grew older. Freddy was far better than I was in assisting them in their outside interests. Camping was something I loathed, so I absolutely was not willing to accompany anybody on overnight camping trips. I had no skills in crafts, so I could never contribute to making costumes or masks or anything of that nature. However, I could bake and cook very well, so bake sales and refreshments I would and did do ad nauseam.

Freddy did not like doing the Scout activities either, but since I could not do them, he did. I am sure there were many times when he would have gladly traded me in for a strong, skillful woman! Sometimes I felt a bit guilty about my shortcomings, but usually I was quite hard-nosed and said to myself, "It's good for Freddy to do these things for and with his children. After all he was the one who wanted a family."

Freddy deserves credit for taking on this challenge. However, I must add that his participation in these activities played a role in his acquiring a greater understanding of American life. This is lacking in many foreign-born people who remain in ethnic groups and stubbornly resist change and new experiences.

After Freddy finished his doctoral dissertation at Yale, Cecil Driver suggested that he send a copy to Princeton Press for them to consider publishing. So one of the copies I typed was sent to them. The press replied that they would like to publish the work as a book, but it would need some revision. Freddy began to work on the revision, so once again I had a great deal of typing to do.

Alice goes to school

Unlike Steve, who had to be pushed into going to school, Alice wanted passionately to go to school. Unfortunately the public schools had strict age requirements for enrollment, and there were few privately run schools. Since Alice had been born in January, she would be five years and eight months old before she could enter kindergarten. It was quickly evident that this would be unacceptable. The morning after her fifth birthday, Alice dressed herself in her best clothes, including her ruffled petticoat, and insisted that I take her to school.

Alice
Gainesville, c. 1956

This was a tough one to handle. The School of Education at the University of Florida had an experimental school, P. K. Yonge, which they operated outside state regulations. Although I was not at all keen on it, we enrolled her in their summer kindergarten program. I was surprised that she wanted to go to school during the summer when her neighborhood playmates were not in school, but she went very happily.

It was harder still to get Alice into a swimming program, because she was so short. All public programs required that children be able to stand in the pool with their heads above water before they could be accepted for instruction. We solved that one by teaching her ourselves in motel swimming pools.

When the regular school year began, Alice went to the afternoon kindergarten session at our neighborhood school, which was named for the southern poet Sidney Lanier. In Florida in the 1950s, the prevailing style was for young females, from college coeds to one-year-olds, to wear ruffled petticoats somewhat in the style of *Gone with the Wind* costuming. Alice loved these ruffled dresses and petticoats. When she started attending kindergarten at Sidney Lanier, she insisted on wearing such dresses to school.

I was startled when at my first parent-teacher interview, her teacher asked me why Alice did not play outside. "Alice not play outside? But she loves to play outside," I must have answered. When I returned home, I asked Alice about this, and her answer was that she could not play outside in a dress, petticoat, and patent leather shoes. So with my hearty endorsement, she wore a top, shorts, and slides to school from the next day on, as long as we lived in Florida.

Looking back, I must philosophize a bit about human behavior and social patterns. How was it that in the south, the schools could be so relaxed about allowing children to go to school in comfortable clothing suited to the climate, whereas "ladies" were expected to wear hats, gloves, and hosiery when going to church or social events? Similarly men wore suits and ties in a formal way. This all in spite of the fact that there was very little air conditioning. On the other hand, in the north, schools required greater conformity in clothing for children, whereas for practically all occasions, adults were allowed a wide latitude in their dress!

Surgery

Early in 1958 Freddy was invited to return to Yale to teach during the 1958-59 academic year and he accepted. So once again we were busy gearing up for a year in New Haven. Though I had been freed from sciatic pain after Alice was born, my overall health was still not good. I suffered from anemia, but I was unable to take oral iron supplements because my digestive system rejected them. So twice a year I received a series of vitamin shots.

I was also troubled by great irregularity in my menstrual cycle. My doctor, Emory Bell, suggested that I consider a hysterectomy. He believed I had either cysts or tumors that grew and subsided from time to time. Freddy and I decided that we did not care whether we had more children, and that a hysterectomy might be the healthiest course for me. I also considered that I would be leaving Dr. Bell's care and relying on a new physician who would be unfamiliar with my situation.

So we decided that I would have a partial hysterectomy, which would remove just the womb. Dr. Bell was jubilant (there is no other description) over the pathologist's report. My womb had indeed been a collection of cysts and tumors. I concluded that he had received a lot of negative flack from his medical colleagues about his advice and actions, and he was relieved to find that he had been correct.

The operation was set for June when Freddy would be less busy. But it complicated life because we also had to find someone to rent our house for that year (I shuddered at the thought), and we had to find a place to rent in New Haven. Because our previous rental experience had been so bitter and costly, I felt very uncertain about renting again and about my ability to judge a reasonable caretaker for our home.

One day a young man came to see the house. He had recently completed service in the navy and was returning to the university for an engineering degree. He had just married a widow with two children. Our house, he said, was just what he was looking for. He was not very talkative, but he impressed me with his quiet sincerity and his love and concern for his wife and her children. We rented our house to them. They were wonderful tenants! They have remained our friends over the years.

New Haven, Connecticut (1958)

We went back to New Haven in 1958 for another year. This time we lived in the house of James Tobin, a Yale economics professor who has since been awarded a Nobel Prize in economics. The house was large, very comfortably furnished, and in a pleasant part of New Haven known as Edgewood. Steve was enrolled in Sheridan Junior High, and Alice was in first grade at Edgewood Elementary School.

Alice had a very good year. She was reading very easily by the end of the first month. Like Steve she read many books on her own but for a long time, continued wanting to be read to as she cuddled next to the reader. The Tobin house had a lovely working fireplace, and frequently either Freddy or I sat by the fire in the middle of the couch and read to them. It is a lovely memory! I feel quite nostalgic about those times.

We attended the Church-on-the-Green, a church I really loved. It was the first Anglican Church established during colonial days and very plain. For many years they had not used candles or flowers on the altar. By 1957 the congregation had become less austere and candles were in place, but it remained a Low Church.

During the Sunday school or education hour, there was an adult forum that we enjoyed attending. I remember most vividly one of the participants, Randolph Crump Miller, a professor of Christian education at Yale. The national office of the Episcopal Church had just published and was distributing his lesson study plan for Christian education. He had developed a new method, complete with literature, for a comprehensive curriculum from preschool through young adults.

That winter Randy, together with a colleague and someone from the Episcopal seminary (also in New Haven), offered a course on Christian education. I eagerly enrolled in the course, which was held at our church in the evening. Often too few people attended (sometimes I was the only layperson there), so the course was abandoned after about a month.

Randy did not abandon me as a student, and I kept up my study of the material he had offered. He was generous with his time and supervision while we were in New Haven and even years afterward when I would write him for his advice about teaching problems. He was one of my favorite people!

We resumed our usual round of entertainment for New Haven, which included going to New York for special events. One memorable event was our visit to the Bronx Zoo. On Columbus Day, there was a special train ride to the zoo offered for school children. Ann Dunn suggested that we go.

We had long owned and read a Little Golden Book called *A Day at the Zoo*, which we soon realized was a day at the Bronx Zoo! Just after we entered the gates, we heard a lion roaring, just as we had read in our book. Alice's face immediately assumed a rapt look and retained it the whole day. Everything was just like it was in the book. I do not remember that I ever spent a more delightful day with my children. For Alice in particular it was a magical day.

Once again we went to New York for the ballet *The Nutcracker* and to see the beautiful Christmas tree at the Rockefeller Center. And, too, I was also able to see special art exhibits at the Metropolitan Museum of Art and the Museum of Modern Art, which I enjoyed greatly. It is almost impossible for me to explain just how much these excursions and events meant to me.

In those years trains into the city were frequent and inexpensive, and both New Haven and New York were relatively safe. I must say that in New Haven I detected a change, in that a new ethnic group had arrived to push the Irish, Italians, and Poles up the economic ladder. These newcomers were formerly southern black people. Their culture was very different from those of the European ethnic groups, who were finding that they had fewer differences than they had once imagined, and who were drawing together to put down the black people.

That tension was only beginning to be felt, but it was surely there. I felt it through Steve, who found his school to be less pleasant than it had previously been. He found outside things to do rather than associating with schoolmates. The Tobins had a piano, so both Steve and Alice took piano lessons that year. Steve ushered at the new ice hockey rink at Yale, which he enjoyed very much. He also resumed his interests at West Rock Park with the nature conservation group.

As before we made picnic excursions in every season into the beautiful New England hills and countryside. In the summer we added the new Shakespeare theater at Stratford, Connecticut, to our list of favorite places to go.

Freddy and I also greatly enjoyed the faculty dinners to which we were invited and the return dinners we gave. I found these dinners delightful, for the people we met were very cosmopolitan, widely traveled, and usually interesting. Since we were last in

New Haven, Fred Baarghoorn, the Russian specialist in the Political Science Department, had been arrested as an American spy in Russia, where he had spent months in jail. It was only at a dinner party that I could have had an opportunity to meet and converse with him. Fred was a bachelor and did not give dinner parties, but he was a pleasant guest.

The Japanese specialist was a native of Japan, as was his wife, and the meals at their home were wonderful, so much better than the food at Japanese restaurants, which were just then becoming popular. I greatly enjoyed and valued the entire faculty at Yale.

Throughout the year, the university brought many exciting visitors to the campus for lectures and seminars. I attended as many as possible and enjoyed them thoroughly. There was one well-known visitor who was very disappointing—Gunnar Myrdal, whose book *An American Dilemma* was praised and discussed at every party we attended. I went with Freddy to a small gathering in one of the residential colleges where Myrdal was conversing with a few faculty and students in one of the lounges. Myrdal had taken too many alcoholic drinks. He was simply an incoherent, slightly disgusting man that afternoon. We were told this happened too frequently with him.

If my memory is correct, this was also the year when Adlai Stevenson was a visitor. I went to meet and talk with him in a small gathering. I am not, nor have I ever been, one who is bowled over by public figures and adoringly amenable to all they say or do. I had liked what Stevenson had said when he was a presidential candidate and had voted for him. However, in this small group, I neither liked nor disliked him or what he had to say, which was precious little. I felt mildly letdown after this impersonal encounter with the man.

As usual I was quite ready to go home to Gainesville when August came. We drove down the east coast, stopping to visit places we had not seen before. We came to Jacksonville, Florida, rather late in the afternoon and could easily have driven on to Gainesville that evening. Remembering our last return and the condition of our house, we decided to stay overnight near Jacksonville Beach.

We likely were also influenced by how much we loved the beach and how superior we found our Florida beaches to New England's. The next morning Alice had to be persuaded into the car.

We all would have liked another day at the beach, but we knew we needed to get home and settled before classes resumed.

Gainesville, Florida (1959)

This time our homecoming was a real joy. Everything was in perfect order! We were delighted to discover that our wonderful tenants, Frank and Betty Chisholm, had bought and moved into a neighboring house, that of Harold and Mary Jean Hanson, who had moved to Austin, Texas. We regretted losing the Hansons, but we were glad to have the Chisholms as neighbors!

Before long, life resumed its routine and pleasures among good friends. There was also the added joy brought by the realization that our children were rapidly growing. We began to think about what we needed to do to assist them into the kind of schooling and skills required for their futures. We had lived for so many years on such a small income that we were years behind most people of our age and education in our financial worth.

By this time, I had learned that even in academia, many people do a great deal of finagling, posturing, and exaggeration about work done or in progress in order to earn promotions or higher salaries. I did not want Freddy to engage in such behavior. At the same time, I certainly realized that it would take many favorable, almost miraculous happenings to boost his earnings to an acceptable level in Florida. We had too many handicaps to overcome, caused largely by Freddy's tardiness in finishing his PhD.

After the winter term ended, we decided that rather than sell our present house and buy a slightly larger one, we would borrow on our equity to enlarge our house. Our greatest need was a laundry area and another bath. So we had our house remodeled and did a bit of redecorating as well. We put a much larger air conditioning unit into our new family room, which had been our old breezeway, and with this addition, it became a much more comfortable house.

Steve was, by this time, in high school, playing violin in the school orchestra and taking a great interest in his science courses. Soon after the Soviet success with Sputnik in outer space, there was an enormous quickening of interest in science at all levels in the schools. Steve was one of those electrified. Freddy and I did all that we could to assist him in his interest. However, we continued to put in our plugs for the arts, humanities, and social sciences.

I remember Freddy helping Steve with a project in photosynthesis that took him all the way to the state science fair, where he received an honorable mention. Steve was not a brilliant student all around, but he was always a very good student. He might well have been brilliant in the social sciences, but he was never given the incentive, either by society or by his educators, to give time and interest to that area of study.

Chapter 7

Haverford

(1960-1966)

Early in 1959 Freddy received a call from Haverford College, near Philadelphia in Pennsylvania, inviting him for an interview for a position in their Political Science Department. He went, was offered the position, and accepted. The decision was made entirely by him.

At this point, I knew so little about his feelings concerning his professional life that I did not question his decision or his right to make it. I always felt that he was the one supporting the family, so he had the right to choose how he would do it, especially since I was not earning money myself. That I had no real profession or degree, I must confess, still causes me some resentment.

We move to Haverford

Once again we had to concern ourselves with the practical problems involved in moving. Moving *to* Florida had involved far fewer problems than moving *from* Florida did. We arrived with only a few possessions and some cash in hand. When we left, we had more possessions, and we had just depleted our cash reserves by remodeling our house!

We had put down roots in our community, and our children had just recently renewed and deepened their friendships and their school ties. As for me, I hated leaving my church and my work with Laura Smith in the kindergarten division of the Sunday school. I also hated leaving my friends and co-workers in the League of Women Voters.

Steve, who was finishing tenth grade that year, was quite unhappy about changing schools again. Probably he discussed his feelings more with me than his father. I was more sympathetic with his point of view and more understanding of his unhappiness than Freddy, though Freddy was not unsympathetic. Steve's greatest concern was that he would have only a very short time in his new school before he would need to start thinking about where to apply for admission to college. Consequently, we had to consider where he would be going to school and how that might affect admission to a good college.

We weighed the relative merits of public versus private schools. Lower Merion High School, the public school Steve would attend, was very large, and it worried us that it might take quite a long time to adjust to it. After many phone calls, many letters, and much discussion, we enrolled Steve in a private school in a suburb near Haverford—Episcopal Academy.

All we knew about it was what we learned from the literature and letters from the headmaster. We had obtained a list of private schools from some kind soul at Haverford College and written to all of them. The only headmaster who was in the least friendly and welcoming was Dr. Quin, the headmaster of Episcopal Academy. I was amazed and distressed by the indifference, if not unfriendliness, of all the others.

That was one of the concerns of our move. Financially, of course, our greatest need was to sell our house. I found the idea emotionally troubling. I really liked having my own house, and that little house in particular. When compared to the homes of our colleagues, our house was probably the least expensive, the least imposing, and in one of the least desired neighborhoods in town. Nevertheless, I was happy there, and I knew very little about where we were going.

Freddy had not thought much about housing when he accepted his appointment. I can understand that it would not have been at the top of his list. I understood his professional concerns and shared them, but I also had concerns of my own.

We found a realtor to sell the house and entered into a very stressful time. It was a great bother to keep the house in order and ready to show at any moment. Worse, to our dismay, there was very little traffic. It was our bad luck that more people were leaving than moving to Gainesville that year. Those arriving wanted a more prestigious neighborhood than ours.

It worried us that if we did not sell the house, we would have trouble paying the Mayflower Company for moving our goods. Freddy solved that problem by calling the treasurer at Haverford College to see if, by chance, we could get some help from them. As it turned out, indeed we could! In fact, the accessibility of the administration was the greatest advantage of our years at Haverford. The Haverford administrative personnel were dedicated to meeting the human needs of the entire Haverford family—students, staff, and faculty—and they have always had my deepest admiration.

Even now, I shudder as I recall the tremendous stress associated with that move. We had to cope with the usual problems of relocating an entire family, but there were also our individual personal reactions. When we set out on our trip to Haverford, we were in less than good spirits. Alice and Freddy were never good travelers; sometimes the motion of the car made them nauseous. It was also difficult for either of them to sit quietly for long periods. Steve was unhappy at the thought of yet another new school. I was tired and apprehensive.

In Florida, by taking an accredited driving course, one could get a limited driver's license at age fourteen. That summer, Steve had taken the course and received a license, so he took his turn behind the wheel during our journey north. The driving lifted his spirits somewhat. After we were safely on our way, we all felt much better and started enjoying our trip as we usually did. We elected to travel the scenic route of the Blue Ridge Parkway. We had the time to do so, and that route eliminated truck traffic.

Our little dog Snoopy was with us. He tried to alert us that we were about to have trouble with the car, but we did not understand. Every time the car stopped and a door opened, Snoopy bolted out and we had difficulty getting him back in again. Steve was driving, but it was Freddy who first noticed that something was wrong with the car. Then the engine began backfiring, and suddenly we were all aware that our feet were too hot. By then Snoopy was on our laps, not the floor, and acting very uneasy.

After what seemed like a long while, we found a pull-off at a scenic viewpoint where we could rest the car and ourselves.

Snoopy did not rest though. He ran away down the mountain. Steve and Alice had a real task getting him to return. To our further dismay, the car refused to start again.

What a Sunday afternoon we spent, cajoling and pushing the car back down the mountain. Fortunately a kind motorist pushed us to a filling station. In those days it was a kinder, gentler nation. It was safe to help a motorist in difficulty! So there we were, stranded on a Sunday afternoon in a small town in Virginia. On Monday the Ford service people worked on our car all day, but they could not find the problem. We had to buy a different car to continue our journey to Haverford. The Ford agency in that small town could not have been more helpful or accommodating! That lifted our hearts a bit.

By pushing the clock and with three of us taking turns driving, we arrived at Haverford in late afternoon—at about the same time as the movers. This was the only time in my memory of moving our household goods that we had absolutely *no trouble* with the movers! They loaded the truck and arrived on time, just as they promised.

Our house on Cheswold Lane

Haverford was a totally new and different experience. The physical settings of both the place and the college are beautiful. The campus is uniquely lovely. The longer we lived there, the more I came to appreciate and love that beauty.

The name itself refers simply to a post office and a train stop on a commuter railway line. Haverford is a city suburb of Philadelphia, but its government is a county and township that adjoin another county and township. There is almost nothing to distinguish where one leaves off and the other begins. The county line runs almost down the middle of campus.

In all the time I lived there, I was never really clear about my directions. I was never aware with any great accuracy whether I had traveled north, west, east, or south. I drove the car so much that I sometimes felt like I spent most of my life in it, but I always carried detailed maps so I could find my way around.

The students lived in dormitories on campus, but faculty members were housed in several different ways. Haverford College has a long tradition of a close relationship between students and faculty members. In its very early days, the college expected all faculty families to live on campus and encouraged faculty to build on college-owned land. In a diversity of arrangements, those houses remained the property of the college when the owners departed. A few of the large old houses were still one-family dwellings, but most of them had been remodeled into apartments. There was also a building devoted to faculty apartments. Housing was not in the least uniform.

Housing assignments were determined by application and longevity of service, so new appointments were at the bottom of the list. Initially they assigned us a two-bedroom apartment. We learned about it while in Gainesville. I said it would not do. Freddy really hates these kinds of arguments and wanted to try it at least for a year, but I was adamant, so he asked for a reassignment.

The college had recently been bequeathed an off-campus property on which there was a large old Victorian house, a double garage, and a small house. The college administration was converting the large house into apartments, but they promised to make the small house, which was on Cheswold Lane, habitable for us.

However, when we arrived at Haverford, our new home was not yet ready for us. There was a stove in the house, but no refrigerator. The windows were just paneless, empty holes! We put up our beds anyway, and we tacked up sheets to cover the bedroom windows. Our house was in an almost entirely residential area, so to begin with, we badly needed a guide just to find places to eat and shop!

As it turned out, the first month was absolutely dreadful, so much so that during the first year, I had recurring nightmares. One of the first things to happen was that Alice stepped on a board with a protruding rusty nail. We had to find a doctor in a hurry!

Fortunately one of the college's perks for its faculty was its contract with two local physicians for routine healthcare and a yearly physical for adults and children. A quick check gave us the name and address of the doctor to whom we were assigned, and we were off to see Dr. William Watson. As prudent parents, we had kept up with all recommended shots, so we did not have to undergo many fights with Alice about injections. However, keeping her quiet and her leg elevated was not easy, given the situation.

In Gainesville Steve had been taking allergy shots for very serious hay fever. Before we left, Dr. Kokomoor had given us tubes of serum and a detailed account of Steve's care and the required dosage, which we gave to Dr. Watson. Steve had his first shot that day. However, either the doctor or his nurse failed to read the instructions carefully, for Steve received an overdose. By the time we returned home, he was swelling rapidly. It was frightening!

The doctor was closing his office when we returned, but he kept Steve there for hours while he worked to counteract the effects of the overdose. The experience left us all spent, hungry, and on edge. To make matters worse, we had to return to that *dreadful* house.

Considering the climates along the East Coast, the location of Philadelphia is not the worst by any means, but in late August, it is usually hot and muggy, just as it was that year. Our little house was shoddily built, not insulated, and full of mosquitoes.

There was an added nuisance, something I had never encountered before and could never have even imagined. Apple trees had been planted around the house long ago, but they had not been tended in many years. That year the trees were very productive, and there was a great abundance of diseased, wormy apples covering the ground. When the builders, repairmen, and furniture movers tramped on the apples, they managed to create a great ground covering of mashed apples. The apple-mash in turn attracted hordes of wasps and bees!

The pervasive odor of those fermenting apples and the loud hum of that great swarm of insects did not enchant me—in fact, it frightened me a lot. But closer scrutiny revealed that we were in no danger of being stung. All the insects were totally inebriated! The kids and I found them fascinating to watch when we found the time. A few faculty wives offered to use the apples for applesauce, but they discovered, as I already had, that it was not worth the effort. In the following years, I hounded the college's gardening staff to remove the apples.

Adversity and adjustment

In time, we settled fairly well into the house and our new surroundings. I found new interests and renewed old ones. But I never felt at home at Haverford. I never felt that I belonged. For quite a long time, I felt hurt and angry with Freddy because he had not talked over the appointment with me before accepting it. I felt that he did not regard me as a full and equal partner in our marriage, and I resented being cast only in what is presently called "the cookie-baking role."

I was very depressed and unhappy, and I had no friend to talk with. Finally I went to see Dr. Watson. I must give him credit for taking me seriously and trying to help me, especially since he could not really understand why I would not love a place like Haverford. He had been an undergraduate at Haverford, had gone to the University of Pennsylvania for his medical studies, and then returned to Haverford to live and practice. Like many others, he thought it was the best place one could live and be a part of. He prescribed some kind of joy pills to lift my spirits, and told me to report back soon.

I suppose the pills must have been a tranquilizer. I took only a few of them. They did not help me in the way that I needed to be helped. Within my own mind, I knew this was something that I, and only I, could deal with. I needed to come to terms with it in my own way and time. What I longed for was a quiet meditation chamber—somewhere I could withdraw and rest and read and feel free of responsibilities for a long while. But I felt guilty that I had those longings.

Eventually, our immediate conditions improved and that helped us feel more settled. I began to feel less sorely used. We bought a refrigerator for our kitchen. The college staff put windows in place and affixed blinds over them. They all were pleasant, able, and friendly people. In September, we had encouraging news from our Gainesville realtor. Our house was sold. Unfortunately, the selling price was quite a lot less than I felt we should settle for. But at least we were free of the mortgage obligation.

Freddy's attitude about the sale bothered me (though I may have been unnecessarily sensitive). He said something to the effect that he cared little about what we sold our house for; he just wanted to be free of it. I had an attachment to that house—I had worked and cared for it for ten years. He had not. It seemed to me that I had spent ten years in a vain enterprise. It took some stiff scolding of myself to get past our difference in feeling about this.

Although our first months at Haverford were not easy, there was one very happy occasion. Some old friends from our Hoosier Courts days in Indiana lived in the area, Ray and Rita Bard and Fred and Barbie Burgess. One Saturday afternoon soon after our arrival, they took us away for a feast and reacquaintance fest. Nothing could have given us more pleasure!

Ray was doing very well financially as head of research at a pharmaceutical manufacturer in the area, and Fred was teaching at Villanova University, which was not far from us. It was wonderful to be with them again. They lived too far away to be on the close terms we had enjoyed in Hoosier Courts, but Barbie and Rita were most helpful in pointing out good shopping areas and things of that nature.

Fred tried to help us find a church to our liking. He attended a High Episcopal Church, which we visited with him. We also visited St. Mary's Church in Ardmore, just on the south edge of the Haverford campus. None of us, especially Steve and Alice, cared for either of them. Finally we established ourselves at the Church of the Redeemer in Bryn Mawr, probably the oldest and wealthiest of them all. The Redeemer took Sunday school (Christian education) seriously, and I expect that was the attraction.

I do not remember that Walter and Mary Jane Baker introduced us to the Church of the Redeemer, but they may have, for they were members. They remained very good friends during our years at Haverford. Walter Baker had attended Haverford College and had, I believe, worked in one of the big city banks in Philadelphia. He came to the college as a financial adviser and fundraiser at about the same time we did. I was very glad they were at Haverford when we were, for they contributed greatly to the enrichment of our lives on the Main Line (as that whole area of suburban Philadelphia is called).

I never learned a great deal about either Walter's or Mary Jane's personal life. Walter probably was a wealthy man (possibly the grandson and great-grandson of wealthy men). About Mary Jane, I could never guess. They seemed a very compatible, loving couple. They had four or five children, and lived in Bryn Mawr in a modern house that was comfortable and pleasant but not in the least ostentatious. They had a full-time maid, and people who could afford full-time maids had to have very good incomes. Mary

Jane and Walter opened a door for me into a Philadelphia I might otherwise have not known.

Steve had been the most reluctant of us to leave Gainesville, and yet he was the first to adapt and enjoy his life in Haverford. He rode the commuter train down to the City Line, and then walked two or three rather long blocks to school. It was tough for him academically at Episcopal Academy, but he found there many interests unknown to him elsewhere. He soon became very enthusiastic about the school and involved with the other fellows.

The school did not include a physical education class as did the public schools, but everyone participated in school sports after classes. Having so much trouble with hay fever for most of the year in Florida, Steve had remained small and engaged in few sports. But at EA, he played soccer and ran track. At first he did not like wearing a shirt and tie to school, but he came to love his navy blue school blazer. He liked the chapel service, and soon joined the glee club. Freddy and I felt very good about our decision to send him there.

Adjustment for Alice was much more difficult. She attended the public school in Gladwyne where she was in third grade. We were far enough away from the school that she rode the bus. The school and her teachers were fine. However, outside school she was so very lonely. From the imaginative, eager, active little girl she was in Gainesville, she changed into a quiet, inactive bookworm who lay on her bed and read. I suppose her behavior change began when she stepped on the rusty nail and had to stay quiet with her leg elevated.

When Alice wanted to join Brownies, I quailed at the thought, fearing I would be called upon to go camping and participate in all the activities I loathed. I need not have worried. Gladwyne was full of young mothers with lots of time, money, and energy, who were quite willing to engage in these activities with their daughters. As usual, my contributions most often were the refreshments.

Through Alice, we came in contact with new wealth. Through Steve, Episcopal Academy, and the Church of the Redeemer, we were in contact with old and established wealth. It was a new experience for both Freddy and me.

Mama buys a new coat

During our two years in New Haven, Freddy and I had managed to keep warm during the winter with our old outer garments. Now the time had come for my old winter coat to be replaced. I had tweeds in mind since on the Main Line one wore good tweeds, and it was a style I dearly loved.

I had to shop carefully. The sale of our house had not yet been completed, and we had been compelled to pay for some expensive unplanned items, such as a car and refrigerator, not to mention Steve's tuition. Rita Bard suggested I come to Media and shop with her, and I did. But Rita and I were too unlike in our tastes and methods for that to prove very useful.

Shopping with Alice came to mean shopping *for* Alice, so I found other things to do with her. We had wonderful times together. She loved musicals and music films. We found that as New Haven had been, so Philadelphia was a place for tryouts for plays and musicals prior to opening, if ever, on Broadway in New York. Then, too, it was easy to go by rail from Haverford to New York. Alice and I went a number of times for Saturday matinee performances.

It seems to me that for me personally our first two months in Haverford were the worst. During this time, I felt very lonely. I felt that Freddy had let me down. My heart was sore and very hurt. It seemed to me that the partnership I had treasured had been a sad illusion on my part, and I could not even talk to him about it.

One day in late October, Freddy said that as we had taken care of the basic needs for all the family, he thought it was time for me to buy some things for Mama.

My reply was that Mama would have to wait, for we had spent as much as we could afford to spend. These were not the kind of words Freddy wanted to hear. As I have often been known to remark (usually sarcastically), Freddy never likes to talk about money, but he does expect it to appear in his hand when he decides to spend it. It was perfectly true that we had only a bit of subsistence money left in our account. But I also knew it would upset him for me to say there was no money to buy clothing for me. I was being nasty.

Freddy's response was that I should go shopping the next day and buy myself a winter coat. So the next day I went to Ardmore. Ardmore's shopping mall was small, tiny by today's standards.

However, it had some of the best shops, branches from department stores in downtown Philadelphia and New York, as well as some specialty stores. I tried on several coats and found one that I liked at Best's. I wanted that coat very much, but it exceeded the amount I could afford. So I went back to Strawbridge and Clothier and bought one that was within my self-imposed budget.

Freddy came home for lunch that day, likely because he intended to tell me again to go shopping. I showed him the coat. He asked me about where I had shopped. I told all, including that there had been a coat at Best's that I liked much better, but that it was almost twice the cost of the one I had bought. I really, truly thought I should not spend that much for a coat.

We left it at that. I went off to do something else and did not even notice when he left the house. Sometime later, I heard a door downstairs open and close. I went down, and there was Freddy with a big box in his arms. He had returned the coat I had bought that morning, and then he had bought the coat from Best's that I had liked so much but thought too expensive.

I did not often burst into tears, but I did then! The ice around my heart melted. We hugged and kissed with a love and enthusiasm that we had not felt between us for months.

Freddy had taken the coat he did not like back to Strawbridge and Clothier, and then he had gone into Best's and applied for and received a credit card. Then he had found the coat I liked, charged it on his newly acquired credit card, and brought it home to me. I had charge cards before then (though in those unenlightened days, they were always issued in the name of the husband, no matter the status of the wife), but this was the first time he had even thought of applying for one. Freddy had entered the plastic age!

Autumn at Haverford

Autumn in the Philadelphia area is far less colorful than in New England or Indiana, but it is longer and a lovely season. The large grounds of which our small house occupied a corner had some great trees that were beautiful in their fall colors. Our house faced onto Cheswold Lane, a private lane that bordered the Lower Merion Cricket Club, an old, exclusive social and athletic group. The gates of the club have a memorial plaque to Alexander Cassatt, brother of the impressionist painter Mary Cassatt and longtime president of the Pennsylvania Railroad. From our front windows, we could see the lovely green area that was the cricket field.

The weather was still beautiful the weekend we went to a park in the Poconos and found that it was a favorite spot for birdwatchers. We wondered at their knowledge and were awed by their eager interest. On that weekend, a certain species of hawk was migrating south, and the viewpoint was above the valley of the flyway. It was a new experience for us all. The Main Line had many birdwatchers, and before we left, we had become birdwatchers, too.

Freddy and I both came to love walking around the campus, enjoying the many different kinds of trees, and learning to identify them. There were about two hundred varieties, both native and imported, a number of them exotic. Among them were a great number of gingko trees. Gingkos are quite lovely most of the year, but they become a smelly nuisance when the fruit falls. I did not have to walk through them often, so they did not bother me personally. However, gingkos lined the walk leading to the overpass walkway from the campus to the Friends School, just off campus. So the children carried the stench of the fruit on their shoes and clothing into the schoolrooms and into their homes.

I wished many times over that we had put Alice in the Friends School rather than Gladwyne. This is in no way intended to be critical of her public school, which was a very good, friendly place. However, it is in school that children find their friends, and she would have been far less lonely in those first months if she had known more children who lived close by. It was my ignorance of the area and my midwestern bias for public schooling that produced that problem.

Our first Halloween while living on Cheswold Lane was a delightful experience for Alice and me. Much of the kind, friendly spirit that came with the pioneer founders remained in Philadelphia, as well as in the detached suburbs such as ours. There was generally a very tolerant attitude regarding religion and a very pronounced resistance to offending people who hold beliefs different from one's own.

So Halloween at Gladwyne School had become a greater time for fun than Christmas. Each age group had its Halloween party during school hours, and the parents' group had a foods and bake sale during the afternoon. I met a great many very interesting women at the bake sales—artists, writers, professionals of all kinds, and often wives of creative persons as well.

On that first Halloween, even after a day of fun at school, Alice wanted to go trick-or-treating, something she had enjoyed so much with friends in Gainesville. She had no friends to accompany her, and both Freddy and Steve claimed to have work to do, so Mama and Alice went trick-or-treating together. I remember that there was a cold, intermittent rain falling, and that I was physically uncomfortable. After ten years of heat in Florida, I had not yet adjusted to late October in Pennsylvania.

The experience was worth the discomfort. It gave me an opportunity to meet our noncampus neighbors. Most of them were people outside our personal experiences. We began next door at an old Victorian house, the home of a lawyer, an executive at RCA whose office was actually across the river in New Jersey. I later learned that many executives live on the Main Line, both for a tax advantage and because their families prefer it to New Jersey with its smoky factories.

We then went on to the house of a wonderful, charming woman who became a friend. She was Ada Campbell Rose, the editor of *Highlights*, a children's magazine to which we had long subscribed. Ada was delighted to see us and insisted we come in. She served us refreshments, put money in the trick-or-treat-bag, and gave Alice a children's book she had written. Although Ada never became an intimate friend, on several occasions we spent pleasant hours together, and she always remembered Alice with special gifts of books.

How could we top this delightful treat? We did not, but we did have more fun. In one house a butler handed out refreshments, and in another it was a housekeeper. In another, a masked party was in full swing, and they happily asked us to come in and join in the games. In one beautiful home, an older couple was delighted to have a little girl come trick-or-treating. They told us about their grandchildren, all boys, living in Baltimore.

Alice was a very pretty little girl, and she could usually be relied upon to behave in a pleasant, mannerly way. Given the more than gracious way we were being treated and entertained, she glowed and twinkled, and made a very good impression everywhere we went.

While we lived on Cheswold Lane, we were always treated warmly and pleasantly by most of the neighbors that we met that Halloween night. The people next door were sometimes less than pleasant, but this was a case with extenuating circumstances, for the woman was ill with cancer much of the time, and her sons were sometimes a problem.

Our involvement in Christian education

Sometime in the late winter or early spring of our first year, Thorne Sparkman, the rector of our church in Bryn Mawr, called at our home. I am not sure how he even came to know who we were. He asked me if I would take the position of supervisor for the kindergarten division of the Sunday school. The present supervisor had held that position for a long time and wished to resign. I was much in the dark about what it might entail and knew little about the Christian education program at the Church of the Redeemer. However, I was intrigued, so I said I would be interested to look into it and see whether I thought it was a job I could do.

Dr. Sparkman arranged for me to meet with Aubrey Teamer, the supervisor who was resigning, in his office one afternoon. We talked about the position and walked through the premises. I inspected the classrooms, the general meeting room, and the teaching materials. I asked if I might visit for a Sunday or two and meet with the teachers before deciding whether to undertake the job.

To say that I was awed by the entire enterprise is putting it mildly. Even before I witnessed this division of the church in operation, I wanted to accept the job—but I was not at all sure that I would be the kind of supervisor the congregation might want. In the end, I did become the supervisor, and I gave many hours to my work. I loved it, and I am sure I learned much, much more than any of the little ones under my care.

The education building was separate from the church and fairly new. The first floor housed the offices of the clergy, a large assembly hall, a kitchen, a smaller hall that doubled as a dining room or a smaller assembly room, and one or two classrooms. My domain was more than half of the second floor. There was a Sunday school superintendent over all the Christian education division. I was supervisor for the children five years old and younger. I served under the superintendent, but I was my own boss.

The kindergarten enrollment was a bit over 300 with an overall attendance generally between 150 and 200. Our area included the nursery, a large room for three-year-olds, two rooms for four-year-olds, and two rooms for five-year-olds. We had one woman with assistants for the nursery, one teacher with two or three assistants for the three-year-olds, and a teacher with an assistant for each group of four- and five-year-olds. It was quite a staff!

Everything was very well organized, probably thanks to Mrs. Teamer. I found no reason to change what she had done. I selected the materials for our use and recruited help where needed. I was also in charge of the children's worship service. Sometimes I had the assistance of a priest in training, but quite a lot of the time I conducted the service myself, putting into use what I had learned from Professor Randy Miller at Yale.

Our chapel was simple and lovely. We had a piano and a pianist who contributed her services. My greatest handicap was my singing voice. It was never great, and years of asthma did not improve it. I could not get any of the teachers to lead the singing, but under my begging encouragement, they did indeed sing out with the children. The enterprise certainly called on my ingenuity any number of times, but I loved doing it.

Sometime after I began supervising the kindergarten division, Freddy was asked to teach the high school group, and he accepted. So we were working together again! At least three times during the school year, an association of church school teachers met together. We always began with Evening Prayer, a service I have loved since I first participated in it. Evening Prayer with this large group of Christian educators was an especially wonderful and moving experience, one that has never been duplicated for me. After that, we usually had a speaker and discussion, which I always found extremely interesting, helpful, and stimulating.

My work with the League of Women Voters

When we first arrived in Haverford, a faculty wife who became a very good friend, Charlotte Cadbury, was in the hospital. So I did not meet her or her husband, Bill, for several weeks. It was Charlotte who invited me to a League of Women Voters meeting.

Charlotte and Bill lived in an apartment on campus, but it was on the other side of the dividing line, in Delaware County. That year, Charlotte was president of the local league in her township, Haverford, in Delaware County.

I worked with Charlotte's group for two years. During that time, I declined taking any board position. Instead I worked on problems of the state, in particular Pennsylvania, and continued the work I had been pursuing on national and international issues.

New places and new people bring new perspectives. I soon began finding that my acquaintances and fellow workers in Haverford differed in many ways from those in Gainesville. For one thing, a great number of the Gainesville LWV members were faculty wives who had come from all over the United States and had been educated in a great variety of institutions. In contrast, the members of the Haverford Township league were wives of doctors, lawyers, businessmen, and government employees. Most of them had been educated along the East Coast, no further south than North Carolina. Their knowledge and views were far more parochial than those of my Florida friends, and they were far less dedicated to looking at both pros and cons before arriving at decisions.

After two years with the Delaware County group, I decided to join the LWV group in my own area, Lower Merion Township in Montgomery County. There I again encountered faculty wives. I worked in the Lower Merion league for four years and came to know yet another group of people on the Main Line. I do not recall any particular in-depth study that I either instituted or engaged in during that time, but I must have done some worthwhile things, because I was contacted by the Pennsylvania state league as well as by the city of Philadelphia league.

Generalizing is a dubious business, but I will engage in it to make some observations about government and the people I came to know through working in the LWV there. The early Quakers who founded the city and its public institutions had very good sense, in particular as regards human justice. As a result, Philadelphians had a very good foundation for enacting liberal social justice laws. To be sure, there were a very great number of rock-hard conservatives. (But remember, I had moved there after living in Connecticut, where birth control practice was unlawful, and in Florida, where segregation had been the law during part of our residence.)

While in Haverford, I certainly met more black people of education and wealth than I had ever met before.

For one year, I acted as the LWV representative on the board of the Pennsylvania Council of Latin American Trade and Commerce. Anyone can imagine how totally unqualified I thought myself to be for this appointment. However, I found, as I went to the meetings, that I knew more than I thought and that I was far more qualified than a great many others on the board. In Gainesville I had learned a great deal about Latin America and Latin American Trade. As well, for a good many years I had been a very active committee member of LWV studies on trade. Participating in league studies is a *very* effective way to gain an in-depth education.

I enjoyed working with the Lower Merion league. During my years with them, I met some interesting people. I came to know the state president of the LWV, who lived in Philadelphia. She had me doing many things. As always, my physical problems and strength were inadequate for all the work and projects I would have loved to do.

Life at Haverford

As we continued living in the little house owned by the college, we used our own money to make it more livable. The college treasurer advised us that it would be unwise to invest anything in structural changes. However, the house was not easy to keep clean or warm or cool. It was so poorly insulated that one winter all the water pipes froze. This freeze also ruined our washing machine. When we bought a new one, we could find no good place to install it, so again we put it on the back porch, which was only partially enclosed.

The house had no basement. It had been erected over a cellar, which had walls of layered dry stone and a dirt floor without drains. We put clothes-drying lines in the cellar, and the pets slept there, but otherwise it was not a useful area. The house was not conducive to good health, in particular for people like my children and me with our various allergies.

We lived there about four months before the sale of our Gainesville house was finalized. Overall we sold the house for less than we had spent on it. But the proceeds of the sale provided us with the means to make life a bit more comfortable.

Ann, Freddy, & Steve (center)
with Ann & Jim Dunn
Cheswold Lane, Haverford, c. 1960

As I said earlier, it was useful having the college for our loan officer. It was also helpful that we could ask the college to buy large items at wholesale prices for us and then reimburse them. We bought a piano. We carpeted the entire downstairs of the house, against the advice of the college treasurer. When Steve wrecked the car we had bought in Virginia during our move from Florida, we even financed a new car through the college. Belonging to the Haverford family was very comforting on many occasions for all of us.

Freddy and I both felt very close to many students there. We heartily enjoyed the college policy of asking students into our home, and we encouraged them to come to us with their problems. The freshmen arrived at Haverford a week before the older students, and during that week, we were assigned a group to entertain and become acquainted with.

As this was something we had already been doing ever since Freddy began teaching, it was not a new activity for us. On the whole, the Haverford students were wonderful young men, and we enjoyed them immensely. We always hoped that we made their years at Haverford a more pleasant experience. We are still in touch with several of them.

We were on very good terms with all the faculty families. We came to know each other quite well. Most times when we had students over for dinner, we asked another faculty couple to join us. Then too, at least once a week, Hugh Borton, the college president, and his wife gave a dinner party in honor of a visiting guest, to which appropriate faculty members were invited.

The college had a fund that supplied money for a scholarly speaker once a week. I went to hear as many speakers as I could manage, for most of them were fascinating. They ranged all the way from a biologist whose sophisticated research involved looking for the "timer" in life forms to Walt Kelly, the cartoonist who drew the much-loved *Pogo*. These speakers usually spent the day on campus and then in the evening, had dinner with the Bortons, along with some faculty members.

There was another fund that brought scholars to the campus for longer visits, allowing them to attend classes and mingle with the students for several days. Most of these were researchers in scientific areas, but once in a while we managed to bring a political scientist or an outstanding political figure to the campus. I remember two of them especially well, possibly because I was responsible for showing them around and driving them and their wives to places of interest.

One was Eugene McCarthy. I think this was before he ever made a run for the presidency. I found him to be a very sweet, gentle, and unassuming man.

Another was a vice president of the Conseil d'État and the father of the French equivalent to our social security system. Freddy and I picked him and his wife up at the train station in Philadelphia, and while we were driving them to the campus, she said that the one thing she wanted most to do during her visit was to visit the Barnes Foundation art collection. This I was very happy to help her with.

We had learned about Dr. Barnes shortly after we moved to Haverford, when he and his many eccentricities were much in the news. As the producer of Argyrol (an antiseptic), he had become a very wealthy man. He had been a great friend and disciple of the educator John Dewey and with him had developed a concept for both viewing and educating about the plastic arts, as he called them. The Barnes home, the foundation, school, and museum were in Merion, Pennsylvania, just outside the City Line and next door to Episcopal Academy.

Dr. Barnes was killed in a traffic accident before our arrival at Haverford. His affairs continued to be in the news for months because settling the estate brought a great deal of controversy. His museum and school claimed a tax exemption as a public not-for-profit enterprise, but the state contested it, saying these enterprises were not tax-exempt, because only a select few could attend the school or view the collection.

The state was successful in making the museum open its doors but only to a limited degree: from September 1 to June l each year, 200 people were admitted on Friday and 200 on Saturday, unless it was a holiday, when the doors were closed. On each of these days, 100 people were admitted by prior reservation and 100 could enter in order of arrival. I went several times and never encountered the least trouble, nor did I even have to wait for admittance.

Someone who was setting up the social schedule for our French visitors had called Mlle de Mazia, the executive director, to arrange a reservation for them to view the collection but was brusquely told that all the reservations were taken for two or three months. Freddy heard about this rebuff, and we decided that I should simply drive our guests to the museum early on a Friday morning. If we did not get in, we would try again the next day. When we went that Friday, we had no trouble gaining admittance. There were perhaps ten of us without a reservation but not more.

I visited the collection perhaps five or six times. I cannot account for my affinity for plastic art. Perhaps my affinity is innate. It cannot have been acquired from proximity or training because I had neither. There is, of course, my relationship to Aunt Lillian Hughes and her cousin, Mary Quick Burnett. Yet, without Freddy, I wonder if it would have ever come to the fore. It was with Freddy that I began to go to museums. I very quickly became absorbed in paintings and painters. I have become an avid viewer, though I have no talent for creating.

After I became familiar with Dr. Barnes' very fascinating but somewhat bewildering collection, I became interested in the school Dr. Barnes and Mlle de Mazia had started. I decided to enroll in it. The enrollment was limited, and the list of entrance requirements very long. One of the requirements was the submission of two supporting letters with the application. I asked a Haverford faculty wife who had taken the classes to write a letter for me.

When I had my interviews with Mlle de Mazia, I learned that only one of my supporting letters had come in—the one from the faculty wife was missing. I suppose I should consider myself fortunate that Mlle de Mazia interviewed me anyway. Perhaps she thought I had some interesting qualities. But in the end, I was not accepted into the school. The unsent letter rankled me. It was, I am sorry to say, another one of the dissatisfactions about living at Haverford that I let bother me.

Friends and acquaintances

Freddy will relate the many intellectual and professional advantages that came to him by virtue of living and teaching at Haverford, and to these I assent. While his salary was certainly better than it had been at Florida, the move might not have been worth it if those advantages had not also been present.

That first summer (1961) Freddy taught a course at Columbia University in New York. He lived in the apartment of our friends the Blaisdells, which was just off the campus. The kids and I visited in Indiana and then joined him there for a week of music and theater before the fall semester at Haverford. We began our second year at Haverford under much easier circumstances than we had our first, and we were better prepared for the school year.

Our second summer, we spent at Haverford, much of it in the small swimming pool on campus, which was faculty owned and operated. That summer, Alice and I came to know the other faculty families a great deal better. Alice became especially good friends with Chrissie, the third daughter of Helen and Ho Hunter. They both loved the pool. I liked and admired both Helen and Ho. Helen taught at Swarthmore during the school year. They were wonderful parents and interesting, valuable contributors to Haverford College life.

It was through the Hunters that we came to see the great relationship that existed among Bryn Mawr and Haverford and Swarthmore, all three of which had been established by the early

Philadelphia Quaker community. I see all three colleges as being wonderful places, connected but unique. Several of our faculty had Swarthmore-Bryn Mawr, or Haverford-Bryn Mawr, or simply Swarthmore backgrounds. I retain a very high regard for all these institutions.

Harvey and Sylvia Glickman came to Haverford about the same time we did and were already in residence when we arrived. Harvey was the only other political scientist on the faculty that year since the chair, Herman (Red) Somers, was on leave for the year. Although much younger than we were, they became and remain very good friends. Both of them grew up in New York City, but they met as Fulbright students in England. Sylvia is an accomplished pianist who graduated from the Julliard School in New York. They had two daughters and a son.

When Sylvia began giving music lessons, Alice was one of her students. It was such a delight to have Sylvia for a friend. She was a professional musician to her fingertips. We enjoyed many hours hearing her play.

Sylvia was such a caring and capable person, and a wonderful wife and mother. She managed all the while to look very attractive. (Had it been in me to be envious, I would have been of Sylvia, but truly that is not one of my traits.) So it was with a number of the faculty wives—they were gifted, professional, and capable.

About this time, we gained what was for us a sizeable financial boost. The Diamant properties in Austria were finally sold legitimately and the money transferred to the living heirs. Freddy and Liesl, his sister-in-law, were all that remained of that family in 1963. We went through an array of national and state taxes as well as a whole gamut of thank-you-for-your-help gifts before we finally put money in the bank.

While this restitution did not bring us wealth, it did bring me a release from the constant stress of cutting corners and carefully guarding every expenditure. In other words, I would no longer have to consider taking the cheaper coat at Strawbridge. I could now take the one at Best's with a clear conscience.

The following year, we inquired into the possibility of building a new house on the college's property on Cheswold Lane, just in front of the house we were living in. However, the trustees said that they were not sure they wanted to retain that property and were thinking of selling it. At the time I was very disappointed, but this probably worked out for the best for us.

In the spring of 1962, Steve graduated from Episcopal Academy. He went to Trinity College in Hartford, Connecticut, that fall.

Steve
Episcopal Academy
Graduation, 1962

We drove him there, stopping in New Haven to see the Dunn family. It was very hard to have Steve go away. It was our first family break, and I knew that our family life as we had known it was at an end. As well, he seemed so young and vulnerable. He was not eighteen until almost a month after he went to Trinity.

Steve had looked forward to going away to college, but his first year was not terrifically happy. He shared a suite that had been built for *two* people with *three* other fellows. Not only were they crowded, but they were not particularly compatible. Nevertheless, he fared well enough academically.

For pocket money, he had a job washing pots and pans in the dormitory kitchen. Steve said he was glad to be in the kitchen where he could get more to eat. That was a big change. Steve wanted more to eat!

Bloomington, Indiana (summer 1963)

Steve returned home after his first year at Trinity, and during the summer, he worked for Guy Davenport, an assistant professor of English at Haverford. Guy was one of the young, untenured faculty members. This was his first teaching appointment. It was I who was first attracted to him when we met during our early days at Haverford at one of the many teas, coffees, or dinners with other faculty members. The cultured southern voice and the trace of gracious southern manners are as attractive to me as the Viennese manner is to Freddy. Though, of course, we both recognize that outward manner can disguise a whole range of thoughts and behaviors that we despise.

I enjoyed Guy very much. He was not married. I believe he had been married and divorced while in graduate school at Harvard. I offered to help him entertain his students with a buffet dinner or two. I used my favorite old recipes from our Gainesville days of either rice and chicken casserole or lasagna. Making lasagna in Philadelphia was much easier than in Indiana or Florida, for the cheeses and the pasta were readily available.

I must mention, too, that in Philadelphia the seafood was excellent. I am not invariably a lover of seafood, but we were able to enjoy a seafood meal of my own cooking at least once a week. For guests I usually offered a kind of curried shrimp baked in a casserole. I also used scallops a lot, and I found that plaice or flounder fillets were always good, too, and much cheaper than beef or pork.

From Florence Bachrach, who was a marvelous cook, I learned how to stuff a leg of lamb with an herb and bread stuffing. It was excellent. The Bachrachs were great friends, too. Peter taught political science at Bryn Mawr as well as a class at Haverford College most of the years we were there. He and Florence lived in a large comfortable home in Ardmore with their six children and family pets. Alice enjoyed being friends with the youngest girl, and Steve liked the company of the older girls. It was a family friendship that we all valued.

To return to the summer of 1963, Steve worked as Guy Davenport's assistant, and Alice elected to go to a small summer camp on Cape Breton Island. The director of this informal youth camp was the daughter of Celia Hinton, the founder and director of a well-known prep school in Vermont. We came to know her because she was acquainted with so many of our faculty families. I felt some reluctance at Alice going to such an out-of-the-way place, especially one I had never seen and would not be able to easily reach in an emergency, but she very much wanted to go. Freddy and I spent that summer in Bloomington, home again.

During our early years at Haverford, Freddy began working with Fred Riggs, whom he had come to know at Yale and who was then at Indiana University. (I will make no attempt to explain this collaboration in detail, but I will try to explain some of the ways it affected us as a family.) The Comparative Administration Group (CAG), headed by Fred Riggs, had obtained a grant for a series of summer seminars, and during the summer of 1963, Freddy participated in the seminar at Indiana University.

We rented a clean and adequate furnished apartment in Campus View Apartments, which had been built on the grounds where our student apartment had been. It was the first time Freddy and I had ever been able to spend such an extended time alone together, so it was almost a honeymoon time for us!

In so many ways it was a very wonderful summer. We still knew many people from our earlier days. We enjoyed renewing those friendships and making new ones. Also, I could easily drive to Indianapolis, Hope, and Columbus to see my brothers and sisters and their families.

The university theater was putting on performances of the off-Broadway musical *The Fantastics* in the Frangipani Room of the Indiana Memorial Union building. It was a charming, entertaining little piece to which I went more than once. On one occasion, my sister Mae came to spend the night, and we went to see *The Fantastics* together. As well, Indiana University had begun their theater in Brown County, and we attended a performance or two in Nashville, Indiana.

That summer, there was one event in particular that neither Freddy nor I will ever forget. The School of Music at Indiana University was then under the guidance of Dean Wilfred Bain, who had come to Indiana in 1947 or 1948, about the time we left. They had begun to expand the voice faculty very rapidly and were staging a wide range of operas. That summer, they were doing a production of *Aïda* in the old football stadium between Tenth Street and the Memorial Union building.

Freddy and I walked over from Campus View to attend a performance. The first act was still in progress when a light shower of rain began to fall. There was a debate about whether to continue or give a rain check for the next night. Before a decision could be made, it stopped raining so the opera continued. But then, all at once, the heavens opened and heavy rain descended upon us. In the twinkling of an eye, we all were absolutely soaked!

By the time we made our way out of the area and across the street, the gutters were already overloaded and we were walking in ankle-deep water. I was wearing a knitted dress and some very attractive straw shoes, neither of which had been intended as rainwear. The shoes slowly disintegrated with every watery step. The waterlogged dress clung and lengthened until I felt like I was hobbled.

We entered the Campus View lobby looking like people from a comic film. We received lots of stares as we sloshed our way to the elevators. On our floor, as we passed the garbage chute opening, I dropped in what remained of my shoes. Later I disposed of my dress in the same way. Freddy's shoes suffered, too, but he was able to wear them again. His trousers were a new nylon fabric, and after washing, they were as good as new. We often think of what happened that day, and we laugh again as we remember how we felt and looked!

During our last week, Liesl, Freddy's sister-in-law, joined us in Bloomington and then drove back with us to Philadelphia. She had come from Sydney, Australia, to visit her mother and sister in New York and another relative in Detroit. She came from Detroit to Indianapolis, where we met her and brought her back to see Bloomington and Indiana University. We had an enjoyable time at a picnic that my family arranged so they could meet her. I love my sister-in-law very much and am grateful for the opportunities we had to be together.

I had hoped, and even promised Alice that we would drive up to Cape Breton to pick her up and bring her home. As it turned out, this was not possible, because Freddy agreed to perform a task for the American Political Science Association that took him to Reno, Nevada, for a week. So Alice was driven home by another family.

Since then, Freddy and I have never found time to visit Cape Breton. However, we do have a little painting, a watercolor that Alice did there. She sent it to us in a letter, folded over many times. I treasure that painting highly! I consider it an outstanding piece of work for an eleven-year-old child.

Ann Arbor and Gulfport (summer 1964)

The following summer, Steve went to Europe with Guy Davenport as Guy's companion and chauffeur. For Steve this was a great time of learning. They went by ship to England, drove to Paris and then Italy, where they visited the eccentric poet Ezra Pound, and then went on to Greece. There they sold the car and flew back to London.

Freddy went to yet another CAG seminar, this time at the University of Michigan in Ann Arbor. Alice and I remained in Haverford until her school closed for the summer. Then she and I flew to Ann Arbor to join Freddy. Later we drove to my sister Mae's farm, where Alice stayed when I returned to Ann Arbor.

Mae's daughter, Julia, had married Mark Hayes, her high school sweetheart, while they were both students at Indiana University. Mark and Julia were now living near Gulfport, Mississippi, where Mark, who was in the Air Force, was assigned to a base. That summer they were expecting their first child, and Mae wanted to go to Gulfport to be with Julia after the baby arrived. I agreed to go with her and assist with the drive. Freddy had a few more days left at Ann Arbor when Mae called to say she had a granddaughter and was ready to leave.

Alice was such a poor traveler that I wanted to leave her in Columbus with my brother, who had three daughters that Alice enjoyed visiting, but Alice insisted on going with Mae and me. It was not an easy journey, either coming or going, for it was so *horribly* hot! Mae's car ran well, but it had no air-conditioning. We were so very hot all the time.

All three of us really enjoyed being in Gulfport. Mark and Julie lived in a trailer in a very big trailer park near his base. Mae, Alice, and I rented another trailer not far away. While we were there, Mae and I took a rest from cooking. We ate most of our dinners at a restaurant on the beach adjacent to the trailer park. It featured many shrimp dishes as well as excellent fish. We all especially loved the Creole shrimp gumbo that was a specialty of the house.

Julie and Mark's baby was a tiny little girl they named Kristi. Julie was home from the hospital with Kristi almost as soon as we arrived. Mae decided that she could not bathe such a tiny baby, so the task was mine. Kristi really was the tiniest baby I have ever bathed, just a little less than six pounds. Both Mae and I were a little in awe of her.

There was little work to do, so our time in Gulfport was like a vacation for us, particularly for Alice and me because we loved the beach so much. There was also a small petting zoo that Alice loved to visit every day. Mae would have stayed longer, but I was anxious to get back to Freddy, and then on to Haverford. Steve would soon be arriving from Europe, and I needed to get everyone's wardrobe ready for the school year. The drive back to Indiana was unbearably hot, even hotter than the drive to Gulfport. We literally almost *expired* from that intense heat!

Alice makes a child

That year was the last for Alice at Gladwyne. As I remember, the highlight of her year was a school play in which she had a supporting role and sang a solo. I remember I went to school to fetch her, so I was there before dismissal time. When the principal, Mr. Fenner, saw me in the hallway, he told me with a twinkle in his eye that I should be sure to ask Alice what had happened that day.

Just then Alice came along and seeing me, flung her arms around me and said, "Oh, Mother! I made a child today."

As I hugged her, I saw Mr. Fenner laughing at us, and I said, "Whatever do you mean, Alice?"

Alice said, "We are giving a play, and I'll be the child. And I'll sing a song all by myself!"

Alice sang her solo in the play beautifully. I was very proud indeed of her performance! So was her father, and his is a very exacting ear musically. He does not tolerate off-notes or off-beats pleasantly. I listen to tunes; he hears notes.

Alice and the IQ test

That year Alice had an especially wonderful teacher, Mrs. Hughes. One day Mrs. Hughes called to ask me to meet with her one day after classes. She wanted to talk about an IQ test that her class had taken. Alice had been next to last on that test. Alice's teachers and the principal were dumbfounded. So Mrs. Hughes and Mr. Fenner had arranged for Alice to take the test again. This time the results were only slightly higher. They decided that I should be told and given advice about how to deal with my daughter and plan a happy future for her. Mrs. Hughes could not have been kinder, more honest, or more lovingly intentioned.

Alice always performed at a top level in *everything* she did at school. Her artwork was of the best. Her music and performance were A+ (just as her performance in the play had been). Her class work as a whole put her in the topmost rank in her grade (there were two sixth grade classes). So they had come to the conclusion that coming from a family such as ours, with the father a professor at one of the country's most prestigious colleges and a brother graduating from Episcopal Academy with honors and now attending a highly ranked college, Alice was able to perform as well as she did because of her family. They concluded that she must be very hardworking, and that she was surely overstretching herself, so she would find her next and succeeding years very stressful.

When Mrs. Hughes told me all this, I was so overwhelmed and my feelings were so chaotic that I could barely take it all into my numbed brain. Mrs. Hughes understood my bewilderment and confused feelings very well. She said they all loved Alice so very much that they had decided to talk with me about it for her sake. She advised us never to push Alice, but rather to let her go along at her own rate. We should guide her not into a college or university, but rather possibly into some technical school or trade apprenticeship.

When I reported all this to Freddy, he was far less bewildered and concerned than I was. We both knew that we had never pushed Alice. Alice had always been so self-propelled that typically, we had to give more energy to slowing her down than pushing her on!

In retrospect, as I consider Alice's achievements and accomplishments, I can only conclude that intelligence tests may often be a good guide, but they are not completely accurate. One should always allow for a margin of error and should never make judgments based only on IQ test results. Alice's inability to score well has perhaps prevented her from entering one school or another, but when allowed to perform, Alice usually out-performs everyone performing with her! By sheer grit, she has learned to overcome even physical shortcomings—something her mother has never been able to do.

By this time, Freddy and I had grown far more compatible in our care and concern for our children. Unless one gives it some thought, it is not easy to recognize how different our early years were. Freddy never knew any babies except his nephew, and even his nephew was very near Freddy's age and lived in a different household, so Freddy's experience with him was limited. On the other hand, I grew up in a very unstructured way and always had a sibling to be responsible for. For me, a baby is a unique human being and deserves to be treated as a person. For Freddy, a baby needs strict training to become a person. So in our early years of marriage, this difference in perception caused us just about our only problems.

There was an incident in our early days in Gainesville which was quickly over for me, but which still bothers Freddy. It was not until I lived in Germany and saw how they caressed their dogs and swatted their children that I began to have an inkling of the atmosphere in which European children were raised. Freddy loved Steve and cared about him, but he could be very belligerent and threatening toward him, and that aroused my protective instincts very quickly. I do wish that it were different, but in spite of my parents' best efforts, I am much like them in this: I have a very hasty and hot temper.

One day Freddy began to shake Steve and say very bitter words for which I could see no reason. I was so incensed that I slapped Freddy. I have wished many times over that I had been more con-trolled, but I am also fairly certain that I would likely do the same thing again today, given the same provocation. I also give it as my earnest conviction that both Steve and Alice have a great deal of love for their father, and that they respect him far more than they do me. Whatever I did in that hasty moment did not diminish him in their eyes. So it should be, for he is a caring and loving father!

During our last year at Haverford, Alice went on to a middle school not far from Gladwyne. We were not at all content with the school and its highly charged atmosphere. The intensely com-petitive and often crude behavior of those with new wealth is not appealing to either Freddy or me, and we did not like it for Alice either. We saw this kind of atmosphere as prevailing in her middle school, and if we had stayed at Haverford, we had already decided to send her to a private school.

We were by then fairly relaxed about our financial situation. We could not be smug, but neither were we tense. Things were going very well academically for Freddy. In fact, Freddy was very happy indeed with his professional life, but he will tell you more about that.

Christmas in Gainesville

Ever since we left Gainesville, Manning Dauer had been urging us to come back for a visit and to consider his home as a place to stay. (His mother had died only a week or two after our arrival in Haverford, at a time, unfortunately, when we felt it impossible to return for the funeral.) So at Manning's urging we went to Gainesville for the Christmas vacation in 1964.

Freddy and I enjoyed being there very much. Some of our old friends had left Gainesville, but many were still there and were the same good friends. I think, perhaps, that Steve and Alice enjoyed it less.

Some of their very good friends had left, and all our immediate neighbors from NE Seventh Street were gone. Then, too, our children were growing and changing, and so were their friends. Although Tommy Petty still lived in Gainesville, Alice no longer enjoyed him in the same way. She said he could talk only about Elvis Presley, and she was not all that interested in Elvis. Freddy and I have visited again, but for Steve and Alice, that was it. They and their Gainesville friends had grown apart.

Berkeley, California (summer 1965)

The summer of 1965 Freddy was invited to participate in another CAG seminar—this one at the University of California in Berkeley. I for one was happy to have him accept.

Steve had decided to change his major at Trinity College and needed to reinforce his Latin skills for entering a Latin course in the fall. So he and Freddy arranged for him to enroll in a Latin course at Berkeley that summer.

Alice did not want to go with us, but she had no fixed idea as to what she did want to do. I could not promise her anything about what she might do in Berkeley. I had never been in California, and I had no idea what or where our residence would be, or what we would find in youth recreation facilities or programs, and I knew no one to ask.

After endless discussions, Alice realized that she was going to California with us, and she asked if she could take a friend along. She felt it would not be too bad if she had one friend with whom she could go places and do things. That seemed logical enough, so I agreed. She chose a friend that she had made at summer camp in Cape Breton, a girl who lived in Philadelphia. She and Alice had spent some time together during the winter, and both Freddy and I liked her quite well. Although we had not seen much of her, we felt sure that they would be congenial since they had spent one summer together. So since they both desired it, we agreed that Alice could invite her to spend the summer with us in California.

The girl's parents were both social workers. Her father taught social work at Temple University, and her mother worked for the city of Philadelphia. Her mother talked with me on the phone about the plan. The core of her questioning seemed to revolve around what kind of "meaningful program" we could provide for the girls. I could offer none. I had not worried much about a meaningful program for Alice. I simply hoped for a happy, healthy time for my daughter.

They did not let their child go with us. Alice was very sad, and I was unhappy for her. I did not worry deeply about it, but I did do a little examination of my duties as a parent in my own heart and mind, and I wondered if I were actually being a responsible parent. Both girls had been at summer camp in Cape Breton, I told myself, and so far as I could tell that had been less than a meaningful experience, so I rather wondered about the real reason for them not accepting our invitation.

Deprived of this companion, Alice insisted on another. The second choice was Hilda, a girl we knew even less well. Hilda turned out to be a less than felicitous choice. Why the two did not get along well together, I do not know. Perhaps it was their age. Whatever the source of the problem, it cost me a great deal of time, energy, and money that I would have been happier spending elsewhere.

We all loved San Francisco and Berkeley. Steve had to be there earlier than we did, so he and his friend and roommate from Trinity College drove there in a new Ford Galaxie that we had just purchased (we feared our old car might not get over the mountains). Freddy and I flew there with the two girls. We arrived a few days before we could get into the house we had rented for the summer, so we stayed in a very modest hotel in San Francisco for three days.

I will never forget my feeling of great joy and exhilaration on that first day! I am so accustomed to my allergies and breathing problems that usually I think nothing of them, except when they really get me down for one reason or another. So when I inhaled that clear, lovely air beside the Pacific Ocean, I was overcome with an almost indescribable feeling of exhilaration and well-being. Those three days were better than normal weather-wise. There was no fog in the morning, the sun shone clearly and brightly, and it was pleasantly warm.

When we went over to Berkeley to inspect the house we rented, we found ourselves in real luck again. The house suited us very well indeed! It was just right for our needs. There were three floors. The top floor, which was at street level, had a large bedroom, a bath, and a small study. Steps led down to the middle level to a pleasantly furnished main living area with a stone fireplace, a dining room, a kitchen, a bath, and a bedroom. Off the entrance hall and two steps up was a small study/library with a fireplace.

Down another flight was a large master bedroom and a bath. The master bedroom had sliding doors onto a patio and a small, lovely garden. The west and south sides of the dining room consisted of windows that we loved, for they looked out across the bay to San Francisco. Especially at night, it was a spectacular view—the bay, the city, and two bridges lay glittering before us!

The rental fee included two maids; one came on Monday, the other on Thursday. There was also a Japanese-American gardener who came once or twice a week. I was so happy to have them. Usually when I am in someone else's house, I spend too much time trying to keep it as the owners left it, so I cannot relax. If I found little time to relax in Berkeley, it was not because I was cleaning the house or tending the garden. Rather, my greatest tasks were keeping enough food in the house and trying to keep the girls happy.

The girls bickered constantly, and Hilda complained about a great many things. As I saw it, she never wanted to try anything new; she only wanted more of the things she already liked and liked to do. I spent a lot of time trying to find a place for them to swim. I never succeeded. I could not locate a public beach or pool in either Berkeley or San Francisco. However, I located a ranch where they could ride. That was a real plus.

My nephew Tom (Roy and Paulene's son) was in basic training at the naval base at Alameda, and I shall always love him and be grateful for his help and kindness to Alice and Hilda. He took them riding, he took them to movies, and he played board games with them for hours on end.

That summer, I seemed always to have lots of hungry mouths to feed. In addition to our family of four, there were Hilda, Tom, and Burnett (Steve's friend who had driven with him to California). Burnett was visiting a friend or relative just outside Berkeley, but he came back often to visit Steve. As well, various friends of theirs were often at our house. Then toward the end of our stay, Paulene (Tom's mother) and her son Roger came to visit, and they stayed at our house. It was a pleasure, really, to have them all come, and it was great to be able to house them comfortably.

Fortunately, I found shopping for food in Berkeley a pleasure, for I did lots and lots of it. Fruits and vegetables were so cheap, so good, and in such an unending variety! There were even vegetable and fruit vendors on the streets, so I was always stopping to buy apricots or sweet red cherries or melons or cantaloupes. My family reveled in all these treats, but Hilda did not. I had to buy shriveled, out-of-season apples and bananas for her when I could find them at the supermarket.

Freddy asked me why I bothered, but I felt an obligation, and a little guilty. It had been a bit of a sacrifice for Hilda's family to let her come, and her mother had been reluctant for her to interrupt her music lessons for two months. Hilda was very gifted musically; she later commuted to Baltimore for lessons at the Johns Hopkins School of Music. Fortunately there was a good upright piano in our rented house, so she was able to practice. It was a pleasure to hear her play, and I must confess, about the only time I enjoyed her.

I tried to stop the bickering between the two girls but I was never successful. Telling Alice that Hilda was her invited guest and she owed her that courtesy fell on deaf ears. In my own mind, I could not blame Alice too much, for Hilda really could be a pill. She was seldom cooperative, and she was highly competitive.

Eventually I found out that Hilda had thought we would be near Disneyland—after all, it was in California! So Freddy made inquiries at a travel agency and found some special package deals through a small California airline for transportation and lodging at Disneyland. He bought a package for the girls and me. This outing was a great success. We all enjoyed it very much! This is not to say that the girls became friendly and amiable throughout, for they were not. But they enjoyed everything, and even I loved it!

I still think of it as an ideal place for a family vacation. Our package was for three days in midweek, but they both begged for another day. This was easily arranged. On that extra day, I had a glimpse of some of Disneyland's future problems. There were many more people in the park on that Saturday, and the crowd was rougher. That made the general atmosphere less friendly, sometimes bordering on rude and belligerent. Nevertheless, the trip to Disneyland was probably the high point of the summer for Alice.

That summer, someone from our Gainesville days was in Berkeley—Susan Tilley, our dear friend and former neighbor. Susan's family had moved from Gainesville to Davidson College in North Carolina. The summer following her graduation from high school, Susan had married her father's star student, who was graduating from Davidson College. They had come to Berkeley for Susan to enter college and her husband to enter graduate school. By working for a year and gaining residency, they could go to school more cheaply by paying in-state fees. I was happy to see Susan. We had always gotten along very well together. She was such a bright girl, and I do enjoy bright people. Indeed, I love all the Tilley children exceedingly.

The CAG seminar gave me further opportunity to interact with bright people. I enjoyed Freddy's colleagues and their spouses enormously. I always looked forward to our dinners and the time we spent together. After the seminar ended, we stayed an additional week so Freddy could finish his seminar paper. Again my typing skills were put to use. It was difficult to find the time for typing, but I was glad to do it, for I was always interested in Freddy's work. At Haverford, the college supplied a secretary whose services he and Harvey shared, so we had fewer opportunities to talk about his professional interests.

After seven weeks, we left that beautiful place. Freddy and I, with the girls, drove back across the country. (Steve had flown back a week before we left.) We started at a leisurely pace, going up the Pacific coast to visit my cousin Dorothy and her family in Seattle. Then by arrangement, we spent an evening with the Tilley family in Spokane, Washington.

In my memory of this journey, one very beautiful experience stands out. We had wanted to drive up Mt. Rainier after we left Seattle, but the park service stopped us after we had gone up only a little way. It was snowing on Mt. Rainier, so we could go no further. As we drove on east, we soon were on the very flat, almost barren plain that is the center of Washington state. Freddy was driving, and I turned to look back at the mountains. Mt. Rainier filled the whole back window, and my breath almost stopped as I gazed on such tremendous beauty.

Out on the plain, the sun was shining, and that great mountain glittered with its fresh new covering of snow. A feeling of such awe and reverence came over me. I was so overpowered by emotion that my eyes became misty.

I told Freddy to look in the rearview mirror. He did; then he pulled over and stopped. We all got out of the car to gaze at the glittering mountain. Everyone was moved by the sight. When I have since tried to describe that experience—how the mountain looked and how I felt—I have fallen short. For it was like a religious experience, as if heaven had opened up to me and I had a shining vision of a father-mother God, so vast, so caring, so loving, and watching over us all. I shall never forget it!

To the girls' dismay, we only drove through Yellowstone Park. By then, Freddy had begun to get impatient and said we had no time to linger. They did get to see the hot springs, the bubbling lava beds, and the waterfalls, but we spent the night outside the park on the east side. Then we drove on through the Black Hills with a very short look at the carved faces on Mt. Rushmore. In a bookstore in Berkeley, we had bought a great stack of Agatha Christie paperbacks, and both girls read them ceaselessly as we traveled home. Those books were a blessing!

Haverford

During the academic year of 1965-66, Alice was in eighth grade and Steve was in his senior year at Trinity College, Hartford. This turned out to be our last year at Haverford College. The following year Freddy was on sabbatical and we lived in Europe. We returned to Haverford only to pack up and move to Bloomington and Indiana University.

We lived on the Haverford College campus on the Main Line for six years. As I mentioned earlier, I never really felt at home there. I never felt that I belonged. Freddy and I found certain aspects of the lifestyle there both bewildering and distasteful. I was also finding that my relationship with Freddy's students was changing.

My philosophy is very much of the live and let live sort, and I am very opposed to putting labels on people and then seeing nothing

Steve
**Trinity College,
Hartford, Connecticut
Graduation, 1966**

around or beyond those labels. But I remember how addiction to alcohol destroyed my father, and I was dreadfully alarmed when I became aware that so many young people were turning to marijuana and hard drugs.

It was about this time that I realized that I was beginning to feel much older in mind and outlook than our precocious young students. I was still happy to give them home-cooked meals, but I think they enjoyed it less and had less to talk with me about.

It is quite true that I could not share their feelings about Vietnam, and that I felt sick about their disenchanted, negative, or hostile attitudes toward the United States and its government. Flag-waving and school prayer may not be very high on my agenda, but flag burning is not at all. I am unwavering in my allegiance to my religion and to my country. So I was disturbed by the upheaval, and I was restless. I needed some new interests, and I needed to find a new personal goal.

Chapter 8

Europe

(1966-1967)

We were at Haverford for six years before Freddy was able to take his first sabbatical leave. He was eagerly looking forward to our spending the year in Europe. I was happy to go to Europe, but I was not as wildly happy or enthusiastic as Freddy and Steve. In retrospect, I realize that part of the problem was my health. We lived in a very dusty house, and the constant exposure to dust caused continuous problems for my lungs. In addition, I had two operations during this time, so my health was generally below par.

Freddy made most of the arrangements for our living in Europe for a year, while I looked after the domestic side of our preparations for departure. Our plan was this. Less than a month after my major surgery, Freddy and Alice would leave for France and Germany. Alice would be attending summer school at Le Collège Cévenol in Le Chambon-sur-Lignon, France. Several weeks later, I would cross by ship, bringing with me a trunk for Alice and one for Freddy and me. Steve would leave after me, crossing the Atlantic on a much smaller boat and going directly to Ireland, where he would be doing graduate work at Trinity College in Dublin.

Preparations and departure (summer 1966)

Our weeks of preparation were very busy indeed, and I frequently had a big decision to make or a new problem to solve. My greatest difficulty was establishing guidelines about the deposit of our income checks into the proper accounts and the transfer of funds to us in Europe for the next year. I wrote out all the details about the deposits for the departmental secretary. However, she did not understand me well and there was a problem. Fortunately Steve was still in Haverford. After graduating from college, he spent the summer with me while working in Philadelphia, so he was still there when the banking problem arose. Luckily he was able to rectify the situation before he set sail for Dublin.

My departure began with an overnight stay in New York, in a motel near the pier. The next day I boarded the Queen Elizabeth II for my first trip to Europe. An officer took pity on me as I struggled up the plank with two heavy suitcases, an overnight bag hung around my neck, and a rather large handbag slipping off my shoulder. I committed my first faux pas almost with my first breath onboard, for I proffered the kind man a tip, which he politely refused. I had read my little book on tips, but I had nothing to teach me to recognize British naval uniform stripes and insignia. I was embarrassed to show my ignorance so soon.

I had a single second-class cabin on the inside. There were no portholes, so my cabin was as dark as a dungeon. However, I was very comfortable, and I was glad to have my own shower, toilet, and basin.

My only complaint was with myself. I wanted to be doing things, but I slept so much. Also, I had brought only dresses, and I soon wished I had slacks and sneakers to wear on deck. I had not realized that a chilly wind blows constantly over the North Atlantic. So even though I had a deck chair, I had to keep it in a corner out of the wind, and I saw little sun or water.

The food was fabulous, and it was tempting to eat more than I needed. Every meal was excellent. I reveled especially in the wonderful fruit, and ate my first greengage plums from France. They were so different from the small sour fruit I had known in Indiana. Overall, I think the voyage was good for me. I needed the good food, sleep, and rest.

I arrive in France

On the day of our arrival, they alerted us early in the morning and hurried us to get ready to disembark, but then we had to wait a long time to leave the ship. I was reminded of Freddy's hurry-up-and-wait experiences in the army. Freddy was there to meet me.

He walked with me through French customs. It was good to have him along, for the customs people harried me a bit.

Most of the luggage was going on to Germany, but the trunk for Alice was going to her school in the south of France. In the light of more years and more experience, I can see that the French customs agents were not at all bad, but then I thought they were illogical and fussy.

I was inclined toward argument and mulishness. Why should they want the big trunk unpacked? It was going into Germany. Why should I unpack all the luggage, and show them all the *new* things I had bought, and tell them what I had paid for each piece? I think they were only baiting me for their own amusement, for ultimately they did not insist.

Soon we were on a small boat train to Paris, where Freddy had engaged rooms for us in a small hotel. Alice joined us there. She had been at summer school in Le Chambon and was escorted by a school representative to the train station in Paris, where Freddy met her.

We stayed in Paris a few days while we transacted business relating to each of us for the coming months. We had to redirect our trunk to Germany and Alice's to Le Chambon, and we had to buy supplies, including bedding, for Alice's upcoming school year.

I found the shopping in Paris not too different from America, but then I had Freddy with me. He spoke French quite well, at least for shopping and for getting around. Alice did, too, but she was not old enough to be taken seriously by the sales staff. This is a facet of French life seldom recognized in the United States. Until the age of eighteen, French girls lead a very restricted life, and they are guarded closely. At least they were in 1966. I have not been in France for twenty years now, and things may have changed, but I doubt it.

We tour Scotland and England

During our short time in Paris, I visited the offices of Thomas Cook, a well-known British travel agency. There I arranged an itinerary for the three of us to tour Scotland and England for three weeks. Afterwards I was pleased that our arrangements had been made this way. We were able to travel and stay with Scottish and

English people rather than Americans, which gave me greater insight into the way the British actually travel, think, and live.

We flew to Glasgow to begin our tour. From there we took a short bus trip to visit a nearby castle and other sights, stopping at village inns for meals. We were fortunate in the weather. I fell in love with Scotland. It was so beautiful. The rhododendrons were still blooming, and I was amazed at how the shrubs were about three times larger than any I had seen in New England or Washington, DC. We were very aware of just how far north we were, because it remained light for about twenty-two hours of the day. I had read about this phenomenon, of course, but it did not become real until I experienced it myself!

I noticed that in the villages, the cottages and clothing seemed rather poor and primitive, but the children were beautiful, rosy and round-cheeked, and healthy-looking. The villagers were still using handlooms to produce extremely lovely woolen cloth. Many such products were for sale at a local shop where the tour buses parked. There were also tearooms galore and lots of bakeries with tempting goodies. Our teenage daughter was interested only in the clothing. We bought her a kilt-type skirt and a sweater, both of which proved to be excellent purchases, for they remained lovely for years.

From Scotland we went south into England and stayed in Stratford for a few days. Freddy felt quite at home there. During his long convalescence after being wounded in France, the ambulatory patients from his hospital were brought to Stratford to visit the theater. We saw *Hamlet* there, and we all loved it, including Alice. I formed the opinion then, and thirty years later I still retain it, that only the British can do justice to Shakespeare.

From Stratford we went to Windermere in the Lake District, where we stayed at the Belsfield Hotel for a few days. It had once been a private home, but its owners had been unable to afford living in it. We liked staying there very much. We especially enjoyed the grounds and the abundance of rose beds. In that cool, moist air, the roses were gorgeous, and their perfume was pervasive. Roses have such a wonderful, light fragrance. I have never been in another place where they were so lovely or so fragrant! Freddy and I, sans Alice, greatly enjoyed long walks all around the area.

From Windermere we went to London. Freddy left us there while he went back to Germany for a few days. He and a European colleague, Herr Schnur, were arranging yet another CAG (Comparative Administration Group) seminar, this time with European scholars. It was to take place in September in Bochum, Germany. So Alice and I were on our own in London for a while.

Since Alice was more interested in shops than historic spots, we looked at shops and stores while Freddy was absent. Freddy is absolutely the worst person in the world to window shop with. He does not enjoy it and has no patience with those who do, with one exception, he loves browsing in bookstores.

Alice and I went all over Harrods, and we enjoyed strolling through the streets. I took note of the theaters and plays, and we decided which ones we would see when Freddy returned. We did indeed see the plays. We also saw other things tourists see when they visit London—Westminster Abbey, the changing of the guard at Buckingham Palace, Kew Gardens, and many historic spots.

Freddy shows us his Vienna

From London we went on to Vienna, traveling by train. After crossing the English Channel, we boarded a wagon-lit in Calais. We woke up in Switzerland, and I had my first glimpse of the Alps from the train. I was utterly delighted! I felt so privileged to see so much beauty! Switzerland was like a glossy picture book. It was such a contrast to France and England, which were still showing the terrible effects of the war. Neither Switzerland nor Austria had been devastated in the same ruthless way that Western Europe had.

From the train we saw one delightful scene after another: towering snow-capped mountains, dark green forests, bright green grasslands, houses of earthen-brown wood, with their balconies hung with boxes of bright red, blue, and white flowers. (I later learned that these flowers generally were geraniums, lobelias, petunias, and alyssum.) For my eyes, it was a superlative feast!

The Alps are very different from our own western Rockies. I found the Alps much gentler in appearance, in spite of their height, for they had many more rolling slopes and many more areas of human cultivation. The Rockies, it seems to me, appear far wilder and more rugged and forbidding. This is not to say that

I prefer one mountain range to the other. To me they are quite different and to be enjoyed differently, in one's own personal way and according to the emotional responses that each evokes.

We arrived in Vienna in the late evening. It was Freddy's first return. We were met by Hans Jecht, a young Austrian professor who had translated Freddy's book into German. (Hans and his family had visited us in Haverford in the spring of that year.) Hans helped us to find the pension at which he had made reservations for us. Unfortunately it was full of young people, part of a walking tour group. The manager was sure it would be too noisy and boisterous for the Herr Doktor Professor, so she arranged for us to stay in her friend's apartment, where it would be much quieter. Once again I satisfied my desire to live among the native people.

How typical our hostess, Frau Forster, was, I cannot be sure. I expect that it was greatly to our advantage to stay with her, but I did not love or admire her. She was most curious about Alice and me, and quite critical. Alice carried a bag of curlers all over Europe and put her hair up on them every night. That "wasn't too stupid of her, but how on earth could she sleep?" Alice's worst crime was that she was not deferential enough to her parents and other elders.

While we did think that Alice was being pretty silly in being more interested in shops than historic sights, and in not using her time more advantageously, yet we also knew quite well that she enjoyed the ballet and the opera very much. Alice was an American girl just at the beginning of her teen years, and given her age, and the place and time, she behaved far better than we dared hope.

We really filled our days and nights in Vienna! Freddy had not forgotten a thing, including the routes of the streetcars. We were there several days before he took us to the street where his family had owned a store and lived in an apartment above it. It was wrenchingly painful for him, so we barely glimpsed the area.

Before that moment, I had not realized the depth of his feelings. Although I had wanted so very much to get some personal feeling for the place, it was very plain that he could not deal with the memories. So we did not linger.

It was abundantly clear that Vienna had been the cultural seat of the Habsburg Empire, and that the Habsburgs had brought the cream of Europe's cultural crop to Vienna for their and their court's intellectual pleasure. The Viennese museums were the former palaces of the royal family, and they contained a marvelous collection of royal armor, robes, and jewels. Seeing such things truly personalizes history, and it extends and broadens one's understanding!

The scope of the collections of paintings was no less than breathtaking. In the countries ruled by the Habsburgs, in particular in the Netherlands and Spain, the paintings, sculpture, and silverwork were the best produced. I had seen an exhibit in New York in the late forties called, I believe, Treasures from Vienna, which had been a wonderful exhibit, but I could see that it had been a mere token. Vienna was full of cultural treasures of every kind—architecture, music, ballet, and all forms of artwork. There was even a modern museum containing work of Schiele and Klimt. Their work was certainly a departure from classicism, but not at all like other moderns I have seen elsewhere. They had distinctive styles of their own.

As long as we did this kind of sightseeing, Freddy seemed to enjoy showing us the sights. However, he frowned upon Alice's desire to see the Spanish riding school performances. We tried to get tickets but were unsuccessful, so one morning, we went to watch rehearsals that were open to the public. Alice loved it. We stayed for an hour, with Freddy getting more uncomfortable by the minute. Not until many years later did I fully comprehend (if I really do) his impatience and discomfort.

As for me, I found that I did not like the Viennese people very much. They had such an exaggerated manner of willingness to serve (whether in restaurants, shops, transportation, or elsewhere) that one suspected insincerity. And so there was! If one was a little slow in comprehension or in bringing forth a tip, or if one made any other slight misstep, the Viennese could be very mean-spirited.

Freddy told me some of the critical comments that our landlady made about me. He laughed about them, but they astonished me quite a lot! For beginners: Why had he chosen to marry someone so small and obviously incompetent? I was thin, so obviously I couldn't cook, and so, she supposed, we must eat all our meals in restaurants. She had heard that this was true in America.

I strengthened her supposition of no housewifely accomplishments when I had Freddy ask her if she could recommend a place to mend a broken zipper in a dress. She would not let Alice or me do any hand washing, yet she berated me for not doing simple things for my family and myself. It was all such ludicrous nitpicking that I could not even be angry. Besides, her comments seemed intended to disguise the fact that her friends were willing to perform all these little tasks for us—for a price!

Bochum, Germany

From Vienna we went by train to Bochum, Germany, where Freddy and I would be living while he taught at the new university for a few months. When Freddy was in Bochum during the summer, he had stayed in the university guesthouse, and he had searched for a place where the two of us could live during the coming semester. He had arranged to sublet an apartment from Frau Kramer.

Frau Kramer had grown up in Vienna. Her family had been prosperous and owned several small factories throughout central Europe. During the years of Nazi rule, they had lived in Switzerland. Her father had died during that time, and her mother, a Belgian, soon after the war. On her own, Frau Kramer had reclaimed factories and apartments in Munich, Bochum, and Belgium, as well as a summer home in the Austrian Alps. She maintained the house in Luzane as her principal residence.

Frau Kramer told Freddy that she had been very ill and had been told that she had little time to live. She had recovered, but her illness had given her a new perspective on living. During her illness, the supervisors in her factories had carried on very well, so she had decided to retire.

One had to admire Frau Kramer, her business skills, her language skills, her hard work, and even her appearance—all were superior. Unfortunately my personal relationship with her was not very good. When Freddy was around, we had pleasant times with her, but when we were alone together, she generally treated me as if I were her kitchen maid. She scolded and found fault with everything I did, and even many things she just assumed I did!

Our arrangement for a sublease was this. Frau Kramer would share her Bochum apartment with us. She would be there only occasionally, one or two days a month at most, and probably not even every month. We were to pay her a monthly rental, and then she would pay us a daily amount for the time she was there.

As it turned out, by the end of our stay she had paid us at least half as much as we had paid her! Evidently she loved her work and could not really retire. She had every reason to be proud of her accomplishments, but our lives were far happier when she was not there.

I was most conscientious in caring for Frau Kramer's apartment and possessions. She was less scrupulous in her concern for our comfort. When we arrived in Bochum with Alice, Frau Kramer was in residence, even though she had told Freddy she would not be. She decided we could use a very small room with a single cot in it for our bedroom. She told Freddy that she had learned he could borrow any furniture we needed from the university. That night she grudgingly allowed Alice to sleep on the couch, and Freddy slept at the university guesthouse.

Fortunately her information was correct. Ruhr-Universität was new, so it included student dormitories (something not done prior to 1945). The dormitories were still under construction, and dorm furniture was being stored in a warehouse. Through Professor Schnur, we were able to borrow a dorm bed and a chest of drawers, which were cheerfully delivered to Frau Kramer's apartment.

We coped well enough with our arrangements, and we were generally warm, clean, and well-fed while in Bochum. However, during our stay there, I certainly depended almost entirely on Freddy. If we had not been well-bonded before, we would have come to be then! Our life there truly demonstrated our compatibility and our love and commitment to each other.

I must comment on my impressions of the Ruhr area. It was then twenty-one years after the fall of the Nazis. The Ruhr area had been heavily bombed during the war, but by this time the rubble had been cleared away, new factories and roads had been built, and the area looked clean, glossy, and busy. I must confess that I felt cynical about that busyness, since it involved a host of Turks and southeastern Europeans doing menial jobs and factory work.

Shopping adventures

Alice would be returning to boarding school in Le Chambon, so we needed to buy the clothing and bedding that she would need for the winter. For that we were relying on help from Jutta Jecht, the wife of Hans Jecht, Freddy's assistant during his teaching tenure at Ruhr-Universität. Jutta, Hans, and their two-year-old son had visited us in Haverford for ten days during early spring of that year. We had housed them in one of the college's guest suites, and I had cared for the little boy while his parents were sightseeing. So I felt no reluctance about accepting Jutta's assistance.

Unfortunately our shopping trip with Jutta was less than successful. She met us in Münster, and we went about to the shops, but Alice and I both wished we had gone shopping by ourselves. Jutta was not a pleasant companion. She treated us like stupid handmaidens that she would rather not be troubled with. Then to make matters worse, she put us on the wrong train for our return trip to Bochum!

Even though I knew almost no German, I somehow sensed we would be going in the wrong direction. To Alice's consternation, I decided we should get off the train and ask for help. We found a uniformed man and showed him our tickets, and I tried to say, "Which train?" in German (though I knew my words would likely be wrong and mispronounced).

Fortunately he understood me. With an exclamation of distress, he urged us to jump down, cross the tracks, and race over to another train faced in the *opposite* direction. He banged on the window of the driver, who was about to leave. The driver opened his door to talk to our guide. Then he scooped Alice and me up into his cab, shooed us off into the passenger car, and before we even found seats, the train was moving!

Alice was very upset. She was sure we were going the wrong way. But as it turned out, I was right. A short time later, we reached Bochum, and there was Freddy, waiting to help us carry our purchases and take us to our apartment in a taxi.

To this day, I remain puzzled by Jutta's unfriendly, almost hostile behavior. I would have assumed she was just having a bad day if it had been only this one instance. But Jutta continued to behave unpleasantly throughout our stay in Bochum. In fact there was one other time when I had to endure her surliness for a day.

Jutta's husband, Hans, told Freddy that she intended to visit some art galleries and hoped to buy a postwar artwork. She would be accompanied by a German art professor, who would assist her to make a selection. Freddy knew I would love going on such an expedition, and he said so to Hans. I suspect that Hans must have told Jutta that she had to invite me. She did so, but she obviously did not want to. I have never been treated with as much disdain and rudeness as I was that day.

Nevertheless, I am glad that I had this experience. It was the only one of its kind I have ever had, and it was very educational. Strangely enough, Jutta's incivility did not bother me that much. I knew I had done no wrong. Indeed, I had been hospitable, friendly, and helpful to the Jechts in Haverford. So I knew that whatever was troubling Jutta must have nothing to do with me. I assumed that she was very unhappy about something I could do nothing about. At the end of the day, I was pleased that I had gone, even though I realized it could have been a pleasanter, more educational experience if Jutta had chosen to be friendly.

We visited galleries in three different cities. The works we viewed came from artists of different schools but with similar styles and insights. They could have qualified as the 1960s descendants of the De Stijl painters. They differed most in color and mood. To myself, I classified them as more ornamental than thoughtful or philosophical.

There was one painting in particular that I liked, and if I had been looking to buy that day, I would have chosen that one. I do not now recall the artist's name, but I have seen his work in museums in the United States, and I have read about exhibits of his work in places such as Detroit and Seattle. The craftsmanship was wonderful and the colors appealing. Some of the canvases had been painted with metallic paint—the entire canvas covered with small squares painted in such a way that one saw it all as covered with triangles of twinkling colors.

After viewing the entire gallery, I returned to look again at my favorite painting and the other paintings by the same artist, which I also liked. The art professor, seeing my interest, came to talk to me. He could speak English rather well, and he tried to probe the depths of my interest and talk about the prices, but I was not interested in buying anything.

I do not recall whether Jutta bought a painting that day, but I do clearly recall her incivility. I recalled it again about ten years later when we visited the Jechts in Munich after they moved. They had a daughter then as well as a son. Jutta was a kind, friendly, pleasant hostess in Munich. Perhaps she had been unhappy living in her mother's home in Dortmund.

To Le Chambon-sur-Lignon

When it was time for Alice to return to boarding school, we looked into various options for getting her to Le Chambon-sur-Lignon. We considered train, bus, air, and combinations thereof, but there was no option that would be appropriate for a thirteen-year-old girl traveling alone. I certainly felt incapable of taking her, and neither did I want Freddy to take her and leave me in Bochum. So Freddy decided we should buy a car and drive her to the school.

We considered buying a Volkswagen Beetle, but it had no luggage space, so we finally bought a used Volkswagen 1500, a model never offered for sale in the United States. It had an abbreviated back seat and a slightly larger luggage area. Unfortunately the previous owner had not used it well, and we experienced many problems with it. However, it was adequate for our needs, and having a car made living in Germany far easier. I never really grew accustomed to European drivers, either then or later, so driving in Europe has never been a pleasure for me. I prefer train trips.

Alice was not interested in sightseeing or visiting along the way, so Freddy drove directly to her village. We enjoyed the drive through the lovely scenic area. After we left Alice at school, we made a more leisurely journey back to Bochum, enjoying the beautiful scenery very much indeed. We returned via St. Étienne, Lyon, Colmar, Besançon, Trier, then on northward beside the Rhine to Cologne.

My historical senses were alive, well, and pleased throughout our trip! I found it all so beautiful and thrilling. The advance of the Roman legions and the Holy Roman Empire centuries before became clear and awe-inspiring. Excavations had discovered relics of a very early church that I found most touching.

I bought a poster that I kept for a good many years, which pictured one of the finds from that early church—a Christ figure

astride a small donkey on wheels. It had been used in church parades and was small enough that a child could have pulled it.
Such relics brought the early Christian parades and rituals to life,
and one could imagine the lives of the people and the role of this
then-new religion in their lives.

Our drive along the Rhine was both lovely and historically re-
vealing. I was thrilled with the great cathedral at Trier. It had
been greatly damaged in World War II but had been rebuilt, and it
was clean and magnificent. We did not have time to tarry there as
long as I would have liked. Trier is a busy modern town, but there
are many markers and reminders of Charlemagne and the seat of
his empire that we (I in particular) would have enjoyed seeing.
Unfortunately I have never been privileged to return.

The CAG seminar in Münster and Heidelberg

We needed to return to Bochum since the CAG seminar would
soon begin, and Freddy still had some work to do in preparation
for it. It is Freddy's task to relate details about the seminar, the
papers, and the discussions, and mine to relate an onlooker's observations. As it happened, very few wives came, but there were
two Italian women whom I remember well. It was not that they
were particularly beautiful, but they were so beautifully dressed.
They were both well educated and had jobs of their own. They
lived in Rome, though their husbands had appointments in universities outside Rome.

I gained the impression that none of these four people would
have considered living any other place—not Athens, not Venice, not
Milan, not Paris, nor London. Rome was for them the ideal center.
I have always been sorry I never had the opportunity to visit or live
in Rome, even for a brief time, so that I might approach some understanding of their attitude.

Blanche Blank, an academic from Hunter College in New York,
was one of the seminar participants. She was our loveliest contribution from the United States. Besides admiring her beauty and
grooming, I came to have the highest regard for her as a person
and friend. She and Freddy eventually collaborated on a research
project, which they decided on during this period in Germany. In
a way Blanche is the epitome of all that I ever aspired to be and
never attained.

The other person whom I came to know quite well and who has remained a friend was C. L. Riggs, Fred's wife. (I think her name is Clara Louise, but she prefers C. L.) I had met C. L. several times before. The first was when Fred, C. L., and their children, Wendy and Ronnie, came to visit us in Haverford. I also saw her many times in Bloomington during the summer of 1963, just a few months after their son, Ronnie, had died in an automobile-train accident. I cannot honestly say that in Bochum, C. L. was a sad, grieving figure, but she had changed into an introspective, mystical one, and had lost a lot of her vivacity and vitality.

Professor Schnur had made the site arrangements for the CAG seminar. It began in an old country inn a few miles from Münster and concluded in an old hotel in Heidelberg. Both places were Old Germany but in very different settings, and I liked them both. We had lovely weather, so I spent hours walking alone in the countryside.

The country inn near Münster was in a farming village. I was probably the only person from the seminar group who had grown up on a farm, and so far as I know, no one else was prepared to endure the smells and meet cows nose to nose through fences!

It was quite a contrast to the United States. The pigs, cows, and horses, as well as the chickens, ducks, and geese, all lived in the village, so the whole place smelled like a barnyard. It was just as I had read: the dwelling place for the humans and their beasts was one—the humans upstairs, the beasts down, all enclosed within high wooden fences.

Usually the fences were too high for me to see a complete enclosure, but there were a few stretches of wire fencing that afforded me glimpses. Later I would be in modern villages closely resembling American suburbia, but this one was still one of the hundreds-of-years-old types.

I also walked in the fields. Unlike the United States, there were walking paths everywhere. I certainly used them. I thoroughly enjoyed myself all by myself.

The whole seminar then drove by car from Münster to Heidelberg. There C. L. joined me in walking and exploring. I enjoyed that, too. I particularly liked going into old bookstores. They depicted the old university town and its traditions so well.

Living in Bochum

When we returned to Bochum, it was time for classes to begin. We settled into the routine of Freddy going to the university while I coped with the usual tasks of keeping us clean, healthy, and well-fed. I seem to remember that Bochum had two Laundromats, one of which I could walk to. When Frau Kramer was in residence, she kept the bathroom covered with her hand washing, even though she employed an old woman and her daughter to wash, iron, and mend for her.

When Freddy asked if perhaps they would do the same for us, she said that the old woman was really not able. She had worked for Frau Kramer's mother for many years, and now she insisted on doing this for Frau Kramer and only Frau Kramer. I feel that she spoke sincerely, for I learned from the old woman's daughter that her mother had come into the city from a nearby village to help nurse Frau Kramer during her recuperation after surgery. I discovered that when Frau Kramer had reclaimed her family's property after the war, she had been kind and helpful to her former maid's whole family. It was a story that I thought about when Frau Kramer was most unpleasant and nitpicking with me!

The first time I went to the Laundromat, Freddy went with me to read the instructions and help me learn to operate the machines. The woman manager was Viennese, so she was friendly with Freddy and always helpful and friendly to me. She had a yappy toy Pekinese that she loved and most of the customers tolerated, even though he nipped someone almost every time I was in the Laundromat. He never bit me, but he surprised Freddy greatly one day when he nipped him.

The manager was most profuse in her apologies to the Herr Doktor Professor. Hans Jecht, who was with Freddy that day when he picked me up, was that rare German who did not like dogs. He laughed heartily with me over the episode and agreed that some customer should give the dog a good kick in the teeth.

In Bochum there was a large farmer's market at least twice a week in the city center. It was always crowded with pushy housewives wielding great baskets that they used expertly to shove their way to the front. Shoving and pushing were probably the German characteristics that I disliked most. In fact, they often angered me. So many Germans that I met had so many admirable, likeable, even lovable traits that I felt it paltry of me to get angry over the shoving. Eventually I achieved a greater tolerance, but I am afraid I hardly ever rated a passing grade.

Even in other countries in Europe, I could always identify the Germans by this overwhelming desire to be first in line! One evening when we were at a theater in Paris, we experienced just such a first-in-line incident that illustrates this very well. It was the custom for people to be seated by a young man and woman, both of whom expected a tip. Finding one's own seat was not permitted; they were very firm about this policy.

On that evening, we were at the theater standing in line, waiting for the attendants to seat us. Eventually we came to the front of the line, and just as the young escorts were approaching us, arms came from behind us waving tickets in front of our faces and bodies shoved us from behind.

I remarked in English to Freddy, "They *have* to be Germans. No one else ever behaves in this atrocious way."

Whoever was behind us must have known English and must have heard my remark. The bodies stopped shoving; the arms and tickets were withdrawn. We were seated almost immediately after this. I never looked back, and I felt as if I had been rude, too. But it is an incident that Freddy and I remember with some amusement.

In our apartment house, there was an older German woman who knew some English and always greeted me pleasantly. She had a son, with whom she lived in her apartment, who had been a prisoner of war in the United States for more than a year during World War II. He had been treated very well, he said, and he and his mother had friendly feelings towards Americans.

I asked her to help me learn some German words and phrases that would enable me to shop alone and communicate in a basic way. She was happy to try. I enjoyed being with her a lot. I learned a few things, but she probably enlarged her English vocabulary more than I did my German one! She was such a sweet, motherly woman. She revealed to me a kind, loving aspect of the German character.

I sample the arts

Freddy was engaged in a study of how the federal bureaucracy operated in the various administrative units of the West German Republic states. So he, with Hans Jecht, traveled frequently to various cities to interview civil servants. I went along, and while they interviewed, I went to museums. In so doing, I came in contact with an amazing amount of folklore and art history, and I learned to appreciate the development of German civilization.

What the Germans had accomplished in restoring, building, and rebuilding was truly miraculous. As they reorganized and set up the states, they budgeted healthy amounts for culture and arts, including the performing arts. This was an established tradition begun long ago when a royal prince ruled each German state.

Interestingly, some cities shared cultural entertainment. For example, one city might maintain a theater troupe while a neighboring city maintained a symphony orchestra or opera theater, and then each group would perform in both cities.

Since the performing arts were state-sponsored, the cost of attending performances was nominal, so we were able to attend performances frequently. The churches had wonderful choirs, and we also went to many Sunday afternoon performances of oratorios. Music and singing seemed to spring spontaneously from most people. It was not an activity for only the elite. There were exceptions, of course. For example, Freddy's assistant, Hans Jecht, did not care for music. However, the majority of Germans love music.

Before going to Europe, I had known about German music, but I knew very little about the painters and architects. Considering that I grew up in Indiana, that may seem a little strange. To be sure, I did know that most of the revered group of Brown County artists had studied in Germany, but I knew almost nothing about the great German expressionists.

My ignorance was probably due in part to the American rejection of all that was German after World War I. Another explanation could be the total suppression of whole schools of art and music by a totalitarian government. It happened under the nazis in Germany, the communists in the Soviet Union, and the fascists in Italy.

In October 1966, there was an exhibit in Essen of the works of Emil Nolde. Freddy and I spent the better part of a Saturday viewing it. It was an immense retrospective and my first plunge into German painting. After that experience, German art and artists became an absorbing interest for me, one that continued through subsequent visits in later years. Just as the French impressionists were the first to capture my intellectual imagination and attention, so the German expressionists awakened in me an empathetic response.

Learning about French artists was easier because both American and English authors have written a great deal about them. Much less had been written about German artists, so my journey of discovery was done firsthand.

I would love to write about this art history journey in greater detail, but it digresses from our central reason for this present writing, and it does not, I think, offer any explanation of the continuing love and caring that Freddy and I have for each other. But perhaps that is not quite true either, for as I talked with Freddy about these artistic interests of mine, he began to look at and view painterly art with greater attention than before.

Freddy loves and requires music in his life. I love music, but I do not require it. I require a kind of beauty and symmetry around me. I think I would speedily die without sunlight and color, and so paintings, especially those of the impressionists, satisfy a spiritual need in me in a way that music cannot satisfy.

Christmas in Paris and Bochum

Christmas in Germany is a very special time, and it was especially wonderful for our family in 1966. Steve came from Dublin, and Alice from Le Chambon. We arranged to meet in Paris. It gives me such pleasure to recall those days we spent together. We were in Paris before Christmas and then in Bonn for Christmas and into the New Year. I wonder if we have ever spent a more joyous and happy time together as a family. Certainly for me, it was a most wonderful experience.

Steve arrived in Paris first, and he had already attended a Christmas music concert in one of the city's huge, old churches before we arrived. He was ablaze with excitement and delight over the city, the music, Christmas (always a very special event to him), and being with his family again.

Alice traveled to Paris with a group of fellow students and a teacher as chaperone. She had requested that Steve meet her train, so Freddy and I waited at the hotel while Steve went to fetch her. They had a tale to tell when they returned. Steve had not recognized Alice getting off the train! And because Alice had spoken to him first, her chaperon was suspicious and reluctant to allow Alice to leave with him. In the end, they managed to convince her. Alice found it all very funny, but Steve was not as amused.

Alice had changed a great deal in those six months since Steve had last seen her. In June 1966, Alice had been a pretty, plump little American schoolgirl. After living among French students for six months, she was a slender, chic, and very French-looking young woman. There really had been a dramatic change. I expect she knew that, and she wanted Steve to be the first to see the transformation.

So there we were, all in Paris together for a few days. Christmas in France is not the wildly exuberant affair that it is in Germany, but it is a celebrated and beautiful event nonetheless. The big event in Paris that year was the first great Picasso retrospective. It was an immense show, and if I remember correctly, it was set up in three different buildings. The early years were grouped with the pink and the blue years. Then came the cubist years, followed by the sculptures, ceramics, and paper cuttings of later years. It was fascinating, to say the least. Freddy was busy for a day or two with his CAG concerns, so Steve and I went to the exhibit first. After that I went again with Freddy, and then probably with Alice, too. In all, I saw the whole exhibit at least twice!

Of all Picasso's works, the one that stands out in my mind as being most moving is the *Guernica* mural. However, it was not in this exhibit but still on loan at the Museum of Modern Art in New York, where I had seen it. That particular painting has the most appeal to me of all his works. If I were a professional art historian, I would claim that the most interesting and creative piece at that show was *Les Demoiselles d'Avignon*. It is a clear departure from traditional modes of artistic expression and a genuine tribute to a creative artist.

As a family we had our greatest fun at dinner in the evenings. We ate at small mom-and-pop restaurants, where the wife cooked and the husband was the waiter. These meals were some of the best I have ever eaten. One evening there was a slight contretemps with a person leaving the restaurant as we were coming in. It set us all laughing, and the merriment lasted the whole evening. We had such a wonderful time.

Freddy and I returned to Bochum a day before Steve and Alice, for Alice had begged for a day of shopping alone with Steve in Paris. What else she bought, I can no longer remember, but I do recall her present to me, a very lovely French umbrella! Part of the handle is wrought silver, and there are two layers of fabric, the top layer a beautiful blue nylon and the second a figured silk. Even then, Alice had her special talent of choosing the right gifts for people of all ages and dispositions. I still have that umbrella. It is one of my dearest possessions.

In Bochum, we had a small Christmas tree with real candles—the only real candles in all our years of Christmas trees. Our American friends the Birneys kindly invited us to join them for Christmas dinner and so, met our children for the first time. How good it was that the only other American family in Bochum was so congenial.

On to Paris

We lived in Bochum only a short while longer before we moved to Paris. We drove there in our Volkswagen by way of Amsterdam. Our journey took us through the Dutch national forest to the Van Gogh Museum, a small building set in the middle of native trees and wildlife. It is rather off the beaten path and not many visitors were there, so it was very pleasant. Some of the pictures and sketches in the museum were familiar, but many were not.

As we left the museum and were on our way to the car, we discovered that two wild boars from the forest had wandered into the parking lot. There they were grunting about. They were very large animals. The one standing beside our car looked at least half as large as the car! Neither Freddy nor I wanted to shoo him away, so we retreated behind the fence until the boars, finding no good forage among the cars, ambled off into the forest!

I presume these boars were the animals hunted by the royals of Europe. Whenever I went to a beauty parlor anywhere in Europe, there were tabloids and gossip magazines lying around, just as in the United States. However, the gossip there centered around the former and present royal families and their aristocratic relatives.

That same year, the Belgian king had entertained at his hunting lodge, and the main event had been a boar hunt in his national forest. To me, such stories were historical novels. Seeing these boars from the forest was an awakening. The past was still there, and 1066 AD did not seem all that long ago!

Freddy had been invited by several scholars to visit their universities and lecture to their students. Our stop in Amsterdam on the way to Paris was made for that reason. I was glad to have the opportunity to spend time there. I feel very much at ease with the Dutch, and I loved being in the Netherlands. Whether my ancestral van Schoyck genes influence my empathetic feelings, or whether the feelings stem from my admiration for Dutch writers after World War I, I cannot say. But the friendly, comfortable feelings are there.

Living among the French

From Amsterdam, we went on to Paris to the Mirabeau, an apartment hotel that we had seen advertised in the *Herald Tribune*, an American newspaper published in Europe, a wonderful newspaper for people who, like me, are not sufficiently knowledgeable in foreign languages. We went to the Mirabeau hoping to find an apartment to sublet within a few days, but it served us so well that in the end, we did not move. We stayed at the Mirabeau until we left Paris in August 1967.

Our apartment at the Mirabeau was less attractive than Frau Kramer's, but we had maid service daily, and the cooking arrangements were far superior. And (Blessed Relief!) I did not have Frau Kramer inspecting the pots to see if they had been properly cleaned or finding fault with my arrangement of articles in the refrigerator or in the bathroom. I was far happier in our Paris home than in our Bochum arrangement.

In fact, we were very content in Paris. Pure, unalloyed joy is granted to us in small amounts most of the time. However, in our months in Paris, it seems to me that we were granted an abundance of such joy. There might have been even more if I had not signed up to attend the Alliance Française, for I did not even with those classes learn to speak French as well as I had hoped. I did try, but my instructor said that I did not become immersed in the language as one needs to do. Freddy and I spoke English together, I read an American newspaper, and I went to a shop that sold British books for my reading material.

Nevertheless, I loved Paris, and I loved the French people. It is hard for me to understand why so many Americans think the French are unfriendly. To me they were not. Let me relate one instance to illustrate. I needed to ask a question, so I summoned up some French words that I thought were appropriate, approached an older man, and slowly asked my question. His eyes twinkled as he answered in very good, French-accented English and in the friendliest, kindest way. Possibly I blushed, for he tried to put me at ease.

This happened several times to me. Young or old, male or female, when they heard my atrocious attempts at speaking French, they took pity and spoke English in a pleasant manner. I found the French admirable in many ways. They worked hard, and they loved beauty and order. They had their own ways, often formal and seemingly rigid, but they also knew how to accommodate gracefully. I liked living among them very much.

Freddy continued with the same research project that he had worked on in Germany. However, France's government was centralized, so most of his interviews were conducted in Paris. During the evening, we often indulged in musical events and ballets. Most of the musical and ballet troupes of Europe perform in Paris whenever they can, so it was possible to remain in Paris and yet see the best of European performers!

At the Mirabeau, my daily life was almost effortless. The maids took care of the cleaning, including the bed linens and bath towels. One of them even did mending for a small extra sum! I did cook, but cooking just for Freddy and me was no chore, and shopping for food in Paris was great fun.

Each morning Freddy went out to buy bread and papers. (He loves having printer's ink for breakfast!) He also discovered little shops with a variety of delicacies—cheeses, processed meats, preserves, and honey. He loved the croissants, but I preferred the crusty long loaves. I could never get enough of their wonderful bread. The butcher shop just a few doors from us was excellent.

They seemed always to enjoy preparing any cut of any size for a customer and making it ready to put directly in the pan.

Then there were the open-air street markets where I bought fish, vegetables, and fruit. The one nearest us was in place two days of the week, but with a little attention, I learned on what days and in which nearby neighborhood I could find other such markets. It rather pleased me to go to the other markets for I loved the variety of the streets, and I was accustomed to walking long distances. For instance, there was a very good market near the Eiffel Tower where I frequently shopped. It was six or eight blocks from us.

The national transportation system in France was very good, and the subway system in Paris was excellent. We traveled cheaply and easily throughout the city and to places outside the city where the trains went. I never went alone outside the reach of the subways. However, I did go alone to Montparnasse, where I wandered around observing the outdoor painters and venturing into a few ateliers.

One of the maids at the Mirabeau, who spoke English very well, was horrified when she heard I had done this. She warned me that Montparnasse was swarming with "A-rabs," and that I should not go there, for they were dangerous!

I am sure she had good reason for her warnings. These "A-rabs" were North African refugees, most of them from Algeria, which had gained its independence from France not many years before.

Who was it who said, "The Poor are always with us"? He should have said, the problems of the poor, the outcast, the refugee are always with us. Twenty-five years have passed since I learned of the "A-rabs" in Paris, and more than fifty since my dear Freddy was also a refugee. Yet this problem remains worldwide and seems greater now than ever before!

Paris was, in a sense, a repeat of our experience in San Francisco and Berkeley. We had an abundance of visitors. In fact more Americans visited us there than we had seen in all our time in Germany. Among them, the Birneys (our American friends from Bochum) stayed with us a few days in late March on their way home to the United States. And then, the son of one of our good Haverford friends (who was in school in England) found refuge with us when he discovered that he had not taken accurate stock of his finances before he came to Paris.

A scholarly visit to England

As a result of the CAG seminars, Freddy had developed contacts with several European scholars. Those contacts, in combination with Fulbright funds used to invite visiting scholars, created many opportunities for travel and experiences that we would not otherwise have had. In late February, Freddy was invited to lecture in some English universities, so we traveled to Manchester, Liverpool, and Bristol. Our hosts entertained us in their homes in delightful ways, just as Americans entertain their visiting colleagues.

Let me never hear disparaging words about English cooking! The dinners served to us in English homes were invariably delicious. And it was delightful to meet and converse with British colleagues and their friends. We are still in touch with Ferdy and Paula Ridley, our hosts in Liverpool, and Peter and Evelyn Bromhead in Bristol.

We visit Steve in Dublin

During a lull in our English travels, we took a long weekend to visit Steve in Dublin. In Ireland more than in other European countries we visited, Americans are welcomed and loved. People at the airport, in the restaurants, even Steve's landlady were so anxious to make us welcome that I began to feel like Queen Elizabeth I, for whom Sir Walter Raleigh had spread his cloak over a puddle to prevent her muddying her shoes. The friendliness of the Irish was amazing. We received it happily and humbly.

Steve wanted us to visit his favorite pub, to delight in the ages-old bathhouse where he loved to go for a hot soak, and to meet his landlady, Mrs. Murphy (yes, really!). As a matter of fact, one of the first things he said to us was that we would "simply have to" rent a sleeping room from Mrs. Murphy. When he had told her that his parents were coming, she had said that she would be delighted to offer us a room.

Steve had tried to demur, saying that his parents were older people and accustomed to central heating. She had brushed it all aside and said she would fill the gas heater with coins early to warm the room and keep it going in the night. She would even put her own electric blanket on our bed! She was friendly and kind in this way and many others. I hope, I sincerely pray, that God has been good to Mrs. Murphy.

We came back to her house after visiting Steve's favorite pub, Ryan's, and then going to a restaurant for dinner. Steve built a coal fire in the little fireplace in his room, and we settled down for a visit. As we did so, Mrs. Murphy sent her daughter down to ask us to come to her quarters for refreshments and television. She had baked a huge American-type cake (carrot, I think). But instead of the coffee or tea we would have served, Mrs. Murphy offered us Irish whiskey in American iced-tea-sized glasses. The glasses were enormous! This really happened.

As you may guess, the evening is a bit blurred in my memory, but I think the TV program was a rerun of the Jackie Gleason type, which we never watch at home. We all tried to be interested and responsive to her efforts to please. In the end, it became a memorable evening that I do not remember too vividly!

Steve had written us about how cold he was in Ireland, and after our visit there, I understood. While palm trees grew along the streets and in Phoenix Park, inside the houses the temperature ranged from forty degrees to a "warm" room of sixty degrees. Neither that night nor the next day, did I disrobe sufficiently to have a real bath. I created clouds in the bathroom just from my warm breath, so I managed to clean only my hands and face. I cannot remember whether Freddy shaved or not, for he found it as cold as I did.

However, our bed that night was far from cold, and that was not only because we were full of Irish whiskey. Mrs. Murphy had put woolen blankets on our bed, then her electric blanket, and on top of that, more blankets. The little gas heater was full of coins and blazing away when we fell into bed. After a short while, we both awakened feeling as though we had been sent to burn in hell.

Scholarly visits to Oslo and Copenhagen

Freddy's contacts with European scholars also took us to Oslo and Copenhagen. It was on May Day that we flew from Paris to Oslo, where Freddy had been invited to lecture. I remember it so well because May Day is a festive day in France. It was the middle of spring, pleasantly warm, and flowers were blooming in window boxes and in the parks.

On May Day, many of the children make their first commu-
nions, the little girls wearing white dresses and wreaths of flowers on their heads. The streets were full of flower venders, from
whom everyone bought tiny nosegays of maybells, which we call
lilies of the valley.

I was still carrying my maybell nosegay when our plane landed
in Oslo where it was snowing. The jonquils in the park were in
bloom, standing up bravely in the snow. As in the Netherlands,
I felt very much at home in Norway. I noticed with interest that
there were many more individual homes than apartment houses
and that the houses were made of wood, unlike most homes on
the continent where we had been.

Oslo has a marvelous folk museum, which I visited first alone
and then with Freddy. There is also a Munch museum devoted
almost entirely to the works of Edvard Munch, a great painter of
the German expressionist school. He had sold only a few paintings
outside Norway and had left his entire collection to his nation. Art
historians now award him his just space in art history.

We also visited the Viking museum, which was wonderfully
constructed around a Viking ship that had been unearthed almost
intact from deep sands just off the shore. I had not known how
much there would be to see in Oslo, and I was happy to find so
much to enjoy. As was our usual custom, I did a daylong guided
tour while Freddy was involved in scholarly activities. Then we
stayed on a few days longer so we could see the best things together. We were so compatible, and it was truly delightful to be
able to travel around in this way together.

We went next to Copenhagen, another unique and delightful
city. The highlight of our stay there was seeing a performance of
the Royal Danish Ballet. As we were leaving for Paris, there was a
rather interesting incident at the airport.

We had already boarded our plane, and it had backed away
from the terminal perhaps 200 yards, but then the plane stopped,
and there we sat for several minutes. Nothing seemed amiss, and
there were no messages from the pilot. There were murmurings
all about us, but no great outcries or inquiries as there would have
been in the United States. Then a small, nondescript car came
across the airfield. It stopped, and a rather tall man and a woman
stepped out of the car, embraced, and kissed. He then boarded
our plane with his briefcase, and she hopped back into her car and
drove away.

As it turned out, the woman was the crown princess of Denmark. She was saying goodbye to her fiancé, a French count. There was a television set in the lounge of the Mirabeau, and I sat in front of it one day and watched the marriage ceremony of these two. The French (or many of them) were ecstatic that one of their aristocrats had been chosen as the consort for the future Danish queen.

Alice and l'asperine

We returned home to Paris only to be confronted by the unexpected. A letter arrived from the French woman who was in charge of the dormitory at Alice's school in Le Chambon. In my memory, this whole episode remains chaotic and frantic, largely because of my lack of competence with the French language. I must also confess that I still feel some irritation, if not anger, with Freddy for not helping me to understand what happened more clearly.

For a long time, I thought that the letter was from the headmistress of the school and that they were asking us to take Alice from the school for misconduct. Freddy tried to talk to the woman on the phone, but he could not understand what she was saying, for in her highly excited state, she was speaking too rapidly and in such a high pitch that her voice resembled a siren—the kind of sound that sets dogs yelping!

Freddy was extremely busy just then, trying to arrange for the final interviews to complete his research study, but we decided to drive to Le Chambon. We arrived in the late afternoon of that day and found Alice happy to see us and eager to tell us about Jonquil Day. Wild jonquils were blooming in great masses in the high fields and woods of the area that we drove through, from St. Étienne to Firminy to Le Chambon.

Spring was only now coming to this mountain region, even though we had already had nearly two months of warmth and flowers in Paris. Girls from the school had picked quantities of the jonquils, made small nosegays of them (much like the maybell nosegays in Paris on May Day), and then handed them out to passersby on the streets and roads in and around the village. To me, Alice looked glowing, happy, and very well.

The next morning, we had our interview with the head of the dormitory. Freddy's French is quite good on the whole, though as he says, he is better at understanding conversations about his special interests than about the more intimate, personal situations in everyday living. Even I had come to understand some French conversation, but I understood practically nothing Madame was saying. Her voice was very excited, high, and shrill, and her words ran together. However, I heard *asperine* emphasized several times.

Freddy said afterward that he too had understood little of what she said, but he did understand that they were expelling Alice from the dorm for attempted suicide because she had taken aspirin. My feelings were that the woman had to be mad.

We then went to see the advisor to the American students, a black American who found the French less prejudiced than Americans and who was very happy there among the Huguenots. His easygoing approach was a distinct contrast with and relief from Madame's. It seems that the school authorities regarded aspirin as a poisonous substance, so students were not allowed to keep it in their rooms. I am quite sure Alice regarded this as a silly rule that she did not need to obey. After all, we always had aspirin in our medicine cabinet and took it without thought whenever we had pain.

I do not remember whether Alice had a bottle of her own, or whether she had borrowed one from her friend Renée. She may have had a sick stomach and headache. At any rate, she had taken more than one or two aspirin. Then she had vomited. Whoever had come upon her being sick had seen the aspirin bottle and taken it to the head of the dormitory, who accused Alice of trying to commit suicide. So they had sent for us to take her away!

I did not understand much of it then, and I still do not know all that was said. Freddy thought it a big tempest in a teapot and wished that he did not have to soothe all these people. He managed to settle the problem, though I have never understood exactly how. Freddy rented a room for Alice in the same house where her friend Renée lived, thus freeing her from the dormitory and its strict rules. In the end, Alice got what she wanted all along. She was allowed to remain at the school, take the exams, and on passing them, get her certificate.

Steve joins us in Paris

Steve finished his graduate work at Trinity in Dublin. We all rejoiced when he was accepted into the graduate program in archeology at the University of Pennsylvania in Philadelphia. He had won a fellowship that paid full tuition and a graduate stipend for four years.

I was less pleased when he declared himself to be in love with a young English girl, who was a student at Trinity College in Dublin. He brought Jan to Paris with him, and I was immediately aware that they were already being intimate. Only someone of my age and background will understand how dismayed I was about this affair. So, too, was Freddy. We found no fault with Jan. We would be happy to have her as a daughter in our family if only they would wait until he had finished his schooling and could support a wife and home. She had another year yet to complete her degree. Jan was nineteen, and Steve was twenty-one.

Steve and Jan occasionally took the car and made a day trip out of Paris. I went with them to visit the cathedral at Rouen. We bought a guidebook and had a good time looking at all the interesting features. Having visited cathedrals under Guy Davenport's tutelage, Steve had learned what was unique and what to look for, and he enjoyed instructing his mother and his girlfriend.

I must confess, though, that there was another event in town that I found more interesting than the cathedral. Rouen was a town famous for its champagne, and samples were being given out at every cave. We did some sampling, and it was next to impossible for me to decide which I liked best. I finally bought two bottles, and to this day, I berate myself because I did not buy a whole case and ship it to the States.

In 1967 I was still afraid to spend money frivolously. (It is a different story now in 1990. Now Freddy and I have exchanged our spending attitudes!) I love champagne, and I have never again had champagne as good as those two bottles. The caves in Rouen were small and produced only enough to supply the families who had been buying from them for generations. To be sure, there were some extra cases for persons like me who came along and bought only once. But who knows? Perhaps I could have established a tradition of buying one case a year from that cave for the rest of my life.

About this time (late May or early June) Freddy went to Munich for two or three days. Although he did not mention it when it happened, while we were in Le Chambon, he had briefly suffered an occlusion in one eye. While in Munich, he suffered an even more frightening experience when the occlusion returned and remained. He saw a German ophthalmologist, who urged surgery. When he returned to Paris, he immediately called his French ophthalmologist, who also advised surgery at once.

This was very upsetting news. Fortunately Freddy called his American doctor in Philadelphia, who said it was best to postpone surgery for as long as possible because surgery increases the chance of cataracts. For someone like Freddy who has acute glaucoma, surgery in 1967 would mean blindness soon after. His Philadelphia doctor felt he should increase the strength of the eye drops and see what the results might be. This he did, and thankfully, the occlusion cleared away.

Alice joins us

Alice joined us in Paris after she had her certificate and while Steve and Jan were still there. She went out a few times with them, but she said, she did not like it much because they were only interested in each other, and she did not enjoy being left out. So, predictably, she and I went shopping. I wanted to buy a suit, and of course, our shopping ended in a suit for me and one for her.

I believe that suit was the only apparel I bought in Paris, but what fun it was to shop for it. How I loved that suit! I would have loved being one of those favored few who go to Paris to buy their wardrobes each year! My suit was wonderful, and I wore it until it no longer fit well. Alice's suit was possibly the loveliest and smartest she will ever have, and she looked beautiful in it.

Soon Steve and Jan went back to Ireland. Jan went on to her parents' home in Mahee in Northern Ireland, and Steve returned to Philadelphia by ship. There he found an apartment and got settled before starting graduate studies at the University of Pennsylvania.

Alice was restless and unhappy, and she wanted to go back to Philadelphia. That was something of a problem, because our house was sublet to some Penn students, and we were moving to Bloomington, Indiana, as soon as we returned.

Alice wrote to her friend Sara and asked if she could visit her until our return. Sara wanted Alice to come, and even though Sara's parents really did not, they said she could visit for a week. Had I received such a reluctant invitation, I would never have gone. But I am quite unlike my daughter, and her desire to go persisted.

When I asked her what she would do after her visit with Sara, her very airy reply was that she would find another place to stay.

She felt very grown up at fifteen and very able to look after herself after spending a year away from her parents in a foreign school.

Though Alice was being tiresome and I was not enjoying her presence very much, I could not send her off on her own. Yet, neither could I change our obligations and arrangements. Freddy was returning by boat with me and the trunks, and our passage had already been booked for the first week in August. As well, Freddy had arranged some interviews to complete the research he was doing with Blanche Blank. His sister-in-law, Liesl, was going to Austria with some of her relatives, and we had arranged to spend a week with her in Switzerland.

Just then, I received a long, newsy letter from Ann Dunn, my dear friend in New Haven. In the spring before we left Haverford, all the Dunns (Ann, Jim, Chris, and Jen) had spent about ten days with us during spring break. We had housed them in the college guest rooms, and they had spent the week exploring Philadelphia. In her letter, Ann recalled how much they had enjoyed their visit and bemoaned the fact that we were moving to Indiana. She wished we could come for a visit before we moved.

I decided to call Ann. Jim answered the phone and almost fainted when he realized I was calling from Paris. Twenty-five years ago, calling from continent to continent was a rarity, not the commonplace event it is today. To my great relief, Ann expressed delight at the prospect of having Alice visit until we returned to the States. So it was arranged, and off Alice went. While she was with the Dunns, Ann painted Alice's portrait and gave it to her. The portrait now hangs over our living room fireplace.

Soon after Alice's departure, we went to Switzerland

Alice
Portrait by Ann Dunn

and spent a lovely week with Liesl. Every day was beautiful and sunny. We took the cogwheel train to the high meadows and walked the trails, a different one every day. Liesl was amused with my delight over the wildflowers and bought me a book to identify them. The weather was unbelievably hot, even as high as we were, so I bought a cotton skirt and blouse to wear for walking. It was so beautiful on the mountains. We all had a wonderful time together. Liesl loved it so much she stayed on alone for a few days at the hotel where she and Oscar had honeymooned years before.

Back in Paris, Freddy and I attended a few more musical events. Most were in restored courtyards of homes of aristocrats who had lived before the French Revolution. I remember seeing a Russian ballet company do a very old-fashioned, formal Cinderella. It was a little boring with its studied movements and lack of spontaneity, as compared to the ballets we had seen in the United States, London, and Copenhagen.

There was also a very early Mozart opera, with the text in the original Italian. I always love Mozart's music, so I found it enjoyable, but I can understand why that particular opera is rarely performed. As an insight into the early days of opera, this performance was an addition to my education.

We journey back home

We intended to take our Volkswagen back to the States on the ship, so we planned to drive it through Normandy to see the battlefield and also the area where Freddy had dropped by parachute on D-day in 1944.

Two days before we left Paris, I developed a back problem. Our trunks had already gone, and only our bags for the ship remained. I was at a new art exhibit when a stab of pain doubled me over. I was alone, and I did not think I could get back to the apartment, but somehow I did, and on the subways to boot.

We did drive through Normandy, but we missed the battle site. I was in almost unbearable pain, and I moaned and groaned all the way. Our ship, the Queen Mary, was already at the dock when we arrived, so we went directly onboard. (That was the last such Atlantic trip for the Queen Mary.)

Fortunately there was a masseuse on the ship, and I was able to have a treatment every day as we crossed the Atlantic. Our cabin was comfortable, and it was the first crossing by ship that Freddy ever made without being seasick, but then, it was also the only one he ever made on a big ocean liner.

When we docked and retrieved our VW, we were dismayed to discover that it had been battered quite a lot during the crossing because it had not been chained properly. As we drove home to Haverford, I found myself viewing driving in the United States a little differently after being in Europe. Previously, I had thought the New Jersey Turnpike a horrible, dangerous place to drive, but now it seemed a pleasant breeze by comparison.

My sister Betty had used our Ford while we were in Europe, and she drove it alone back to us in Haverford. She stayed a few days, and I went with her to see various historic sites. Unfortunately her visit was more abbreviated than I would have liked, because life for us was then extremely hectic. We were moving, and we were very concerned about Freddy's eyes. He had to see his ophthalmologist about the new problems he had experienced in Munich.

It was not until some years later that I could look back on those extremely busy days with any clarity of vision. I then realized that at this particular time in our lives, we were at a crossroads. From then on, we would never be our tightly knit little family group again. Steve preferred to be on his own. He was of age, had an AB, and could direct his own life. Alice was not of age, but neither was she the little girl she had been before she lived apart from us that year in France.

Steve was disappointed by our decision to move to Indiana. He has always been one who dislikes change. We tried to explain our reasons to him, but he could not understand that we could be so gross as to move for financial reasons.

Those of us who lived through the Vietnam War years will understand his feelings. There was that very large group of American youth who rebelled against materialism and accumulation of wealth. They used ruthless methods and stupid, often dangerous modes of behavior to express their contempt for old ways of living. Neither of our children was ever radical, but they were of an age to be influenced by their peers.

Chapter 9

Bloomington

(1967-1993)

The reason for our return to Indiana was simple: financial. In 1967 Indiana was working hard to transform its universities into first-class institutions, so they were attracting faculty by offering better salaries and more attractive perks than most of the other Big Ten universities. Freddy had been late starting his career, and as we were in our middle years, we knew the time was short to accumulate for retirement.

There were other considerations, too. We knew many people in Bloomington. We also knew the School of Music at Indiana University, and all that it offered in musical entertainment. We felt sure that the musical offerings would probably be superior to those in Philadelphia. Neither were we wrong. We have been very happy in Bloomington.

We come home to Indiana

The move to Bloomington was not easy. Once again we had trouble with the movers. In fact they were still loading our furniture into the moving van when we started driving to Indiana. We put Steve in charge of seeing that the job was finished. We had already rented a house in Bloomington. Fred and C. L. Riggs were moving to Hawaii. While in Europe, we had arranged to rent their house with a view to buying it.

As it is with moving, though we planned well, there were many problems. Our furniture arrived almost three weeks late. Fortunately although we had left Bloomington more than twenty years before, we still had many kind friends there. My family all lived nearby, so we might have stayed with any of them. But high school was starting that same week, and Alice had to enroll for classes. So we stayed in a motel a while, and then we camped out in our house. We bought household items from the Riggses before they moved to Hawaii, and we were able to borrow a few things. So with the help of kind friends and family, we managed to survive until our furniture arrived.

It was a busy time. Freddy had seen his ophthalmologist in Philadelphia, who did not agree entirely with the French doctor. His Philadelphia doctor prescribed increased medication and advised Freddy to locate an ophthalmologist in Indianapolis as soon as possible. So that was a top priority.

Then there was the car accident—my first car accident ever. I remember the day very well. A football player and his buddies came out of a side street and rammed into my car. I was stunned. Later that evening, Steve called to say that his love, Jan Eaton, was back in Washington, DC, and that they were getting married. So, in addition to being stunned by the car accident, I was now almost in a stupor from this news.

That same evening, the Political Science Department gave a departmental dinner to welcome us and James and Natalie Christoph, who had also just arrived. The dinner turned out to be a happy event in spite of the day's earlier blows. It was indeed lovely to be back in Indiana.

When Alice reported being happy at Bloomington High School, we knew we had made the right decision. Alice's counselor, Ida Medlyn, had interpreted her transfer grades from France and Pennsylvania and remained her good friend through high school. Even now, Ida and her husband, Bill, are our friends and coparishioners at Trinity Episcopal Church.

Steve and Jan

Jan Eaton, our daughter-in-law-to-be, had arrived in Washington, DC, with her parents in September. Her father, John, was an attaché at the British Embassy. They had been on vacation in Northern Ireland that past summer. Eleanor (Nan) Eaton phoned me soon after the news had been announced and introduced herself. She asked, a little plaintively, "What are we going to do about these children of ours?"

We had a friendly talk together and agreed that if they did marry, we would each make our own child an allowance so that Steve could continue working toward his PhD. After all, his fellowship paid his tuition and a stipend, but it was hardly enough to support a wife, too.

We hoped that Jan would finish her degree before their marriage. But they had decided to marry, and marry they did just a few weeks later, in a small ceremony that took place in a chapel in Washington Cathedral. I am ashamed to say I did not give their wedding ceremony the attention I should have, indeed, that I would have given it under ordinary circumstances.

My life had suddenly become very complicated. There was endless paperwork and worry connected with my car wreck. Also, we had just moved, and every house one moves into is different than the one moved from, so getting settled is never an easy process. It is not accomplished in a day or two.

To make matters worse, so many things were much more difficult without a car. Yet even though I very much needed a car, I had to wait two months more for a replacement because of a strike at the Ford Motor Company in Detroit.

Freddy also had a great deal to do as he settled in at the university and prepared for his classes. Since he was coming from a school where he had twelve students at most in each class, preparing lectures for a class of two hundred was a staggering leap. Getting established in a new place is, of course, very important, and Freddy has always been almost single-minded in his dedication to his work.

As a result, neither of us felt we could possibly go to the wedding. However, we sent Alice, and we invited everyone to come to Bloomington for Thanksgiving.

At Thanksgiving all the Eatons came, except Jan's younger sister, but including Gran, Nan's sweet mother. Freddy and I gave a large party for Steve and Jan to which we invited all our Bloomington friends and all my relatives living close enough to come. Alas, this was not enough. I think we were never quite forgiven for not being at their wedding.

Montclair Avenue

We lived in the Riggses' house only a short time before deciding we did not want to buy it. So, we engaged a realtor, and I spent a large part of our first year in Bloomington looking for a house to buy. I thought I would prefer an older house. When we had moved into our new house in Gainesville, we had bought furniture appropriate to the house. Now we lived in another climate and a different kind of house, and we had acquired other furniture that would look better in an older house.

The house on Montclair Avenue
Bloomington, Indiana, c. 1968

Alice had just one stipulation. We must not move into another school district. She refused to change schools again. I honored her wishes and restricted my search to her school district. I thought she had every right to complain that she had been moved too much.

I did not find a house suitable to our needs, so we decided to build a new one on Montclair Avenue. The house that the builder planned and induced me to accept suited the lot and the neighborhood, Sycamore Knolls, and it covered our needs as they were then. We still live in it. Financially, it was a tremendous bargain, and because everything in and about it that we have repaired or replaced has been of far better quality than the original, it is now quite a good house. We moved into it late in May 1968, and we have been very happy in it.

Alice searches for her Jewish roots

While Alice was in high school, she spent a summer in Israel. She went with a group from New York City to work on a kibbutz for six weeks. Her great friend Sara from Gladwyne had instigated the idea. Though they had planned to go together, it turned out that only Alice went. Alice had been so moved when she read *The Diary of Anne Frank* at the age of ten or eleven that she had been determined to look for her Jewish roots. She loved living on the kibbutz. She became caught up in the purposefulness and zest for living of the young Israelis.

Alice's reaction is very understandable. During the Vietnam years, many young persons became so hostile about American life and the pursuit of the American Dream that they dropped out of the mainstream and pursued what seemed to be a purposeless existence. Only young persons who have lived through those years can understand how appealing the positive attitudes and intense lives of the young Israelis would be. There was much to admire. Alice ultimately decided that she wanted to attend school in Israel.

I understood Alice's feelings, but I felt bereft and very much alone while she was in Israel. Freddy and I were not then the close companions we had been. I was no longer an integral part of his academic life. For years I had typed his notes and papers, and read and criticized his writings. Now as at Haverford, he had the services of a clerical staff in his department, so I no longer had much typing to do.

I did continue to read what he wrote, but as he now wrote quite well, there was little for me to criticize or to recommend. These were Freddy's busiest, most productive years, and he loved it all. I was, of course, pleased for and with him. But I had to find new interests for myself.

Our first grandchild

Our first grandchild, Gordon Niall, was born on our twenty-fifth wedding anniversary. His other grandmother, Nan Eaton, had only two girls and had always wanted a boy very much. Gordon was just the little boy she had always longed for, and she loved him whole-heartedly at once. He was such a sweet, beautiful child.

Since they lived in Washington, DC, for two years after his birth, Gordon spent a lot of time with Jan's parents. But during his first summer, he and Jan spent a month with us while Steve was in Greece on an archaeological dig, doing fieldwork required for his graduate program. Steve finished his course work at Penn in three years in residency at the university, and then Steve, Jan, and Gordon went to live in Greece where Steve did his research and wrote his dissertation.

The Diamant Family
Freddy, Alice, Ann, Steve, Jan, & Gordon
Bloomington, October 1968

Pursuing my interests in art and art history

Our move to Indiana; Freddy's deepening involvement in research, travel, and teaching; Steve's taking his family to Greece; Alice's increasing interest in Israel and her Jewish roots—all these things intensified the full impact of my dismal fifties. Our year in Europe, however, had increased my already great interest in art, and had aroused in me a longing to know more about art and artists.

During our first year in Bloomington, I was, of course, too busy to even think about enrolling in any university courses. However, I did enjoy a very special exhibit of sculpture at the university art museum. The show consisted of works by three of the world's most famous contemporary sculptors, all of whom had a previous connection with Indiana University: David Smith, George Rickey, and Isamu Noguchi.

It was a very special exhibit, and I was so very surprised and happy to see it there. Such an exhibit would never have been mounted in our previous years at Indiana University. Fortunately the show was still in place when Blanche Blank spent a few days with us.

Blanche and Freddy were tying up loose ends on publications based on Freddy's research in Europe. Blanche and her husband, Bud, had started a collection of sculpture, and she was ecstatic about the works on exhibit, especially those of George Rickey. She would have bought something, but when she phoned Bud, he vetoed a purchase.

The exhibit gave me such confidence in the School of Fine Arts that I decided to enroll in an art history course for the fall semester. To enroll in only one course and not in pursuit of a degree, I had to be interviewed in admissions. I had a very good interview and learned what I would need to earn an AB. Unfortunately very few of the courses I had taken previously could be applied to either an arts or science degree. I was far closer to a degree in economics.

I was appalled to discover that earning a degree would take me two full years at least, and that I would be required to take courses in which I no longer had any interest. Meanwhile, I had permission to enroll in the art history courses that I was interested in.

The year that Alice was a senior in high school, I took an extremely interesting course, Art in Western Societies from 1880 to the Present. The class was immense and filled the auditorium of the Fine Arts Building. The course was taught by a young British instructor, who was getting a doctorate from the University of California at Berkeley. She was wonderful, but the scope of the course was so wide and the coverage so thin, that I felt a little dissatisfied at the end. Then, too, we lost some classes because of student strikes and like interruptions. This made me further aware of my age. I was more interested in my studies than strikes!

I made an A- in the course, and I was glad I took it. Not only did I learn a lot, but it helped me to make some decisions. For so many years, the core of my ambitions had been to earn an academic degree, or so I believed. Here now was my opportunity, and I consciously did not take it. I have known many women who earned a degree in later life, and I admire them for it. As for me, I came to realize that earning a degree would require me to change the kind of life I lived with Freddy and to put aside all my other interests.

I am not sure I can articulate all the reasons I marshaled for this conclusion, for not all of them are logical. Essentially I loved my life with Freddy, and I did not want it to change. Freshman algebra and English no longer had much appeal for me. I am sure they would have had more appeal at age eighteen or even thirty, but at age fifty-seven? I was a bit appalled at my conclusions. But those were the conclusions I reached.

Prior to our return to Bloomington, I seldom went with Freddy when he traveled anywhere as a visiting lecturer or to professional meetings (except for his sabbatical year in Europe and the CAG meetings I have already noted). Now with Alice in Israel and Steve in Athens, I had no lasting commitments, so I frequently went with him when he traveled.

Most national meetings were in New York, Chicago, San Francisco, or Washington, DC, and I began to look forward to them with great eagerness. Not only did we meet old friends and colleagues, but former students as well. There were opportunities to have dinner with friends at good restaurants and to visit art museums.

I came to enjoy Chicago far more than I ever thought I would. The Art Institute there has a great museum with an excellent and varied permanent collection. Every year they stage special exhibits that are worth a trip to see.

Travel to most American cities does not offer many unique differences, or at least the differences are not as pronounced as in Europe. In European cities, there are such differences in culture, architecture, and historical background that I find them far more interesting. Nevertheless, here in the United States, I always seem to find a new, interesting learning experience in each city I visit.

It was a professional meeting that took us to Atlanta. Aside from the pleasure of meeting and visiting with friends, I was pleased and excited about a museum exhibit. Of all places to find it, this one was of Abigail Adams—her life from pictures, journals, letters, artifacts, and old newspapers. Sometimes Freddy gets tired of all my "peering" at this kind of exhibit. To this one, I went alone and I "peered" to my heart's content, and I loved it. When I was home again, I read as much as I could find about Abigail Adams.

So many people love New Orleans, and when Freddy had occasion to go to a meeting there, I went along. It was my first trip there and probably will be my only one. It is difficult to explain to others, except Freddy, why I felt such a great disquietness of spirit there—indeed, very nearly an abhorrence of the ambience! There were two very small incidents, but they shook my heart and soul enough to make me never want to go there again.

One day we were walking peacefully down a main street when two cars came along from opposite directions, one filled with white people, the other with black. I could not discern that the black people had done anything wrong, but some small thing must have happened. The white people began to shout angrily and pulled their car about in such a way as to block the car of blacks. I had never, ever heard such hateful, horrible obscenities as the ones the white people hurled at the blacks. It not only curdled my blood, it made me ashamed to belong to the same race as those white people. I will never forget it.

The other incident was less dramatic, but it made me very sad. One day I was out walking alone when I turned into a little courtyard to rest on a bench by a flowerbed. A window opened in an apartment, and a black woman stuck out her head and addressed me, "White woman, what do you want here?"

"Nothing," I said, "I'm just a visitor and have been walking about. I thought I'd rest a few minutes."

"Ain't no place for you to rest here," she said. "We don't like white people here. Go rest someplace else."

I was surprised, but I could understand her feelings. As I left, I glanced around the courtyard and saw several black faces leaning out windows, watching me leave. I found New Orleans to be a sad city, full of hatred. Never mind the great restaurants with the jazz-playing black entertainers.

I visit Greece and Israel (spring 1971)

Through a variety of honors earned or tasks performed outside his usual duties, Freddy had put together a tidy sum beyond our scheduled expenses and savings. He insisted that I use some of this to travel to Greece and Israel to visit Steve and Alice. I made this journey in the early spring of 1971.

At the time, Western Europe was on alert about some unsettling incident. Whether it involved communists, Arabs, or Israelis, I do not recall. I do remember that ongoing passengers were not allowed off the plane at Geneva. It is a very long flight from New York to Athens, and I badly needed to walk about, so I was incensed at being restrained.

In view of the many bombings and killings that have taken place since, I now have a greater understanding of the precautions taken at that time. As Freddy has reminded me, it was only the year after that when a group of Muslim Arabs invaded the Olympic Village in Munich and succeeded in murdering nearly every Israeli team member.

When I arrived in Athens, Steve met me at the airport and took me to their apartment, where Jan and Gordon were waiting. My three weeks in Greece were wonderful. We had given Steve a car, a small VW that he had picked up in Germany the year before. He was forced to use it sparingly because the cost of gasoline in Greece was very high, several times over that in the United States, but he was able to drive me several places.

The ancient ruins of classical Greece are both lovely and sad. It is easy to recognize the skill of the sculptor and the ingenuity of the people who created the statues and the temples such as the Parthenon. In the museums, the artifacts from the preclassical periods were most interesting. I was extremely happy to see it all.

Since Steve needed to go to Delphi, we all went by car, stopping for a short time in Thebes. The countryside was all in bloom with spring wildflowers. I feel almost guilty in confessing that I found the wildflowers the most enchanting, the most pleasing sight I saw in Greece!

Jan, a true Englishwoman, understood my delight. She knew a lot about flowers and said she believed it to be true that more species of flowers grew in Greece than anywhere else in the world.

She and Steve gave me a very good and lovely book on the wild-flowers of the Mediterranean world.

Delphi was a lovely place. The town itself was tiered on a high rocky hillside, and on the same hillside, rested the ruins of the shrine to Apollo. Steve pointed out the harbor below where victorious Greek warriors had come to bring tributes to the god Apollo. Now the way from the harbor to the ruins was covered with an olive grove, giving us a gloriously scented drive down to the small seaside town.

After three weeks in Greece, I went to Israel. Alice met me at Lod, the airport, and we went by taxi to Jerusalem. Alice was so enamored of Israel that she had begged to go back to perfect her language and attend Hebrew University. Before she could enroll in the university, she was required to spend a preparatory year patterned after the freshman year at an American university. That is what she was doing when I visited.

Clearly Alice was finding it a waste of time. From the day she was conceived, or so it seems to me, Alice has never been quiet. She has always exceeded the requirements in every school she has attended. At Bloomington South High School, she had not only been the class valedictorian, but she had completed the three years of requirements in two and a half years and had taken several courses at the university as well. Her courses in high school were not easy ones, either; she had taken more science and math than were required. Although her present classes were all in Hebrew, she still found them too easy, for it was material she already knew.

In Jerusalem, Alice was sharing an apartment with a lovely young American named Miriam, who was the daughter of a wealthy American-Jewish family from Kansas City. Miriam had already graduated from college and was there to learn He-

Alice
Israel, early 1970s

brew. She was a dear, sweet girl, and she and Alice lived together very amicably.

I have adored my daughter all her life, but she and I are not simpatico. She and her father are. Alice turns to her father for understanding as Steve does to me. When our acquaintances meet our children for the first time, they invariably say how much Steve is like his father and Alice is like me. That may be, but I had an unhappy time in Israel and a beautiful time in Greece. We did have quite a good time together in Haifa, my favorite city in Israel. The gardens of Bahá'í and the shrine there were lovely and peaceful, and to me, at least, the people seemed less noisy and pushy. In Jerusalem during the celebration of Easter in the Syrian Orthodox Christian Church, it was an absolute madhouse. I could sense no feelings of reverence, love, or happiness whatsoever.

I do not doubt that I was bringing with me an expectation of the joyous gladness of an Easter service at home, with an added exaltation because of this holy place. I was severely disappointed, and I had a sulky child beside me who had no sympathy or understanding for my feelings.

Alice had classes, so I went alone on a bus tour to Bethlehem and Eilat, including the Dead Sea, where there was a roadside indication of the caves in which the scrolls were found. The roads were not passable just then, so we did not see the caves.

Later Alice and I visited the kibbutz near Galilee where she had spent her first summer in Israel. We looked over it to the Golan Heights, to the squat dwellings of that small group of Muslims, the Druze. Then we went on to a very lovely place—a green spot where clear water bubbled out of springs as it has for centuries.

The Greek leader Alexander had kept a large encampment there by those springs. We also saw the cave said to have been used by Alexander for shelter. It still shows some very old drawings and inscriptions that are said to have been made by those Greeks. To me they were illegible. I thought a great deal of imagination had to be used to think they were man-made and not just the ravages of weather!

Overall, I had a miserable time in Jerusalem. The root of my misery was that Alice and I were at such odds. The weather did not help. It rained every day, very unseasonably I was assured. I became soaked through, and every day I donned damp garments because nothing ever dried overnight! The apartment's only source of heat was a small kerosene heater with a broken leg. The heater was forever scaring me witless because it frequently fell over, spilling kerosene.

I was physically uncomfortable and spiritually ill. We were not hurling epithets at each other; nevertheless, Alice and I were confronting each other, and our wills were in combat. She was angry, sad, and petulant because I was not embracing Israel and the Israelis as she had done. I had, and I have, the greatest respect for Jews and their religion. After all, it is the basis of both the Christian and the Muslim religions. But I viewed Israel as a historically interesting place and that was all.

To this day, I have the greatest admiration for Israel. No one viewing that part of the world from an economic perspective can deny that they have indeed made the desert bloom. The contrast between the industry of the Israelis and that of the Palestinians is unbelievably striking.

Personally, though, I would not want to live in a religious state. I would not want even another Christian's views to impinge on mine. Perhaps they were not compelled to do so, but in Israel, the Arabs rode in the back of the bus just as the black people had done during our early days in Gainesville. I found it repugnant.

I was glad when the day arrived for me to go home, for I needed Freddy's love and care desperately. Of my various physical ills, the dominant one has always been my lung problems: my allergies and asthma. So it was perhaps not surprising that being physically tired and mentally stressed, I arrived home very ill with pneumonia.

The day after my homecoming, Freddy was going to Chicago for a professional meeting, and he had arranged for me to go with him. However, on the plane from Athens to New York, I realized that the tightness in my chest was not from tension alone. I knew I was ill. From New York to Indianapolis, I dozed most of the way. That was very unusual for me.

Freddy was most reluctant to leave me at home. He kept telling me I was just tired; I could sleep in Chicago, too. But I knew I was sick. So then, having a commitment there, Freddy called one of his students. Jan Frohman was an undergraduate whom we had seen a lot, and with whose parents we had exchanged visits.

Freddy asked her to spend the nights with me while he was in Chicago. She was happy to come.

That first night I became very ill indeed, so the next morning, Jan drove me to the doctor. He listened to my chest and sent me immediately to the hospital. For a day or two, I was in an oxygen tent and dosed with antibiotics. Jan was so very kind and resourceful. We kept in touch with her for several years, and then we ceased hearing from her. Wherever she is, she still retains my gratitude.

I was a very long time recovering from that illness. I seem to remember that my therapy and return to health came through spending many hours gardening. I vowed then that I would never travel alone again. If Freddy could not go, then neither would I. I need his balance. The part of the marriage service that warns you that two have now become one was certainly true in my case. While I retain my own personality and much of my independent behavior, still part of me is Freddy, and I am happiest when we are together.

The Diamant Family
Bloomington, 1978

Europe (summer 1972)

In 1972 we were in Europe for two months during the summer. Freddy had meetings to attend in Glasgow and Bonn. Then we went to Paris so he could confer with a colleague. He also attended a seminar in Aosta, Italy, but I did not go with him. Our grandson, Gordon, was at Mahee in Northern Ireland with his Eaton grandparents, so I went there for a few days to spend some time with him.

Freddy joined me there, and Nan drove us around Ireland. There are so many ruins of old cathedrals in Ireland. History has a way of becoming alive when one can view these sites with one's own eyes. What a missionary St. Patrick must have been! He inspired the people on this island to build so many great churches and cathedrals and in such a relatively short period of time before the Danes came, occupied the land, and destroyed them.

Bonn, Germany (1973-74)

For Freddy's second sabbatical leave, his first from Indiana University, we went to Germany again, but this time we were there for the whole year. Freddy had applied in several places for academic research grants and received two: a Guggenheim and a Fulbright. The Guggenheim Foundation advised him to accept the Fulbright, which they then supplemented.

Fulbright pays only expenses for the recipient not the family, so this time with the Guggenheim supplements, my travel and living expenses were paid, and it made a world of difference in our daily lives. During the sixties, the American dollar was the most valued currency in the world. In 1974 in Germany, the exchange rate was still good, but it was lower than in 1967 and has declined in the years since then.

We were fortunate to obtain very good living quarters this time, just by chance as a kind of gratuitous favor. Indiana University has had for many years one of the best German studies programs anywhere in the nation. German academics and directors of German learning programs visit regularly.

That spring when Freddy received his awards, an assistant director of the Humboldt Foundation was visiting, and I rather think we had him with a like-minded group for dinner one evening. Before he left, he offered us an apartment in which to live during our year in Bad Godesberg.

Freddy was delighted but flabbergasted. He could hardly believe it. But it was true. Soon after our visitor went home, we received a note saying only that Freddy had been assigned an apartment in the foundation's apartment building in Bonn. Housing was very scarce in postwar Germany, so the foundation had built an apartment building for their visiting scholars and students. We regarded this rather casually offered gift as manna from heaven.

Our life in Bonn differed quite a bit from our months in Bochum, not only because of our living quarters, but also because of the differences in the cities themselves. Bochum was an industrial city and most of its people were of the working class. Bonn had been a small academic town in the years before the war, and its adjoining suburb of Bad Godesberg had been comprised of the summer river residences of wealthy people from Cologne.

Bonn was the home city of Chancellor Konrad Adenauer, who had made it the seat of government for the Federal Republic. We were surrounded by embassies from around the globe, including the American Embassy, which was within walking distance.

We had some acquaintances already living in Bonn. Wolfgang Dexheimer, who was originally from Berlin, had attended Indiana University. He was writing a dissertation for a PhD from Indiana University, and Freddy was his dissertation supervisor. Wolfgang was working on the staff of a member of the German parliament. He and his wife, Carol, an American, lived across the Rhine River from us. Carol was writing a dissertation for a PhD from Brown University in Rhode Island. We were with Carol and Wolfgang many times that year.

Freddy also was supervising the dissertation of another young man, Hans Michelmann. As a boy, Hans had left East Germany to live with his father in Canada. He and his father had become Canadian citizens, and Hans had graduated from the University of Alberta in Edmonton. Fred Englemann, our good friend from Yale, taught in Edmonton, and several of his students came to Indiana University for graduate studies. Hans was one of them.

Hans and his wife, Martha, were living in Brussels, where he was gathering data for his dissertation concerning the Common Market. Hans' mother and sister lived in Bonn. Since Hans and

Martha often came to Bonn for Hans to consult with Freddy, we came to know his relatives fairly well.

There was also Franz Fürst, Freddy's childhood friend from Vienna, and his wife, Marlis. As when the Hartmanns had lived in Bonn years before, the Fürsts lived in the American apartments, and Franz tutored American Embassy personnel in German. Marlis was a wonderful cook. We had marvelous meals there, and often coffee, cake, and pastries after lovely Sunday afternoon walks.

Some Germans spent their Sundays by piling the family into their car and driving as fast as the car could go in half a day, eating dinner wherever it was, and then speeding home again. Others took long walks or ambles, ended with having coffee and cake in homes or cafés with friends.

Many of our Sunday afternoons were spent this way, too, sometimes with Franz and Marlis, but more often alone. We loved it. There are so many great places for walking on both sides of the Rhine. We must have covered them all.

Tübingen

Once again, Freddy was invited to give lectures or seminars in quite a number of places, most of them in areas we had visited before. One new place was Tübingen. Roman Schnur, who had invited Freddy to Bochum, was now at Tübingen, and he invited us there. I was so pleased he had, for it was unique.

I am not sure how many Americans realize that before federation each German princedom was an individual nation with its own culture, including its own dialect of German. Tübingen lies beside the Neckar River and next to the Black Forest. It is very beautiful and shows much evidence of its special crafts of woodworking and carving. It seems less bustling and has a far more tranquil ambience than the cities of the Rhine and Ruhr.

Frau Schnur took me for a day trip into the countryside and forest in her car. In spite of the fact that I knew little German and she knew little English, we had a wonderful day together. We visited a small German castle atop a steep little mountain (such as must have been used for the movie *Graustark)*. It was something of a tourist site, but it was not crowded when we were there.

We ate a noon meal in a restaurant, and we had a pleasant day. Maybe it was even the *most* pleasant day I ever spent in Germany. I am grateful to the Schnurs for giving it to me. I was never able to return their personal hospitality, but I hope that the many Germans I have driven around and fed may in some measure be regarded as recompense.

We were in Tübingen only a few days. I bought two quite good colored etchings of the castle, the river, and the center with its fountain, all of old Tübingen. When we returned to Bloomington, I hung them in Freddy's study.

Athens

By this time, John and Nan Eaton were living in Brussels, where John had an appointment as a British representative to the European Common Market. When we arrived in Europe, Gordon was with them in Mahee, where they were vacationing in their lovely home. Nan wrote me that she would be taking Gordon back to Athens in time for school and invited me to go with her. So I went back to Greece.

Later that year, we gathered in Athens at Christmas with the Eatons, their younger daughter, Sue, and her fiancé, Peter Dewar. Steve had arranged for each family to live in a borrowed apartment belonging to American friends who had gone back to their families for Christmas.

We slept in our apartments and had breakfast in them. Then for dinner, each couple took turns buying and preparing the food. I seem to remember that John and Freddy, assisted by Jan to put away the leftovers, generally cleaned up the kitchens. This arrangement worked well, and we had fun together.

Oil shortages

During the winter, sometime after Christmas, we lived a novel experience for a few weeks. As often happens, a problem spewed up in the Middle East that resulted in oil-producing countries declaring an embargo on oil exports.

Germany had come to depend substantially on oil for energy. Instead of using their native coal as they had for many years, they had converted almost exclusively to oil, even for house heating. The federal government reacted immediately by restricting the use of oil and curtailing the personal use of automobiles altogether, with only a few necessary exceptions.

You would scarcely believe how extremely quiet the city became. Even during working hours, there was less noise and little traffic. They also observed car-less Sundays, which were really quite delightful because they brought out good humor and comradely feelings. Families filled the walking paths and crowded the cafés and the coffeehouses. We enjoyed that time.

Betty and Harold visit us in Germany

During the spring, my sister Betty and her husband, Harold Hustedt, came to spend two or three weeks with us in Germany. Harold's grandfather had emigrated from Germany to the United States. Harold, who grew up in Indianapolis, had learned German in elementary school. He had always wanted to visit Germany but had never worked up the courage to do so.

We arranged for them to use the apartment of another American couple in our apartment house, and we planned an itinerary we hoped would interest them—an overview of different but interesting German cities, a week in Switzerland, and a few days in Vienna. The German cities we visited were Nürnberg and Rothenburg, two places that retain much more of old Germany than those in the north.

As a child, I remember reading a story called "The Nuremberg Stove" that I found very appealing. It was about a boy and his love for his family's tiled stove, which was so beautiful and kept him cozy and warm. In the museums of Nürnberg, we found many examples of beautiful tiled stoves, as well as other uses of the lovely tile manufactured there.

Nürnberg was also the city of toy makers and clocks, not the cuckoo of the Black Forest but other enchanting types. In fact the clock in the city hall tower, which has little gnome figures that spring out to sound the hour, is the one always depicted in pictures of Nürnberg.

Harold seemed to most enjoy the evening we went for dinner at an old tavern that featured hearty German fare, beer drinking, and music. The entertainers were three or four men with an accordion, who played and sang old German drinking songs, with a number of patrons often joining in. Freddy slipped them some money, and they came to our table and sang to Harold. He was moved to tears as he recalled how his father and uncles had sung the same songs when he was a boy.

Harold had a wonderful collection of old records, especially recordings of old jazz and blues singers, and he belonged to an exchange club with collectors from around the world. For several years, he had been in correspondence with a collector in London and wanted to visit him. So Freddy arranged for Harold and Betty to fly to London to spend most of a week there, and then go back to the States from Heathrow.

Harold and Betty were somewhat aghast that Freddy and I were not going with them, but Freddy was quite firm that he could not spare any more time; he had work to do. They went to London alone, and we learned later, they had a wonderful time there.

Since that year in Europe, Freddy has returned several times. I have often planned to go as well, but something has always intervened to keep me at home. During the late seventies and early eighties, Freddy and I were both plagued with health problems and operations. He has made better recoveries than I seem to have done.

Still when I read of some intriguing place to visit, I long to go. But then I think of all the medications I must lug along now, and how very easy it is for me to catch a cold, and how very ill I am when I do—and I decide to stay home. Bloomington is a very good place to be.

Activities at church

During our years in Gainesville, New Haven, and Haverford, I spent many hours in Christian education, both learning and teaching. However, my experience in our church in Bloomington has been very different. Our first Sunday at Trinity Episcopal Church was the last Sunday for Reverend Eddy, who had accepted a call to a church in Lansing, Michigan.

In Indiana there are fewer Episcopalian congregations than any other place we have lived. The church building in Bloomington is small. It was built under the aegis of Reverend Cole, who so loved the rural Anglican churches in England that he patterned his church after them. As I understand it, Reverend Cole ran the church very like an exclusive club of which he was the head. He cold-shouldered out all the people he did not care to have in his club. After his death, his first successor was Reverend Eddy, who had a rough if not contentious time of it.

Alice was a senior in high school when Reverend Charles Perry came to be our rector. I expect that Charles was the best person for the church at that point in time, but he made enemies of many in the congregation. He made a clean sweep of all the old club ways and instituted Low Church practices for all the services. Alice liked him a lot. She talked with him, and he encouraged her to go to Israel.

I was quite willing to go along with Charles and render any service I could to the church. I mentioned to him the training I had with Randy Miller and the work I did for the Church of the Redeemer in Bryn Mawr. But he seemed highly uninterested and made no suggestion of any service I could offer.

However, Charles persuaded Freddy to run for the vestry. The same evening that Freddy was inducted into the vestry, Charles announced his resignation as our rector. He went from Bloomington to the staff of the Washington Cathedral, where he remained until he retired.

Through the years, we have come to love our church in Bloomington very much, and we have made many good friends there. I served for a short period with the altar guild, but Freddy fussed about the time I spent before and after the services (one has to come half an hour or so before the service to prepare for the communion and remain after to wash up). So when I had to take leave for our year in Europe, I did not volunteer again when I returned. I have served as a visitor to our members who are confined at home or in nursing homes, and I have taken meals to families while there was illness.

I must sadly confess that I have never found a niche where I felt I could play a meaningful role. I do bake cookies now and then, but most of my cookie-baking has been for our neighbor children and for Freddy's students!

I put on my gardening hat

Our newly built home gave me an opportunity to undertake a new enterprise. During our years in Haverford, I had no place to garden or work outdoors. So when we moved into our new house in Bloomington, I had not dug in the earth for a long time. As it turned out, the lot on which our house was built offered greater scope for my hands, back, purse, and ingenuity than I could ever have dreamed!

When we first saw it, our lot was bare except for wild grasses and weeds, and it was somewhat irregularly shaped. It is almost fan-shaped, for it is nearly twenty-five feet wider at the back than the front. Unfortunately the builder, who did the siting, did not properly place the house. It is a few feet too close to the neighboring house on the north side to accord with city ordinance regulations. At least that is what I was angrily told by the builder on that lot.

I had our builder remeasure, and he agreed that he had made a mistake. So I had him drive down discernible markers on all four corners, and I have since tried not to overrun my borders and create nuisances for my neighbors. Fortunately, through the years we have been blessed with kind, friendly neighbors on either side, good friends all of them. The house on the north has changed owners three times during our residency and the one on the south only once.

This part of the country is quite beautiful. There are lots of trees and it is very hilly. But the hills are not the kind created by volcanic action. They are piles of debris left over from the ice age. Ten thousand years ago, Bloomington was just fifteen or twenty miles beyond the lower edge of the last ice sheet to come from the north. Debris pushed southward by this ice sheet covers all southern Indiana, from Monroe County, where we live, to the Ohio River.

Our county in Indiana and the county just to the south of us have quarried more limestone than any other area in the United States. Much has been written about the industry and the famous buildings in the state and the nation that are built of our local stone.

As a result of the glacial activity, there are a great number of limestone boulders strewn all over the county. They range in size from a few pounds to hundreds of pounds, and they can be a costly nuisance for farmers and builders alike! Part of our house sits on just such a boulder.

When Freddy cuts our lawn, he complains that there is no level area. It is uphill or downhill all the way. As part of our contract, the builder was supposed to level the yard, clean up, and do some planting. The house was begun in December and by April it was nearly finished, but then the plumbers went on strike, which held things up a few weeks. When the builder asked us to settle at the end of April, I pointed out that he had still not leveled the yard, removed the debris, and done the planting as contracted.

I went to check their progress after the plumbing was finished and when the walls were being painted. They had done a very slipshod job of cleaning up. They had been equally careless in leveling off the land and had done only the front of the house and about half the backyard.

Let me explain a little about this strip of land. It is on the side of a small hill. The north end of the house, possibly eight feet of it, actually rests on a large limestone boulder, which slopes downhill to what was once a small stream. On the far side of the usually dry stream, there is a fairly steep rise to a fence across the back. This barbed wire fence divides us from farmland that is still not incorporated into the city.

When we moved in, cows were grazing in that field, and then there were horses. For a long time now, it has been untended, and it is full of diseased trees, scrubby growth, and tall weeds that harbor small wild animals. So rabbits, opossums, raccoons, groundhogs, and deer come across the fence to nibble at my flowers.

I could write an entire book about my landscaping and gardening trials and tribulations. If I had put in the bank all the money I have spent on landscapers, workmen, and materials, I would not need to worry about money for nursing homes, should Freddy or I ever need one. I would have a small fortune!

Our lot was a difficult piece of land in the first place, and the builder did not fulfill his contract properly in the second place. So we began wrong, and from there I made tons of mistakes. But no matter, I loved working on the landscape and the garden. Although very little of our landscape looks as I first planned, we now have a fairly distinctive property that is quite lovely.

Soon after we moved in, when we had nothing at all growing around us, we stopped at a nursery in Brown County to buy a corkscrew willow tree. I thought it would grow nicely beside the mostly dry stream in our backyard. The nursery had just changed hands, and the new owner hoped to build a landscaping business. The former owner had grown Christmas trees, and over in one corner were a number of gallon tins with tiny fir trees in them. The nurseryman told us, "If you're interested in trees, you can have that lot for $10."

We took them all. When we unloaded them, there were twenty-three. I assumed that at least half would die, but they did not. The willow tree never grew well, and when we finally cut it down, it was full of tree borers, which were probably there when we bought it. But only one of the fir trees has died. In fact, we recently cut some down, for we now have too many!

Over the years, a lot of volunteer trees have grown up. We could have a grove of walnut and sassafras. Each spring they try to spread from the jungle beyond the fence and I ruthlessly dig them out. Black locusts, too, keep popping up. They are rather pretty, but I have enough trees without them.

Two other volunteers I have encouraged—a sycamore and a maple have now grown tall. Every year I have a fight with the electric company, who claim they endanger the power lines. So far I have won the fight. If they take those trees away, the ugly jungle sprawl on the other side of the fence will be exposed.

In the years when we were away, the tenants who lived in our house cut the lawn around the house but did nothing else. The upslope at the back received no attention whatsoever, so the weeds grew high and bore seeds. After each year we were away, it was as if we were starting over again, except for the trees.

I move a mountain to build our rocky creek bed

Possibly my best idea in the beginning years was to create a full rock-lined creek between the down- and upslopes in the backyard. The large boulder underlying our house surfaces at the bottom of the downslope. One day as I was digging around there, I discovered lots of rocks that were covered with about only a foot of earth. I went along uncovering rocks about two-thirds of the way across our yard.

We had hired a landscaper to redo our front lawn, and I showed him what I had done in the back. He was enthusiastic about my rocky creek idea and gave me an estimate of what he would charge to do the work. I nearly fainted at the sight of his figure—it was so high! I told him I could not possibly afford it.

However, I did pay him for a few stones, and two young fellows he had working for him came back one evening and showed me how to lay them. We put these stones at the south side of the lot where there was soil and no stones.

Over the next year, I accumulated flat limestone rocks from all over. Freddy told everyone I had rocks in my head. He had reason to say it, for whenever I saw flat stones lying beside the road, I stopped the car to put them in the trunk to add to my rocky creek bed.

I also got some rocks from the area just to the south of us. It was undeveloped for about three years, so I was able to cross the field to the stream known as Rock Creek and dig flat rocks out of its bed. They were too heavy for me to lug across the field, so my sister Betty drove her husband's truck down from Indianapolis, and she and her son Rick helped me get them to our yard. Then, too, there was the builder working on a nearby house who saw what I was doing and kindly brought me a small truckload of his scraps.

Gradually, through various ways and means, I accumulated what I needed. I had a bit of help from a student we housed for a time, but other than that, I built our rocky creek bed by myself. It took an incredible number of stones and a great deal of labor.

I still like our rocky creek bed. It gives our garden a kind of distinction that I have not seen elsewhere. I must relate one little incident that warmed my heart and gave an indication that I have had some success in my landscaping efforts.

Our first neighbors in the house on our north side were Higdon and Ruth Roberts. One day Ruth and I attended a lecture given to the gardening group of the University Women's Club. The woman giving the lecture was a landscape architect who had her own business in Bloomington.

The landscaper had been showing slides of her designs, shrubs, flower beds, and so forth, when she paused and said almost as an aside, "I was visiting in a house the other day, and I happened to look out a back window. The house next door was an ordinary little tract house, but the owners had created something unique and interesting." The woman proceeded to describe my rocky creek bed.

Ruth said, "That's *your* house." We could scarcely contain our laughter. It was the "ordinary little tract house" that we found so funny. Our husbands found it equally amusing, and we all had many laughs over our little tract houses.

Of course, the landscaper was accurate in that description. Through the years I have had to endure jibes, particularly from those on the East Coast, about the tract houses of the Midwest. There was a story some years ago in the *New York Times Magazine* called "Levittown, Twenty-five Years Later." Levittown, New York, had been built soon after World War II to provide housing for some of the many young veterans coming home and starting families.

This development so near New York City had received a lot of national attention and was generally derided for its monotonous ugliness. A few years later, after the owners had remodeled and landscaped in their own way, they made of it quite a beautiful neighborhood—just as we had done here in Bloomington. Of course, in its beginnings, our Sycamore Knolls was more diversified and less monotonous than was Levittown. I find it still a lovely and pleasant neighborhood.

My perennial garden

Before long I discovered the joys and advantages of perennial gardening. When I began to realize that my joints were stiffening, and that I could no longer crawl about on my knees for very long, I started planting only perennials in every open spot on the upslope. I hoped that in time, they would outgrow the weeds and create some beauty without too much work. Only the gardener whose plot it is will pull the weeds! With the single exception of one young woman (no males), I have never been able to hire anyone who would do weeding.

My perennial garden has gradually become well established. During spring and summer, that slope is now quite lovely. The first to bloom are the daffodils, and before they are finished, the bluebells appear. Then there are lots of wild columbine, not blue but coral and yellow. After them come the day lilies. I began with just two colors, yellow and orange, both double petaled, which were grown from starts that Aunt Bee gave me years ago. Since then I have added many other colors and also lots of hostas, which grow well in the shade.

By late July the black-eyed Susans are in bloom, and they last through September. I have been scattering their seed all about, hoping that eventually they will cover every vacant spot! The fall asters are the last flowers to bloom. I have had asters just a few years. They are only now beginning to spread.

Wild violets grow profusely in our yard. When our lot was in its natural undisturbed state, a large patch of white violets grew there. Through the years, I have planted a few violas and parma violets. Now covering the ten feet of leeway that the electric company claims but does not tend, violets of many hues cover the ground: deep purple, lavender, blue, white, and white with blue eyes. The pollen from the nursery plants must have blended with that of the wild plants to create this lovely blanket of violets that delights me every spring.

Freddy grew up in an apartment house in a city, so at first he had little interest in gardening. He did not understand the joy that caring for growing things can bring. Through the years, his interest and appreciation have grown, right along with our garden. Being an extremely neat and tidy person, he began doing yard work as a necessary chore to keep our home neat and tidy. Now he tells me he actually enjoys it. So even where our joys and interests were not the same, we are now joined together. I hope we can keep it so for many more years!

Freddy's students

Freddy's students have always been an important part of our life. Over the years, we have become friends with and participated in the lives of many graduate students. In fact Freddy has probably directed more theses and dissertations than anyone else I have ever known!

When Freddy was the director of graduate studies in his department at Indiana University, I tried to have all the students and their spouses to our home for dinner. One year we had so many graduate students that I could not comfortably seat them all at one time. I had to entertain them on three different evenings. Since then we have been more selective.

In Florida we began entertaining students with beverages and cookies at Christmas time. At Haverford, we were encouraged to have students in our home. Add to that Freddy's many years as a participant in Danforth Foundation programs, which promoted a close student-teacher relationship, and you will understand how we became so involved with students.

By the time Freddy joined the faculty at Indiana University, we had come to feel that this particular activity was justly a facet of his responsibility. I enjoyed the students very much, even more so after our own children had departed our home. I loved feeling that I could be a participant in academic life.

In our early years at Indiana University, we tried entertaining Freddy's undergraduate honor students on Sunday evenings. The dormitories did not serve meals on Sunday evenings, so I thought that would be a good time to invite them. However, it was a dismal failure. I was a whole generation and more removed from these students. They did not want anything of Mom and home cooking at this time in their lives. Many of them were probably escaping Mom, her restrictions, and her cooking. They preferred McDonald's and their peers.

Perhaps I am a slow learner. I should have realized our own children were not wanting to rid themselves of us so much as they were simply behaving as part of the crowd. I rather think I expected our children to be like us, whom I think of as nonconformists. Perhaps I was wrong on all counts.

The attitudes of the graduate students were totally different. After all, they were adults. They looked upon Freddy as a friendly mentor. My position was slightly different. Often I was a friend, someone who listened to their problems, sympathized with their heartaches, and provided boxes of tissues for their tears.

Some have become lifelong friends. With some, our contacts are rare but always friendly. As I said, we came home to Indiana primarily to improve our financial future, which the move did indeed accomplish. However, our greater gain came from the students and our personal friendships with them.

On art and art history

Indiana University has given me much intellectually. My travels in Europe had awakened my passionate interest in art and art history, and at Indiana University, I have been able to continue deepening my knowledge in that area. After taking an art history course for credit, I audited two others. Of the two, the one in Renaissance art interested me less, perhaps because with my many medical problems, I missed too many lectures.

I found the course in early Christian art far more interesting, especially the reading list. When Steve first became interested in archeology, I expanded my reading to include a great many books on that subject, so I had a stronger background for the study of early Christian art.

Over the years, Indiana University has had many good public lectures and exhibits. The university's art museum has an unusually large collection of African art, which parallels its strong African studies program. Gus Liebenow, our friend and Freddy's colleague, created and headed the program for many years and was possibly the top Africanist in the United States. He had studied with Gwendolyn Carter at Northwestern University. After Gwendolyn retired there, she came to Bloomington, where she continued teaching for several more years.

Just recently, the African art collection received a great boost when Rita and John Grunwald donated much of their large collection. Henry Hope, the director of fine arts for many years, also gave the museum much of his collection, which contained many paintings from French artists of the late nineteenth and early twentieth centuries.

The present museum building was erected since our return to Bloomington. It was designed by I. M. Pei and is a smaller replica of the East Wing of the National Museum in Washington. Personally, I think Mr. Pei deserves no praise for this particular design. He insisted on the exterior being concrete. I find that an ugly contrast to the two buildings it is set between, which have exteriors made of our own beautiful Indiana limestone. The building design also looks quite wrong next to the building to which it is attached.

It is, I am sure, arrogant of such a little pebble as me to criticize present-day critics and art historians, but I have come to despise the language that many of them use to describe art. To me, the jargon sounds artificial and pompous. Furthermore, young artists who wish to express an appreciation of beauty, color, and joy must feel totally depressed when they realize that their work will only be regarded as meaningless unless they record the ugliest, the grossest, and the most hopeless phenomena of the human experience.

Let me add quickly, though, do not blame the School of Fine Arts at Indiana University for my bitter words. Quite simply, my words come instinctively out of me—someone who loves beauty and color and finds joy in their expression!

My work with the League of Women Voters

Over the years, I have found a great deal of pleasure in all the work I have done, but the most enduring satisfaction has come from my work with the League of Women Voters. It was from my work with the league that I derived the most intellectual satisfaction. Perhaps this has something to do with Freddy and his interests, since I was always able to talk over whatever study I was pursuing with him. He never failed to be interested.

I invariably liked my sister members in the league. Generally speaking, these women were alert, intelligent, and likeable. They were sincerely interested in having good government that worked well for themselves and their families, friends, and communities.

The League of Women Voters has one goal: informed voters voting. To achieve this goal, members work to become informed about issues, and then they act to inform voters and encourage voter turnout. Becoming informed is the work of the study committees, the aspect that I have most enjoyed.

In all the places I have lived, including Bloomington, I have served on study committees for national and international issues. I have a genuine interest in both areas. The issue being studied is under the guidance and direction of the national league board, which always has excellent people serving on it.

When I first started working in the LWV, the Equal Rights Amendment was not yet an issue, so many able, well-educated women were barred from positions of power in government and business simply because of their gender. It was women of this caliber who served on the LWV national board. For our studies, they always provided us with very good materials and extended reading lists.

The Bloomington league had several women of that caliber, who had considerable knowledge and experience in national and international areas. Working with them was a pleasure, and I learned a great deal over the years.

My first two or three years in Bloomington were intensely busy with house and family care, so I did not then become greatly involved in league work. However, in 1971 a younger league member asked me to work with her on a committee on a state project having to do with state taxes and financial disbursements to the counties. I am not quite sure why I agreed to work with her, but I did. From this beginning came the most important study work I have done and my greatest contribution to the league.

To my great surprise, during this study I discovered some talents in myself that I had not known were there. Untangling the various tax laws, and then the time and reason for their enactment was a bit like finding one's way through a maze. But I found it a fascinating, engrossing study.

It was about this time, the early seventies, that groups of citizens in various states were beginning to question whether or not their children were receiving equal access to quality education from one school district to another. In a few places, citizens who felt they were being treated unfairly were even going to court to ask for redress of their grievances.

In Texas such a case was taken to a federal district court, which refused to hear the case on the grounds that the federal constitution had nothing to say about education. Control over schools and education had been left to the states.

As a matter of history, it probably never occurred to the writers of the constitution of either the federal republic or any of the thirteen colonies that they needed to be concerned with education. Their own experience and learning had come from church-related schools. Their objective was to avoid the institution of a national religion, but at the same time, they omitted laying down guidelines for the states in regard to education.

As new states were formed, particularly in the Northwest Territory, the state constitution writers must have been men with other attitudes, for they made provisions for setting up and funding public schools. I must hasten to say that though the provisions were there for public schools, local governments often ignored them. Nevertheless, public schools appeared willy-nilly through-out Indiana. Likely it happened in much the same way in other places as well. As states formed west of the Mississippi, public schools were always provided for. Funding for them usually came from property taxes, as public lands became private property.

During the seventies, people began to complain that not only were landowners being taxed unequally, but school children were not receiving equality in education. When federal courts found that state governments, not the federal government, were re-sponsible for education, educators asked Congress to provide funds for states to study their own educational systems. They wanted to find out whether their programs for financing schools were equitable and whether they produced equal access to qual-ity education for each student within the state.

A professor in the School of Education at Indiana University drew up a plan for such a study to be done by a group of profes-sional educators. He received a grant, and those preparing the study were paid grant money for their work. He asked that all organizations working in the public interest for public schools send a representative to monitor, advise, and participate in this study.

The president of the LWV of Indiana asked me to represent the state league in this study. I was happy to be asked. I loved doing it, and I was pleased with the results of my work when it was finished. I was not paid for my services or my time, but I did receive some money for mileage and for meal expenses while away from home.

Over a period of eighteen months, the whole group of partici-pants met four times. The first meeting allowed the supporting groups to meet the persons who would be preparing the research papers. Professor Buehler, the director, presented his outline for the scope of the study and gave us dates for future meetings. He asked the monitors to participate by questioning, whenever it seemed appropriate to them, any pertinent omissions, or even the directions the researchers were taking.

All the meetings were lively with discussion. As a layperson, I gained a great deal of understanding about the concerns and problems of the superintendents, the principals, the tax board chairperson, and others who worked within that now vast governmental enterprise called Education. It was also useful to see in how many ways the state system differed from the modest structure envisioned in the first state constitution.

As I was doing my background reading, one thing in particular struck me. In the earliest provisions, those pioneer Hoosiers had been very clear that there should be institutions of higher learning funded by the state. Evidently they had reason to feel concerns about higher education being left to church denominations. I found this historical tidbit both ironic and thought-provoking.

At the final meeting, the researchers gave an oral brief of their work, and then there was some discussion. Copies of the research papers were offered to the monitors. My next task was to prepare a report on the results of this very big study for the state league and the local leagues, so I took a copy of each paper and read them all.

If I had not been so compellingly interested in participating in this project and pursuing it to the end, I might have given it up early on, for I had two medical operations during those years. I had a hiatal hernia that became so serious that I could neither eat nor sleep comfortably. While performing the medical tests for the hernia, my surgeon became concerned about a stone stuck in the gall bladder duct. He said it should come out immediately.

I declined to worry about the gallstone. It had not troubled me. I said, "Repair the part that's troubling." The poor doctor was Iranian-born, and he found his language skills inadequate as he tried to explain the problem to this ignorant, exasperating woman. He did as I desired and performed the operation. That operation was a most painful and devastating experience. I was a very long time recovering from it.

In fact it took me more than two years to get my courage up for the next one. I suspect I would have kept postponing it, but my internist discovered inflammation and swelling when she pushed around on my abdomen during my routine physical. She practically shoved me into the hospital and said, "Shut up and get on with it."

Fortunately my gallstone operation really was minor, and I recovered quite rapidly. Still it was my second operation during this period of the school financing and taxes study. However, my quiet times during recovery gave me leisure to read all the research papers, and to sort out the facts that were pertinent to league issues.

I was serving on the state board of the LWV while I wrote the report that was sent to the local leagues for their use. I was asked to speak on the subject a few times, and my report was used for two discussion periods at state general meetings. I also spoke to the education committee of the state legislature, which almost totally ignored the study.

Even the legislator from my own district was very derisive during a general meeting at which I related the findings of the report. Only one official zeroed in on the report, the school superintendent from my own school district. He was the one person who really gave it an intelligent reading and asked pertinent questions.

Perhaps I should explain some of the findings, so that politically speaking, you can understand why the legislators found it expedient to ignore the whole thing. It is very simple. In areas where property is valuable, a relatively low rate of taxation produces far more revenue than a much higher rate produces where property is of little value. For example, in a school area where there are oil refineries and steel mills, a rate which taxes $2 out of every $100 can produce thousands in revenue, whereas $6 out of every $100 produces only hundreds where there is only minor manufacturing and rocky clay soil for farming. Of course, the rich resist sharing with the poor!

Other practices had also been brought forward for attention. No one was about to suggest that rural Indiana return to its one-room schools again. However, the fact was that consolidation in the countryside and desegregation efforts in the cities had more than *tripled* the cost for transporting school children. Of course, no politician was about to ask for legislation to reverse the changes, but neither were they interested in adjusting the taxes to finance those changes.

It was very plain that while there were more buses and the bus drivers were being paid more, the teachers were losing salary, compared to cost-of-living increases, and their burdens had become even greater—the teacher-pupil ratio had risen several times over.

It was a discouraging report. Too many people did not wish to hear it. Nor did they feel that it was incumbent upon them to change the present inadequate funding for education. A partial explanation for this lack of response is that Indiana has declined dramatically in school population when compared with other states. In Indiana the number of children in school may be two percent greater than it was ten years ago, whereas in Ohio, for instance, the rate of increase would have been five or even eight percent. It is difficult to persuade an aging population that taxes should increase for the sake of children.

So although I found personal satisfaction in the work that I did on this study, I did not feel the same satisfaction about the effect that the study had.

It is now twenty years later, and the legislators have put a cap on property taxes, although they have also allowed that cap to be raised. Laws require the state to supply the money lost by property tax restrictions. However, they have never been able to entirely replace those lost funds to local school corporations. They continue to pass laws placing additional requirements upon the schools, but they continue to refuse to increase taxes for financing those requirements.

In recent years, to my great sorrow my various physical infirmities have prevented my engaging in LWV studies and enterprises. I miss that stimulation. However, I have continued my interest as an observer. From this perspective, I have watched various changes occur in the league. One of particular interest I will share here. The LWV was never properly financed, perhaps because it was a woman's enterprise. A few years ago, men were admitted as members, but that has made little difference in LWV finances.

For national and even state projects, the league has used outside financing to hire professional researchers to prepare materials for the discussions on issues. I am a little sad that this must be so, but these days many more women are in the workforce, and they have less time for volunteer work. Having been a feminist all my life, I must not complain that women are being given more earning opportunities than ever before, but I am sad that fewer very able women have less time to give to the League of Women Voters.

Family times and family ties

I have mentioned that finances were an important factor that contributed to our decision to return to Indiana. Another contributing factor was family. Returning to Indiana brought me in closer contact with my brothers and sisters and their families. While we lived in other states, we returned to visit with some frequency. Still, I felt that I did not know my nieces and nephews at all well.

Steve and Alice had spent a lot of time with Mae and Glenn on their farm, and had come to love and care for them in an enduring relationship. They knew the remainder of their relatives less well. Although it was a little late in their lives for them to become close to my relatives, perhaps they have achieved a better acquaintance with my origins than they might otherwise have done if we had not come home to Indiana.

Over the years, the tenor of my and Freddy's life has taken us rather far from the experiences of my family. Still, I felt as loving and loyal as I had always been. So I was glad indeed to be near them in Bloomington for an occasional meal and day together!

My brother Paul was divorced while we were still in Gainesville. He had married Eleanor Metcalf a short time before Freddy and I were married, and they had a son, John, nearly a year older than Steve. Eleanor and I had worked together at Fort Harrison. In fact I had introduced them. Their marriage was not a success almost from the start, and their divorce was a fairly bitter one, fueled by Eleanor's mother.

John was less than ten when his mother was tragically killed in a car accident. The insurance to John from the accident was quite good, and his grandmother, who was his guardian, sent him away, first to boarding school and then to college. John never returned to Indiana, and we heard nothing more about him. Paul married and divorced again. Then he married Lucille Curtis, and they had a beautiful girl, Toni, whom we still know and love.

The rest of us have remained happily married. George and Thelma had three daughters, Mary Ellen, Joyce Elaine, and Anita Kay, who all remain very dear to us. Sadly, Thelma died from colon cancer while their youngest was still in high school. George remarried and gave us a dear, sweet sister-in-law. Mildred and George had about ten years together before he died of a stroke. Dear George was a very loving, religious, happy, gregarious fellow all his life. He was the first of us to go. Less than two years later, Paul died.

My greatly loved brother Joe, who had kept the family together for so many years, left us in 1989. I suppose we should rejoice that he remained among us as long as he did, for he had been diagnosed with emphysema before our return to Bloomington. It was agony for him to give up cigarettes, but he did it, and he lived far longer than many do with that disease. Joe's wife, Helen, had also been my friend before their marriage. She is an exceedingly bright person with many talents. They had two daughters, Rebecca and Roberta, two beloved nieces of mine.

The brothers fared less well physically than the sisters in my family. My youngest brother, Roy, still lives, but he is afflicted with Alzheimer's disease. We love his sweet wife, Paulene, and their two sons, Tom and Roger.

The four sisters keep in close touch by phone at least, but I cannot claim that we are hale and hearty. As I related above, my eldest sister, Mae, and her husband, Glenn Klipsch, had one daughter, Julie, whom we love dearly. Sadly, Mae lost most of her sight. She is legally blind, and she has been very crippled by arthritis.

My sister Betty and her husband, Harold Hustedt, had two dear boys, Chuck and Rick. Betty lost her husband several years ago, and she has had two huge tumors removed from her body, neither cancerous, but both life-threatening. The first tumor, very large, was removed from her chest, and the second, from her brain. They were successful operations, but the second left her with problems, mostly in speaking and communicating. She continues to be her sweet, loving self.

My youngest sister, Martha, and her husband, Albert Horn, had more children than the rest of us. They had five, Marilyn, Nick, Marty, Tim, and Linda, most of whom have children of their own! Now Martha is kept very busy with her grandchildren. She also is unusually kind in many ways with our blind sister, Mae. Family is extremely important to Martha.

Family is also very important to Freddy. Unfortunately his mother, aunts, uncles, cousins, half-sister, brother-in-law, and nephew were all lost or scattered in the Nazi-created Holocaust. We have kept in touch with those who survived and visited whenever we could.

Ann with six of her siblings
George, Joe, Roy, Ann, Martha, Mae, & Betty
Columbus, Indiana, 1984

As I have already mentioned, they were always extremely friendly to me, and I have always had a special love and admiration for Liesl, the wife of Freddy's half-brother. Even though they settled in Sydney, Australia, Liesl has visited us in this country quite often. For almost five years now, she has been in a nursing home in Sydney, and we have only infrequent news of her.

Friends and neighbors

As Freddy has lost family, he has gained friends. We have acquired so many wonderful friends down through the years. In fact, our greatest expense at Christmas time is always buying stamps and cards for that once-a-year time of catching up and exchanging news with our friends!

In addition to the many couples who are our friends, I have personal friends, many of whom have been my neighbors or my associates in the League of Women Voters. But if I should try to list them, I know I would often repeat myself, and I might possibly leave out some who are extremely dear to me.

In the summer of 1991, five friends from my elementary school in Petersville met at a motor inn just outside Columbus, Indiana. We had lunch and a gabfest.

I wish we could have had a week together, for this one afternoon was not enough! It was such a heartwarming, wonderful afternoon. We quickly found that our lives and husbands were quite different, but we still had so much in common. I wish we could do it again.

This meeting has, perhaps, something to say to the fifty years of my life with Freddy. That life has been exciting and stimulating, and we have had many, many wonderful experiences together. We still do.

I cannot say that we have grown together, for in a sense, we have always been a part of each other. Yet at the same time, in spite of our life together, I remain very much *me*. My roots, my beginnings, remain. They are all a part of the wonderful life that has been mine.

Ann Redmon Diamant
Bloomington, Indiana, c. 1995

Part IV

Our Life Together:
Freddy's Story

Chapter 10

Bloomington & New Haven

(1945-1950)

Although my wartime exploits probably rate as something out of the ordinary, my academic career has been much more conventional. However, my career clearly forced decisions on us about where we would live and how well we would live given the confines of my academic salary. Where we lived influenced our lives and those of our children through the neighbors we would have and the community culture we would be exposed to.

As a result, the manner in which my career developed, or failed to develop, affected Ann and the children in significant ways throughout the years. Of course, to the extent that Ann enthusiastically supported my pursuit of that career, the bonds between us were strengthened.

Although I have not wanted my academic career to overshadow everything else, I have to admit that first as a student, and then as a faculty member, my studies, teaching, research, and academic service all occupied an important place in my life. This was possibly to the neglect of my family, but also to the neglect of other intellectual pursuits, with the exception of music and politics.

Bloomington and Indiana University

When I began my studies at Indiana University in June 1945, the university was at best a third-rate institution, though it subsequently blossomed in the expansionist fifties and sixties under the spectacular leadership of Herman Wells. Nevertheless, when I went to Yale in 1948 for my doctorate in political science (having decided I did not want to teach history after all), I found that in comparison with many of my fellow graduate students who had come from more prestigious institutions, I had received a very solid and sophisticated education at Indiana University.

In 1945 at Indiana University, classes were still small. The flood of veterans did not come until 1946 or 1947. I received mostly favorable attention from my teachers in history and political science. I was devoted to my course work and never missed a class. I took copious notes, which I then transcribed on a typewriter.

John Stoner, who taught the American state and local government introductory course during the 1945 summer session, would tell anyone who would listen that I took down everything, including his "good morning." He also recounted more than once the time when I contradicted him on a point he had made by referring to my class notes on his previous reference to the same subject. Later I worked as a grader and research assistant for John Stoner. We did some work on voting in Indiana that won us an acknowledgment in Charles Hyneman's magisterial *Voting in Indiana*.

Since I had always wanted to study history, I elected history as my undergraduate major. In that first summer session, I took the standard survey course from Lee Benns. He showed great interest in me and my work, and he would have sponsored me as a graduate student if I had chosen to continue in history after my undergraduate degree.

I took additional courses from Benns and found him a very demanding teacher. As the author of a widely used standard text on modern Europe, he insisted on verbatim reproduction of material from that text on examinations. Whatever intellectual objections one might have to such pedagogy, as far as I was concerned, Benns was a kind and caring teacher. We remained in touch for many years. When he retired from the university and went to live near his daughter in Rensselaer, we visited him during the summer whenever we returned to Indiana for visits with Ann's family and with university friends such as John Stoner.

Having been exposed thoroughly to Greek and Roman history in *Gymnasium*, I found my way to Prescott Townsend's courses in these subjects. He, too, took much interest in me. I thoroughly enjoyed his classes, which brought classical history and culture alive. He showed slides in profusion, and on exams he included questions based on the slides to ensure that we paid as much attention to them as to his lectures and our readings. A darkened room made note-taking difficult, so I sat near a window, where a sliver of light made the endeavor easier.

Very early on, in a discussion in his office, Townsend inquired into my foreign language competency. I admitted I had four years of French in secondary school, but that it had been ten years ago and I had surely forgotten it all. He told me to read a certain entry in the Daremberg encyclopedia of classical antiquity in French. I protested that I could not possibly do so, but I tried it. I found that, lo and behold, I *could* read French!

With this newfound confidence, I presented myself for the French proficiency exam when I entered Yale and passed it. Having also taken the German proficiency test and passed it, I was the only entering graduate student that year who had put all foreign language requirements behind him upon entry.

Townsend paid little attention to his appearance. He wore jackets and pants from different suits, and the belt buckle peering from under his vest was bent and tarnished. I had formed some definite ideas about teaching as a career, so I began to wonder whether after a lifetime of work, I would be able to afford a suit of clothes and a decent belt for my trousers. However, I found out later that Prescott Townsend's wealth came from the Pennsylvania Railroad well before its demise, and that during the deep Depression years, when the budget of the History Department was stretched to its limits, he would take frequent leaves without pay to ease the strain on the department's budget. So much for judging a man by his belt buckle.

The most exciting course in the program was Francis Wormuth's yearlong course in the history of political thought. It left the graduate students determined to become political theorists like him. Francis Wormuth also pointed the way to my first published article and suggested topics for my master's thesis, which very directly led to my doctoral dissertation.

Thus it was that my life literally stretched from our apartment on South Washington Street to the building that housed the Government Department (now Rawles Hall) and the library (now Franklin Hall).

South Washington Street

The other exciting dimension of my early Bloomington days was at South Washington Street. Steve was nine months old when we moved to Bloomington. As an only child, and having grown up in a different culture, I was absolutely at sea about raising children, especially in American society. How fortunate I was that Ann had been one of eight, with five younger siblings for whom she had helped care.

On the one hand, I studiously pored over Arnold Gesell's publications about what was "normal" for a nine- or twelve-month-old, but on the other hand, I surrendered to the charm of Mother Goose and the stories in the Little Golden Books, then priced at 25¢ each. It came to be a routine for me to feed Steve at 6:00 a.m. as well as other times, though I left toilet training to Ann. That Steve was an unusually placid baby, I did not realize fully until seven years later when the perpetual motion machine we called Alice was born.

Given my political and ideological parentage, I was on the side of nurture in the eternal conflict about whether nature or nurture should determine child-rearing philosophy. I was certain that babies were tabulae rasae on which society (that is to say, parents) could write whatever it thought best. I held to this view firmly until I watched my own children growing up. Babies might not be fully formed human beings as they emerge from their mother's womb, but the slate is quite well filled, and society's impact has sharp limits.

Early on, one noticeable trait that Steve exhibited was conservatism: he liked things the way they were and intensely disliked change and anything new. This included new clothing necessitated by his growth. One day we

Freddy & Steve
South Washington Street
Bloomington, 1945

had to buy him new shoes because his old ones were simply too small. The result? Howls of protest and total refusal to put on the new shoes! What were we to do? If having new shoes was considered a sort of punishment, then what reward could overcome his resistance?

He dearly loved to go for a walk with me, still holding onto a finger to steady himself. So the next morning, I offered to go for a walk with him after his 6:00 a.m. breakfast. Eureka! After I fed him his oatmeal, he permitted the new shoes to be put on without protest, and off we went around the block. That solved the problem, for obviously, once worn, they were no longer new shoes. I was reminded of that episode many times in later years when first my students and then my colleagues came to be the age of my children.

In those early Bloomington years, we attended First Methodist Church on the invitation of George Shaffer, who worked at the university's speech clinic. I attended speech clinic faithfully for most of our three years in Bloomington. There is general agreement that I was helped considerably to lower the pitch of my speaking voice and to smooth away my German speech patterns and sounds. That is chiefly to George Shaffer's credit.

In 1945-1948 Bloomington was a small town, whose friendliness we experienced in many ways through people we came to know both inside and outside the university environment. Even then, music was an important part of community life and of our life, too. The Indiana University School of Music was not then what it became much later, but Bloomington and Indiana University were a stop on the Metropolitan Opera's annual spring tour. I heard my first operas since 1938, and for Ann, these Met performances were a true first.

University lecture events were not then as numerous as they are today, but several prominent visitors appeared through the year and covered a great variety of subjects. We attended many such events.

Peace and learning

The themes of these Bloomington years were peace and learning. The war was over. Our life together brought us much happiness. I did exceedingly well in all my courses and received strong recommendations when I applied for fellowships at major universities. I received the AB degree with highest honors (elected to Phi Beta Kappa) with a major in history and a minor in government. I went on to obtain my master's with the principal emphasis in political science, but I was still undecided about the concentration for my doctorate.

I found a variety of ways to postpone the choice. I decided to apply to do doctoral work in history in some institutions and in political science in others. I reckoned I would get at best one fellowship offer, so I would be spared the task of making a choice. As it turned out, I was offered a fellowship in history from Cornell University and one in political science from Yale University. My dilemma remained.

In those years, the Government Department had a very small number of graduate students and no particular machinery for directing their work. Oliver Field, a senior member of the department, served as an informal advisor to the graduate students. In my years at Indiana, Field had lost most of his sight but continued to function very effectively.

For teaching his course in constitutional law, Field employed a number of readers to read court decisions to him, and then typed précis of the cases. Before each class, he took relevant cases home with him, where Mrs. Field would read the case briefs to him. On that basis, he then taught the class on the following day.

During my period of indecision (the two weeks allowed to fellowship candidates to accept or reject offers), I was one of the readers Field employed. He had been talking to me about my forthcoming decision and knew about my dithering in this regard. With the two weeks just about up, I arrived at his office for one of my reading appointments. He greeted me with, "I guess, Freddy, you have decided to go into political science!"

He took me completely by surprise. All I could do was stammer, "Y-yes, Mr. Field." That is how I decided to accept Yale's offer of a fellowship in political science.

Field's strategy was rather ruthless, but he had shrewdly recognized one of my chief characteristics: worrying endlessly over decisions. Obviously, he had decided that I needed a push to get me off the proverbial dime. But Field should not get all the blame—or credit. Increasingly, I had been finding historical scholarship tedious and lacking in concern for the broader questions of events and people. Political science, on the other hand, more nearly matched my interest in political ideas, ideology, and what the discipline now calls policy studies.

When I started at Indiana University in 1945, my notions about teaching were quite unformed, and I still thought, essentially, about teaching secondary school. However, my teachers (John Stoner, Lee Benns, and others) insisted that my academic performance indicated a clear capacity for doctoral work and university-level teaching.

There was no question in my mind about where I wanted to be after I was given the opportunity, as a first-year graduate student, to teach two independent sections of an introductory course (with about fifty students in each). These two sections, for which I was fully responsible, constituted half of a graduate student's load, with courses and thesis on top of them.

It will provide some perspective on this assignment to note that the year was 1947, and Indiana University was experiencing a deluge of World War II veterans taking advantage of the GI Bill. There were not enough dormitories, not enough married housing, not enough classrooms, not enough textbooks, and not enough fully qualified instructors.

The nature of this emergency will help to explain why the department decided I should teach two sections of state and local government, for which I had as sole background John Stoner's one-semester introductory course. I had been in the country for a little over five years, most of it spent in the armed forces. Thus, my familiarity with American local government (Indiana's included) was truly minimal. I will only add that the hoary chestnut about what a teacher should do in such a situation fit me to the tee—get a big book for yourself and a small book for your students.

As a lighter note to my first teaching adventure, after I was told about my teaching assignment, the first thing I did was to visit a local clothing store to buy a double-breasted suit. I suppose I still had very European notions about teachers as authority figures in the classroom.

I am sure that it was John Stoner who sponsored me for the teaching appointment. What he saw in me at the time as a potential teacher-scholar, I certainly did not see myself. But he started me on an enterprise that has filled my life ever since.

University housing

Our first year in Bloomington, we lived on South Washington Street. For the remaining years, we lived in university housing. We were among the first to occupy Hoosier Courts, the married housing that was converted from military barracks placed among fields and woods at the far edge of campus.

The accommodations were surely Spartan, but we were happy to have cheap and adequate furnished housing. During these years, we were introduced to the delights of Italian cooking and the many-course Italian family meal, and Steve had a variety of playmates from neighboring families.

Today it is difficult to convey the full flavor of life among the veterans and their families—their determination to make up for lost time, their delight in their children, and their generally meager budgets. Most of us were held together by the bonds of our war service and the GI Bill. There has not been a college generation like it since. Yet, if the return of such a student generation would have to be preceded by another world war, we should stop and reconsider our nostalgia about the good old days of the GI Bill student generation.

New Haven (1948-1950)

Moving from Hope to Bloomington in 1945 had been a simple matter. Ann's familiarity with southern Indiana had eased the move. There was also the small-town quality to life in Bloomington, which enabled us to settle in easily, all our problems with housing in 1945-1946 notwithstanding. Our move to New Haven was another matter. The East Coast was more or less familiar to me, but it was alien territory to Ann.

In late spring, we traveled by train to New Haven to look for housing. It was a dispiriting experience. Yale's student housing had no vacancies for us, so we looked at the private rentals listed in the housing office. The rents were expensive, especially for what seemed like slum housing. Ann shuddered at the thought of Steve growing up in such settings.

Eventually we found a vacancy in a rather nice neighborhood near the university. An Italian family had converted Victorian era, single-family residences into apartments. The first-floor unit in one of the houses was available, but the rent was three times what Indiana University charged for student housing units!

Ann dissolved into tears and angrily wanted to know why we had to undergo all these agonies. Why could I not complete my studies in Bloomington?

This sent me into a tailspin. I could not fully explain why this move was necessary for my career, but yet I knew that it was what I should be doing. In the end, we decided that whatever financial sacrifice was required, we would take the apartment.

As it turned out, we thoroughly enjoyed our life there on Orange Street. We became good friends with our Italian landlords, who actually lowered our rent for the second year when we considered moving to a cheaper apartment.

Joe Schlesinger, a fellow graduate student who moved into one of the other units, ate breakfast with us and became one of Steve's favorite adults. We also came to know Ann and Jim Dunn, a young couple on the second floor. We formed a lifelong friendship with them and later, their children.

As it turned out, our two-year stay in New Haven was only the first of three sojourns. Our sojourns in New Haven enriched our lives and those of our children in various ways. There was a high level of intellectual activity at Yale. New Haven was a pre-Broadway tryout spot, and above all, a short distance to New York with its art museums, ballet, Bronx Zoo, and Christmas decorations at Rockefeller Center. Such things enriched our lives and broadened our horizons.

At Indiana University, I had moved from freshman to a completed MA in three years. My career at Yale was considerably less smooth. The Yale Political Science Department in the late 1940s was, essentially, leaderless. International relations constituted a separate department, and political science (essentially only comparative government and political theory) was of very uneven quality.

The intake of graduate students was minuscule. Though the graduate student cohort immediately preceding mine had been larger and possibly had a better completion record, in my year, 1948, there were only six graduate students. Of these, only two, George Totten and I, completed doctorates.

Yet two of the incompletes were men of genuine intellectual stature, more original and creative, at least potentially, than either George Totten or me. Charles Lichenstein wandered off to Washington and the right wing of the Republican Party, rising to ambassador rank under Jean Kirkpatrick's tenure at the United Nations. John Ponturo became entangled in a failed marriage and eventually became a brilliant international security operations research analyst in Washington, DC. He was a gentle, kind man with an intellect to match his human goodness. We saw each other often during the year we spent in Washington (1980-1981). Soon after, he was killed in a traffic accident.

I also developed a close friendship with Fred Engelmann, who was at our apartment often, as were several other single graduate students. Fred was from Vienna, and when his mother visited from Los Angeles, she prepared one of Vienna's favorite desserts, *Kaiserschmarrn*, for us. She also identified an alpine watercolor that Ann had been given by Aunt Lily as being the work of Maria Egner, a distinguished Austrian water colorist.

Initially we were troubled by New Haven's housing costs because our financial resources were so limited. Yale had awarded me an $800 fellowship, its largest in political science. But the fellowship more than doubled when I was appointed as a teaching assistant. We breathed a great sigh of relief and began to take a more positive view of life in New Haven. I believe I justified Yale's confidence in me by completing my course work in two years with all honors grades and passing my written and oral qualifying examinations in the spring of 1950.

New intellectual vistas

In that first year, Yale's graduate seminars opened up new and exciting intellectual vistas to me and gave my thought directions that have influenced me ever since, especially those seminars taught by Driver, Kendall, Dahl, and Lindblom.

Cecil Driver was a transplanted Englishman who had only contempt for what he called "the American PhD machine." His year-long seminar provided a thorough grounding in European political institutions. It was essentially a course in constitutional history and would be scorned by today's comparative political behavior specialists. Yet it provided a foundation on which I was able to build.

Dahl and Lindblom taught a joint seminar while they were working on *Politics, Economics and Welfare*, a most important but terribly written and poorly edited book. They provided an exploration into what today would be called political economy and introduced us to the works of a group of major thinkers from Karl Polanyi to Frank Knight.

The class consisted of doctoral students from both political science and economics, but the discussion was mostly political, or in today's jargon, policy oriented. From time to time, Dahl would suggest that we take up issues raised by the economists on our reading list, but Lindblom would squelch such suggestions with comments like, "Why waste time on economics?"

The year I took their seminar, Skinner published *Walden Two*, which was assigned under the rubric of planning the lives of human beings, I suppose. The excitement caused by *Walden Two* was such that several members of the seminar began to lay plans to establish the sort of utopian community Skinner envisaged. Truly my graduate education did not really *begin* until after I got to Yale.

Willmoore Kendall

The most disturbing element in my years at Yale was Willmoore Kendall, whose intellectual brilliance both attracted and destroyed, or at least damaged, the lives of a number of my fellow students.

Kendall, the son of a blind, Oklahoma Baptist preacher, had won a Rhodes scholarship and written a brilliant, yet wrong-headed, doctoral dissertation that set out to prove that Locke's *Second Treatise* was really a defense of absolute majority rule. Today his approach to political texts would be labeled deconstructionist.

Kendall's yearlong graduate seminar, Critique of Liberalism, foreshadowed precisely the conservative counterrevolution to the American liberal establishment that reached its apogee in the wake of the 1994 congressional election. The impact of that seminar on its members was best summed up by Duane Lockard: "After the seminar on Tuesday, it takes me until Friday to get over being mad. Then I begin to read next Tuesday's assignment, and I get mad all over again."

My own reading of the failure of democratic/liberal government in Central Europe made me more receptive to Kendall's antiliberal strictures than many of my fellow students were. For example, I held the position then, and still do today, that free speech is not to be extended to those determined to do away with free speech once *they* are in control. That position owes nothing to political correctness, but rather to a strong and militant defense of democratic institutions against a variety of know-nothings who want to impose their notions of political, moral, or other correctness on the rest of society.

Kendall was a Socratic teacher par excellence, which meant that he totally dominated his seminars and thus was able to demolish counterarguments presented by anyone else. Once during my second year, I finally found enough voice to raise a counterargument. He heard me out for a while and then cut me off with a smile, "Freddy, two can't play a Socratic game in the same room."

In that second year, Kendall took some of us on in individual Oxbridge-type tutorials, and effectively taught us to argue a passage in a Platonic dialogue in four pages. It was a truly memorable experience. The first time or so, it took me almost an entire weekend to read the passage and write the required short paper. Gradually practice made me if not perfect, then certainly very proficient.

However, there was a dark side to Kendall. He was well on his way to alcoholism and became a troublemaker in the department. He denigrated his colleagues in front of their students, and created such tensions that some graduate students left the program and went elsewhere to complete their degrees. He was also monumentally irresponsible in mentoring students who had him as their dissertation adviser. As a result, several careers and lives were destroyed when people could not complete their dissertations.

Worst of all, Kendall was not just a critic of liberalism. He was well on the way to becoming a fascist, if not an American brand of authoritarian. Any thought I ever had of asking him to supervise my dissertation disappeared when he suggested that for the dissertation, I should do a study of Nazi concentration camps as a model for the institutions in Plato's *Laws*. Surely Karl Popper's characterization of Plato as the "enemy of the open society" applied fully to Willmoore Kendall.

Cecil Driver

Students of Yale's prewar Political Science Department, such as Marian Irish and Dwight Waldo, fondly remember Cecil Driver and his wife as being most hospitable to graduate students. The Drivers entertained students at their home and were supportive in other ways.

Then during or right after the war, Mrs. Driver fell victim to Parkinson's disease, and Cecil Driver became increasingly preoccupied with caring for her. He refused, often brusquely, all offers of assistance from colleagues or students. He became increasingly erratic in his seminars, one year giving all the students in one seminar *pass* grades—a grade generally viewed as *not pass* in the graduate school.

Yet in my years at Yale, I was able to maintain an open, and to me, most profitable relationship with Cecil Driver. The reason for that might be that even in 1948-1950 at Yale, I still carried with me some of the same awe that I felt for American universities and their professors when I started at Indiana University in 1945. My image of the student-teacher relationship still bore a strong European mark, and Cecil Driver likely responded favorably to the manner in which I conducted myself in my relations with teachers.

Cecil Driver gave my work then, and really for the rest of my life, a direction that did not seem to find favor with most of my Yale contemporaries. The roots of this development go back to Indiana University in 1945-1946. As I mentioned, because of the small graduate enrollment, Oliver Field acted as an informal mentor to all the graduate students. At the beginning of my senior year, Field suggested that I take a course in public administration from a new faculty member.

I was reluctant to do so. I told him that I was not really interested in public administration. I wanted to do political theory, like Francis Wormuth.

Field countered by saying that in the near future, as a newly-hired faculty member, I would probably have to teach such a course, so I had better know something about it. Being still very respectful of my teachers, I took the yearlong course, as well as a yearlong graduate seminar the following year. That made me something of a wonder when I arrived at Yale, where no one ever considered anything but political theory and comparative government proper subjects for study.

Apparently Driver knew all this about me. When I wanted to discuss a topic for the term paper required for his seminar, he simply said, "Freddy, I want you to do a paper on the French Conseil d'État."

When I responded that I knew nothing about this obviously important institution, he indicated that it was time to learn something about it. From this paper came my first scholarly article, and soon after another one on French administration. Much of my subsequent career took off from this work.

I should add that I certainly would not have continued this line of inquiry had I not found it both interesting and challenging. I have continued to teach seminars on comparative administration and public policy even after my formal retire-

Cecil Driver
New Haven, c. 1949

ment in 1988. That work clearly identifies me as an institutionalist, and from that base, I moved on to studies of public policy and policy processes more generally.

Whatever was at work, I became very much attached to Cecil Driver. He came to play a central role in my subsequent intellectual and professional development, extending his concern and interest to Ann and the children, especially during my two subsequent sojourns at Yale in 1955-1956 and 1958-1959.

Family life in New Haven

After Ann became reconciled to our move into a high-rent area, our two years at Yale provided her with a most stimulating environment. She acquired new friends such as Ann Dunn, and she devoted herself to Steve's continued development. She also enjoyed the company of my fellow graduate students, such as Joe Schlesinger, Fred Engelmann (though she found his Viennese superiority attitude rather grating), John Ponturo, George Totten, and Walter Carr (who was already working on his dissertation, and who became a victim of Kendall's irresponsibility).

Steve played occasionally with the children of my fellow students. He also acquired a playmate on his own, or rather was acquired by her, a little girl named Judy, who lived down the street and was a few years older than him.

The friendship between the two children came to have a most profound impact on our lives. Judy's parents were nominally Roman Catholic and mostly nonpracticing, and she had on her own begun to attend St. John's Episcopal Church, and had become friends with its rector, Father Gummere. Judy decided that Steve should attend her Sunday school, and in the end, Steve's parents went along, too.

When we first arrived in New Haven, we had gone to the Methodist church on the Green but not found it satisfactory, so we were unchurched when Judy introduced us all to St. John's. The congregation was quite small and contained a number of Yale faculty families who had not yet fled to the suburbs. Father Gummere called on us, but the only part of the conversation I remember is his concern that Ann with her Midwestern Protestant background would object to a church that was, so to speak, next door to Rome. Ann assured him on that point, and we became regular attenders at St. John's.

I had indicated to Ann from the start that Steve should be baptized if she so wished, but she always responded that she would not do that unless I clearly indicated my own move in that direction. The discussion usually ended there. Given her profound religious commitment, I thought Ann would want Steve baptized.

As for myself, I had not yet clarified my own mind and my own feelings. Essentially I was still the same secular Central European who had been shaped by his Viennese environment. At the same time, I had absorbed enough of my Jewish upbringing with its distant, jealous God, and the finality of the death of the physical human being, that I found Trinity, Virgin birth, and resurrection to be so much mumbo-jumbo peddled by an established state church determined to keep its hold over a superstitious peasantry. Science had the answers about the physical universe, and man was surely able to shape his existence without some form of divine intervention.

Ann's commitment was not to Methodism but to a Christian religious belief system, and Steve obviously responded to Father Gummere. Judy's enthusiasm and the appeal the Christian story has for children when it is well told by caring individuals also played a role. So our family began attending an Episcopal church, but all the pieces did not fall into place until 1950 when we moved to Gainesville.

Steve's first loves

What marked not only these first New Haven years, but also much that followed, was Steve's love affair with reading, or rather, Ann's having successfully instilled her own love in him. From then on, Steve's and later Alice's books tied us together as a family. Steve could sit still endlessly (Alice less so) to be read to, and their books became central to our lives.

We all particularly enjoyed the Pooh books, which had just made their appearance in the United States. The two Pooh books became our constant companions, as did the *Chronicles of Narnia* later on. We reread them endlessly, and all three of us could recite whole passages from memory.

Steve always ended his day with a bath. One night we heard him laugh uproariously, so we hurried to find out what caused the hilarity. There was Steve sitting in the bathtub,

Freddy & Steve
Orange Street
New Haven, 1948

reciting particularly funny lines from a Pooh book and doubling over with laughter about the episode where Pooh's head became stuck in a honey jar, and Piglet thought he espied a Heffalump! We enjoyed our subsequent years in New Haven in other ways, but it all started on Orange Street in 1948.

During our Bloomington years, we had acquired a record player so we could enjoy music even though concert-going was expensive and difficult because of the need for a babysitter. Although Steve had records of children's songs, he was already becoming incorporated into our musical world.

One day Steve visited our upstairs neighbors Jim and Ann Dunn, as he often did, and returned with a 78-rpm record of Rossini overtures. Apparently he had listened to it so often on their record player that they made him a present of it. Perhaps they could not stand to hear "La Gazza Ladra" again and decided it was our turn to suffer. Steve was indeed a sort of monomaniac. He played that record over and over, vigorously conducting the orchestra, something he still does at age fifty.

Steve responded to other music as well, both serious and comic. He and I fell completely under the spell of Spike Jones, much to Ann's disgust. He also became infatuated with Mahler's First Symphony. I had bought the multi-disc 78-rpm album at a department store sale assisted by Steve, who helped me lug home all the heavy multi-disc albums I bought. In the next few years, whenever Steve succumbed to any of the usual childhood ailments and was confined to bed, his first demand was always, "Read me a book." But then, especially when he felt particularly miserable, he would command, "Play the Mahler."

In the decades since, Steve has acquired musical tastes and understanding far broader and more sophisticated than those of his parents, and he has passed them on to his son Gordon, who (now that he is living with us and working on a degree at Indiana University) has become our companion at musical events. Gordon, too, has developed musical tastes of his own, especially medieval and renaissance music. To think it all began with "La Gazza Ladra," Mahler's First, and Spike Jones.

Oscar and Liesl visit

Our stay on the East Coast also marked the beginning of contacts with the few members of my family who had survived the Holocaust. The great family event of our New Haven years was a visit from Oscar and Liesl in 1949. They arrived in the United States after traveling to Europe, where Oscar was engaged in settling our property affairs in Vienna, a lot of headaches and little to show for it. Liesl was eager to see her mother and her two sisters living in the United States.

A Gathering of Freddy's Family
Standing: Judith Diamant holding grandson Freddy Losch,
Oscar Diamant, Ann Redmon Diamant, Eric Diment,
Fritzi Diamant Losch, Herta Diment, Liesl Diamant.
Sitting: Freddy Diamant, Steve Diamant,
Erik Strindberg-Diment
Newark, New Jersey, 1949

When Oscar and Liesl arrived in New York, they contacted us, as well as Liesl's sister Mary and her family, Liesl's mother, my cousins Fritzi Losch and Eric Diment and their families, and the Willy Unger family.

Willy Unger was Oscar's closest personal friend among the Unger clan. Through Oscar, we came into contact with Willy's two daughters, Marianne and Lilly. Marianne and her family lived in Connecticut, and we visited them frequently during our New Haven years. Lilly was married to John Kautsky, who was completing a PhD in political science at Harvard and later spent most of his academic career at Washington University in St. Louis.

Oscar and Liesl visited us in New Haven at least once, loaded down with presents for Steve. Other times we went to New York, and at least once, we went to Newark for a reunion with the Losch and Diment families.

Possibly I had exaggerated my earlier description of my family's criticism concerning my lack of ambition. Whatever might have been the case earlier, it was now unmistakable that Oscar and Liesl were pleased, even proud, of my intellectual and professional life and goals.

I had last seen Oscar and Liesl in London in August 1939, while they were en route to Australia. Sadly, their visit in 1949 proved to be the last time we would see Oscar. He died late in 1951, shortly before his sixty-first birthday, when a heart condition incurred during his younger years finally took its toll.

Since then, Liesl has visited us here in Bloomington, and one weekend, we flew to New York to be with her. On that occasion, she had been in Europe to celebrate her eighty-fifth birthday with dinner at the Café Sacher and a memorable performance of the *Magic Flute* at the Staatsoper. She is now well over ninety and in a nursing home near Sidney.

Mine is the fate of survivors: thankful for the circumstances that have kept me out of harm's way until seventy-five, yet increasingly alone in a rapidly changing world.

Liesl & Alice
Bloomington, 1975

We settle our property affairs in Vienna

One of the principal reasons for Oscar's trip to Europe in 1949 was settling our property affairs in Vienna. By then we had tracked Mama's tragic end in Eastern Europe, and we were able to get her death certified legally. With that, we could settle the estate, now to be shared by Oscar and me as the only survivors.

However, one should not conjure up any grand vistas of great wealth falling into our laps. There was, first of all, our store and the very painful history of our relationship with Rudolf Fuchs, who had been one of our salesmen. Fox was an appropriate name, as it turned out. When Fuchs had fought for the Socialists in the civil war in 1934, Oscar had protected him from harassment by the government-controlled patriotic front, which wanted us to fire all known Socialists.

But when March 1938 came, it turned out that Fuchs had become a member of the pre-1938 illegal Nazi Party. He had proceeded to Aryanize our store and was still operating it when Oscar went to Vienna in 1949. Because Fuchs actually had made payments to us under the table, there was no way we could make any claims against him regarding the store in the Brunnengasse.

The rest of the estate consisted of two pieces of property my father had acquired for investment purposes: an apartment house in Vienna and some undeveloped land near Baden, the famous spa. The land had been bought cheaply with the expectation that the spa would expand in its direction. Not only had this been a futile expectation, but the parcel of land was an odd shape, long and narrow, so the only facility that it could have accommodated would have been a bowling alley.

The apartment house was an even more questionable acquisition. It had been built around 1780, and the state of its basic utilities was commensurate with its age: shared toilets and common cold water faucets. Very little had been done over the years except the minimally required repairs.

The reason for this was Vienna's famous rent control law, which had been enacted at the beginning of World War I and never repealed. The Social Democrats, who governed the city after World War I, kept controls in place, and even after the Social Democrats had been replaced by conservatives, nobody dared touch the rent control sacred cow.

I vividly remember the annual visits of the retired civil servant who managed the property, in which he made his report to my father. After the fee for the administrator, taxes, and minimal upkeep, there was never any positive balance for the landlord. Fortunately the building received some bomb damage in World War II (though parts of it continued to be habitable), and the city of Vienna finally condemned it as unsafe for human habitation, with no protest from historic preservationists, and tore it down.

Finally we had a saleable property, and in short order, the piece of land that had held a house the same vintage as Franz Schubert became a used car lot, but with no Franz Schubert to sing the praises of the beautiful manageress of the used car mill. Sic transit.

Oscar set the legal wheels for restitution in motion in 1949, but it took until 1965 to get it settled and for us to receive our share of the settlement. There were, of course, fees and taxes to pay: legal fees, income and real estate taxes, and most galling, the fee collected by the Austrian government for restoring our rightful property to us, after it had been taken away from us by a government of war criminals.

Whatever more serious and productive uses we might have made of the $10,000 remaining from this magnificent estate, we spent most of it the following year to make life in Europe more comfortable than it might have been without this topping off.

I am offered my first academic job

To return to Yale and 1949, at the beginning of my second year in graduate school, the Political Science Department installed a new chair, V. O. Key, the most distinguished scholar of American politics of his generation. Key was a Texan to whom the ways of the Ivy League were strange and puzzling. His mind was focused only on his research. He appeared in his office at 7:00 a.m.—practically the middle of the night by Ivy League standards. Key disliked administration, and after a short stay, he fled to Harvard, where he could pursue his research, largely unmolested by all the Ivy League foofaraw. However, Key's time at Yale was of some significance for graduate students because he had contacts across the country and so was able to help place students who were on the market.

In that year, we heard of only two vacancies in political science in the field of comparative government. One was in the Ivy League and was filled by Dan Rustow, generally considered the best among several cohorts. (Willmoore Kendall used to tell me, only half jokingly, that after Dan Rustow, I was the best.) The other position was at the University of Florida, and I was nominated by the department for it, with Key's support. Key's ties to the region were particularly close because of his great work on politics of the south.

When I learned of this, I went to see both Key and Driver to point out that I would be taking my qualifying exams at the end of my second year, so I had not yet had any time to define my dissertation topic or to do any research. I argued that I should have support for another year to work on my dissertation. University support was becoming especially crucial because my GI benefits would be exhausted midway through the second semester of the 1949-1950 year.

I was told quite bluntly that there were now other claimants for the fellowship, and that I could not expect any departmental support for placement the following year if I rejected an offer from the University of Florida. So there was nothing I could do but accept the department's help in securing the Florida position.

Accordingly, after Christmas I attended the APSA (American Political Science Association) meeting in New York, and there I was interviewed by two people who became lifelong and most dear friends, Fred Hartmann and Manning Dauer. Dauer was designated to become chair in 1950, when the existing Department of History and Political Science would be divided into two autonomous departments. I learned subsequently that I made a poor impression on them, and that Manning Dauer wrote to his friend V. O. Key, seeking reassurance about Yale's recommendation, which Key promptly supplied.

Nevertheless, they decided to offer the position to Julian Towster, who had just published the first systematic study of the Soviet system in the postwar period. This was a perfectly rational decision, given the choice between a candidate with a completed degree and a book and one who would be simply an ABD (all but dissertation).

Manning Dauer drafted a letter offering the position to Julian Towster and submitted it to James Miller Leake for his signature.

Leake was about to retire as chair of the combined History and Political Science Department, but at that point was *still* chair. Leake tore up Dauer's letter, declaring that he would not offer a position to a person who had written a book about communism, and he substituted my name for Towster's. So in the end, I was offered the position at the University of Florida, $4,000 for a modified 12-month appointment.

One might ask whether I now approve of anticommunist hysteria if it is to *my* advantage? I have only one rebuttal: with that book, Towster was tenured at Berkeley. He has not published a line since.

As I noted earlier, my academic studies moved rapidly from freshman to ABD in five years, but at that point, they came to a screeching halt. I took a full-time position teaching four courses per semester with no more than an outline of what my dissertation might be like. It would take five years for me to get back to completing my dissertation.

Faced with the prospect of beginning a full-time position in the fall, I decided that I should use at least the summer to begin my dissertation research. So Ann took Steve with her to Florida to find us a place to live. Meanwhile, I moved into a dormitory room and worked in the Yale library and the New York Public Library, which had the country's best collection of political pamphlets, ideological tracts, newspapers, and the like documenting Austrian political ideas and development.

Ann and Steve went to Florida by train, stopping first to visit the Brumfiels, our former neighbors from Hoosier Courts, who were now teaching music in Bradenton. They went on to Gainesville, where Ann succeeded in finding a place for us to live, and then returned to the Brumfiels. I met them there in August when I finally set out for my first academic job.

While still in Gainesville, Ann had called me in New Haven to report that she had contracted to buy a house, and that we would have to buy a car as soon as I got there, so I had better learn to drive and get a driver's license. That produced a shock comparable only to the 95°F heat that greeted me in Bradenton. I had a $4,000 job and was about to incur debts totaling $12,000. Reality of life in America had finally caught up with me.

Chapter 11

Gainesville & New Haven Again

(1950-1960)

I t was during the Gainesville years that our family took the shape in which it subsequently functioned. The house that Ann had contracted to buy was eventually built and furnished, and we moved into it early in 1951. It was a mass-produced subdivision house, and we lived surrounded by other young academics and professionals, and with lots of playmates for Steve and later Alice.

Gainesville and the University of Florida

Steve, who had attended private kindergarten in New Haven where he had taught himself to read, started grade school in Gainesville, and he seemed to do well, both in and out of school. With Steven in school, Ann began to take steps toward getting her own degree, only to have her plans disrupted by pregnancy.

At least this time I was not engaged in some airborne tomfoolery a continent away. I was right there when Alice was born, a delivery with far fewer complications than Steve's. Once again, I got a nature-over-nurture lesson that is still with me. While Steve had been a placid baby, Alice moved, seemingly from the moment she was conceived. She has not stopped moving, now past her fortieth birthday.

One day when she had misbehaved for the umpteenth time, eliciting deep sighs and "Oh Alice!" from Ann and me, Steve, who watched it all, asked, "Will we have to go through life saying, 'Oh Alice!'?"

Our first five years in Gainesville were truly harsh ones. It took time to adjust to life in a tropical climate, then still mostly without the help of air-conditioning! The greatest burden fell on Ann, who managed the household and had to stretch my very meager salary for a family of four.

During these years, our only vacations were annual treks to Indiana in late August for a stay with Mae and Glenn. In some years, we sent Steve ahead by plane so he could spend as much time as possible with Uncle Glenn, a tie that has remained firm and close to this day.

Beyond that, food, clothing, and housing more than exhausted my Florida pay, which started at $4,000 and reached only $4,800 by 1955. There was, of course, no way Manning could make greater salary adjustments until after I completed my degree.

In all these years, it was Ann's chore to worry about money, to find ways to feed us with what she had on the shelf, and to wait for the next paycheck. She balanced the checkbook and worried while I maintained a posture of no or little concern for our common balance sheet. Since retiring, I have relieved Ann of that burden, and now it is my turn to worry about money. If there were not a prior claim of authorship, I could sum up these first five Gainesville years as "the best of times, the worst of times."

Baptism and family unity

When Ann and Steve were in Gainesville looking for housing, they enjoyed the help and hospitality of Fred and Reggie Hartmann, who became our steady companions throughout the Florida years. Fred and I shared an office during that decade, and if I became a clean-desk man, it is largely because it is simply impossible to be a messy-desk person while sharing an office with Fred.

During the war, Fred had fallen in love with Reggie and with the US Navy, attachments that have endured throughout his life. Just as onboard ship where everything must be stowed away properly folded in the proper place, so Fred kept his office. Perhaps I am tempted to say that he shamed me into being a clean-desk

Freddy (left) with Fred Hartmann
In their University of Florida office
Gainesville, c. 1955

man, but I do not suggest that such a thought ever entered Fred's orderly mind.

When Ann and Steve first arrived in Gainesville, Fred and Reggie had taken them to University Methodist Church. (They have since seen the error of their ways and become active Episcopalians.) Then one day when Ann and Steve were in downtown Gainesville, they passed a church, and Steve stopped and said that he wanted to enter and say a prayer. When they emerged, Steve announced that this was the church that he wanted us to attend.

The fact that he had chosen Holy Trinity Episcopal Church could, of course, be explained by noting that both Holy Trinity and St. John's in New Haven were typical of English country churches, an architectural design widely copied by Episcopal churches in the United States. Perhaps this was a manifestation of Steve's conservative traits. He had simply opted for a familiar building.

Yet, this simple action triggered a set of events that both Ann and I later identified as being typical of how I function in a variety of settings. For instance, in my research, I will go for a long time without putting anything on paper. During this time, I think about an issue and turn it over in my mind to look at all sides, and I even rehearse what I might write. Then finally, when I become so full of the accumulated evidence that action becomes inevitable, I put it down on paper.

Steve's actions resulted in just such an event for me. I found that I was now ready to be baptized and confirmed in the Episcopal Church. Lots of Jewish middle-class intellectuals migrate to the Anglican end of Protestant Christianity, if they do not veer completely into Quakerism or Unitarianism. This may be simply because its ritual is vaguely familiar to them from their former Roman-dominated environment, and because it imposes few if any doctrinal demands. No doubt, some such change process was at work in my case. The crucial difference for me was Steve and Ann, who provided models that I came to respect and ultimately to embrace fully.

Do I believe in the Trinity? Do I believe in the resurrection and the life everlasting? Do I take Jesus Christ as my savior? I did not know the answers in 1950, and I still do not know them today. Do I even believe in God? Or do I want to shout angrily, "If there is a God, why did he permit the enormity of the war crimes in World War II? And even today, the inhumanity of men to other men that spreads like a plague around the world, often in the form of a religious war?" Obviously this is the agenda of a lifetime, and it is still incomplete today. It could not be otherwise.

Nonetheless, all this anguish has not prevented me from devoting time and energy throughout the years to the Episcopal church. Steve and Alice certainly grew up in the Episcopal church, though as adults they have kept at a distance, more or less. Steve is more open to the ritual of the High Church than Alice, who had to work through her own path when she went in search of my roots in Israel, even though by that time, for me those roots had certainly withered.

I have served the Episcopal church in these past decades in a variety of ways, including annual pledging, service on vestries and other committees, and even as chalice administrator on occasion. Do I indeed assist in the transubstantiation of wine into the blood of Christ?

There is no doubt in my mind that Steve's actions set in motion a chain of events that helped to unite us as a family. Of course, much more happened to unite us together more tightly, and to all these developments, I now turn my attention.

Manning Dauer

The dominant figure during our years in Florida was Manning Dauer. Whatever doubts he might have had at first about my potential and performance must have been resolved before long, for he became my closest intellectual companion and ultimately a supporter of my cause. He remained a lifelong friend.

If my academic career took off at the University of Florida (albeit after a very slow, bumpy start), most if not all the credit must go to Manning Dauer. His personal and intellectual companionship continued without interruption until his untimely death, long after I left Gainesville. There was nobody whose death I mourned more deeply than Manning's.

Manning was a southerner by birth and background. He was raised by his divorced mother, a high school Latin teacher and a suffragette. Martha Dauer was a southern lady in both her strengths and limitations. She was strong-willed, outspoken, and a fighter throughout her life. They lived together through all the decades he spent at the University of Florida, first as a student and then as a faculty member. Manning's longest absence from home was his military service with the US Air Force in the Pacific during World War II.

Except for the minimum number of years necessary to complete the residence requirement for his doctorate in history at Illinois, Manning spent his entire career and all but the first eighteen years of his life at the University of Florida. I met many academics in the south whose careers closely resembled Manning's. However, without exception, they were men of limited vision and intellect, and they were burdened with all the usual southern prejudices. By contrast, Manning possessed an intellectual inquisitiveness, a thirst for new ideas, and a commitment to liberal political values that made him a most exceptional person.

Manning Dauer
University of Florida
Gainesville, c. 1958

Manning traveled widely, something done more easily by a bachelor, and he poked about in places he probably had no business trespassing. My favorite story concerns his display of sang-froid when he gained a most spectacular vantage point to watch a Nazi Party congress, the one filmed by Leni Riefenstahl. Unlike some very prominent Americans, Manning did not succumb to fascist siren songs, and he also kept a very level head about the true nature of the Stalinist horrors, which he did not confuse with the "brave new world."

As a graduate student in history, Manning taught himself basic quantitative skills for use in social sciences. He then applied them to a study of political behavior in the earliest years of the American Republic. S. M. Lipset has called that work, *The Adams Federalists*, the first modern application of quantitative methods to research in political science.

When political science was established as a separate department at the University of Florida with Manning as its chair, he introduced into the curriculum and taught a required graduate seminar called Scope and Method, in which he consistently took account of the changing dimensions of political science research.

I know of no major university that had a comparable requirement as early as 1950.

But Manning was not simply an ivory tower scholar. He virtually reveled in getting his hands into Florida politics. Manning had taught generation after generation of Florida governors, legislators, and judges. Many of them turned to him regularly for help with such chores as constitutional revision, electoral law reform, and state code changes.

Manning was both cosmopolitan and local concerning the university and his discipline. His loyalty to the University of Florida was deep, though never uncritical. He was troublesome no end to a succession of deans, provosts, and presidents. In essence, there was *nothing* that competed with the University of Florida for his time and loyalty. When he died, he left almost all his estate to the university—but he took care to ensure that the funds were used for well-defined academic and intellectual purposes.

When he became chair, Manning became a devoted and conniving fighter for more money for the departmental budget. I had taken a special interest in library appropriations because the university's holdings of European materials were almost nonexistent when I arrived in 1950. The strategy Manning taught me ran something like this: always have lists of desired accessions ready, complete with source and price, so that if there is a windfall at the end of the fiscal year, you will be first in line with your requests. Of course, it helped that the university librarian was an old buddy of his who let us know just when to expect the next windfall.

Yet as much as he was a local, Manning was also a cosmopolitan, that is to say, he cared genuinely about the academic world beyond Florida's walls. He had a profound interest in the intellectual development of political science both in the south and nationally, and he concerned himself with developments along the interface of science and government.

Of course, I would not have been able to articulate any of this post-hoc appreciation during my years in Gainesville. Clearly Manning played the role of a mentor to me, but we might have been embarrassed had this been pointed out to us.

My closeness to Manning developed principally because of the intellectual affinity between us, an affinity we quickly discovered. There were a number of bright, productive people in the department at that time, but I had a strong sense that only Manning shared with me a range of interests and ideas regarding the discipline and the wider intellectual universe.

Dissertation blues

When I arrived in Gainesville, I had no more than a preliminary outline of my dissertation and only a few weeks of research in the libraries at Yale and New York. Like so many newly minted ABDs (all but dissertation), I relished my faculty status, and I let myself be absorbed by a myriad of duties.

I had a four-course teaching load, which was reduced to three when I was assigned duties as assistant managing editor of the *Journal of Politics*, the first journal started by a regional political science association. Manning was its virtually permanent managing editor. That assignment turned out to be a terrible bargain! I exchanged teaching one three-credit course for the virtually *unlimited* task of running the business end of the quarterly scholarly journal. I found it fascinating, but I worked at it probably twenty hours per week year-in, year-out.

Particularly during the first year, it was difficult to cope with Florida's near-tropical climate, which sharply limited my physical and intellectual performance. However, even after I became acclimatized, work on the journal, teaching, and all my other academic chores kept me occupied. As Parkinson's Law suggests, work expands to fill the time allotted.

It seems to me now that Manning must have become increasingly concerned and cross-pressured about my future. I am sure that he recognized that I had two major scholarly articles accepted in the *Journal of Politics* (fully refereed) within my first two years in Gainesville, both of them on topics not connected with my dissertation. And I am sure he valued what I did as a teacher and for the department generally. He even pushed through a promotion to assistant professor while I was still without a doctorate. However, he became increasingly worried about my dissertation, a concern he shared privately with Ann.

I found myself avoiding my dissertation increasingly, until work on it almost totally ceased. I was, of course, concerned about it, and I was made even more miserable by the notices from Yale that the clock was running out for completing my dissertation.

My procrastination made Manning's life more difficult. There were complaints within the department that I was being given preferential treatment. Although I was still without a doctorate, I taught graduate seminars for doctoral students, and I participated in doctoral qualifying examinations. How much longer would the department tolerate my lack of the terminal degree?

The depth of Manning's concern for us (he truly cared for all of us as a family) can best be appreciated by measuring it against the standards increasingly enforced currently and in the recent past. Incoming faculty are given a maximum of one and a half years to complete the doctorate. If the degree is not awarded by then, they receive a six-month termination notice.

Yet there I was in the fall of 1954: I had been allowed *four years* and my dissertation still was not done. I could not produce the draft of even a single chapter. My persistent cry was that I needed to do more research.

At this stage of my and his agonies, Manning performed the ultimate feat on my behalf. In the fall of 1954, the Danforth Foundation announced a new teacher study grants program aimed at ABDs (all but dissertation) who after three years of teaching still had not completed their dissertations. The award provided for the equivalent of a year's salary, all fees, tuition for a year in the degree-granting institution, and roundtrip travel to that institution.

One day while waiting to have a discussion with the dean of the College of Arts and Sciences, Manning saw the grant announcement on a table in the dean's office, waiting to be duplicated and sent out to the college faculty. Manning unobtrusively appropriated that one copy and brought it to me, thus depriving all other ABDs in the college of a chance to apply as well.

As a result, mine was the only application from the University of Florida, and though I am quite prepared to credit myself with having submitted a strong application, to this day, I cannot help reflecting on Manning's willingness to help us, even to the extent of committing what was surely an unethical act. I cannot imagine how differently our lives would have evolved if I had been unable to complete my dissertation.

We were away from Gainesville during 1955-1956, while I completed my dissertation, and then again during 1958-1959, when I was invited to return to Yale to teach for that academic year. Not long after that, I was invited for an interview at Haverford College, the oldest of the Quaker-sponsored colleges, which then had an enrollment of five hundred students.

I heard from others that Manning was deeply upset when I accepted Haverford's eventual invitation. Why Haverford wanted someone whose entire academic life had been in large universities is something that I did not understand then, and only imperfectly understand now.

My students

The University of Florida was authorized to offer the political science doctorate when the separate department was created in 1950. At that time, the undergraduate program was already quite solid and attracted many first-rate students. Several have achieved professional recognition in a number of academic disciplines. I have remained in touch with many who continue to recall my work as their teacher and intellectual mentor.

By contrast, the graduate program, being new, struggled to attract enough students to make the program viable. Often these students were of questionable quality and had to be continuously propped up. At the very beginning, there was even competition among faculty members to see whose doctoral candidate would be the first to complete his degree. After several years of such efforts, I was determined that I would never again join a department where the graduate students had to be nursed through their degree program.

In my very last years at Gainesville, I had a chance to direct a doctoral dissertation for the first time. The candidate, Ramon Arango, was a most unusual one—the son of a high-status Spanish (not Cuban) family from Tampa. He eventually received a Fulbright grant for work in Belgium, and his final product was published by Johns Hopkins University Press.

His mama was a striking grande dame who made annual shopping trips to Paris to replenish her wardrobe. We came to love her and her son, even though Ann always wanted to hide herself and her housedresses when Mrs. Arango came to visit.

Ramon completed his dissertation with Manning supervising the final stages after I left Gainesville. I remember that we held his defense while the movers were loading our furniture. Ann was quite right in saying that the university always seemed to come first.

Hegelkugel

Although Manning played a major role in my intellectual life and development at Florida, another great influence was the monthly discussion group organized and inspired by Wes Tilley. Wes was a true product of the Chicago humanist tradition of Robert M. Hutchins. He was a man of nearly unlimited talents, who procrastinated over his doctoral dissertation even longer than I did. He read voraciously in literature, philosophy, and science, and was an accomplished pianist and occasional trombonist. He was devoted to teaching the introductory humanities course year after year.

Wes inspired a group of his friends to meet regularly to discuss important books or ideas. When we started the discussion group early in the fifties, the paperback revolution was still in the future, and obtaining multiple copies of books to read was a serious obstacle. However, that problem was solved in time. At our initial meeting, we clearly aimed high, Hegel's *Philosophy of History*, which we never discussed because there were not enough copies to go around. Nevertheless, that selection provided the name for the group: Hegelkugel.

An important feature of the group was the rule that there could be only one person from a given discipline or group of disciplines. Thus the HK consisted of a humanist, a physicist, a political scientist, a band director, the director of the university libraries, the director of the university radio station, and others who came and went depending on their University of Florida connections. I always thought that Manning would have been a splendid addition to the HK, but I respected the no-two-members-from-the-same-discipline rule.

From the abortive Hegel beginning, one could say that the life of the HK after that was all uphill or downhill, depending on one's philosophical preferences. We met year-round, making some concessions to Florida's climate by lightening our fare during the summer with, for instance, a play reading, not aloud though.

Wes Tilley's intellectual reach and appetite were the heart and soul of the HK. The enterprise continued after we left Gainesville and even after the Tilleys' departure a few years later. I gather that it still functions in some form, more than four decades after its founding. Its survival is testimony to the powerful thrust of Wes' intellectual energies.

Wes was one of the last to complete a doctorate in the interdisciplinary humanities program created and inspired by Robert Hutchins, who had only contempt for the disciplinary compartmentalization of graduate studies in American universities. Wes clearly shared this Hutchins credo, which in a way, is great fun intellectually but is hard on the academic careers of its devotees.

Other intellectual diversions

My intellectual development in Gainesville proceeded on multiple but harmonious tracks. During these five years, I also found time for other intellectual diversions when I should have been working on my dissertation. I found time to pursue my growing interest in comparative studies of public administration, as well as doing book reviews regularly for several journals, and attending regional and national political science meetings.

Because there was never enough money to go around for meeting expenses, we car-pooled whenever possible. For the Southern Political Science Association (SPSA) meetings, Manning often provided the car, and Fred and I rode with him. These were nearly daylong rides from north Florida to Gatlinburg, Tennessee, where the SPSA meetings were held during the fifties. It was the only place that would accommodate our integrated (three or four African-Americans) meetings.

In those years, SPSA meetings were a friends-and-neighbors affair. All 120 or so attenders knew each other. The rides to and from the meetings were occasions for endless arguments about US policy in Europe, in which Fred always upheld a pro-German view while Manning and I tried to get him to see the error of his ways. It was obvious to us that German stubbornness had survived through several generations in the United States.

The most significant products of my work during these years were my articles on French administration that appeared in the *Journal of Politics* in 1951 and 1954. The first was based on the

Conseil d'État paper that I had written at Driver's suggestion for his seminar at Yale. I incorporated into it some work I had done in another seminar, thus giving it a comparative dimension (France and the United States).

In 1948 Congress had passed the Administrative Procedure Act (APA), through which the legal profession, in and out of Congress, attempted to rein in the increasingly significant administrative law jurisdictions of the US regulatory agencies. This suggested to me a most intriguing contrast between a common law and a Roman law country.

Many years later, I showed my paper on the APA to a specialist, who asked immediately why I had not submitted it for publication when I had done it originally. The answer was that the Political Science Department at Yale in those days did little if anything to encourage the scholarly activities of its graduate students. I am sure that it was Manning's more realistic perspective on the profession that prompted him to encourage me to revise and submit these seminar papers.

Inspired by this first success, I submitted another manuscript to the *Journal of Politics*. This one had no graduate seminar provenance. It arose from a discussion with Hubert Marshall, one of my nicest colleagues at the University of Florida, or anywhere else for that matter. (Unfortunately he remained at the University of Florida only a year or two and was then recruited by Stanford, where he remained for the rest of his academic career.) I had made a comment to Hugh about certain headquarters-field relationships in French public administration that struck him as very much at odds with the US experience.

So I went back to my sources and took another look. Sure enough, I had taken the formal statements about these relationships as reality. The French reality was in fact widely at odds with the official French formula and very much like the US reality that Hugh had described. I did some other articles in collaboration with various Florida colleagues, but these two really became the foundation for much of my later work.

New Haven (1955-1956)

While I was in Florida, the Yale Political Science Department underwent a dramatic change. The credit for that must go to Jim

Fesler, who had been recruited to chair the department and bring it into the mainstream of political science. Fesler did that most successfully, for that was the department of Dahl, Lane, and Lindblom, and the student generation of Greenstein, Wildavsky, Polsby, and Wolfinger.

When I returned to Yale in 1955 to work on my dissertation, the department also displayed great strength in administrative studies: Walter Sharp, Herbert Kaufman, Fred Riggs (as a visitor), and Fesler himself. The first three were offering a graduate seminar in comparative public administration, and I decided to sit in on it, even though a rational decision would have been to avoid all such diversions of attention from my dissertation. Nevertheless, by participating in the seminar, I became known to Fred Riggs and Walter Sharp.

Walter Sharp, who had written *the* book on prewar French administration, called me the country's greatest expert on postwar French administration—on the basis of my having authored the only two articles on the subject in the English language. Once again, long-term benefits flowed from that diversionary activity, but none of it contributed to the completion of my dissertation.

The dissertation

In all the preceding years, I had put nothing on paper. I had piles of notes, some of them quite faded after five years, some microfilms, books, reprints of articles, and so forth. I kept insisting that more research needed to be done. Nevertheless, I finally sat down and produced four chapters, about two hundred pages, which I presented to Cecil Driver. He said not a word about the five-year hiatus and promised to read it all.

When Cecil returned the chapters to me, the top page of my brainchild looked like a big blot of red ink. He had taken it all apart, sentence by sentence. He had demolished the structure of the argument. He had castigated me for my Germanic sentences, with their endless subordinate clauses. It must have taken him at least an hour to go through just that first page! Nevertheless, he had gone on to the subsequent pages, and there I was glad to see that the Red Sea had thinned out considerably.

I must have heaved a sigh of relief, for Cecil cut me short with, "Freddy, from here on, I have marked only *classes* of mistakes."

Then Cecil stopped mercifully and subjected me to his standard dissertation routine, which was nothing more than an old English grammar school device. He instructed me to put the first chapter into the form of a topical outline, where the chapter itself must be encapsulated in a complete sentence. Each subcategory, for example (1) (a) (i), must also be expressed in a complete sentence and must be logically subsumed under the immediately superordinate clause.

I did not know what to make of it all, but it was clear that I had not produced acceptable work. If Ann was as discouraged as I was, she did not show it. She never did in all these years. She clearly attempted to be supportive in every possible way, even when I seemed not to be responsive to her efforts.

I worked long and laboriously at producing the topical outline. When I presented it to Cecil, he showed me in short order that I still did not have a logically coherent set of propositions. This meant, essentially, that I was still not clear in my own mind about what I wanted to argue. He told me to try again. I went home and cried long and bitterly, afraid that I would never be able to produce an acceptable dissertation.

As it turned out, that was the nadir! I did indeed manage to produce an acceptable outline for Chapter 1, and subsequently, for the other three monsters. Cecil ordered me not to write another line until he had approved the first four chapters in their final form. After that I produced acceptable outlines for the remaining chapters and was able to do them right the first time around.

Still it was slow going. During spring break, Ann took the children to Washington, so that I could have an uninterrupted week in which to work. Unfortunately I did not write a single line during that week. That brought Ann near the breaking point. Would we or would we not be able to leave New Haven with a completed and accepted dissertation?

During all this time, Cecil was unstinting in his support, while still as critical as ever of my work. Eventually my chapter outlines became so detailed, and their structure so near perfection, as he saw it, that Cecil approved them for final typing simply on the basis of the outline.

By then we had rented a second typewriter so Ann could do the final typing of the early chapters while I composed outlines for the later chapters. Ironically I had planned to cover the period 1918-1938. When I came to a crucial point in 1934 and was approaching four hundred pages of text, Cecil decided that we had enough. Yet for five years I had been lamenting the paucity of research resources for my work!

I missed the deadline for the June 1956 commencement, but nevertheless, we had bound volumes when we left New Haven. Cecil had written a letter certifying the completion of my dissertation and lined up two very friendly readers. One of them, Hajo Holborn, later recommended it to Princeton University Press for publication.

It had taken six years, but the result was a publishable manuscript. Would I have produced such a result under conditions of what is usually called normal progress? Was it worth the years of penury and uncertainty?

I am sure it was not. However, it seemed to me that the process went along at a pace I could manage. I can only hope that the deprivation I caused Ann and the children did not do them lasting harm.

In all other respects, our return to New Haven was very positive. We spent a good deal of time together with the Dunn family, which had doubled in size by the addition of Chris and Jennifer since we lived on Orange Street. St. John's had finally moved to the suburbs, and we found ourselves another Episcopal church. Christmas provided an opportunity for a visit to New York and the inevitable New York City Ballet production of *The Nutcracker*, as well as other ballets at other times.

I made a lot of new professional friends, among both students and visiting faculty. Through the comparative administration seminar, I came into contact with Indiana University again and was invited to give a seminar on French administration. It took almost ten years for these contacts to lead to my return to Indiana University.

What was very satisfying in a different way was my relationship with Cecil Driver. Cecil had acquired a reputation for being arbitrary and vindictive, and he had become isolated from both students and colleagues as he devoted all his spare time to the care of his invalid wife.

Nevertheless, in 1956, being one of the senior members of the department, Cecil was asked to take over as chair. He threw himself into that task, and he broke under the double load of home care and department responsibilities. While he lay unconscious, Mrs. Driver died in a nursing home, and the news had to be broken to him when he recovered.

Almost as if driven by a death wish, Cecil insisted on coming back to work and resuming a full teaching load. Senior people in the department then decided that one of Cecil's recent students should be recruited as a visitor and be ready to take over his classes should he overtax himself again. Bill Livingston came from Texas in that capacity for the 1957-1958 academic year, and again Cecil was struck down but recovered and insisted on resuming his regular routine.

In the fall of 1957, Robert Dahl, who had assumed the chair, called me with an invitation similar to Bill Livingston's and for the 1958-1959 academic year. When I asked around the dinner table, "Who's in favor of another year in New Haven?" there were "Yeas" all around. Thus in the fall of 1958, we returned to New Haven for our third, and as it turned out, our last stay.

New Haven (1958–1959)

I suppose that my own pleasure in being asked to return to Yale as a faculty member might have been diminished by the knowledge that both Bill Livingston and I were sort of pinch hitters. Yet as long as Cecil insisted on returning to a full teaching load, it was only prudent for the department to have people on the spot who could take over his duties on short notice. Of course, I was pleased to have been asked, and I considered the invitation an important step in my academic career.

Accepting the invitation was made easy because the rest of the family was obviously delighted at the prospect of another year in what we thought of as an exciting, stimulating environment.

Alice, having been in kindergarten in Gainesville, took first grade in New Haven in stride. However, having grown up in the predominantly Protestant south, it came as a surprise to her when she was one of only two in her class who appeared in school on the Jewish high holidays. She was provided with further insight by our next-door neighbor, the young rabbi who presided over the New Haven Hebrew day school.

Steve was in junior high, and although he was never explicit about it, he found himself among a non-Italian minority. Yet I do not remember that he expressed any regrets about the New Haven year. There were enough compensatory pleasures.

As I have mentioned, Cecil's relations with his graduate students had deteriorated. His grading had become arbitrary, and he had fallings-out with some of those writing dissertations under his direction.

By contrast, our weeks together before his death in mid-October were placid and comfortable. We took long walks in East Rock Park, we talked about a range of common interests, and he continued to take an interest in Steve's reading choices. At one time, he had criticized Ann for reading to Steve from the works of Sir Walter Scott, which he referred to as Scottish propaganda.

At the height of the fall colors, we decided to take a day trip into northwest Connecticut, Litchfield, Sharon, and so forth. I invited Cecil to come with us, knowing that he had spent summers in Sharon with Mrs. Driver.

At first he readily agreed, but on the Saturday before the departure, he called and begged off, saying that the recollection of times and places he had spent with Mrs. Driver would be too painful. I tried some gentle persuasion but was unsuccessful.

Late the following Monday morning, Bob Dahl called me. Cecil's housekeeper had come in that morning and found him dead. He had died during the weekend.

Cecil had, as usual, been carrying a full teaching load: the graduate seminar and the introductory comparative politics lecture course that filled the big auditorium in Strathcona Hall every time his name appeared in the schedule of courses. He would receive standing ovations after some of his lectures.

By contrast, the *Yale Daily News* dismissed the rest of the department as a bunch of "non teachers." Cecil clearly did not use his classes to flog narrow research interests. I suppose Cecil Driver has been the model I have followed in many respects, including being a demanding critic of the written word.

There is a most wonderful example of Cecil's dramatic presentations that I did not witness personally but I heard several accounts of. It begins with his personal acquaintance with Aleksandr Kerensky, who lived out his life in New York City.

Apparently there was an arrangement that Kerensky would travel to New Haven to lecture to Cecil's class when the syllabus called for a presentation on the Russian Revolution in the context of a unit on Soviet government. I have direct proof of that arrangement in the form of a handwritten note from Kerensky to Cecil confirming it. The note was among Cecil's papers, which the department asked me to sort out after his death.

On the appointed day, Cecil would open the class and begin his lecture on the Russian Revolution. He would set the stage for the scene in the Winter Palace and then say dramatically, "At this point, Aleksandr Kerensky walked in." With these words, Kerensky, who had been standing in the wings of the Strathcona Auditorium stage, would walk onto the stage and share with the class his personal recollections of these dramatic events.

Researchers in the profession never tire of pointing out that nothing remains of the work of *teachers*, whereas the product of *researchers* resonates through generations as others build on it. I tended not to question this assertion until I had occasion to check the ages of citations in an Indiana University dissertation in the field of American politics. The average age of journal citations was five years, and of books ten years.

In my own teaching-oriented career, I have carried forward the values and the influence of John Stoner, Cecil Driver, and Manning Dauer. In turn, I hear from my students that their own teaching has reflected my work with them. So then, perhaps the half-life of a teacher's influence far exceeds that of a researcher. That is why the book that embodied my dissertation was dedicated to Cecil Driver.

After Cecil Driver's death, Dahl indicated that the department would bring in R. T. McKenzie, a British visitor at Harvard, for Cecil's British politics seminar in the first semester and that I would continue that seminar in the second semester. As for Cecil's lecture course, the introductory comparative politics course with its huge enrollment, Dahl offered to cancel the course for a week to give me time to prepare. I told him that I could do without the hiatus, that I only needed to be in touch with Cecil's grader to find my place in what was really a familiar course to me.

Considering that no class I had taught before this time had numbered over fifty, this might well have seemed a daring if not foolhardy move. The class discovered quickly that I was no Cecil Driver (though I believe that today, I might have brought it off better than I did in 1958). The students surely missed Cecil, yet they took my lecturing good-naturedly and even applauded politely at the end of the semester. But there were no standing ovations.

During that academic year, Princeton University Press accepted my dissertation manuscript. It is a testimony to Cecil's editorial guidance that except for asking me to abridge the two background chapters, they imposed no further revision demands.

My lecture on the French bureaucracy at Indiana University appeared as a chapter in a book edited by Bill Siffin, and another version of it made it to Britain into the pages of *Political Studies*. I also completed a major book review essay for *Public Administration Review*, which won a prize and earned me the long-lasting friendship of the *PAR* editor, Dwight Waldo.

Now finally I could with good conscience devote my energies to the comparative study of public administration and public policy. Since the University of Florida lacked a sabbatical leave system, the year in New Haven had been second best. It was a change of scenery and a new set of intellectual stimuli. We returned to Gainesville and invested considerable resources in remodeling and air-conditioning our house, only to leave it all the following year when we moved to Haverford College, the penultimate station in my academic wanderings.

Chapter 12

Haverford

(1960-1966)

The balance for the Haverford move must be considered positive: we all gained from those years in a variety of ways. However, the move itself was surrounded by various difficulties of sufficient magnitude for Ann to lay down the dictum, "We will not move again unless I see the place *before* we make the final decision."

The Main Line and Haverford College

The difficulties started with the sale of our Gainesville house, which coincided with a downturn in the housing market. In a university town, this is usually a reflection of a tight university budget and few new hires. We had just invested heavily, for us, in renovation and air-conditioning. However, the sale price we eventually obtained did not reflect these improvements, and the sale was not finalized until Christmas.

Even before we left Gainesville, we lived with the stress that is created by living in a house that is on the market. The tension lasted all summer and was not at all conducive to family harmony.

As well, we were uncertain about where we would be living once we got to Haverford. The college had created a setting in which the faculty resided on or near campus along with the students. Since the assignment of faculty to college housing was based on seniority, we could not be assured which unit we would get until the other faculty members had indicated their preferences.

Eventually we were assigned a house a short distance from the campus. The house needed repairs, but when we arrived, the work had not yet been completed. The windows did not even have windowpanes.

From our house, we could look out on the Merion Cricket Club, founded in 1856, and the Haverford Station of the Pennsylvania Railroad's Main Line. The college prided itself on providing subsidized housing, a necessity if faculty were to be able to afford to live in the midst of the Philadelphia Main Line. Later we found out that the cheapest house near the college sold for ten times my annual salary. The rent we paid the college was less than $100 per month, and the college provided all repairs and maintenance.

One could say that the Quakers ran a small welfare state for the faculty. For the first time, we had employer-provided health care. Two GPs were available for office visits and even house calls for all family members, and the college acted as self-insurer for all other medical expenses. One could also get interest-free loans for big-ticket purchases and could order them through the college at considerable discounts.

Obstacles and adjustments

While we were en route to Haverford, a temporary disaster struck. We were driving along the Blue Ridge Highway when the car started backfiring. After much agony, we were able to coast into the nearest town. Because it was Sunday, we had to wait until the next morning for the local Ford service people to look at it. They could not fix it on short notice, so they suggested that we trade it in if we needed to get to Haverford no later than the moving van. We did so and arrived in Haverford just as the moving van was pulling into our driveway.

Schooling for Steve and Alice constituted yet another major obstacle. Steve was entering his junior year in high school, and Alice the third grade. We proceeded on the assumption that Alice's adjustment would be the easier one and became rather preoccupied with choosing a school for Steve. The chair of my department at Haverford sent us a list of day schools, but only one, Episcopal Academy, was at all welcoming; it even offered some tuition relief. So we arranged for Steve to enter Episcopal Academy in the fall.

At the beginning of the summer, Episcopal Academy sent us a reading list for Steve's English class. We misinterpreted it to mean that all of the several dozen great books (Beowulf to Hardy) should be read during the summer. In the fall, while his classmates reported reading one or two books on the list, Steve nonplussed everyone with his response.

Episcopal Academy turned out to be a good choice. Classes were small, and most teachers had advanced degrees. Steve made the editorial board of the school paper and found a sport in which he could make at least the JV team, soccer.

Steve's strong record at Episcopal Academy eventually won him financial support from Trinity College. Since Haverford had a tuition support program for Haverford faculty children, we did not find Steve's four years of college to be a great financial burden.

By contrast Alice had a most difficult time. She had grown up in a setting where many children lived nearby, where they played in each other's houses, and where the climate made outdoor play possible most of the year. Now, to play with other children required advanced consultation and transportation. Life on the Main Line was very different in many ways.

Still another difficulty was finding a church. We were invited to church by some friends from our earliest Bloomington days who were now connected with Villanova University, but their church did not satisfy us. Why we finally settled on the Church of the Redeemer, one of the wealthiest churches in the area, I cannot say.

In good part, we felt comfortable because the service was decidedly Low Church, as it had been at Holy Trinity in Gainesville. Much of the credit must go to the rector, Reverend Thorne Sparkman, a conservative South Carolinian whom we came to know and respect as a churchman, even though we must surely have disagreed on social policy. I guess we carefully separated church and state.

Before long, Ann was in charge of the Sunday school for those five years of age and under. Thorne Sparkman asked me to be the superintendent of the entire Sunday school, which was a sizable enterprise housed in a well-equipped building. I declined, primarily because of the time demands the job would entail. However, Ann and I worked with the Main Line church school association, and I served on a major diocesan commission under a liberal bishop who subsequently participated in the first (unauthorized) ordination of women to the priesthood.

I point all this out because in most other ways, the Main Line was not a hospitable place, particularly for families with as small an income as ours. We could not even afford the annual membership dues at the Main Line YMCA!

Haverford College

Haverford is not only the oldest Quaker college in the United States, it is also the most Quakerish (at least it was in the early sixties). Students were required to attend Fifth Day (Thursday) meeting. This seemed a truly radical demand to me, given that Haverford Meeting was silent. It was a lot to ask of eighteen-year-olds to sit quietly for an hour and contemplate the condition of their inner selves. I attended occasionally and found it a most troubling experience.

Haverford is not only a Quaker college, but a Philadelphia Quaker college. Thus when Gilbert White was appointed its president in 1948, at the age of twenty-eight, it created something of a scandal. White was indeed a Quaker, but not a Philadelphia Quaker. Under his leadership, students and faculty were recruited nationally and at such a rate that in 1960 when I arrived, no more than ten percent of the student body were birthright Quakers.

The Haverford ethos and pattern of living focused on campus life. (I began to refer to Haverford as a kibbutz, having just read Bruno Bettelheim's *Children of the Dream*.) The lives of most faculty centered on the campus, where most of them lived, and on the students, a bright and mostly bookish lot.

Some of the students opposed the war in Vietnam and took up the cause early on. They formed an organization that collected funds to buy medical supplies for the Viet Cong. Their leaders traveled up and down the East Coast, spreading their gospel and showing a film that purported to portray the life of the Viet Cong and their resistance to American militarism. Experts on Southeast Asia who examined this documentary pointed out that part of it was filmed in studios in Prague and the rest was from pirated newsreels.

At Haverford, opposition to the Vietnam War sprang from a dual source—the Quaker principle of pacifism and the left's anti-war radicalism. In this milieu, Ann and I found ourselves pushed from the left, where we had been at Florida, to the center-right at Haverford (but we managed to shuffle back to our old stance once we returned to the heartland).

Gilbert White's objective had been to make Haverford a national school of high scholastic standing, and he succeeded brilliantly in that effort. Haverford's freshmen had nationally competitive SAT scores. Its senior classes won the highest percentage of Woodrow Wilson fellowships during the sixties, and virtually every senior indicated plans to enter graduate or professional school.

The faculty that Gilbert White recruited began to leaven the Quaker-Penn PhD nature of the instructional staff. The epitome of this new kind of faculty was Herman M. Somers, Red Somers (his hair, not his politics), who was in and out of Washington, dabbled in public policy, and left for Princeton's Woodrow Wilson School in 1963. Somers was convinced that Haverford needed an infusion of people who were not Quakers, not student-oriented, and did not make the campus the center of their lives.

In 1959 when Haverford's three-person Political Science Department lost John Roche and his acid wit to Tufts, Red decided that I should be his replacement. Gerald Freund, the third man in the department, was opposed to my coming, but he was aiming to be Haverford's next president, and when he was not chosen to succeed Gilbert White, he left Haverford.

In 1958 Gilbert White had announced that after ten years, he had done all he could do for Haverford and wanted to return to geography. He did so and subsequently fathered the Mekong River Delta plan for the American Friends Service Committee. White's successor and Haverford's next president was Hugh Borton, a Philadelphia Quaker, thus confirming the laws of managerial succession: after years of innovation, a community usually wants peace and quiet. Hugh Borton was eminently qualified to meet this pretended need.

As a result of these events (of which I was ignorant at the time), the three-person Political Science Department was down to one person: the chair, Red Somers. At Haverford, every faculty vacancy receives faculty attention across the college. In a faculty as small as Haverford's (about eighty), the addition of even one new member constitutes a significant decision for the college as a whole. I believe there was strong opposition to my appointment, but I suspect that Red, a congenial operator and shmoozer, talked them around in my favor. He then also recruited Harvey Glickman from Princeton.

Not long after we arrived, late in the summer of 1960, Red informed us that he would be on leave during 1960-1961, and that he had hired various visitors from the area to take his place, that is to say, make up the third person in our department. That move brought us Paul Mishkin, a very interesting public law person from the University of Pennsylvania; John Logue from Villanova, a near-contemporary of mine from Yale; and best of all, Peter Bachrach from Bryn Mawr, a political radical with a sweet disposition and endless taste for talking politics and political theory.

Harvey and I were flabbergasted to be left leaderless in such a fashion just after our arrival. However, our dismay was nothing compared to the discomfort of the senior year political science majors, who were confronted with a set of strangers in their major field just a year before graduation. Harvey and I tried to comfort and reassure them, but I gathered from later conversations with a member of that group that we did not completely succeed.

I believe that Harvey made a better adjustment to Haverford than I did. He must have, for he is still there, truly an elder states-man by now, with the current Haverford president having been one of his students in the late sixties. I adjusted less well, if by judging only from the number of years that elapsed before I left. The class of 1961 put it very well in their yearbook, which poked fun at Red Somers by likening him to a travel agent who kept rail-roads busy shuffling people back and forth across the country and in and out of Haverford.

About me they said, "He gives brilliant lectures to small class-es." I was not a successful teacher at Haverford, but I never lost my devotion to that enterprise. I clearly did not get off to an aus-picious start. My intellectual interests were not in harmony with the intellectual universe of the college.

I never had the extensive literary and philosophical interests that are the common coin of bright undergraduates and their teachers. Even when it came to political philosophy, my questions were always directed at how the philosophy impinged on human institutions rather than at the quality and direction of the philo-sophical argument itself.

My liberal arts education

I am grateful to Haverford for providing me with the sort of genuine liberal arts education that I largely bypassed en route to my AB at Indiana University. This came about through two related Haverford institutions.

The first was the faculty lounge, a good-sized room furnished with early nineteenth-century furniture, where the college provided a full coffee urn both mornings and afternoons. In the course of any morning, just about all eighty faculty members would drift through for a chat. There was little said on current affairs. Most of the discussion centered on what people were reading or on exciting developments in their disciplines that occupied their minds.

The talk ranged from biochemistry to particle physics to *The Catcher in the Rye*. Thus one of the advantages of frequenting the faculty lounge was that one could be spared the task of reading any current bestseller. That is why I never read *Catcher*. It would have been anticlimactic after having heard it dissected in the faculty lounge.

The other institution was the Phillips Visitors Fund for Scientists and Statesmen. As a bequest from an alumnus, a lawyer from Philadelphia, a sizable sum was left to the college, half of the income to go for library acquisitions, the other half to be used to invite scientists and statesmen to the college. The college had fitted out two suites for visitors, and the faculty could recommend suitable candidates. Both faculty and students profited greatly from the stream of truly outstanding figures in the worlds of learning and public affairs.

The link between these two Haverford institutions was this. Because the Phillips honoraria were very generous, we could ask visitors to stay for a week or longer, and during these stays, morning visits to the faculty lounge were part of the routine. Thus a parade of visitors in the faculty lounge provided countless opportunities for extended conversations that would have been impossible in any other setting.

Surely this was a most unorthodox format for catching up on my misspent youth, but it was an enjoyable and effective one. In the faculty lounge, I came to appreciate not only the visitors, but my colleagues and the liberal arts enterprise as a whole. If I became a much more successful teacher after my Haverford years, I should be grateful to Haverford for having helped me become a more well-rounded person and intellect.

The CAG seminars

During the Haverford years, I became deeply engaged in a research enterprise that neatly complemented my years at a liberal arts college where there was only one other full-time political scientist. In 1955-1956 when I was at Yale, I had sat in on a seminar codirected by Fred Riggs, then a visiting professor. In 1960 Fred, who had moved to Indiana University, took steps to secure funding from the Ford Foundation for a multi-year research enterprise in comparative administration. Thus the Comparative Administration Group (CAG) was formed.

Fred asked me to serve on the CAG executive committee and kept me on even after Ford required him to focus the proposed research on problems of administration and development and thus, supposedly, exclude Europe. The heart of CAG was a series of six research seminars, two each summer for three years (1963, 1964, and 1965), to be held in various university locations around the country. Each seminar was to consist of six to eight scholars who would be joined by senior graduate students serving as research assistants.

I was the only member of the CAG core group who was invited to a seminar in each of the three summers—the invitation coming from the individual director of the seminars. These were the seminars at Indiana University, the University of Michigan, and the University of California at Berkeley, directed by Fred Riggs, Ferrel Heady, and Dwight Waldo respectively. I consider the timing of the CAG seminars and my participation in them so fortunate because they provided me with ample opportunity for scholarly communication at a time when my work and location at Haverford provided so little of it.

Each seminar lasted eight weeks. The scholars were committed to delivering a paper for discussion in sessions that included the graduate students. As always happens, some contributors were on schedule, but many were not. I prided myself on completing my paper in time to hand to the director at the end of the seminar. Each paper was subsequently published.

I am not the person and this is not the place for a postmortem of the work of CAG. That task has been done, and most critics have not spared the rod. Even in the sixties, most of us were still filled with enlightenment ideas of development and modernization. If none of these ideas has worked in the third world, not much else has done any better. Even a casual glance at the former Yugoslavia and the former USSR suggests that hardly anything works anywhere.

However, I have no doubt that it was my work with CAG rather than my earlier connection that played a role in my eventual return to Indiana University. The formal invitation was not extended to me until after Byrum Carter had been designated departmental chair in 1966. Thus it seems to have been Byrum's estimate of my total career and my broader interests in political theory that turned the decision in my favor.

I derived other benefits as well from my involvement with CAG. When a German academic contacted CAG and asked about scholars interested in Europe, he was referred to me. As a result, Roman Schnur, then the director of the Institute for Political Science at the newly founded Ruhr-Universität Bochum, established contact with me. Before long he offered me a tenured professorship *(Lehrstuhl)* at Bochum. That was clearly out of the question, but we did reach an agreement that made me change my plans for my 1966-1967 sabbatical year.

Another benefit was derived from an inquiry to CAG from Blanche Blank, a specialist in American public administration, then at Hunter College. Blanche was surely the most elegant political scientist I ever met, and she was a highly intelligent and wonderful human being. She had some ideas about measuring administrative performance that she wanted to test out in Europe. She obtained a grant from the National Science Foundation to do so, and I became her senior investigator in France, Spain, and Germany.

Blanche became badly disoriented, as any born and bred New Yorker would be, when we moved to Indiana. Fortunately she recovered sufficiently to come to Bloomington. She was happily surprised by what she found, especially an exhibit of George Rickey's work at the Indiana University Art Gallery.

Still another benefit resulted when Jim Fesler and I managed to coax funding from CAG for a set of European activities (this followed some lengthy colloquies concerning the legitimacy of the enterprise under CAG's terms of reference). These activities brought me in touch with the then-younger generation of researchers in public administration and public policy: Michel Crozier, Brian Chapman, Renate Mayntz, Fritz Scharpf, and others.

It was a truly exciting period for me. Along with many others, I profited from Fred Riggs' intellectual drive and entrepreneurship, which seems to continue unabated in him while many of us have fallen by the wayside.

APSA seminars

There was still another set of activities that helped me to remain in contact with the political science discipline and to earn considerable professional visibility: the regional seminars organized by the American Political Science Association (APSA) in the early sixties. These were weeklong seminars for political scientists teaching in liberal arts colleges and lower-level graduate institutions (MA and MPA degree-granting).

These seminars presented leading scholars in the various fields of the discipline. Their objective was to help their audience become familiar with new and important developments and thus strengthen their teaching by keeping them in touch with the constantly changing shape of the discipline.

Comparative politics was one of the topics scheduled for presentation in the APSA seminars. The first seminar was scheduled for Syracuse University, and Carl J. Friedrich of Harvard was to make the presentation. Friedrich reneged at a very late date, and I was asked to take his place on short notice.

I have never found out how I was selected as a worthy replacement. I accepted the invitation without hesitation. Apparently, I made a very successful presentation, because I was scheduled as the regular comparative politics resource person for the remaining three seminars, in each of which I made an equally successful presentation.

Howard Penniman, the organizer of the APSA seminars, decided that his department at Georgetown should not miss my performance, so late in November 1963 (a week after Kennedy's assassination), we went to Washington to fill that engagement. For many years thereafter, colleagues would stop me at national meetings and speak in a most laudatory way about my presentation.

I feel particularly proud of this performance, because it reassured me that my being at Haverford had not diminished my professional skills in the field of comparative politics.

Perhaps the early sixties was the last time it was still possible to be a comparative politics generalist without limitations as to geographic area and research methodology. Ten years later, that would no longer have been possible.

The elusive vacation

In all our years in Florida, we never had a vacation. Actually, one could say that apart from three sabbatical leaves, we did not have vacations until after I retired. At the University of Florida, the standard contract was a 12-month arrangement in which we taught year-round for two years and had the summer off in the third year with paychecks continuing throughout.

One such summer, 1953, we spent in Florida while I worked on my dissertation. The summer of 1956 was spent in New Haven completing the dissertation. Then it was back to summer teaching until we returned to New Haven where we spent the summer without teaching duties but also without any funds that would make a vacation possible.

When we moved to Haverford in 1960, I had for the first time a 9/10-months contract and schedule. However, early that fall, I had a call from Columbia University asking me to teach in its summer program. So for 1961, our summer vacation consisted of my teaching at Columbia, while Ann and the children spent time in Indiana. For Steve, any place but Uncle Glenn's farm was unthinkable in any case.

The summer of 1962 we spent as a family in residence in Haverford, while I did my communal tour of duty as the president of the Haverford Swim Club, worrying about pH levels, municipal certificates, and pumps breaking down during the summer's only heat wave. Alice lived at the pool and fussed at me when the pool remained closed because the air temperature was below 70°F. As president of the pool, she argued, I ought to be able to do something about it.

It was in the summer of 1963 that Steve (who had graduated from Episcopal Academy and spent his first year at Trinity College, Hartford) began to work for Guy Davenport, then an assistant professor at Haverford on a term appointment. Guy is one of the few persons who may rightly be termed a polymath. He was a Rhodes scholar, a Harvard PhD with a dissertation on Ezra Pound. He published the first English translations of some of the earliest Greek poetry and illustrated the work with his own pen and ink sketches. He wrote literary essays for the *National Review,* had a steady output of novels and literary studies, and served on the country's principal literary juries.

Steve had met Guy in our home, and he came to take Guy as a role model in things great and small, things I approved of or did not mind, and things I minded but could not do much about, such as Steve absorbing views of the *National Review.* A small but highly visible Davenportiana concerns the dramatic change in Steve's handwriting, which was as atrocious as that of most of his contemporaries until influenced by Guy, an accomplished calligrapher. As well, I am fairly certain that Guy provided a goodly amount of sexual initiation, something in which I had been deficient. At least some of Uncle Guy's friendly advice was not what I would have wished. But I really cannot complain: I did not provide an alternative.

Much more important was Guy's contribution to Steve's intellectual maturation, the extended range of his literary, artistic, and musical tastes and understanding. During the summer of 1963, Steve worked as Guy's assistant in Haverford, and the following summer, Steve chauffeured Guy around Europe. The highlight of that tour was a visit with Ezra Pound and Steve's going for a swim in the Mediterranean Sea with Pound. We are greatly in debt to Guy Davenport for helping our teenager establish a foothold in his manhood. Guy did better than we could have done, but then parents are not always the most effective change agents in this process.

Perhaps it is worth noting one of the more memorable contributions I was able to make to Steve's education. In his first year at Trinity College, Steve took a required history survey course, which was presented to the students in successive lectures that examined major turning points in history from contrasting perspectives.

Steve was quite enthusiastic about the course. One evening during final exam week, our telephone rang. It was Steve calling from Hartford while reviewing for his history exam. They had been presented with a pair of lectures on the Spanish Civil War, one from the Loyalist perspective and one from the Franco.

Steve, in preparing for the exam and anxious to give the right answer, asked me, "Daddy, in the Spanish Civil War, who was right?" It was comforting to know that Daddy was still considered a competent resource in some matters!

Still in pursuit of the elusive vacation, I devoted the summers of 1963, 1964, and 1965 to CAG seminars. These seminars provided a change of scenery all around, if not real vacations. During the summer of 1963, when Steve was occupied with Guy, Alice spent time at a family camp on Cape Breton Island and Ann joined me in Bloomington for the CAG seminar.

There we lived in an apartment in Campus View House, which looked down on the Hoosier Courts complex, where we had once lived, and which was continuing to serve impoverished graduate student families. (It was still in use in 1967 when I joined the faculty.) I certainly enjoyed the CAG seminar, but whether it qualified as a vacation, I doubt very much. But we did see a memorable outdoor performance of *Aïda*, mounted in the old football stadium, now the Arboretum.

In the summer of 1964, while I was occupied with a CAG seminar at the University of Michigan, Ann spent her time in Ann Arbor with me, as well as in Gulfport and Indiana. The CAG summer seminar in 1965 took us to Berkeley, where we were all together as a family.

There we were visited endlessly by friends and relations, including a nephew from the Alameda Naval Station and Susan Tilley, our former Gainesville neighbor. It certainly was not a vacation for Ann, who had to cook for six people or more every day on a not very generous budget, but then the budget was never generous in those days.

The summer of 1966 we were busy preparing for a year in Europe. The summer of 1967 we spent in Europe. On returning, we packed and moved to Bloomington. From then on, I either taught summer school because we needed the money, or I was on a 12-month appointment as an administrator.

During the seventies and eighties, Ann began to accompany me to professional meetings, especially in cities with museums. As our friends and family began to recognize that pattern, they said pointedly that the only time "poor Ann" gets to travel is when Freddy goes somewhere on business and she can go along.

Thus when we announced on my retirement that we would spend some time in the Bahamas during the coldest part of the year, everyone exclaimed that for the first time Ann gets to go to a place where Freddy does not have any academic business to transact.

Chapter 13

Europe

(1966-1967)

There is a story in the Hebrew Bible of a young man who was required to labor for many long years to gain the hand of his beloved. My academic career featured just such an extended servitude with regard to sabbatical leaves. After ten years at the University of Florida, I was still without a sabbatical leave and a full year's respite from my academic labors. Yet when I raised this issue in my negotiations with Haverford, I was told firmly by President Borton that I would have to labor six more years for my first sabbatical leave. That caused me to have much sympathy for the young man of the Bible story.

In 1966 the time finally came for my first sabbatical leave. Having been deeply involved in the work of CAG (the Comparative Administration Group) for so many years, I wanted to refocus my attention on Europe and especially on France. So I applied for Fulbright grants to spend a year in Paris. Ann would come with me, her missing birth certificate notwithstanding.

Planning my sabbatical leave

Steve was graduating from Trinity College in 1966 and was leaning toward graduate study in classical archaeology. His mentor at Trinity, a classicist, insisted that because of his late start in the field, he should do a post-AB year to strengthen his command of Greek. He recommended that Steve work with a renowned Homeric Scholar at Trinity College in Dublin. This was a good move financially, for it was then still cheaper to live and study in Dublin than anywhere in the United States. Besides, that would put us all in Europe for the year.

Under our original plan, Alice would live with us in Paris and attend an appropriate state school. We arranged for a Haverford student to tutor her in French, but she did not take her tutorials seriously, so she arrived in France understanding little and speaking less of the country's language.

Our plans changed when Roman Schnur asked me to teach in Bochum for a semester. I would be paid by the German university for the first half of my leave and draw on my sabbatical pay for the second half, which we would spend in Paris as planned.

When Ann suggested all this to Alice and pointed out how exciting it would be to go to a German school for one semester and to a French school for another, Alice rebelled. Her principal concern was completing ninth grade work while in Europe, so that she could move on to senior high with her junior high friends when we returned to the States. Given her priorities, this was a most rational position.

Our inquiries into private schools in Europe soon told us that such schools must cater only to the offspring of oil sheiks or GM executives. Fortunately the curate at the Church of the Redeemer and others told us about Le Collège Cévenol, an international boarding school operated by a group of Huguenot ministers with help from the National Council of Churches and the American Friends Service Committee.

We were warned that after Cévenol, Alice would likely refuse to see the inside of any church for years to come—what with twice weekly required church attendance and hour-long sermons in French. Nevertheless, Cévenol was affordable, so we registered Alice for both a summer session and the full school year.

Le Collège Cévenol

I traveled to Paris with Alice at the beginning of the summer and delivered her to Cévenol for the summer session, which turned out to be an extended slumber party, as far as we could determine. Alice's year at Cévenol was not without upsets. To begin with, in the institutional culture of Cévenol, ninth graders were treated as children who had to be in their dormitories, not just on the school grounds, by 9:00 p.m., not exactly what American junior high cohorts would accept without protest.

Then in the spring we got a note from the school telling us to remove Alice from the school. We drove there in considerable anxiety, but we were able to settle the matter by having her move in with another American student who lived in the village. Apparently the trouble was entirely with the dormitory housemother, a veritable dragon, we all agreed.

Fortunately Alice did well in all her classes, in spite of the original language handicap (though she admitted that it was almost Christmas before she fully understood what was going on in class). She totally nonplussed her history teacher by volunteering to do a paper based on her research in the school library. On the other hand, it took her a while to figure out the rules under which the neatness of one's notebooks determined part of one's grade.

Alice went to Cévenol a pudgy, insecure junior high girl and came away a trim, self-assured young woman who spoke French fluently. She was so self-assured, in fact, that living with her became increasingly difficult. Alice's transformation was assisted when she and Ann had some clothes tailor-made in Paris. I suspect that Alice was not blind to the attention she attracted.

My return to Vienna

After Ann arrived by boat, bringing our trunks, and in between Alice's summer session and our fall semester obligations, we did some sightseeing. I drew up a schedule, which included a week in England and two weeks in Vienna—my first return since 1939.

The tour was marred by some slipups in our schedule, as well as by Alice's determination to wash and set her hair every day, using a big bag of rollers that traveled everywhere with us. She was also totally uninterested in any sights, historical or otherwise. A genuine teenage pain!

Vienna in 1966 had not yet attained the glitter and prosperity that one sees reflected in more recent images. Considerable drabness still remained from prewar depression days and war damage. Although the *Anschluss* of 1938 was nullified politically and internationally, such was not the case with the economic incorporation of Austria into the German economy. Thus the Austrian schilling has become as hard a currency as the DM, and Vienna has become one of the most expensive cities in the world.

Returning as I was, the city was still familiar to me in a way that astounded Ann. (Alice was still preoccupied with her rollers.) For instance, public transportation functioned much as I had left it, except that in the inner city, everything was dug up for the subway. There was much I could show Ann, and I did, including the "ancestral" home in Brunnengasse 45.

More troubling than the physical or economic dimensions of Vienna were its human dimensions. The Viennese struck me as quite unchanged. They were still essentially a people of *Raunzer* (whiners or complainers). To make things worse, the older genera- tion had decided that they had been unwilling victims of the Third Reich. So whereas I had the good fortune to have been able to leave, they had to stay behind and suffer untold hardships!

I expected that at any moment, they would suggest that those who had been forced out should pay reparations to the unfortu- nate ones who had remained! No wonder Ann felt that I was tense and on edge during our entire visit. However, we returned to Vi- enna once more, in 1974, and during this second visit, I managed to take it all in stride.

Bochum and RUB

We spent the fall semester at Bochum and its brand-new uni- versity, then in its second year in operation. The conditions in German universities have been the subject of extended political debate and institutional reform, to which I can add little that would be original. But it should be remembered that my time at the Ruhr-Universität Bochum (RUB) predated the great reform and upheaval period of the late sixties and seventies.

Although Roman Schnur claimed to be an innovator in the field of public administration, I found that he was really a traditional, law-trained and historically-oriented, administrative law scholar. He was also a political conservative, as were most of the faculty members who were recruited as the founding cadre of institute directors.

The university had been conceived and started while the land Nord Rhein Westfalen was under CDU (Christian Democratic Union) political control. The founding Rektor, chosen by the CDU education minister, had to resign shortly after his designation when the full story of his Third Reich record became public.

What disturbed me most was the unchanged nature of the university's power-authority structure. Thirty-five-year-old PhDs working for *Habilitation* (tenure) were simply assistants. They were treated worse than any first-year graduate student in the United States.

Some of that changed in later years, but at Bochum in 1966, I could still witness a scene where two such assistants, both published professionals, fought over who should hold my coat. And when I refused to have the assistant assigned to me carry my notes to class and walk deferentially behind me en route to class, he was reprimanded by a senior faculty for his insubordination.

The rain and fog of northwestern Germany made the physical setting of RUB even more depressing. In 1966-1967 the university consisted of two ten-story high-rise buildings that housed both offices and classrooms. The buildings were identical in every respect, and there were another dozen in various stages of construction, all from the same cookie cutter. Each floor had a hallway running the length of the building, giving the mixed effect of a Holiday Inn or the Queen Mary. At times when I walked the length of these central corridors, I felt as though seasickness was about to overtake me.

The university was located on terrain sloping down to the Ruhr River. Most of the time it was foggy, a combination of the weather and the coal-steel smog hanging permanently over Bochum. In the fog, the dozen or so buildings completed or under construction looked like so many battleships lined up on the high seas!

An interesting aspect of my teaching at RUB was that although hardly anyone signed up for my lecture course on American public administration, I had a full room for my seminar on administration and development. Most of the students were foreigners sent by their governments to study at RUB's Institute for Development Studies. I had a good relationship with that group, chiefly because neither they nor I were constrained by the formalism in German universities. This formalism was of the sort that Roman Schnur and I remained at the formal *Sie* level of address during all that time, and Schnur always addressed his wife as Frau Schnur.

The CAG conference

Early in the fall of 1966, there was a conference on comparative administration organized by the Europe committee of the CAG, which was chaired by Jim Fesler and Roman Schnur. This conference brought a sizable delegation from the United States (Jim Fesler, Fred Riggs, Blanche Blank, and Ed Bock) together with German and other European participants.

We started out with sessions in a charming Westfalian village, proceeded to Heidelberg for additional meetings, and ended up at the Hochschule für Verwaltungswissenschaft at Speyer. There our host was F. M. Marx, who had returned to Germany after a successful career in public administration in the United States.

This CAG meeting set in motion quite a bit of cross-Atlantic activity that continued into my Indiana years. If it did not bear better fruit in later years, I fear that the blame lies with me. I became so deeply involved in departmental work and graduate student supervision that I did not carry out the follow-up required to keep the enterprise alive and flourishing.

Christmas in Paris and Bochum

Ann and I planned to meet Steve and Alice in Paris, and then for our family to spend Christmas in Bochum. Ann went with me to Paris, where I attended a working meeting of the CAG Europe committee (Schnur, Crozier, Chapman, and me). Steve had already arrived there from Dublin and was floating on air after hearing the *Christmas Oratorio* performed the previous night. Alice arrived by train escorted by school personnel, and we sent Steve to the station to meet her.

At the train station, Alice purposely walked past Steve, and he failed to recognize her. As a result, the Cévenol people initially doubted that Steve was her brother, and they did not want to let Alice go with him.

It was no wonder that Steve failed to recognize her. Alice and her classmates had traded clothes, for they wanted her American garments and she their French ones. She had lost a lot of weight, had her hair arranged like her French friends, and wore a trade-in French blue trench coat with the belt tied in the back. Alice had changed enough that her own brother had not recognized her.

We went on to Bochum to celebrate Christmas together, and to the great delight of all of us, we had a Christmas tree with real beeswax candles. One of the most memorable events of the Christmas break was when Steve went to Heidelberg. He traveled the highway along the Rhine, singing Siegfried's Rhine Journey music. He also found what he was looking for in Heidelberg, a Sanskrit dictionary.

Scholarly visits to Dutch and British universities

En route to Paris in early February, we stopped in Amsterdam at the invitation of Henk Brasz, who had been at the CAG conference. This invitation was a prelude to a string of such invitations to British universities during the spring, which were organized through the Fulbright program office.

The Fulbright program paid for my travel and a per diem, and the host institutions were to provide an honorarium. Some did and some did not, but that did not really matter. With this arrangement, Ann could travel with me at little extra expense (travel only). In some places, our hosts offered us the hospitality of their homes: Fernie Ridley in Liverpool, Peter Bromhead in Bristol, and others. We arranged the tour to end with a trip to Dublin to visit Steve and see the Emerald Isle.

Living in Paris

When we arrived in Paris, it was still winter, but most of our stay was during Paris' best season, spring. More than anything else, for me spring was symbolized by the little bouquets of lilies of the valley that I bought for Ann, or by the special candies children received as gifts for their confirmation, which were displayed at the confectioners' stores.

Paris, at any time of the year, means art, but it also means shopping for food in the street markets, where the fresh produce comes from North Africa, the Iberian Peninsula, and France. Language was something of a barrier in shopping, but clashing cultural norms also produced some tense moments.

The most dramatic one was when Ann instructed me to buy a chicken, which came plucked but with feet and head still attached. After all, French cooks made use of all these parts. Ann wanted nothing to do with the extra parts. She asked me to tell the vendor, a tough-looking countrywoman, to remove them. This elicited an angry stream of invective about the wasteful habits of American housewives.

Paris was the climax of our year of art in Europe. It began in Germany when we happened upon the first postwar retrospective of the work of Emil Nolde. This opened to us the world of German abstract expressionism. Because of the Third Reich, and because of the general American preference for French art, German art of any school was pretty much a closed book for Americans, including the two of us.

For me, the formative experience had been a series of visits to the Museum of Modern Art in the summer of 1950. That it did not occur until I was well past thirty is not really surprising, considering that I grew up in a city whose major museum had nothing beyond the period of the Dutch masters whose works had been looted by the Habsburgs when they controlled the Low Countries.

Marital harmony

Art created yet another bond between Ann and me during our stay in Europe in 1966-1967, and then again in 1973-1974, especially painting and sculpture. Up until then, that bond was fragmentary at best, simply because there had been so little opportunity for us to explore it earlier. That was still another consequence of having to wait sixteen years for my first sabbatical leave.

Thus, art was added to our already firmly established bond of music, to our common faith and belief, and to our high degree of consensus and understanding of history, politics, and public affairs. Of course, we did not know then that these bonds would form and unite us to the degree that they have in these past decades.

My academic superiors and my colleagues may say, with some justification, that I failed to use my sabbatical leaves to bring major works to fruition. I concede the validity of that charge. However, my sabbatical leaves did strengthen and refresh me.

They provided me with firsthand views of various political scenes, and thus enabled me to teach and to continue scholarly inquiry in a more sophisticated and effective manner. I was nearly fifty years old before I enjoyed my first sabbatical leave, and sixty-three during my last one. The need for recuperation and refreshment at that age becomes even greater.

When we returned to the United States and prepared to move back to Bloomington, we were approaching our silver wedding anniversary. Steve had finished college and was about to enter graduate school. He was also about to be married and father a child, Gordon, who was born on the day of our silver anniversary, March 18, 1968. Alice, whom we had watched transforming into a young woman, was about to start the last three years of high school.

Thus far in my recollections, I have not confronted the one area of our family life that gave rise to sharp disagreements and loud words between Ann and me.

Although we clearly lived on a meager academic salary, we did not seriously disagree about spending patterns until we moved to Haverford. There my higher salary was swallowed up by the high cost of living in the midst of the Philadelphia Main Line. We had also clearly achieved harmony regarding our ultimate religious faith, although Ann must have recognized my continued skeptical and secularist tendencies.

Our years together also revealed a profound sense of agreement on matters of public policy, including party preference, economic policy, separation of church and state, birth control, abortion, and so forth. Perhaps I did not always fully share the public policy positions of the League of Women Voters, but then neither did Ann. Nevertheless, we both supported the work of the league, which had given Ann great scope for her public policy concerns. We clearly were politics junkies and public policy wonks long before these terms were ever dreamed of.

The one issue that led to repeated clashes between us was how to raise and treat our children. Most of those incidents occurred during our Gainesville and Haverford years. For one, I was quicker than Ann to resort to physical punishment and to loud-voiced scolding and exhortations.

In many instances, Ann considered these actions ill advised, if not totally wrong. She would confront me sharply and demand that I stop, and in some instances, slap me sharply on the face. I would step back from what I was doing, and later on, I would try to argue that she should not humiliate me in front of the child. She would dismiss that by insisting that I deserved "what I got."

It never entered my mind to retaliate physically. My reaction, as I recall, was one of fear that what I had done might estrange

Ann from me, and that I might lose her. This is probably a more coherent statement of what were then rather inchoate feelings.

My central difficulty was that I had no model to guide me. I clearly had not managed to shed European notions of how children are to behave. I should quickly absolve both my father and my mother, neither of whom ever laid hands on me or even threatened me verbally, at least not to my present recollection.

My confusion regarding how to deal with my children was the subject of some often-lighthearted comments by Ann when my colleagues or students would rhapsodize to her about what a kind, supportive colleague and teacher I was. Her response to such praise is best summed up by her comment, "You don't know what he is like at home."

Whatever damage I might have done was more than outweighed by the manner in which Ann put into practice her own conceptions and values. She believes that children should be treated as autonomous human beings with their own peculiar strengths and weaknesses, that commands should be kept at a minimum, and that reasoning and discussion will more likely produce acceptable results than threats and punishments.

I believe that Ann had a quicker and surer grasp than I had of the profound difference in temperament and character of our two children. Thus, she was better able to deal with them than I was.

I suppose it is correct to say that we grew out of this realm of serious disagreement. In later years, we were pretty much as one in deploring the fact that Steve fathered a child just as he was beginning his doctoral studies, and thus would need both sets of grandparents to provide financial assistance on a regular basis. From time to time, I blustered about cutting off the funds, but Ann paid no attention. After all, she wrote the checks.

We were also united in deploring, even more strongly, Alice's monomaniacal search for her roots in Israel, while her Indiana roots were near at hand in Bloomington, though obviously much less romantic.

However, by then I believe that I had internalized Ann's fundamental values about individuals needing to find their own way, accepting or rejecting whatever advice and help we could offer. I certainly treated my colleagues and students according to these precepts. Not having always done so with my children contributed much to the one area of serious disharmony in our marriage.

Chapter 14

Bloomington

(1967-1993)

Moving a family, a household, and a career from one academic institution to another is always difficult and somewhat of a risky venture. In fact it can turn out to be a downright mistaken decision. Our move to Bloomington and Indiana University came at the end of my first sabbatical leave. This meant that we returned to Haverford from Europe only to pack and move as soon as it could all be arranged.

In retrospect, I would have to say that at Haverford, we were less happy and less in harmony with our environment. This was true for us as a family and for me professionally. Nevertheless, my accepting Haverford's invitation opened doors for all four of us that might well not have opened if we had stayed at Florida.

And so, overall, we consider the return to Bloomington our happiest move. We said at that time that it would be our last move, so it had better be good. It was.

How the decision to move came about
Over the years, I have made it a point not to refer to our move to Bloomington as a return. Almost twenty years had elapsed since we had left Bloomington for New Haven. During that time, not only had I completed my terminal degree, but I had also established myself as a teacher and scholar quite independent of my academic origins at Indiana University. If the department wanted me to join, it was not as a prodigal son, but on the basis of my academic record and standing. Yet this is not a totally accurate description of what happened.

In 1966 and 1967 when I conducted discussions with the department, it was still the department of John Stoner, Ed Buehrig, and Byrum Carter. The Comparative Administration Group (CAG), under Fred Riggs' leadership, was headquartered in Bloomington, and its executive secretary, Peter Savage (who had been a member of the Yale seminar I taught in Cecil Driver's place), was on the faculty and became a close friend. Bill Siffin, who had graduated from Indiana University before my time (though his wife, Cathy Fox, was my undergraduate classmate), became another companion during the 1963 CAG seminar in Bloomington.

The department had not, however, followed my career with close attention. I discovered this during 1955-1956 when I audited the comparative administration seminar at Yale co-taught by Sharp, Riggs, and Kaufman.

During those years, Indiana University had extensive contractual technical assistance obligations in Thailand to help create schools of education and public administration among others. It sent teams of faculty to Thailand and received a number of Thai students and government officials to complete advanced degrees in Bloomington.

Walter Laves was the chair of the Department of Government at that time. He had arrived in the early 1950s from his position as undersecretary general of UNESCO, and he had transformed the department into an internationally oriented enterprise with a heavy emphasis on public administration and third world development.

During 1955-1956 the Government Department organized a graduate seminar on administration and development. Since they had generous funding, mostly US government development aid, they invited a series of outside scholars to conduct each weekly seminar. One week was to be devoted to French administration, and Walter Sharp was invited.

Sharp informed the department that he was no longer doing France. (He eventually contributed a seminar paper on Egyptian administration.) He suggested they invite the current leading authority on France, who was at Yale. John Stoner later told me that it was not until I appeared in person that the department realized who that great "authority" was!

From then on, I remained in close touch with the department. During the summer of 1963, Bill Siffin began to sound me out on my interest in returning to Bloomington. At that time, our reluctance to make any move was largely due to Steve's college finances.

Like many private colleges, Haverford provided scholarship aid to faculty children. That amounted to two-thirds of the Haverford tuition or of the tuition for the child's school, whichever was lower. (Faculty children could also attend Haverford tuition-free.) We could not see our way to abandoning this benefit, and Indiana University could not adjust for it since tuition subsidy was then not taxable to the parent.

I have always suspected but have no clear evidence that Walter Laves did not share the regard some of his colleagues had for me and my work. Bill Siffin's efforts did not produce results until 1966 when Walter Laves stepped down as chair and Byrum Carter succeeded him. It was Byrum who invited me to Bloomington to talk in earnest about a move. By that time, Ann and I were talking seriously about leaving Haverford. Not only would Steve complete his AB in 1966, but we felt ready to move and had begun to look at various alternatives.

During my last years at Haverford, my name was submitted to the Michigan department by Ferrel Heady and to the Yale department by Jim Fesler. I had already turned down an offer to chair the department at the University of Oregon, in spite of the urgent pleading of the president, Arthur Fleming. We might have responded favorably to either Yale or Michigan but were not given a chance. Just about then, I was subjected to some high-pressure salesmanship by Duke University.

It seemed to us that we surely did not want to return to the south. Yet I clearly did not have a chance in an Ivy League university, and apart from Michigan, we found none of the other Big Ten schools attractive.

We wanted this to be our last move, and we wanted it to be a good one. In 1966 when I received the invitation to join the department at Indiana University, I told Byrum that I would like some time to sort it all out. During the fall while we were in Germany, I gave him our decision.

So in the end, although I did indeed "return" to Indiana University, I did so as an established member of the profession. I was able to do it in the manner that I have described, because Haverford did not require faculty on sabbatical leave to return for a subsequent payback year.

Nevertheless, there is no doubt that for both Ann and me, the move to Bloomington was in some ways a "return." For her, it reestablished physical proximity to her family, still mostly in Indianapolis and around Columbus. For me, it was a return to a university that now had national standing and whose size and quality made possible a kind of academic life that neither Florida nor Haverford could offer me.

It is not very difficult to make honest judgments about the work of others. I have certainly done so in numerous ways: in class grades, in seminar papers, in qualifying examinations, in journal refereeing, in tenure and promotion decisions, in salary determinations, to name a few. It is much more difficult to be honest about myself and my work, especially during the Indiana years, which comprise, essentially, the second half of my nearly half-century life as a student and faculty member.

I clearly gained a measure of national standing in the organized profession, although not enough to be elected to national office in the principal professional organization, the APSA (American Political Science Association). My curriculum vitae includes a number of refereed articles in journals and a number of chapters in volumes edited by others, but I did not produce a published book after the Austrian Catholics study. In this regard, Indiana University was right in being disappointed in my academic productivity.

Yet I had been one of the last students of Cecil Driver, and very likely, I have carried with me his scorn for "the American PhD machine" and his devotion to teaching and to study in the broadest sense. I learned from sorting his papers that Cecil Driver's summers in Sharon were devoted to preparing his lectures for the coming year.

I felt, quite inchoately, that I had reached a point in my career where I could proceed at my own pace and could devote my energy to those aspects of university work that I found most satisfying. Thus, my scholarly output continued at a steady pace and at a rate I found comfortable when balanced against the responsibilities of teaching, directing graduate work, administration, and other academic service.

Still, it is said that biographers always fall in love with their subjects. Could writers of autobiography be immune to this frailty?

The West European Studies program (WEST)

When I first returned to Indiana University, I did not foresee the extent to which my life would evolve around West European studies, in Bloomington as well as nationally. My formal appointment and budget authority was the Department of Political Science; however, I devoted much of my interest and energy to the West European Studies program (WEST), which was created a short time before my arrival. Later I was given the formal title, Professor of Political Science and West European Studies. For me, the genuinely interdisciplinary intellectual life at Haverford led naturally to the interdisciplinary world of WEST.

Under the leadership of Herman Wells, Indiana University developed a variety of programs that were international in orientation. Beginning in 1960, the Ford Foundation provided sizable financial support for area programs that were interdisciplinary in nature and provided teaching and research resources focused on major world areas. The WEST program was created in 1965 with Ford funding. Its orientation clearly bears the mark of Henry Remak, its first director.

WEST was the only European area program in the country that accorded equal standing and legitimacy to both the humanities and the social sciences. From the time I arrived in Bloomington, I was involved in the WEST program through my research, my teaching, and eventually as an administrator.

The Council for European Studies (CES)

A survey of WEST-type programs in the mid-1970s awarded Indiana University's WEST program high marks in several aspects. This survey made me aware of the existence of a Ford-financed consortium for research on Western Europe, the funds of which were limited to a few major universities, both Ivy League and Big Ten. At each of these favored institutions, a few faculty were the sole beneficiaries of that funding.

I considered Indiana University's program equal to those in the favored institutions and felt that we should share in the benefits. However, it took an extended campaign of banging my shoe on the table to get attention! Eventually the funding was opened up in a variety of ways, including a change from an inter-university consortium to a national membership organization headquartered in

New York at Columbia. The organization is now called the Council for European Studies (CES), and its annual scholarly meetings are major events for European area specialists.

My involvement in CES required that I commute quite often to New York. I was elected the first national co-chair of the organization, and I contributed to its work and eventual success. I believe that such organizational work is a legitimate dimension of a program of inquiry and research. This dimension of my professional life, though unforeseen when I moved to Indiana University in 1967, proved to be most gratifying for me. I valued it greatly.

On teaching and students

It seems to me that there is an intriguing parallel between my going to Haverford in 1960 and my return to Indiana in 1967. I went to Haverford College, an undergraduate liberal arts college, identified as a state university research-type scholar. I returned to Indiana University, a state university research institution, as a liberal arts teaching scholar.

At Haverford College, I had no particular reputation as a teacher. At the University of Florida, I performed reasonably well as a teacher, but I was not in the same league as the department's two popular teachers, Fred Hartmann and Ernest Bartley. Nevertheless, I enjoyed good relations with both the undergraduate and graduate students, and we are still in contact with some of them.

Whereas Florida had some good undergraduates but a weak graduate student body, Haverford had truly first-rate undergraduates. Only at Indiana University did I encounter both first-rate undergraduate and graduate students. Perhaps it was this very quality of the student body that inspired my teaching and prompted me to assume the position of director of graduate studies.

At the same time, I continued teaching undergraduates in increasing numbers. I built up the West European politics course from an enrollment of forty in the early 1970s to over three times that size when I retired. I also continued to share in teaching the American government course, often volunteering to do so while the specialists were offering their advanced seminars through which they pursued their research.

Whatever the cause, my confidence as a teacher grew steadily in my years at Indiana University. I had reached a point in my career where I could do what I liked best, and my teaching was twice rewarded. For the AMOCO award in 1975, my work with graduate students was the principal determinant. The award in 1985 from the College of Arts and Sciences reflected the college's regard for my undergraduate teaching.

For nearly half of my active duty years at Indiana University, I held administrative appointments, so during those years, my contact with undergraduates was limited simply because I taught fewer classes. Work with graduate students, however, is not so directly tied to formal class work, especially in the standard doctoral program.

I developed close personal and intellectual ties with many graduate students, ties that continued long after graduation, especially with those students who went on to have active academic careers. There were also a number of students who pursued various careers in policy in Washington, whose friendship we have treasured over the years.

My use of "we" is quite deliberate, for Ann was an active participant in this web of relationships. Her role was not limited to feeding multitudes of students and their spouses with rice pilaf or lasagna, salad, and apple crisp. In a few cases Ann helped by making rooms available to students in the final throes of dissertation writing. In one case, we accommodated first the husband, then the wife this way. They have repaid this hospitality many times over in their Falls Church house.

Graduate students

In the normal course of academic specialization, one chairs qualifying examination committees and directs doctoral dissertations only in one's own narrow specialization. I certainly did not fit that scholarly mold. Students asked me to direct their studies and dissertations because they believed that I could provide intellectual and personal guidance in broad areas of comparative politics or political theory. And if truth be told, also because they had been rebuffed by some of my colleagues pleading overwork, unfamiliarity, or other causes.

At one stage, we lost our Latin America area person when she was denied tenure. Before her replacement could be secured, given time to finish his dissertation, and settled in, I had fallen heir to six dissertations! Their topics included agrarian reform in Chile, the radical priest movement in Argentina, bureaucratic authoritarianism in Brazil, and political parties.

I directed a small number of dissertations focused on Europe, but otherwise the dissertation net was cast widely, ranging from Sri Lanka to black political thought in the United States. I had adopted the unorthodox position that a dissertation ought to produce knowledge, theory, and methodology that was not already at the fingertips of the dissertation director. The metaphor I like to use is this: the dissertation director is to be a midwife (midhusband? midperson?) and not the father of the child about to be conceived, gestated, and born.

It is easily apparent that all this ate up countless hours and days of my years at Indiana University. Equally apparent is the fact that as a consequence, there were fewer hours and days for other tasks.

My involvement with graduate students has diminished since my retirement in 1988, but it has continued. Because I taught my standard graduate seminar in bureaucracy and public policy every year from 1988 to 1994, I continued to be asked to serve on graduate committees, in both political science and WEST. However, now that I have ceased part-time teaching, this involvement will also come to an end.

Meanwhile, I have become more involved in directing master's theses in WEST because of the increased number of degree candidates in that program. Many are army officers destined to become West European area specialists when they return to duty after earning the master's degree.

These men and women are accustomed to completing assignments as required "by authority" even though their intellectual reaches vary considerably. They have a set date by which they are expected to complete the degree (three semesters), and failure to do so would constitute a black mark on their record. I know of only two among perhaps two-dozen officers who left without the degree; one is pending, the other completed the thesis after leaving Indiana University.

Undergraduate students

In the course of over forty years of teaching, I have taught undergraduate classes of varying sizes, ranging from the American government course enrolling four hundred mostly freshmen and sophomores to upper-division seminars of twenty. During these forty years, undergraduate teaching has undergone dramatic transformations, including the use of films, slides, overhead projectors, group dynamics laboratory techniques, and other things too numerous—and to me, sometimes too *discouraging*—to mention.

In that time, my own relationship with undergraduates has undergone the inevitable age-distance transformation. The first classes I taught in 1947 were filled with World War II veterans near my own age or sometimes older. But when I retired in 1988, the parents of my undergraduate students were the age of my children, and the students were the age of our eldest grandchildren. In these recent years when I see people on campus who are quite obviously parents, I am amazed by how young parents seem to be these days!

Another dimension of undergraduate teaching that caught me unawares was the considerable "de-skilling" of the freshmen. Even my own children's experience did not prepare me for that. I had noticed that many of my younger colleagues would put an outline of their lectures on the blackboard or on an overhead projector, or would hand out a photocopied version. I demurred, insisting that taking notes was an essential element of the learning process! They looked at me and responded, "Freddy, these kids never learned to take notes."

After some thought, I joined the procession. One year I produced purple copies of each lecture's outline and placed them on a chair near the door of the lecture room. The result: attendance fell off sharply. My associate instructors reported that students would pick up a copy of the outline and leave.

That was the same course, held in Woodburn Hall 100, where after a few meetings, I noted that a male student would sleep soundly in the same aisle seat throughout each lecture. One day I arrived early and noticed that very student walk in, head for his favorite seat, and promptly go to sleep.

A great load was lifted from me. At least it was not my lecturing that put him to sleep! Still, some unkind soul might suggest that my lecturing lacked the necessary verve to wake him up.

I should, finally, note that I went into retirement without ever showing a film or using a video cassette player. In this regard, the world clearly passed me by and left me behind.

The West European politics course

I taught the West European politics course every year I was on campus. Originally it was a technical course open only to graduate students. I transformed it into a broad-based survey of European politics and society since 1945.

When the college established the culture requirement, that is to say, students should accompany their required foreign language training with courses introducing them to the culture and society of the language and area in question, I easily convinced the college authorities that my approach to the politics and society of the area had a firm cultural foundation.

In this course, I tried to persuade students that Western Europe was both interesting and relevant, and that learning about Western Europe could be almost as much fun as walking down the Champs Élysées or drinking beer in Munich. At the same time, the readings for the course were fairly stiff. They included weekly assignments in *The Economist*, a serious treatment of social policy, the relations of business and government in Europe, and the European Community.

The course required short papers for which I encouraged students to develop topics that related their major to the course subject matter. Because the course was populated mostly by majors from across the spectrum, these assignments tended to produce some rather offbeat topics, such as theater majors focusing on Brecht and other European playwrights examining the political scene. Clearly I was proceeding at my own pace and in the light of my own sense of what is significant in shaping European politics and society!

The Holocaust seminar

The last course I developed at Indiana University was an undergraduate honors seminar on the Holocaust. The reasons for developing the course and the timing of its introduction require some explanation.

For several generations, schools in the United States have received an influx of immigrants from Europe. These students and teachers have brought with them both respect for learning and a desire for the higher status accorded to learning and learned persons in the old country. In the hard sciences, personal and social background entered little into the work of such émigré scholars. However, in the social sciences and the humanities, the situation was quite different.

For instance, although the development of nuclear weapons in the United States was profoundly influenced by the presence of Einstein and Teller in this country, their scientific work was not influenced by their cultural origins. However, in the work of historians and political scientists, both the personal history of the investigators and their values and preferences *shape* the course of inquiry, the selection of data, their interpretation of it, and the final result.

My understanding of research biases has developed through the years. During my undergraduate years at Indiana University, Francis Wormuth urged me to explore some nineteenth-century figures whom he and I labeled as prototypes of fascism. He was, of course, quite correct in seeing fascism as an anticommunist but also more broadly as an antiliberal movement. It was quite natural for me to work on these leaders and movements. I focused on Austria because I believed I would have an easier task mastering the materials.

I continued this work begun at Indiana University in my doctoral dissertation at Yale. I had been sufficiently inspired with notions of social science inquiry *sine ira et studio* (that is, impartial inquiry) that at one point in my work on Austrian Catholic social thought, Cecil Driver reminded me, "Freddy, don't bend over backwards. These *are* nasty people."

Then, too, I certainly recognized the limits of scholarship when Willmoore Kendall suggested as a dissertation topic a study of the social system of the KZ (Nazi concentration camps) as a manifestation of the scheme Plato articulated in the *Laws*.

Later on in my work, I encountered major shifts in the *interpretation* of the history of Austria-Hungary in the post-World War II scholarship emanating from Austria. I sought counsel from Hajo

Holborn, who pointed out that control of historical scholarship in Austrian universities after 1945 had been wrested from Pan-Germans by pro-Roman Catholics who put the kindest possible interpretation on the history of the Habsburg monarchy.

As I began to understand more fully the working of such biases in the social sciences, I decided that I would not pursue a career as an Austrian specialist, a sort of native informant, and that I would not transport biases reflecting the rivalries of the old country into American social science! Thus, my work on French administration and on industrial democracy is testimony to my success in striking out on an independent path.

In my teaching, both graduate and undergraduate, I never hid my liberal and social democratic values and policy preferences, and I tried to present postwar Europe as honestly as I could.

All this has been a necessary if somewhat lengthy introit to a segment of my undergraduate teaching that took place in the last decade before my retirement. Like so many survivors of the Holocaust, I had buried my own history deeply in my subconscious. My children learned about the Holocaust only indirectly. This omission might well have been responsible for Alice's search for roots. Steve's only open complaint was that if I had taught him German, he would not need a month to read a single scholarly article in his field in German!

I cannot pinpoint the time when I decided that I wanted to offer a course on the Holocaust from my perspective as a political scientist. There was both interest in such a course and encouragement from the increasingly active and visible Jewish Studies Center directed by Alvin Rosenfeld, whom I consider not only a fine scholar, but the most successful academic entrepreneur I have ever met. A sensitive student of literature, he is a first-rate organizer and fundraiser who never sacrifices the seriousness of academic inquiry for the sake of fundraising.

I discussed the course with him, and he encouraged me. He listed it in the Jewish studies program offering, and he included me in the program's multifarious activities. I offered the course a half dozen times as a sophomore honors seminar, but I do not believe it was successful. This was partly because of its orientation and partly because I was not successful in communicating the monstrousness of the Holocaust as an exercise in the making and execution of a public policy.

Indiana University already offered courses on the literature and history of the Holocaust and also one that consisted of films about the Holocaust. So what could I offer? I took as my central text Hilberg's *The Destruction of the European Jews*, a vast study based entirely on German documentation.

I sought to present a policy study of the Holocaust, that is to say, how the Germans came to decide on that policy and how they carried it out. What perhaps overwhelmed the course was the students' implicit acceptance of Hannah Arendt's characterization not only of Eichmann, but of all the terrible events, no matter how evil, as "banal."

Perhaps my choice of a focus for the course was a continuation of my earlier denials but in a different form. Did the course's focus reduce the Holocaust to merely a matter of policy, of people sitting behind desks shuffling papers, of the RSHA of the SS quarreling with the Reichsbahn about who would pay for transporting the victims to Auschwitz?

If so, then did my choice of this focus constitute a form of burying it all as deeply as possible so I would not have to face the enormity of these events?

For reasons that I do not understand fully, the Holocaust course did not satisfy either me or the students enrolled in it. Elie Wiesel is right: the enormity of the Holocaust defies all our efforts to come to terms with it.

I am sure that other courses or presentations, such as the recently opened Holocaust Museum on the Mall in Washington, have been more successful than I was when I struggled with it in the last years of my active teaching career.

The various layers of our life and experience are not simply disconnected bits. They form a coherent whole, whether for good or for ill. We are not really capable of discerning that pattern while we are still in the midst of it all!

Thus, my teaching is an inescapable element of my total life experience. It could not be any other way, and I would not want it to be.

On administrative duties

University faculty complain endlessly about administration, an evil only slightly less repulsive than the Black Death. They see administrators as a cabal out to increase their own salaries and constrain the freedom of faculty to conduct their work. They declare piously that universities would be an Elysium if one could only rid the place of the administrative pest! Yet few faculty, when offered administrative positions, refuse them.

They are also less than honest when they contend that the complex systems of modern universities could be operated without full-time administrators, or when they complain about losing teachers and researchers to administration. They never, or hardly ever, *pace* Gilbert and Sullivan, admit that they would like it even less if universities were staffed solely by professional bureaucrats.

In fairness, one must concede that there are many examples of splendid teachers or researchers who turn out to be wretched administrators, and also that faculty members turned administrators quickly lose their faculty perspective on the workings of the university and become acculturated to the administrative world.

Nevertheless, in spite of the problems associated with the faculty person turned administrator, the American university continues to be governed by its faculty, the fiscal and other powers of state legislatures and/or boards of trustees notwithstanding. Like so many of my colleagues, once I had attained a certain national stature in my discipline, I began to be approached for administrative positions.

To chair or not to chair

The first such outside offer that I considered seriously came in 1963 from the University of Oregon for the chair of their Political Science Department. The university's most attractive person was its president, Arthur Fleming, a genuine social liberal, a charming man, intelligent, and a fascinating conversationalist. I flew to Oregon for extended interviews and was truly attracted to the possibility.

I talked it over with Ann. She insisted that after the trauma of the move to Haverford only three years earlier, she would need a firsthand look before we could make a decision!

I discussed it at length with Manning. I must have conveyed my positive reaction to the offer, for he produced an unusually large number of "ums" and "ahs" before he conveyed his very accurate judgment that I would be a fine, hardworking chair, but that I should probably stay away from administration because I was basically a worrier who would find making decisions, especially tough decisions, tortuous and agonizing, and that the job would eat me up (not his exact words).

When I talked to Arthur Fleming and to Bert Wengert, the outgoing chair, I literally hid behind Ann's skirts by telling them of her concern. I indicated that I would not expect them to bring both of us across the country so that Ann could have her look. But that did not stop Arthur Fleming. Ann and I trekked across the continent to Oregon for a long weekend.

We had Sunday dinner with Fleming and a group of administrators. As we walked back to our motel, Ann turned to me and said, "Freddy, do you really want to work with all these stuffy people?"

Ann went to visit in Seattle, and I came back directly. The day after my return, I picked up Alice from school and returned home to find a long telegram from Fleming stuck in the door. I read it immediately. Alice wanted to know what it said, so I read her Fleming's plea for me to accept the appointment, which concluded with, "together you and I will build the best political science department in the country." Alice looked at me with admiring eyes. It is hard to resist such admiration.

In the end I resisted Arthur Fleming's plea, wisely I am sure. Unfortunately I did not resist similar entreaties later on. I should have continued to listen to Manning's advice.

For nearly half of my twenty-eight-year academic career, I have chaired an academic unit of some sort. However, only my appointment as chair of the Political Science Department at Indiana University could really be considered to carry the administrative load and responsibilities one usually associates with such an appointment.

The first of these appointments was at Haverford, which in spite of its small size maintained a panoply of academic departments, each usually consisting of three members. When Red Somers left, I was designated his successor, thus "presiding over" Harvey Glickman and a vacant position. I always worked in complete harmony with Harvey, and when W. D. Burnham joined us, there was simply nothing that involved any decision not made collegially. This sort of chairmanship was effortless and worry-free. Indeed my experience at Haverford might have led me to believe that Manning's concern about my ability to master such a job was exaggerated.

When we moved to Indiana, we had the great fortune to arrive simultaneously with Jim and Natalie Christoph, with whom we forged ties of friendship and collegiality that have remained unbroken to this day. Jim's work in British politics and his eventual specialization in the British civil service made him a colleague in the complete sense of the word.

Jim was recruited to chair the department when Byrum Carter became dean of the College of Arts and Sciences. Halfway through his four-year term as chair, Jim asked me to serve as the director of graduate studies, and we worked together to revise the department's graduate program. At the same time, he took the lead in placing departmental governance on a fully democratic foundation.

Being department chair was a heavy burden for Jim for the very same reasons that Manning had warned me against taking it on. When Jim announced that he would not continue as chair beyond his original four-year term, the dean's search process produced me as the department's not necessarily unanimous but apparently overwhelming choice. However, I encountered Manning's repeated warning when I consulted him again, as well as Ann's reaction, "If you accept, I'll move out!" I decided not to test the firmness of that assertion.

I also felt that temperamentally, I could not work with Big George Wilson, who had succeeded Byrum Carter when he assumed the position of chancellor and head of the Bloomington campus. This new position was created by the reorganization of the university into a system in which Bloomington was only one of a number of more or less equal units.

I was destined not to remain chair-less for long. When Henry Remak, the founding director of WEST, was appointed vice chancellor and dean of faculties, I was asked to succeed him in the WEST position. Luckily, Ann agreed to continue cohabiting the house we had built not so long before.

I served as the WEST chair for six years. These were rather lean years, in part because I did not pursue the federal funding needed to replace the Ford Foundation support that had been terminated. However, I used the visibility of the WEST position to play a role in national affairs in the West European studies area.

The scarcity of funding during these years reflected a position shared by federal granting agencies and private foundations that there was nothing of significance in Europe that warranted the sort of infusion of funds that had been devoted to the third world in previous decades. When Norman Furniss became the WEST director in the early 1980s, he profited from a decisive turnaround of funding policies regarding Europe. He also wrote focused and highly effective grant proposals.

Chairing the Political Science Department at IU

After I refused the political science chair in 1971, Leroy Rieselbach assumed the position and held it for six years. During this time, the fissures in the department continued to deepen. However, Rieselbach, who ran a loose ship, was able to navigate easily among the shoals. In a divided department, personnel decisions (appointment, promotion, tenure) are invariably the factional battleground. Rieselbach carefully balanced the appointed personnel committee and asked me to chair it for the six years of his tenure (excepting only the year I was away on sabbatical leave).

At the end of his second three-year term, Rieselbach stepped down, pleading battle fatigue. To my genuine surprise, the message that the department sent to Dean Jack Shiner was that they wanted me to replace him. Manning, Ann, and I decided that perhaps my time had come: after all, I had not only aged, but I was less a worrier than I had been. So I agreed to serve for a three-year term.

I made a scrupulous effort to give each faction a voice in my administration. I created an advisory committee to which I appointed some of the strongest voices hostile to my conception of the discipline. Unfortunately these three years were marred by my health problems, including surgery several times (glaucoma, kidney problems, and a hernia), which limited my activity. Reappointment for another term was complicated by my age. I would turn 65, the age by which one must relinquish administrative appointments, before the end of the term.

Dean Kenneth Gros Louis was genuinely supportive but he was under pressure from the university's top research administrator to appoint a person with a stronger research and fund-raising record. While I was at home recovering from my most recent surgical adventure, he visited to inform me that he would appoint Elinor Ostrom as my successor. Under her and subsequent chairs, the department shifted its focus radically, a process accompanied by contentions over tenure decisions, appointments, curriculum, and so forth. But that is another story.

Over the years, I have also performed a number of other services for Indiana University, though none has touched my academic existence as much as my teaching and my departmental service. In 1967 Byrum Carter, as a brand-new dean, appointed an educational policy committee, the purpose of which was to look at everything the college was doing. I was appointed to it when I arrived in 1967. It was a group of imaginative and innovative people. Some of our recommendations were even adopted and are still alive and well.

In addition to this, I have been elected to campus and university-wide faculty councils, and I have served on an executive committee for a term. I have also served on committees in the general area of international services and international studies. I have supplemented these university committees with service on the executive committee of the Bloomington chapter of the AAUP (American Association of University Professors).

I note all this only as a testimony to my practicing what I preach. Faculty must be prepared to help govern and operate the university, or eventually it will all be done by appointed career civil servants.

Colleagues and friends

A university is not simply a collection of administrative entities; it is a community of people. The faculty are, ultimately, the university. For me this community involved chiefly the faculties of the Political Science Department and the West European Studies program. If life at Indiana University was worthwhile, it was because of these colleagues and friends!

In 1967 when I returned to Indiana University, there was still a group from my earliest days: Byrum Carter, John Stoner, Edward Buehrig, Louis (Scrappy) Lambert, and E. B. (Mac) McPheron. Byrum had arrived in 1947 as an ABD (all but dissertation) from Wisconsin. He and his wife, Beth, had lived in Hoosier Courts, and Byrum and I had shared an office in what is now Lindley Hall during 1947-1948.

When I returned in 1967, Byrum was dean of the college. He continued in full-time administration for another ten years. His is truly the most powerful intellect I have ever encountered. He is a voracious reader across a wide range of subjects, an avid golfer, and in her days, a great admirer of Miss Piggy.

In 1945 when I started my university studies, Ed Buehrig was away on service with the State Department, but he returned within the year and taught me international relations and international law. Ed should bear no blame if I have steadfastly refused to go anywhere near these fields in my life as a political scientist. After their war service, Scrappy and Mac returned to complete their doctorates. Scrappy has frequently recounted how my tutoring enabled him to pass the German language proficiency test.

One lesson I learned from John Stoner, as I kept reminding him to his chagrin, was to have a fund of jokes and stories, good stories. This is what students remember when all else is forgotten after the final exam! I have ample proof of the validity of his advice, for example from a Haverford student, Jerry Schwertfeger. Years after taking my course in which I produced a very funny line involving bar closing hours in Australia, Jerry sent me a newspaper clipping reporting in earnest the problem with bar closing hours in Australia.

Over the years the department has changed. With the deaths of Buehrig, Stoner, Lambert, and McPheron, the links with the department of my student days have been severed. During the late 1950s and 1960s, a number of people were recruited and made up a middle contingent: Leroy Rieselbach, Ilya Harik, Darrel Hammer, and John Lovell. I have good relationships with all of them.

During the early 1970s many people that the department recruited were fresh from graduate school: Norman Furniss, Tim Tilton, Jack Bielasiak, Jean Robinson, Richard Stryker, Russ Hanson, and others who have since moved on to other universities. With the exception of Hanson, these are all specialists in the field of comparative politics and thus close to me both personally and professionally.

With their arrival all within a few years, I had a group of colleagues to whom I came to feel close, yet who were about the age of my children. Thus our relationships required some adjustment on my part.

I must have shown some impatience with proposals for changes in the department advanced by my younger colleagues. One day Tim Tilton and Norm Furniss pointed out that I always put down their ideas with, "We tried that twenty years ago, and it didn't work."

I realized then that even if your colleagues are the age of your children, you ought not to treat them like children. In fact you ought not to treat children like children in any case.

I have worked particularly closely with Norm Furniss, who was recruited as a joint appointment in political science and WEST. He succeeded me as the WEST chair, and I have always marveled at his success in making that program flourish, attracting outside funding and students nationally.

Although neither Norm nor I ever referred to our relationship as mentoring, that was the case nevertheless. I was profoundly touched when Norm wrote to me years later that I had taken the place of his father, who had died when Norm was a teenager.

I cannot very well describe my life at Indiana University without mentioning Vincent and Elinor Ostrom. In the early years, the Diamants and the Ostroms were together frequently. Vincent is about my age, and in fact our birthdays coincide on September 25. Elinor is considerably younger; she had been his doctoral student at UCLA.

Vincent is an original thinker determined to contradict prevailing wisdom, much like Willmoore Kendall. Like Kendall, he migrated from a position of radical socialism to a position of anticentralism and market capitalism, positions that came to have a strong resonance in the Reagan-Bush years. I have always had considerable respect for Vincent's mind, though it has seemed to me that his writing could stand the sort of treatment that Cecil Driver had administered to mine.

Elinor diligently taught herself the new political science and has generally worked to frame research that would substantiate Vincent's formulations. They carefully funneled funds into an independent research organization, the Workshop for Political Theory and Policy Analysis. Elinor proved to be a most successful research entrepreneur, especially after the 1981 election when decentralization and market capitalism were the favorite mantras of Washington, where a good part of research funding originated.

During the time I was department chair, all my efforts to accommodate Vincent and Elinor misfired. When they strongly objected to a candidate for our Latin American position because, as they insisted, he knew nothing about water rights issues (the topic of his dissertation at Stanford), I listened to them rather than to the majority vote of the faculty who favored his appointment. In subsequent years, this man made a first-rate record as a researcher and was the recipient of major grants for his research!

My research during the Indiana years

My reading, inquiry, and research during the Indiana years constituted both continuation and departures. The work of CAG was wound up in 1970, but volumes containing the work of the summer seminars continued to appear during the 1970s. My work for the CAG seminars at Indiana University and Berkeley appeared in these volumes. The Michigan seminar suffered from last-minute resignations and failures to deliver promised papers. My own contribution, which had been completed in time, was eventually included in a volume edited by Fred Riggs. It was a miscellaneous collection under the brave title, *Frontiers of Development Administration*.

By then I believed that I had reached the limits of any useful contribution I could make to the CAG enterprise, so I turned my attention back to Europe. With a sabbatical leave ahead for 1973-1974, I decided to shift my focus from France to Germany, which has one of the oldest and most influential systems of higher civil service. In that way, I could make use of language and area skills that I had developed over recent years, while still not succumbing to the siren call of the native informant role.

When the time came, I found myself most successful in my grant applications. Both Fulbright and Guggenheim awarded me yearlong grants, which combined to make our stay in Germany most comfortable. Perhaps too comfortable, because even though

I pursued inquiries diligently, I cannot point directly to any finished product that resulted from that year.

Still, my immersion in German affairs and a year at the seat of the federal bureaucracy served to broaden my perspective on the European higher civil service systems and to direct my attention more to questions of public policy and the public policy role of senior bureaucrats. This shift was reflected in both my undergraduate and graduate teaching during the last years of my active teaching career.

After my return from Germany, my research turned in a completely new direction. Peter Bachrach organized a series of panels on industrial democracy for the annual APSA (American Political Science Association) meeting, and he asked me to do a paper on the recently enacted German codetermination legislation. I found the subject appealing, in part because it gave me an incentive to return to basic issues of political theory to which I had paid little attention since my dissertation. The paper was duly delivered and appeared in a collective volume about industrial democracy across Europe.

In subsequent years, I delivered papers at both national and international meetings, some of which were published in collective volumes or in international journals. I have continued to read widely and have done a number of book reviews covering the general topic of industrial organization.

I suspect that the wide interest in workplace democracy was an extension of the ideas of the radical 1960s and 1970s and of the prosperous decades when the so-called pie tended to increase and the relations between employers and workers were peaceful. This peace existed simply because the more substantial pie made it possible to meet worker demands, not only for better pay and benefits (mandated by law in many European countries), but also for an expanded voice in workplace decision-making.

The gains of the 1970s are, however, being whittled away if not slashed with the technical and economic developments of the 1980s and early 1990s, especially the growth of a global economy, computerization-robotization, and the seemingly egalitarian Japanese management style.

As is often the case in the history of democracy, formal checks on power are diminished, if not eliminated, in the guise of "true democracy," which often turns out to be the very opposite of what it claims to be. That is now the case with such seductive slogans as "quality circles" and "worker empowerment." In the same way, the earlier calls for true democracy proposed to replace the raucous voice of universal suffrage with the clear voice of the authoritarian leader.

I can only be saddened by the developments I have just sketched, but my finger in the dike of workplace democracy will not stem the tide of market forces and technology that seem to make industrial democracy outdated and irrelevant.

Sabbatical leave in Europe (1973-1974)

My sabbatical leaves of 1973-1974 and 1980-1981 were still another element in my research program during my years at Indiana University. As I have mentioned, the first of these was spent in Germany. It was a good year, not only because of successful grant applications but because I had been invited by the Alexander von Humboldt Stiftung to be a resident fellow in their guesthouse in Bad Godesberg. This meant a modern, fully furnished apartment provided at subsidized rent.

Our apartment building was located in the diplomatic area of Bad Godesberg, which meant constant patrols by armored cars protecting threatened embassies. The occupants were a veritable United Nations of scholars, including a clinical ophthalmologist from Chile who attended to my glaucoma.

As in 1966-1967, we traveled to fulfill several speaking engagements. This time our Norwegian schedule included Bergen and Tromsø, as well as Oslo. Sadly, Tromsø canceled at the last minute because of a local flu epidemic. We had been looking forward to visiting the only university north of the Arctic Circle. In Liverpool, Bristol, and Nottingham, we were houseguests of our university hosts. Since the visit was in February, we were reminded again of the stern virtues of living without central heating! I also participated in a very interesting conference organized by my Bochum host, Roman Schnur, now on the law faculty at Tübingen.

One of the more fascinating moments of the year was Willy Brandt's resignation as chancellor in the midst of the spy affair. It seemed to me then that Brandt, feeling burned out after the success of Ostpolitik and the award of the Nobel Peace Prize, was simply grasping at the opportunity to relinquish a burden he no longer wanted to carry.

I watched the Yom Kippur War from a German vantage point while Ann was in Greece, having helped convey Gordon back to his parents after a visit with his other grandparents in Brussels. Both of us traveled to Greece for Christmas to celebrate the feast together with the entire family of our daughter-in-law, Jan. At that time, Alice was serving her army tour of duty in Israel and could not get away.

During the spring, we squired Ann's sister Betty and her husband, Harold, on a tour of Germany, Switzerland, and Austria. This time I was able to take Vienna in my stride, so I was less troublesome company than I had been in 1966.

Harold, a third-generation German-American, had become increasingly nostalgic about the old country. We gave Harold and Betty tastes of Rothenburg/Tauber, Nürnberg, and Munich, where I consented to do what I had sworn I would never do, go to a *Hofbräuhaus*. I made sure the strolling musicians stopped at our table to play for Harold. Somewhat to my surprise, I found myself touched by this vivid demonstration of ethnic sentimentality across generations and oceans.

The most significant benefit of the year was my exposure over an extended period to the life and political culture of the Bundesrepublik. I realized that I could view this postwar Germany free from the distortions of my personal fate, as was the case also with Vienna and Austria more generally. I am not suggesting that the Rhineland was not a willing and obedient part of the Third Reich, but rather that I could live and work there without the interference of my personal ressentiments.

This extended intimate interaction with postwar Germany enriched my subsequent scholarly activities in several ways. It enabled me to offer the Holocaust course. It also made me an organized, effective writer and lecturer on German affairs. My notes and handouts for the Indiana University annual alumni institute, the Mini University (which I have conducted over the past two decades), constitute a running commentary on modern Germany, both before and after unification. More strictly scholarly products have also resulted from these efforts, but the important element is my sustained inquiry into the politics and society of post-World War II Germany.

Sabbatical leave in Europe & Washington, DC (1980-1981)

My sabbatical leave of 1980–1981 came at the end of my term as department chair. I applied conscientiously to a variety of funding sources, proposing to continue my work on industrial democracy. I wanted my inquiry to cover both American and European patterns of workplace democracy.

I realized at the beginning of my term as department chair that my record would not be as strong as it had been in 1973, so I took a semester of administrative leave, to which I added my sabbatical leave. That enabled us to break our Bloomington pattern for an entire year, with much of that time spent in Washington, DC.

The Brookings Foundation appointed me as a visiting scholar, an arrangement that included office space, secretarial services, and most importantly, close contact with a group of political scientists, economists, and other policy analysts who had intimate knowledge and understanding of the federal government. The foundation was an ideal spot to watch the initial stages of the Reagan revolution. Though I had taught American government for over thirty years, I had never spent more than a few days at the seat of that government. What a contrast it was to Bonn, Paris, London, Oslo, and Vienna, among others!

Being in Washington made it easier for Ann to enjoy music and all the arts, and that was another good reason for this choice of venue. We were also able to interact with many former and current Indiana University students, as well as visitors from England, and a variety of friends we had made in the course of a thirty-year academic career. We even had Alice with us for Christmas.

I had a late start with my sabbatical leaves, but Ann and I treasured them as opportunities to spend time together, uninterrupted by my academic and her community responsibilities. In particular, we were able to explore and deepen our interests in the arts. Because of the riches of music at Indiana University, we devoted ourselves more to the visual arts in the museums of Germany, France, England, and Washington.

Thus, my sabbatical leaves served not only to refresh and expand my academic horizons, but they enriched our relationship and our marriage and so, served to bind us even more closely together.

Student unrest in the 1960s and 1970s

There remains one dimension of my academic life that cannot easily be subsumed under the teaching-research-service trinity: the climactic years of the Vietnam War and the consequential tidal wave of student activism in the United States and Europe. I did not directly experience the most dramatic of these episodes—Berkeley, Columbia, the Sorbonne, Freie Universität. However, I certainly felt and was influenced by the forces unleashed by these events, first during my years at Haverford and later at Indiana University.

I have already mentioned the student committee at Haverford that collected funds to send medical supplies to the Viet Cong. This was one of the earliest antiwar organizations on the East Coast. Several of its leaders took courses in political science. They usually opted for reading courses, which interfered less with their activist agenda, in which they pursued various themes in the protest literature and in Marxism.

The most visible figure in that group was Russell Stetler, one of the few genuine working-class offspring I have encountered in the protest movement. Stetler was at Haverford on a scholarship awarded to the top graduate of each Philadelphia public high school by the city board of education. His vanguard role in the protest movement drew the attention of the local press, which had come down increasingly hard on Haverford for being a hotbed of radicalism and communism.

That was enough to move the most conservative members of Philadelphia's school board into action. They called a public hearing at which they intended to strip Stetler of his scholarship. Several faculty members attended the meeting, and President Borton stoutly defended Stetler's right to speak and demonstrate while maintaining academic standards.

Stetler eventually graduated. However, he continued to be in the public eye when he worked for Bertrand Russell in London, helping staff Russell's "war crimes tribunal," which prosecuted the United States for war crimes committed during the war in Vietnam.

Haverford's continuing tradition of protest and activism merited special attention from *The New York Times* when colleges and universities were swept by the great protest movement that was triggered by American incursion into Cambodia and the killing of students at Kent State University. According to the *Times*, Haverford faculty, staff, administration, and students voted to suspend all operations, move to Washington as a body, and present their pleas for an end to the war to the legislative and executive branches of the federal government.

Both Ann and I have often reflected on what we would have done if still at Haverford when confronted with this set of events. Having always taken a harder anticommunist line than many of my liberal colleagues, I had supported the war in its early stages, become ambivalent as it dragged on, and ended up opposing it. However, I was never moved to militant antiwar action myself, though I always supported the rights of others to conduct their opposition to the war as freely as possible.

Student unrest at Indiana University

When we moved to Bloomington in 1967, the Indiana University campus was quiet, as one might expect from a midwestern university in a conservative state. Eventually the "year of the young rebel," as Stephen Spender called 1968, began to be felt in Bloomington, too.

Excitement mounted along several fronts: opposition to the war with teach-ins and demonstrations; increasing dissatisfaction with curriculum; demands for the "democratization" of teaching, learning, and grading; demands for student input into university decision-making; and dissatisfaction with university efforts to recruit minority students. I cannot possibly provide a comprehensive account of developments on all these fronts, so I will focus on those where I was directly involved.

A sizable segment of the student protest leadership consisted of graduate students in political science and other social sciences. Because I served as the department's director of graduate studies during the crucial years (1969-1971), and because I chaired numerous doctoral committees, I was close to a number of these students and to faculty members who were sympathetic to their efforts.

One of my earliest memories after returning to Bloomington is a meeting at the home of a young faculty member where students reported on the great Chicago conference of the SDS (Students for a Democratic Society). Black members had presented a program that opened a gulf between black and white participants. The black members demanded that their program be adopted en bloc, including a plank declaring Zionism to be racism.

A sizable portion of white participants, though not practicing Jews, balked at this demand and were in considerable agony. Some ultimately voted against the platform. I recall a husband-wife team that split on the issue, the wife supporting the platform and the husband opposing.

At Indiana University, the student protest leadership group was in the fore of demands to broaden the opportunities of minority students. The university had already taken steps in this direction by initiating the Groups Program, which provided for recruiting an additional two hundred disadvantaged minority students per year through nontraditional channels outside the usual high school grades/SAT route. These students would be fully financed and given special counseling and other forms of assistance to ensure their academic success.

It was the confluence of Groups Program students and a largely white radical leadership cadre that provided one of the tensest episodes of this turbulent period. Some Groups students led by white radicals confronted campus administrators in the faculty lounge of Ballantine Hall and physically prevented them from leaving until their demands had been met. Eventually the standoff was resolved, but not before tension had become nearly unbearable and police contemplated action to break the "lock-in."

My most direct involvement in the events of these difficult times was through members of the radical group who were graduate students in political science, and for whose academic welfare I was responsible as director of graduate studies.

One such student was Joel Allen, who had come to us from Washington University with the highest recommendations. We awarded him a four-year package of financial support, but whether he was really as promising as Washington University had predicted, we were never able to find out.

Allen was the leading figure in a protest incident in which he shouted obscenities at a university vice president and a group of university trustees as they emerged from the Union building. The Bloomington chancellor, Byrum Carter, ordered Allen removed from his duties as an associate instructor.

Subsequently the department divided into hostile camps, with Charlie Hyneman leading a group supporting Byrum's action and Jim Christoph and I arguing for academic freedom.

I know Byrum was deeply offended by the eventual department majority that supported Jim Christoph. I still feel that I was right to support Jim, even though it meant hurting a man whose mind and character I have always greatly admired.

Later Joel Allen got into additional difficulties when he received a summer grant to study German at the Goethe Institute in Munich and instead spent the summer at a socialist kibbutz in Israel. He tried to justify his actions by presenting me with an obviously phony reading list, which was to be proof of the work he had done in Israel when he should have been in Munich studying German.

There was a public disciplinary hearing that filled the Law School moot court room with pro-Allen partisans. Joel Allen was represented by a member of the Law School faculty, whom I had angered by my refusal to testify that Joel's work in Israel was legitimate and acceptable to the department. I had no trouble defending Allen's free-speech rights in the department, but it was equally easy to maintain my judgment of what Allen did during that summer without having to consider whether my position was liberal or conservative.

After that, Joel Allen took a leave of absence from which he did not return. We heard stories of him entering studies for the rabbinate and then for medical school. Sometime later, a member of the dean of student's staff who had frequently dealt with Allen was in New York, and he happened to be watching a pro-Israel demonstration near the United Nations. If I remember correctly, the events were staged by followers of Meir Kahane, the far-right Jewish leader who was later assassinated. After a while, the police began to arrest the more obstreperous demonstrators. As they dragged them to paddy wagons, they passed by the spectator from Indiana University, who instantly recognized Allen as one of the demonstrators.

Perhaps the most impressive event—in a positive sense—of this turbulent period was a peaceful monster rally following the Kent State events. By that time, the protest leadership had incorporated a number of Vietnam veterans. The veterans organized a corps of guides who marshaled the protest crowd and maintained order and dignity. At the same time, the rally effectively gave expression to the students' revulsion over the Kent State killings and their opposition to the continuation of the war.

Changing complex organizations is a difficult and time-consuming process with uncertain outcomes. Whether universities themselves initiated the changes or whether they were forced by outsiders and/or organization members made little difference in the end. As long as the public purse remained open to institutions of higher learning, and the products of their educational processes were able to find employment related to their skills and at an acceptable social level, no truly ground-breaking changes were made as a result of the year or years of the young rebel.

However, times change; the public purse yields ever-shrinking amounts, and places in society are not assured for university graduates. So it is only now that changes might well be forced on the universities, changes of a magnitude not even dreamed of by the young rebels.

On faith and learning

In our twenty-seven years in Bloomington, my service to and participation in community life has been almost entirely through Trinity Church and the ways in which Trinity ministers to the university community, faculty, and students.

For one who claims to be a politics junkie, I certainly have not always put my energy where my mouth is. Still I have done some things over the years. I have discussed public affairs and public policy though the League of Women Voters, and I have faithfully voted in local, state, and national elections. We have also contributed regularly to congressional, state, and local candidates, though certainly not to the extent of bankrolling them.

Trinity Church, and for some years university ministry, were the principal outlets of both my community service and my strong commitment to a religious dimension of my personal and family life and of the community life of which I have been a part for over a quarter century. It is perhaps misleading to phrase all this in the first person singular, for Ann shared that commitment, and she was the inspiration for it from the beginning of our married life!

When we arrived in Bloomington, Trinity was in the midst of calling a new rector. Charles Perry attempted to wrest the congregation from what he thought were its all too comfortable middle-class ways. He reversed the decision to build a new edifice in a suburban location (the Blue Ridge area) and insisted on retaining the downtown location and the attendant responsibilities to the mixed community-student life that ebbs and flows along Kirkwood Avenue. I came to support his liberal-to-radical views about the Vietnam War and the cultural revolution that engulfed the student body.

Charles Perry was an energetic, driven individual. He immediately started a building-fund campaign, and he shifted the focus of parish life from worship to social service. I remember him scolding a group of students for suggesting special services during Lent. He told them they should go out and minister to the poor instead of hiding away in the church from the pressing problems of society.

At the annual parish meeting in 1970 (shortly after the Kent State killings), I was elected to the vestry, having become a candidate at his urging. After the election, Perry stood up, told us he could not abide the inward orientation of the parish, and resigned. He spent the remainder of his clerical career in Washington as dean of the National Cathedral responsible for community relations, a post for which he was ideal.

As often happens in such turnovers, Perry was succeeded by an ultra-conservative rector, who was picked by the bishop to "clean up the mess in Bloomington." Donald Davis did just that, but he was actually aiming chiefly for a bishop's mitre. He succeeded before long and became Bishop of Erie.

With Davis' successor, Trinity finally found a rector who was able to create an effective balance between worship and social activism. Hugh Laughlin's long-range impact on Trinity was not immediately evident. Twice he had to take leave to confront and ultimately conquer his alcoholism. Eventually he developed into a truly superb preacher who cared for the nature and quality of worship. He has consistently spoken out on the central problems of society, from AIDS to wars to poverty and the threats of secularism and normlessness.

He was able to inspire the congregation to finance the additional facilities needed for parish life by a growing and now much younger congregation. He has opened the church buildings to community groups and has nurtured the congregation's involvement in community concerns, from homelessness in Bloomington to the need for optical services in Nicaragua.

Episcopalians are among the smallest main-line Protestant churches, especially in Indiana. During most of our years here, Trinity members have occupied significant community positions in such areas as homelessness, questions of war and peace, and the hospice movement. Yet I wonder whether Trinity in its outreach to the community has been able to strike the right balance between "comforting the afflicted" and "afflicting the comfortable."

Trinity has been a good place for our faith and for our life in the city-university community. My principal service to Trinity has been my four three-year terms on the vestry, including a term as people's warden.

College ministry

My life in the Episcopal church has revolved to a considerable extent around the church's ministry to the university community. In both Gainesville and Bloomington, the mainstream Protestant churches operate student ministries—either through the churches or through university chapels or student centers located in close proximity to the university campus.

The latter was the case in Florida, but there as a family our life centered entirely on Holy Trinity Church. This came about for two reasons. The first was the age of our children, for whom Holy Trinity provided the appropriate religious education. The second was Ann's devotion to Sunday school work with preschool children, which she began at Holy Trinity and continued at the Church of the Redeemer.

The pattern of ministry to the university community that I found in Bloomington resembled that of Gainesville, and one would find it duplicated on most state university campuses. On the other hand, the situation at Haverford and in the colleges along the Main Line was radically different.

To begin with, our affiliation with a mainstream Protestant church placed us in a minority among both students and faculty. The college administrators and many faculty were active members of Quaker meetings. Many of the non-Quaker faculty were attracted to Quakerism by its social activism and the plainness of its religious observances.

My involvement in college ministry came soon after our arrival at Haverford. Though I refused Reverend Sparkman's offer to become Sunday school director, I agreed to co-teach a high school class for most of my years at Haverford. About that time, several Protestant churches along the Main Line, led by a strong lay contingent, began to consider ways to minister to the many colleges along the Main Line. With the exception of Roman Catholic Villanova University, all the other institutions had small enrollments, mostly undergraduate, and ranged in quality from top national institutions, such as Haverford and Bryn Mawr, to junior colleges of the finishing school type.

Reverend Sparkman asked me to represent the Church of the Redeemer in the council governing this enterprise. The leadership and funding came chiefly from Bryn Mawr Presbyterian Church, which is supported generously by the Pew family (Sun Oil and the national Republican party).

The college ministry group began its activity by opening a coffeehouse, which was then a very trendy way to establish communication with students. Fortunately nobody insisted that the coffeehouse become a place for proselytizing. Rather it was to be a place for students to talk, play their music, read their poetry, and find other young adults to talk to.

Although it was never stated or even implied, the college ministry group was most concerned with reaching the students of the two Quaker colleges, Haverford and Bryn Mawr, who had the largely deserved reputation of being the most secular and politically radical of the Main Line college populations. Unfortunately the coffeehouse was largely spurned by this target group. But it was very effective in attracting students from other colleges, including the Roman Catholic ones.

Both Ann and I were on the coffeehouse work schedule, which meant long hours late into the night, plus learning how to operate an espresso machine. We did pretty well with the coffee machine. How well we did as *communicators*, I cannot say. I found the idea inspiring the coffeehouse worthwhile and spent many a post-midnight hour cleaning the espresso machine. Whether any higher purpose was served will probably be determined by a higher authority.

The concern of the mainstream Protestant churches for the three Quaker colleges—Haverford, Bryn Mawr, and Swarthmore (which is actually located a considerable distance from the Main Line)—also took another form: the provision of funds to appoint a full-time chaplain for these three colleges. The funds came from the mainstream churches (Presbyterian, Methodist, and Episcopal), with the lion's share coming from the Presbyterian college work commission.

A call committee was established. As a representative of the Church of the Redeemer, I was its only lay member. Reverend Michael Porteus, an Anglican cleric, accepted our call. Michael and his wife, Gertrude, a German Lutheran deaconess, became our dear friends. Michael set about finding ways to minister to students on three campuses where mainstream Protestant churches were viewed with suspicion if not hostility.

Since I was the only faculty on the call committee and also faculty from one of the Quaker colleges, it fell to me to explain this ministry to the college president, the dean, and some senior Quaker faculty. They sharply questioned the legitimacy of such a mainstream Protestant ministry on a Quaker college campus. They doubted whether a genuine need for it existed. Yet in the end, the strong Quaker commitment to religious liberty prevailed, and the three colleges formally recognized the ministry and provided administrative support.

The ministry ended after I left Haverford. The financial arrangements for it collapsed, and Michael Porteus wished to return home to England. If this ministry is said to have failed, which I deny, it was because of a combination of two factors: the nature of the student bodies at the three Quaker colleges and the general turning away from organized religion by the college generations of the 1960s and 1970s. Judging only by the length of Michael's current service at the University of Arizona, he has found there a more congenial environment and a much transformed student generation.

Having become closely involved in college ministry at Haverford, I continued that involvement in Bloomington within a short time of our arrival. In Bloomington as in Gainesville, the university (students, faculty, and staff) by its very size tends to dominate the community in which it is located. The Indiana University faculty, staff, and their families constitute a sizable portion of the Trinity parish community and generally do so without giving rise to town-gown issues. However, service to the student body is more problematic for Trinity's ministry.

The diocese of Indianapolis, fortified by the wealth of the Lilly family, finances a student chaplain, thus giving Trinity in effect a second clergy person. The student chaplain during our first decades at Trinity was a highly gifted, eccentric gay man, who was able to ingratiate himself with the older members of the congregation. Ultimately his service to the student body became service to a coterie of gays and lesbians, which alienated straight newcomers.

Over time his behavior became ever more irresponsible. It all blew up in Bloomington and on the diocesan level while I was a member of a diocesan commission on higher education. During this skirmish, I was attacked along with Hugh Laughlin for persecuting the chaplain.

Fortunately his successor, the current chaplain, proved to be a solid choice, and he has functioned effectively in the parish and on campus, taking leadership roles on such issues as Holocaust remembrance. I no longer play an active role in Trinity's university ministry, and that is how it should be.

University ministry and the cultural revolution

Any reflections on the role of the church in campus life must take into account the changing tides of student interests, preferences, and lifestyles. When we came to Bloomington in 1967, there was a sizable and active Canterbury organization. Within a few years, it collapsed under the impact of the cultural revolution sweeping university campuses—though certainly Indiana University was a "backwater" when compared to Berkeley and Columbia, or even Michigan and Wisconsin.

Students simply did not want to be seen in a church. I remember vividly one student's response to a query about what he would like in worship services: "a folk mass on Dunn Meadow." But that phase, too, passed, as is always the case. Before long, folk masses were out and High Church liturgy complete with incense and Gregorian chant was in. Thus Trinity's worship style moved from Low to at least "Medium High."

The campus revolution was characterized by increasing indifference to denominational boundaries, particularly those demarcating the multitude of Protestant sects. Led by Charles Perry, some of the major Protestant churches in Bloomington decided to pool their chaplaincy funding to create a campus-based university ministry, an undertaking that I supported enthusiastically.

They established a lay governing board representing the participating churches, which functioned like a lay vestry for the enterprise. I was chosen by Perry to represent Trinity. I made the fatal mistake of saying something substantive at the organizing meeting and was elected president of this revolutionary enterprise.

However, denominational lines are difficult to erase, and denominational dollars that go to an undertaking that supports, at least in part, another denomination are viewed with suspicion. Thus it was not long before the Baptist team member asked me to justify to his Baptist church support group the expenditure of Baptist dollars for this multi-colored enterprise.

My position became even more precarious after Donald Davis (Charles Perry's successor) appeared on the scene. He was charged by the bishop to "clean up the mess in Bloomington"—that "mess" being chiefly Charles Perry's decision to participate in university ministry, and the transfer of diocesan funds for the Episcopal chaplaincy to university ministry without the bishop's approval.

Being a student of politics and administration, I saw all this as fascinating but not really fatal. The kingdom of God on earth functions through some mighty fragile earthly vessels, and I doubt that our ultimate fates are seriously affected by such accounting and fund transfer problems!

More seriously, I came to see a number of problems with the very concept of the student chaplaincy. Ultimately these problems led to the dissolution of this federated effort, even though an entity called University Ministry continues to function in Bloomington.

The Danforth Foundation

In reflecting on my increasingly stronger links to Christianity and Christian religious institutions, I should pay tribute to the Danforth Foundation. My earlier reference to the Teacher Study Grant program that enabled me to complete my dissertation does not do justice to the foundation or its influence on me over the years.

My account must begin with William H. Danforth, who built an agribusiness fortune out of a single feed-mill in rural Missouri, from which grew the Ralston Purina/Checkerboard empire. Danforth epitomized midwestern Protestant Christianity: a simple faith with strong emphasis on good works, especially as regards young people of high school and college age. During World War I, Danforth was a YMCA volunteer in Europe who drove a wagon from which he dispensed coffee and doughnuts to soldiers behind the front lines.

Danforth's business skills must have been considerable, because he continued to prosper even during the inter-war Depression that hit American agriculture especially hard. Eventually Danforth established a foundation. One of his earliest advisors was President Hutchins of Berea College, a unique institution that provides college education in exchange for work to the children of the Appalachian hill country people.

Danforth supported YMCA and YWCA activities at the high school level, including a large summer camp on Lake Michigan. Later he extended his activities to the college/university level. There, too, his activities reflected his personal religious faith. He donated money for the construction of nondenominational chapels and established a program in which a selected group of women college graduates, the Danny Grads, were appointed to staff college YWCA centers.

Another early and long-lasting program was the Danforth Associates program, in which faculty were appointed to four-year terms, during which they would open their homes to students and spend time interacting with them. Associates would receive a stipend to help them entertain students or otherwise devote themselves to fostering closer student-faculty relationships.

Twice during their term, Associates would attend a weeklong conference at Camp Miniwanca on Lake Michigan, at which the foundation invariably produced first-rate lectures on topics of interest to people from all disciplines. The activities included daily religious services, and attendance at the services was required.

These services were clearly Protestant, even though selection for the foundation's grant programs had no religious criteria. The foundation's Christian orientation was well established until World War II. As the country's Protestant consensus came to be questioned, the Danforth Foundation tended to dither. Was it a religious foundation with educational concerns or an educational foundation with religious concerns?

I served a four-year term as an Associate in this program after my teacher study grant. We attended a Miniwanca conference, which I remember fondly, except for its Spartan lifestyle! The various lectures were intellectually stimulating. The evening worship service on a dune near the lake was truly moving. By then I had embraced that Protestant consensus and felt at home in it.

In later years, there was much controversy over required worship attendance, especially from Roman Catholic and agnostic grantees—strange bedfellows, these!

After World War II, the Danforth Foundation underwent a radical shift in focus. Harold Brown, former president of Dennison University, became executive director. Under his leadership, the foundation began to focus on higher education and created the Danforth Graduate Fellowship program, one of the most generous graduate fellowship programs. The fellowships were awarded to outstanding graduates who showed genuine commitment to college teaching in any discipline. Each covered four years of tuition and full living expenses, as well as attendance at annual conferences devoted to central issues of university teaching and research.

The foundation assumed quite correctly that various programs were available for those seeking careers as researchers or researcher-teachers, but no comparable programs were available for those who would demonstrate their primary commitment to teaching. About 120 fellows were chosen each year and supported for four years—an expensive program indeed.

I had a close-up view of the program during 1963–1966 when I served as a member of the national selection committee. The committee was chaired by a contemporary of ours from our Florida days, who also served as one of the foundation's associate executive directors.

I have watched the careers of several fellows, and how they have indeed been devoted to teaching and inquiry in the best sense of the terms. As a result, I have great admiration for the skill with which the foundation has over the years identified its fellows.

Eventually the federal government entered the field of financial assistance for advanced study with a program looking very much like the Danforth fellows program—four years for work to the doctorate, all fees and tuition paid, plus living expenses. It did so as a result of the national "shock" over the Russian sputnik success.

To justify entry into higher education financing, the federal government had to invent a link to defense and the cold war. Thus the basic legislation was the National Defense(!) Education Act. It was a veritable cornucopia for students and universities. As a result of the NDEA, the Danforth fellows program lost a good part of its raison d'être.

As I recounted earlier, the Teacher Study Grant program was started in 1955. Lasting about ten years, the program was a response to some special consequences of World War II. Veterans, returning from the war, had started families and began to utilize the GI Bill, much as we did.

Many of those who continued their education beyond the AB degree found they had exhausted their government benefits before they could reach their terminal degree and were forced to take jobs, teaching or otherwise, to support their families. The Teacher Study Grant program was created to enable these ABDs (all but dissertation) to take off a year to complete their doctorates, without which they could not hope to attain tenure appointments and secure academic careers.

The study grant program ended when the foundation directed its attention to problems of America's cities, especially to the foundation's home base, St. Louis. Eventually the foundation's assets were liquidated and distributed to two St. Louis institutions: St. Louis University and Washington University, the latter presided over by a descendant of William H. Danforth. Various changes in American society had made the foundation's orientation not obsolete, but no longer as much in natural harmony as it was during the lifetime of its founder.

The difficulties created by this dissonance became apparent as early as my own involvement in the 1950s. That dissonance became stronger, as I have recounted, and ultimately led to the demise of the foundation.

As a practicing social scientist, I understand why this came about, but I continue to have great respect for the founding father, whom I met briefly at the 1955 Miniwanca conference. He died later that year.

I was pleased to serve as an Associate. I should say "we," for the Danforth Associates program initially appointed only married couples, who were meant to function as a team. Only much later and reluctantly, did the foundation appoint single Associates—still another illustration of the foundation's struggle to find a modus vivendi consistent with a changing national consensus.

Both husband and wife were to attend the Miniwanca conference and were to participate in the Associates program activities equally. If I remember correctly, "baking cookies" often entered discussions about Associates' activities, but no sharp lines were drawn between that and other activities of the Associates' wives.

Eventually a network of regional conferences for Associates was created and alumni Associates were invited to attend. Ann and I attended several and came away intellectually and spiritually refreshed!

Quite obviously, the foundation took for granted the institution of the married couple with the wife as homemaker. Could or should a wife with a career of her own (often the result of financial necessity) open her home and dare one say it *pace* the 1992 presidential campaign, "bake cookies"?

Nevertheless, stripped of such time-bound conceptions, the foundation's commitment to *teaching* as the central concern of higher education remains fully valid. But what is "great" or even "good" teaching? At one Associates meeting, my discussion group set out to define "good teacher."

Before long we had a consensus, but then came the poser: "What is a good Christian teacher?" We concluded that being a Christian did not add any dimension central to our definition. We could not agree that being a non-Christian, say a Jew or a Muslim, would prevent one from being a good teacher. That unresolved puzzle is the best clue I can offer to the strengths and weaknesses of the Danforth Foundation.

The Danforth Foundation undoubtedly helped me to clarify and strengthen my commitment to teaching. Likewise, it helped me to deepen my faith as a Christian.

The relationship of one's faith to one's work is essentially an unfinished business. Thus, for me the conundrum of the "good Christian teacher" has remained unresolved to this day, after nearly half a century of work in my chosen profession, teaching.

The Student Advocates Office

When I retired in 1988, a thoroughly new field of activity opened to me. I was invited to join the staff of the Student Advocates Office, a group of retired faculty who are available to students who find the 35,000-student monster an intractable bureaucratic maze. The Student Advocates Office consists of a dozen retired faculty who help students with complaints that they are unable to get resolved anyplace else in the university.

Although each advocate spends only a half day per week in the office, the follow-up and resolution of a student's complaints may take many hours of consultation, meetings, and so forth. I have served as an advocate for seven years. Each year I have dealt with as many as eighty-five cases. I have found that no two complaints resemble each other.

To be sure, complaints about instructor fairness or cases triggered by charges of academic or personal misconduct tend to resemble each other, and some academic units of the university generate more student complaints than others. Yet each student's problem is unique and requires a different strategy for resolution.

The advocates program likely originated from some of the same concerns that gave rise to ombudsman programs at other universities. These programs took their name and function from the government ombudsman in Scandinavian countries whose governments have been sensitive to the voices of their citizens, and who have wanted to make available to citizens an instrument for complaints against government officials.

I see the role of the advocates as similar. We help students resolve problems that the regular university bureaucracy finds difficult to handle. Each of us has given decades of service to the university. We know how it functions and can fail to function. We can deal with a range of administrators and faculty on a personal basis. Thus, I see the advocates program as a fitting, appropriate coda to my life as a university teacher.

Retirement

My retirement in 1988 was marked by a send-off that I consider the equivalent of a whole collection of solid gold watches! Not even the usual infatuation of the autobiographer with his own subject would permit me to record this event.

Since then, I have continued my teaching, inquiry, and service to the university. However, my contributions have been at a level that has permitted us to be in a warm place, in Treasure Cay on Abaco Island in the Bahamas, during the coldest part of the year.

Freddy & Ann
Treasure Cay, Abaco Island
The Bahamas, 1988

In particular, WEST has made use of my graduate seminar to serve a student body that has been much expanded as a result of the federally financed language program and of the Defense Department sending officers to be trained as area specialists for Western Europe.

Now that the Political Science Department has recruited re- placements for me and for Jim Christoph, who took early retire- ment, there will be less need for my seminar and for my services on master's and PhD committees. I have truly enjoyed my con- tinued teaching and graduate committee service because it has enabled me to remain in touch with university life in its various forms.

Aside from teaching, my earlier inquiry and research have continued in the form of papers at national and international meetings, articles in scholarly journals, book reviews, and some manuscript evaluation. Much of this writing still gets done in an- tediluvian form: using ballpoints and lined tablets.

I am very much a local, as Manning Dauer had been, focusing my life around university institutions. I remain enchanted with the Indiana University campus, much as I was nearly fifty years ago when I first tramped through the wooded campus from the Government Department to the library.

Conclusion

Autobiographies, even those published posthumously, are by their very nature open-ended. One recounts the course of one's life, and one reflects on it, but there is really no obvious coda to the particular *Helderleben* one presents. Yet we believe that we have found an appropriate note on which to end *our* reflections—the celebration of our fiftieth wedding anniversary.

Our fiftieth wedding anniversary is appropriate for two reasons. First, because it is such an obviously memorable event. And second, because it embodies the central theme of this joint autobiography. As such it constitutes still another way of providing additional answers to the second of the two questions that gave an impetus to this enterprise: *What has kept you together over a lifetime, in spite of contrasts in religion, social background, national origins, and so forth?*

We had abandoned the idea of celebrating our fiftieth wedding anniversary on its actual date, March 18, 1993. We wanted to have our children and grandchildren present. That made a summer date the only possible choice.

The inspiration for our anniversary celebration came from Freddy's comment about our wedding some fifty years ago. He observed that the ten days delay en route granted by the US Army dissolved into a kaleidoscope of events in which the two participants seemed to be pushed inexorably on a course that they did not fully understand.

No doubt there have been thousands of young men and women who thus blundered into wartime marriages that began to dissolve before the ink had dried on their marriage licenses. Yet there we were fifty years later still happily married. Freddy suggested that the only appropriate form in which to observe this milestone was a reaffirmation of our marriage vows in the setting of a Eucharistic service of the Episcopal church.

Freddy continues to joke that he suggested this observance because he had been totally befuddled during the original observance, and he wanted another chance while he was still compos mentis. When pressed further, he observed that reaffirming our marriage vows seemed quite naturally the only possible way to affirm and reaffirm the work of our joint life together.

What made it all even more remarkable was that the idea touched a chord in both of us most profoundly, and it was quite obvious that we had found still another manifestation of our sensitivity to each other's deepest feelings.

We met with Hugh Laughlin, our rector, to find out whether such a thing as we proposed was even possible in the Episcopal church. He pulled a book from his shelves and opened it to a page headed *Reaffirmation of Marriage Vows.* Not only that, he expressed great pleasure that Trinity Church should have an occasion for such a celebration.

The reaffirmation service is an abbreviated wedding sacramental service. The participants stand before the congregation rather than before the altar. The prayers and the questions and answers all focus on the reaffirmation of the original vows. At the end, the bridegroom kisses the bride. Then they both receive the congratulations of the congregation.

We set the date for a Sunday afternoon on August 22, 1993, and then set about making our plans. We chose not to send out printed announcements, but rather we extended invitations to the congregation through the church bulletin, and to friends by word of mouth and through brief announcements in LWV and university calendars. We asked some of our friends to read the lessons, and others to provide appropriate music for the service and for the reception, which we held in the Great Hall of Trinity Church following the Eucharistic service.

With our chosen date, we ensured the presence in Bloomington of Steve, his wife Tasoula, and their son Alexis from Greece, as well as that of Alice and her three children, Paige, Colin, and Christopher, from Texas. Only Pete, Alice's husband, was unable to be away from San Antonio for professional reasons.

More than we could have imagined, this celebration of our Fiftieth Wedding Anniversary epitomized the nature and the depth of the bonds that have united us. A spark of an idea by one partner produces profound echoes in the other partner and triggers a result—a result that reflects the essence of our marriage better than anything else we could say about the constellation of events and forces that brought us together and the enduring bonds that grew from that original union.

The Diamant Family
Alice, Freddy, Ann, Steve, Gordon, Alexis,
Colin, Christopher, & Paige
Bloomington, 1993

Epilogue

Ann was my love and companion for more than sixty years. Beginning with Rudolf Serkin playing Beethoven's *Emperor Concerto*, we shared art and music in Europe and America, and we debated politics and public policy.

On February 27, 2003, the attending nurse said to me, "Freddy, she wants to see you." When I came to her bed, she stretched out her arms and kissed me three times, and then she sank back onto her pillow.

A minute later, the nurse checked with the stethoscope and said, "She's gone." The happiest part of my life had come to an end.

Bloomington, Indiana
March 2004

Ann & Freddy
Bloomington, Indiana, 2001
© 2001 QuickPic Photo Lab & Portrait Studio

Family Trees

Family Tree for Ann Redmon & Freddy Diamant

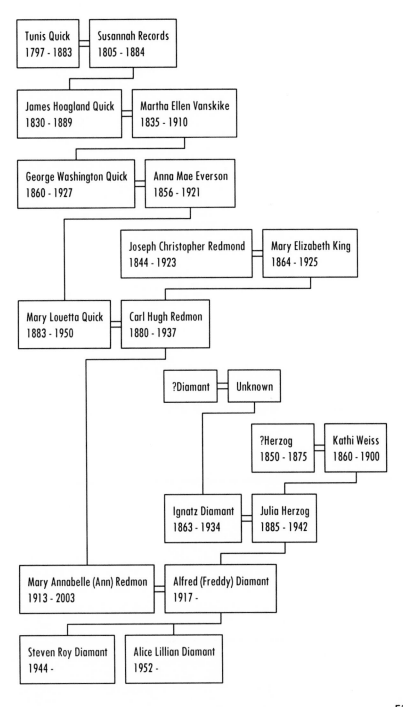

Tunis Quick
1797 - 1883

Susannah Records
1805 - 1884

James Hoagland Quick
1830 - 1889

Martha Ellen Vanskike
1835 - 1910

George Washington Quick
1860 - 1927

Anna Mae Everson
1856 - 1921

Joseph Christopher Redmond
1844 - 1923

Mary Elizabeth King
1864 - 1925

Mary Louetta Quick
1883 - 1950

Carl Hugh Redmon
1880 - 1937

?Diamant

Unknown

?Herzog
1850 - 1875

Kathi Weiss
1860 - 1900

Ignatz Diamant
1863 - 1934

Julia Herzog
1885 - 1942

Mary Annabelle (Ann) Redmon
1913 - 2003

Alfred (Freddy) Diamant
1917 -

Steven Roy Diamant
1944 -

Alice Lillian Diamant
1952 -

Descendants of Tunis Quick & Susannah Records

Tunis Quick
1797 - 1883

Susannah
Records
1805 - 1884

Smith
William
Quick
1823 - 1824

Morgan
John Quick
1825 - 1913

Harris
Quick
1827 - 1827

Spencer
Records
Quick
1828 - 1920

James
Hoagland
Quick
1830 - 1889

Martha
Ellen
Vanskike
1835 - 1910

Tunis
Gorrell
Quick
1833 -

Josiah
Quick
1835 -

Hannah
Gorrell
Quick
1838 -

William
Quick
1840 -

Samuel
Thompson
Quick
1843 -

Rachel
Nelson
Quick
1847 -

Samuel
Butz

Mabel Butz

George
Washington
Quick
1860 - 1927

Anna Mae
Everson
1856 - 1921

Evan Snead
Quick

Unknown

William
White Quick

Lillian (Lily)
Quick

Harold (Hal)
Hughes

Descendants of James Hoagland Quick & Martha Ellen Vanskike

Vanskike (Van Schoyk) Family Tree

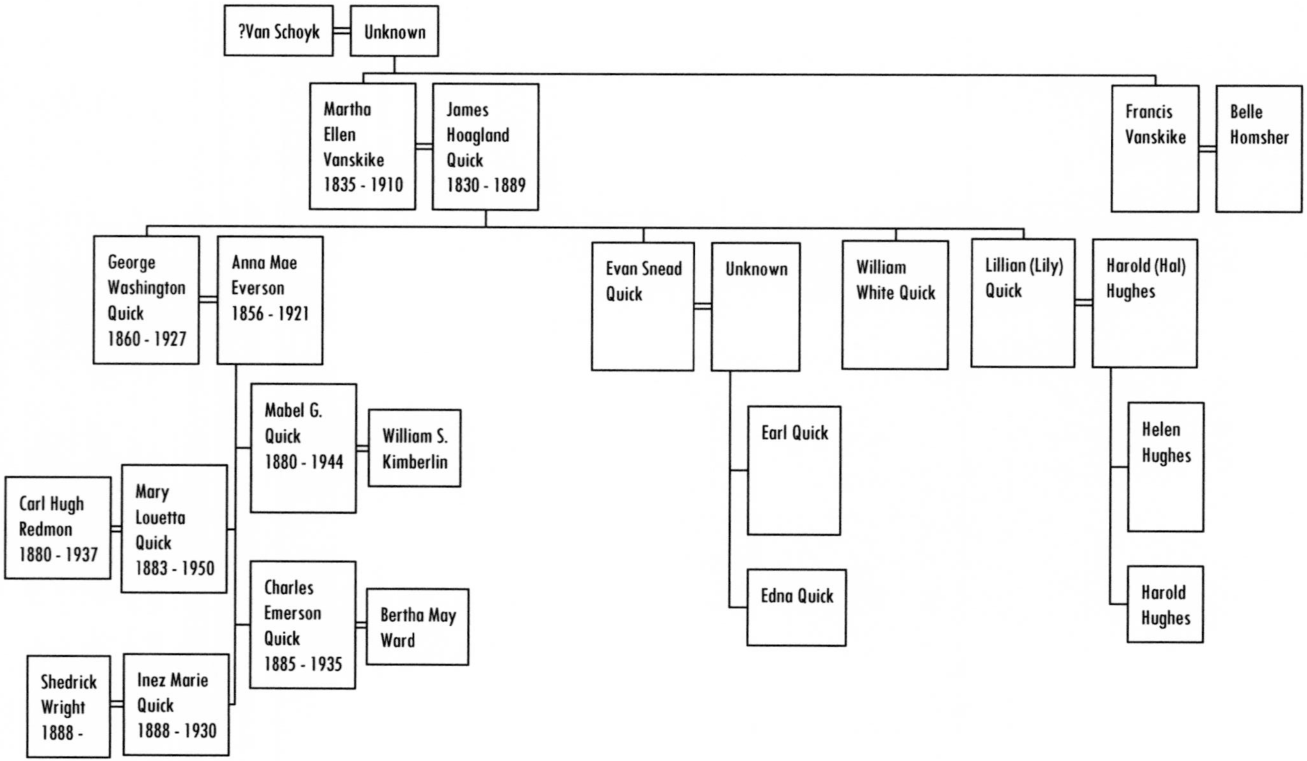

Everson Family Tree

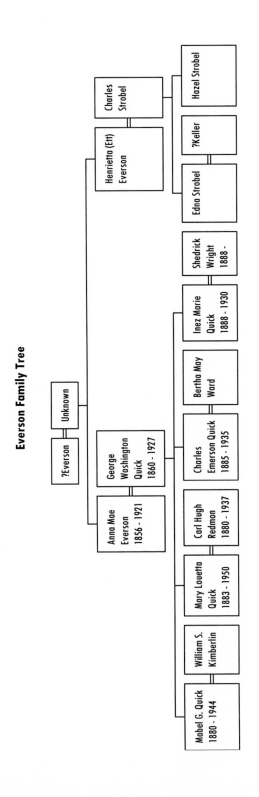

Descendants of George Washington Quick & Anna Mae Everson

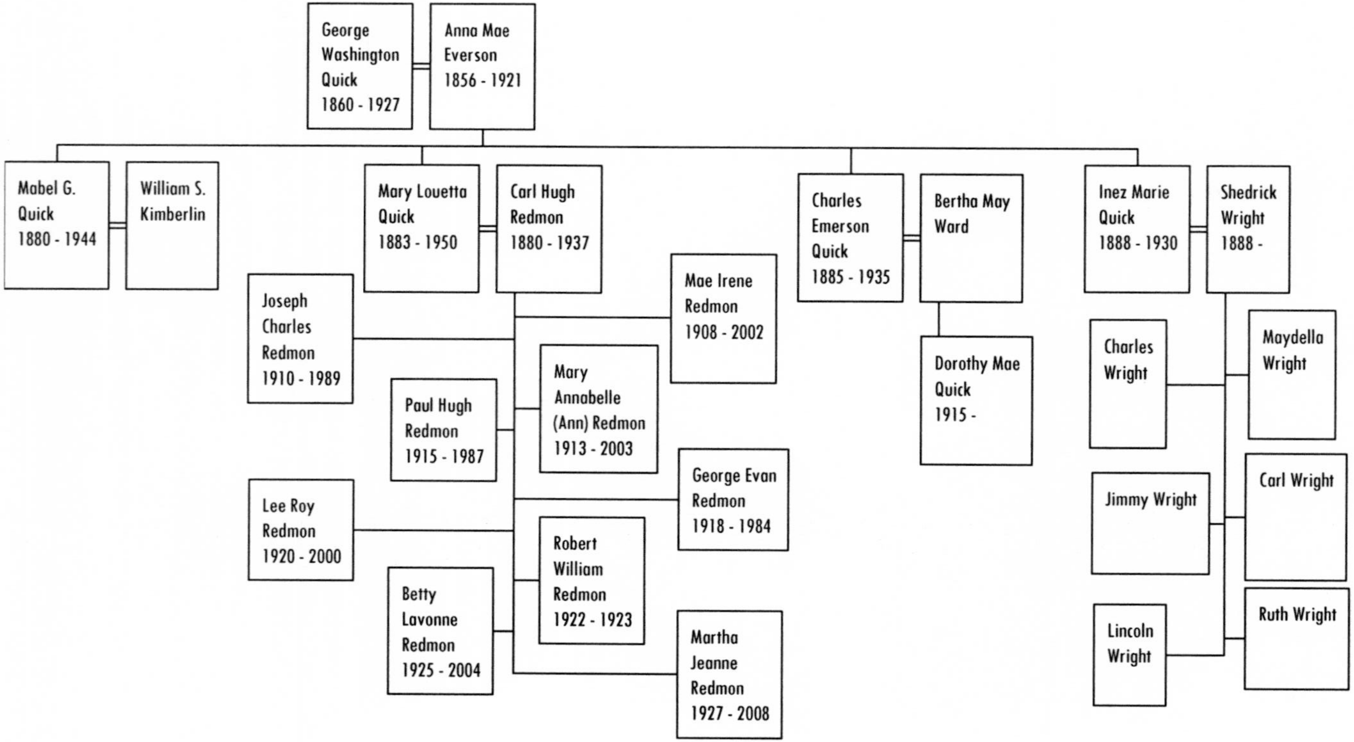

Descendants of Mary Louetta Quick & Carl Hugh Redmon (1 of 6)

| Mary Louetta Quick 1883 - 1950 | Carl Hugh Redmon 1880 - 1937 |

Mae Irene Redmon 1908 - 2002
Glenn Klipsch 1912 - 2000

Joseph Charles Redmon 1910 - 1989
Helen Gertrude Carver 1918 -

Cont. p. 2

Julie Ann Klipsch 1941 -
Mark Hayes 1940 -

Rebecca Redmon 1941 -
Will Cheesman

Roberta Redmon 1945 -
Gene Speaker

Kristi Hayes 1964 -
Bruce Yunker

Paul?
Kimberly Hayes 1969 -
Nick Guerrini 1967 -

Holly Cheesman
Paul ?
Joe R. Cheesman

Amy Lynn Speaker
Tom Dowd
Erin Speaker
Tony Miller

Descendants of Mary Louetta Quick & Carl Hugh Redmon (2 of 6)

Mary Louetta Quick 1883 - 1950

Carl Hugh Redmon 1880 - 1937

Cont. p. 1

Mary Annabelle (Ann) Redmon 1913 - 2003

Alfred (Freddy) Diamant 1917 -

Eleanor Metcalf

Paul Hugh Redmon 1915 - 1987

Lucille Curtis

Cont. p. 3

Steven Roy Diamant 1944 -

Tasoula Dimitriou Voutsina 1948 -

Alice Lillian Diamant 1952 -

John Peter Pfeiffer III 1952 -

John Hugh Redmon 1943 -

?

Toni Redmon 1957 -

Jim Hayes

Elizabeth Jan Eaton 1946 -

Alexis Alfred Diamant 1992 -

Paige Alison Diamant 1983 -

Colin Andrew Pfeiffer 1986 -

Christopher David Pfeiffer 1989 -

Jennifer ?

Ben Hayes

Gordon Niall Diamant 1968 -

534

Descendants of Mary Louetta Quick & Carl Hugh Redmon (3 of 6)

Cont. p. 4

Cont. p. 2

Mary Louetta Quick
1883 - 1950

Carl Hugh Redmon
1880 - 1937

Thelma King
1918 - 1971

George Evan Redmon
1918 - 1984

Mildred Bryant
1928 - 2005

Lee Roy Redmon
1920 - 2000

Paulene Harden
1922 - 1999

Robert William Redmon
1922 - 1923

Mary Ellen Redmon
1946 -

Bill Wittenmeyer

Joyce Elaine Redmon
1952 -

Scott Crowder

Anita Kay Redmon
1957 -

Danny Lee Burton

Hugh Thomas Redmon
1946 -

?

Roger Redmon
1948 -

Mary Ann McNealy

Zackary Evan Crowder

Lucas Crowder

Brittana Crowder

Lindsay Burton

Andrew Burton

Andy Redmon

Brian Redmon

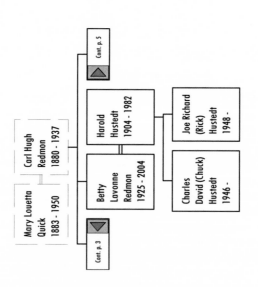

Descendants of Mary Louetta Quick & Carl Hugh Redmon (5 of 6)

Mary Louetta Quick 1883 - 1950

Carl Hugh Redmon 1880 - 1937

Martha Jeanne Redmon 1927 - 2008

Cont. p. 4

Albert Walter Horn 1915 - 2003

Marilyn Jean Horn 1952 -

Larry Stark

Bruce Stuart

Nicolas (Nick) Marc Horn 1955 -

Barbara

Martin Roy Horn 1957 -

Timothy Joe Horn 1958 -

Vicki Lynn Biddinger

Cont. p. 6

Samuel John Stark 1979 -

Erica Jean Stark 1980 -

Tonya Kaye Horn 1975 -

Nathan Hagerty

Nicole Marie Horn 1977 -

Jason Hamilton

Brittany Ann Horn 1984 -

Nathan Raymond Horn 1990 -

Alexander Mark Horn 1993 -

Keith Joe Horn 1985 -

537

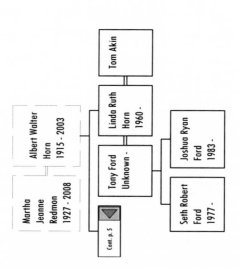

Descendants of Joseph Christopher Redmond & Mary Elizabeth King

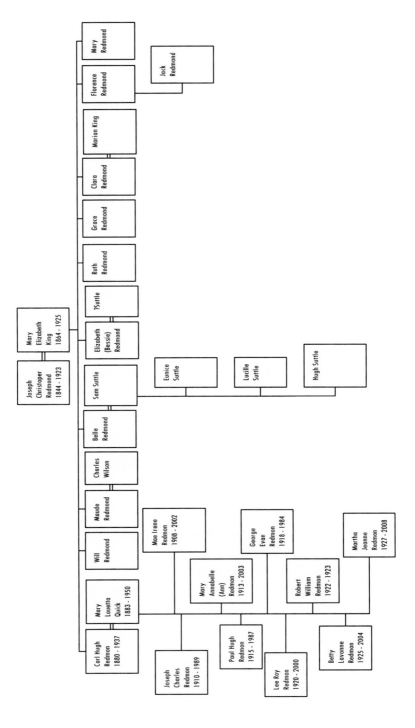

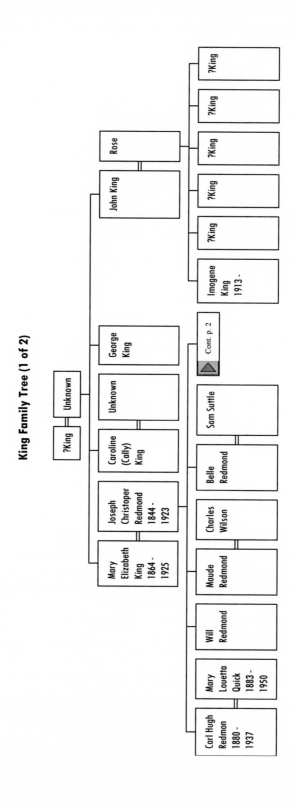

Cont. p. 2

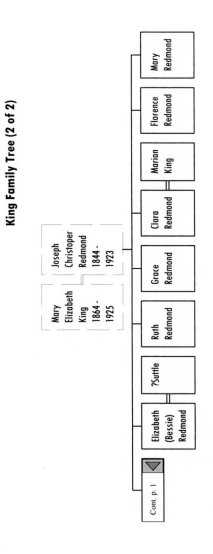

Diamant Family Tree

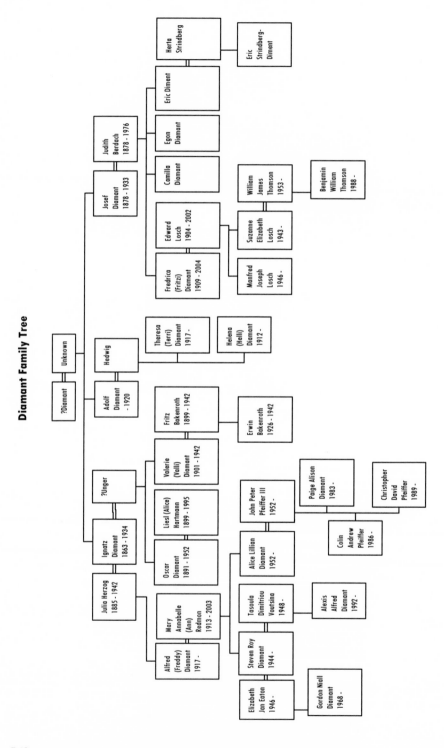

Weiss-Herzog Family Tree

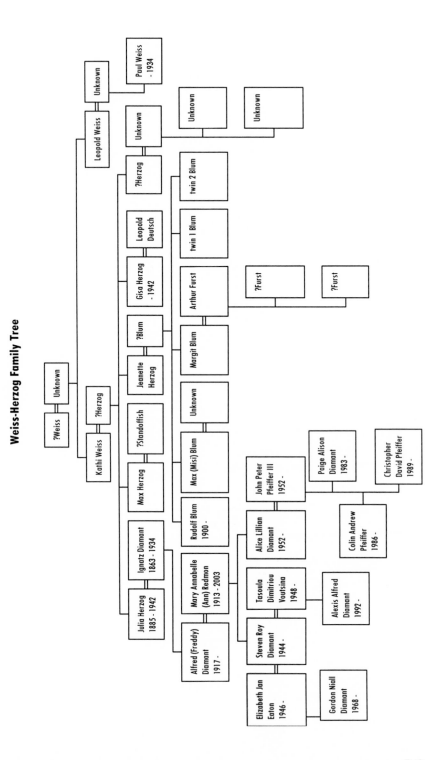

Descendants of Julia Herzog & Ignatz Diamant

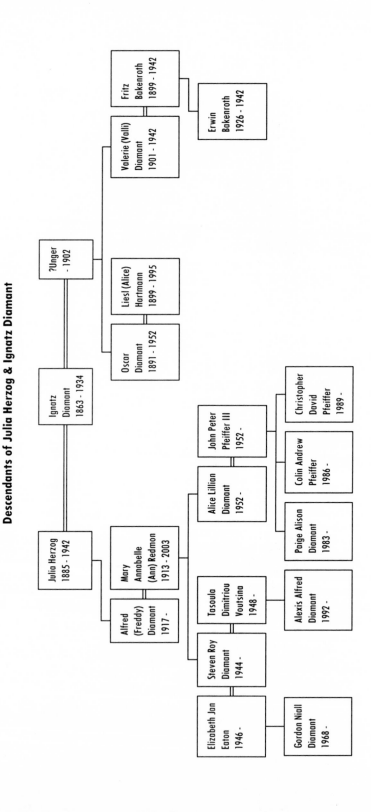

Diamant-Unger Family Tree

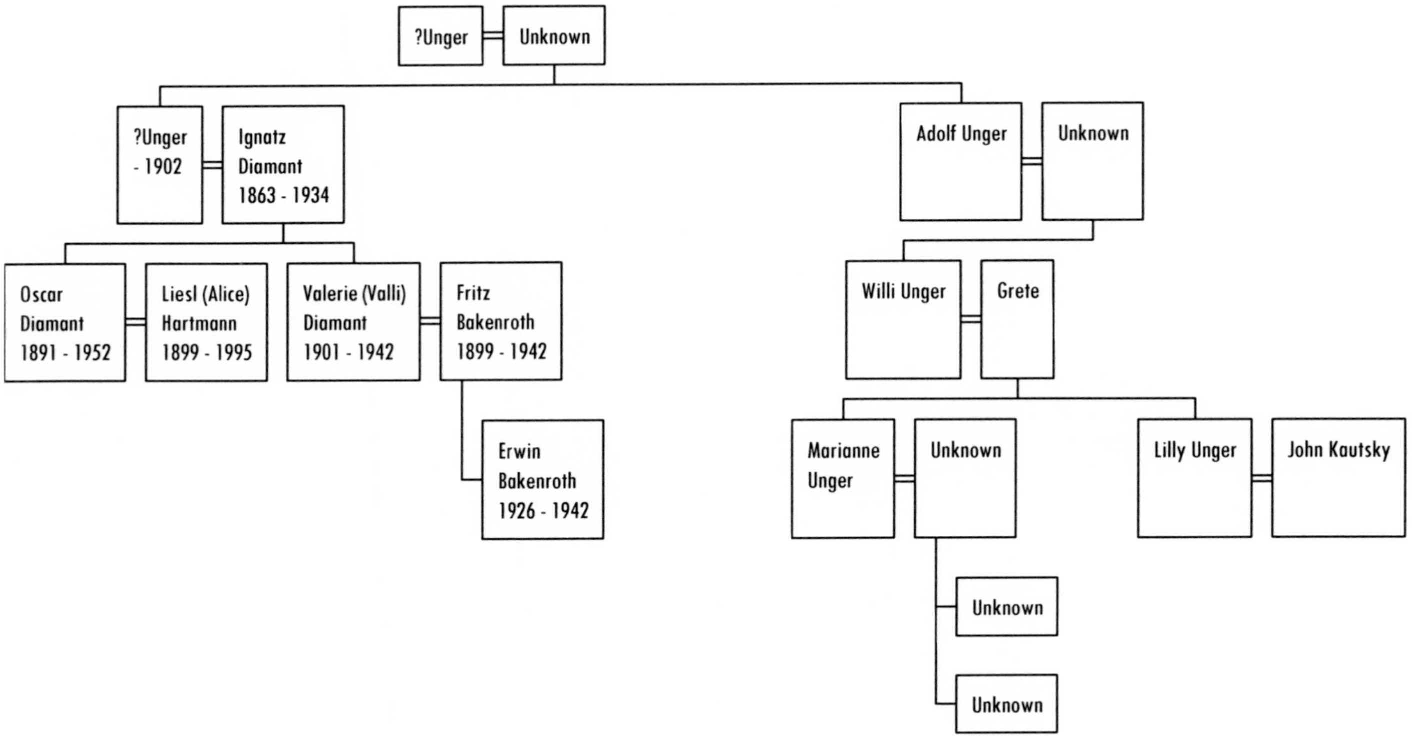

Diamant-Hartmann Family Tree

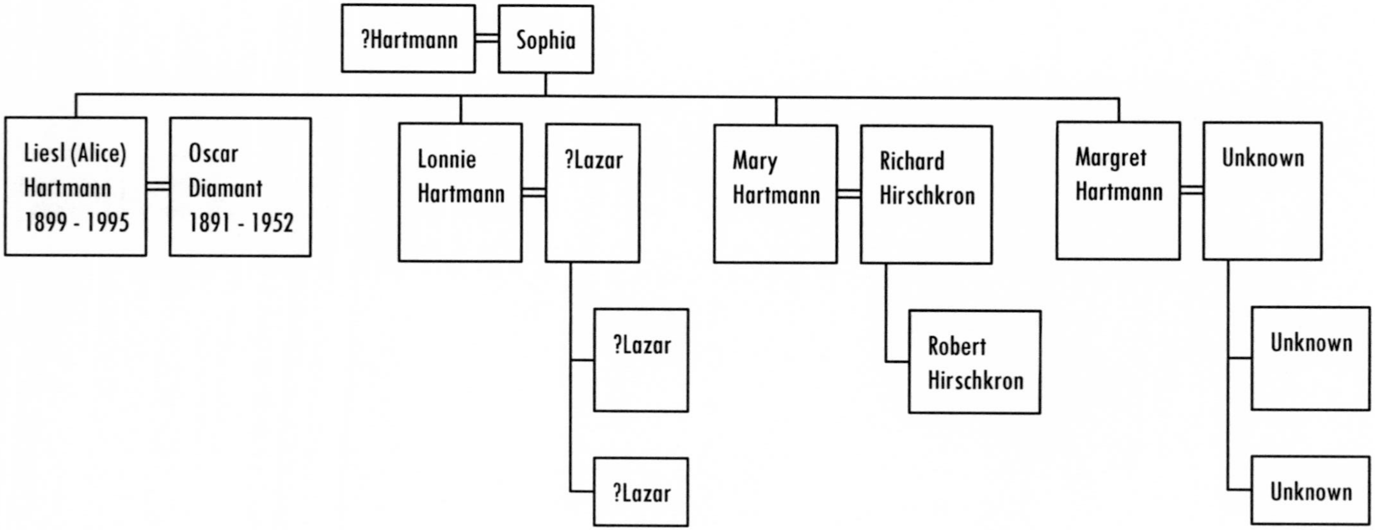

LaVergne, TN USA
23 August 2010
194349LV00004BA/2/P

Lecture Notes in Com...
Edited by G. Goos, J. Hartmanis and...

Springer

Berlin
Heidelberg
New York
Barcelona
Hong Kong
London
Milan
Paris
Singapore
Tokyo